BLUEPRINT FOR DISASTER

BLUEPRINT FOR DISASTER

The Unraveling of Chicago Public Housing

D. BRADFORD HUNT

The University of Chicago Press | Chicago and London

D. Bradford Hunt is associate dean and associate professor of social science at Roosevelt University in Chicago.

The University of Chicago Press, Chicago 60637
The University of Chicago Press, Ltd., London
© 2009 by The University of Chicago
All rights reserved. Published 2009
Printed in the United States of America

18 17 16 15 14 13 12 11 10 09   1 2 3 4 5

ISBN-13: 978-0-226-36085-0   (cloth)
ISBN-10: 0-226-36085-7   (cloth)

Library of Congress Cataloging-in-Publication Data

Hunt, D. Bradford, 1968–
    Blueprint for disaster : the unraveling of Chicago public housing / D. Bradford Hunt.
        p. cm.
    Includes bibliographical references and index.
    ISBN-13: 978-0-226-36085-0 (cloth : alk. paper)
    ISBN-10: 0-226-36085-7 (cloth : alk. paper)
    1. Public housing—Illinois—Chicago—History—20th century. 2. Chicago Housing
Authority—History—20th century. I. Title.
    HD7288.78.U52C45 2009
    363.5'850977311—dc22

                                                                    2009006297

∞ The paper used in this publication meets the minimum requirements of the American
National Standard for Information Sciences—Permanence of Paper for Printed Library
Materials, ANSI Z39.48-1992.

To my family

CONTENTS

ILLUSTRATIONS

What Went Wrong with Public Housing in Chicago?

In 1956 the Ashford family happily took up residence in the Harold Ickes Homes, a recently completed public housing project on Chicago's Near South Side. The project had wiped away part of the old Federal Street slum, including an assorted collection of warehouses, a run-down hospital, and nineteenth-century tenements that had long housed African Americans. In their place the Chicago Housing Authority (CHA) constructed a series of seven- and nine-story concrete and brick buildings. Years later Vonsell Ashford recalled her first year at the project: "I moved into Ickes in April. The building was new, and they had a beautiful playground for the children. You couldn't ask for a better location, and the place was just marvelous. I had three bedrooms, a nice storage area, and a linen closet. . . . And I had wonderful neighbors. . . . I thought I was moving to paradise."[1]

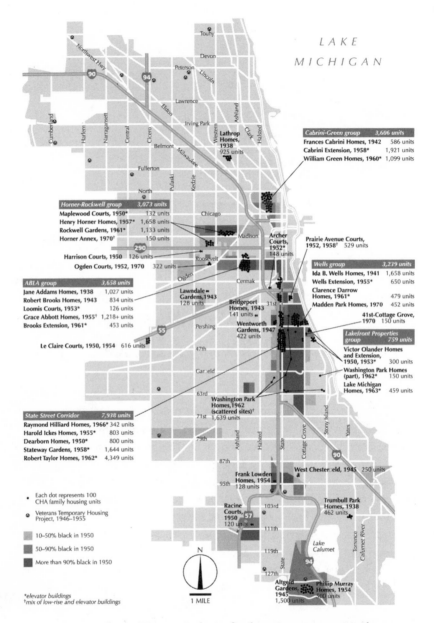

Figure 1. Chicago Housing Authority family projects, 1938–70. Map by
Dennis McClendon.

Figure 2. Harold Ickes Homes, August 1956. Courtesy of the CHA.

Ashford's reminiscence is not unusual. Early public housing residents responded with an intense affinity for their new communities, and the word "paradise" surfaces repeatedly in interviews. "We never looked at Altgeld Gardens as public housing," recalled Maude Davis, a retired public school principal. "We felt it was just paradise. We felt this was just the greatest housing that we could live in! There was pride in it." Addie Wyatt and her husband Claude were among the first tenants at the sprawling, semi-suburban Altgeld project built for African American war workers in 1945 and remembered that it "was the greatest community we had seen, and we were just delighted. . . . We had just found this heavenly place. We loved it and wanted to stay. . . . Let me tell you. We have since owned two lovely homes, but we never had the pride in either one of them that we had in Altgeld Gardens." At the Ida B. Wells Homes, the CHA's first slum clearance project in the city's old black belt, completed in 1941, Arnold Weddington relished his childhood: "In Ida B. Wells, when I grew up, we thought we were rich. We never envisioned ourselves as being poor people. As a child I believed we were more fortunate than many people because of where we lived and the way we lived."[2] Waiting lists were long,

Figure 3. Altgeld Gardens, 1945. Courtesy of the CHA.

and those who gained admission felt lucky to escape the city's slums and live in apartments with modern appliances, multiple bedrooms, and subsidized rents.

Over time, however, the CHA's projects slipped downhill. Ashford sadly described the decline: "We got through the 1950s pretty good, then slowly through the 1960s things got worse. . . . What really started destroying things is when the family structure broke down. But the most important thing, I think, really, is the kind of people they were putting in. The CHA wasn't being as careful." Still, she stayed for twenty-three years, until 1979. "It's not that I didn't like the apartment, I loved my apartment. . . . But then you go across the hall, and this person doesn't have a door on the bathroom, the oven door is pulled off, and the sink is broken. Lord knows how. And you'd be saying, 'What in the world . . . ?'" Addie and Claude Wyatt were forced out of Altgeld Gardens in 1953 after her rising wages as a union organizer made her family ineligible for public housing. She attributed social deterioration at Altgeld to "concentrating too many people in the same economic category. . . . I don't think it is good for the society as a whole to have mostly people on public aid" in projects. Arnold Weddington left the Wells Homes at age eighteen and rose through managerial ranks to become an executive at a telephone company. Returning to his childhood home in the early 1990s, he was distraught. "We had everything at Ida B. Wells. And now if you go down there, what do they have? They don't even have a field house. The last time I went down to look at 653 East 37th Place, I had tears in my eyes. I couldn't believe it."[3]

By the late 1980s, Chicago's largest public housing projects were dysfunctional. Poor, African American, female-headed families were "stacked on top of one another," as residents put it, surrounded by appalling physical neglect, random violence, and social disorder. Criminal gangs fueled by the drug trade controlled several projects while basic systems—elevators, roofs, building heat, trash collection—failed constantly. Vacancy rates soared, reflecting both the undesirability of public housing and the inability of the CHA to repair damaged apartments. Moreover, two decades of budgetary turmoil had left the CHA in managerial disarray; accountants were unable to give a clean audit, and consultants labeled it "incompetent." Concentrations of poverty reached acute levels, and in 1995 Henry Cisneros, secretary of the U.S. Department of Housing and Urban

Figure 4. Ida B. Wells Homes building, 1941. Courtesy of the CHA.

Development, reported to Congress that CHA projects comprised eleven of the fifteen poorest communities in the nation.[4]

These conditions had tragic human consequences. Numerous accounts uncovered the physical and psychological damage inflicted upon children growing up surrounded by destitution, violence, anxiety, and fear. Reporter Alex Kotlowitz followed the lives of two young brothers, Pharaoh and Lafayette, at the Henry Horner Homes, a West Side project, and his important 1991 book, *There Are No Children Here*, details an environment devoid of hope. The title references their mother's statement that her sons never had the opportunity for an innocent, carefree childhood. Instead, the boys' minds were scarred and numbed by repeatedly witnessing destructive acts around them. Kotlowitz enumerates the struggles of institutions—the CHA, the schools, the community centers, the police—trying to help the boys but failing at the most basic levels. Life in public housing by the 1980s was bleak, dangerous, and isolated from American mainstream culture.[5] In one generation, "paradise" had transformed into "housing of last resort," arguably even more hazardous and more debilitating than the slums it had replaced.

* * *

This book wrestles with a deceptively simple question: how did a well-intentioned New Deal program designed to clear the nation's urban slums and build decent housing for low-income families become, in a relatively short period of time, a devastating urban policy failure? Put bluntly, what went wrong with Chicago's public housing?

Historians and critics have offered a long list of explanations for public housing's deterioration in most major U.S. cities. The stripped-down and unwelcoming architecture created a poverty aesthetic that stigmatized residents, especially in large-scale, monolithic high-rise buildings. Located largely in black ghettos, public housing perpetuated racial segregation and symbolized second-class citizenship. Inadequate funding resulted in shoddy construction and deferred maintenance. Conservative opponents sabotaged legislation and tarred the program as "socialistic." Corrupt or incompetent managers did not screen out "undesirable" families and failed to provide basic security and repairs.[6]

Many items on this list have merit, though others, as will be seen, are exaggerated. Moreover, the causal links connecting these explanations with project failure are often more implied than adequately described. Numerous questions deserve deeper scrutiny: Why, exactly, were high-rise buildings a poor choice for public housing? Who determined subsidies and why were they inadequate? Did racial segregation cause project decline, or was class separation more important? Why did public housing's tenant base shift from the working class to the deeply impoverished? What caused public housing's social disorder? And how did public officials respond as public housing slid downward?

These questions require a close examination of policies and decisions by those in power. However, scholars have argued that actors at all levels, including not only elected legislators and agency administrators but also interest groups and program clients, influence policy formation and implementation.[7] In the case of the U.S. public housing program, a coalition of reformers played the principal role in crafting housing legislation in Congress and then drew up the program's rules at the newly formed United States Housing Authority. These rules were then administered through a federal-local partnership, with Washington officials supervising local housing authorities such as the CHA. Next, local housing authorities built and managed projects, interpreting mandates through their own context and experience, while further down the chain, project managers made on-the-ground decisions that were even more location specific. For their part, public housing's clients—low-income tenants—could chose to live in public housing or to leave, and at times they organized in an effort to force change. To understand public housing's decline, then, requires an understanding of decision making by these various actors and the multitude of forces shaping their choices.

Policy decisions and their contexts are the central focus in this analysis; it is not a social history of life in public housing. Others have produced richly detailed studies of public housing communities in Chicago and other cities and demonstrated how residents fought for reforms, carved out communities, and empowered themselves in the midst of often horrific conditions.[8] Those who stayed in public housing through its downfall and struggled for a better life have a vital story to tell, and their historical agency has grown, beginning in the mid-1960s. Overall, however, policymakers rarely asked tenants what they wanted, and residents had almost no power over the site selection, design, budgets, tenant selection, or rental policies that would define their communities. Tenants had agency in other ways, especially by voting with their feet or, after 1970, by staying and demanding change. But on policy matters of crucial importance, tenant voices were largely ignored. That few administrators listened is a distinct element of public housing's tragic downfall.

A central contention of this book is that contingent and compounding policy choices made by actors at the federal and local level led public housing in Chicago down an unsustainable path. Sometimes choices amounted to self-inflicted wounds made by liberal administrators for well-intentioned reasons. These include the pursuit of large-scale slum clearance and the planning of massive projects of thousands of units rather than smaller, less imposing developments. Similarly, the switch to a rental policy where rents varied by tenant income (rather than by apartment size) had negative, long-term implications. Moreover, the decision to develop projects with high proportions of multi-bedroom apartments to accommodate large families was a fatal misjudgment. When combined, these internally driven policies led to social and fiscal disorder. At other times external political and social contexts restricted administrative choices. White racism constrained site selection, union control undermined maintenance efficiency, and political conflicts damaged the CHA–city government relationship as well as the federal-local one. In most public policy arenas, feedback and pressure from interest groups and clients foster a dynamic policymaking process where learning leads to incremental improvement. But in public housing, policy evolution was limited; bureaucratic knowledge often did not get translated into reform in a timely manner. Instead, policy was frozen in place during much of the 1950s, even as insiders recognized misguided strategies and predicted future failure. Public housing administrators in Chicago during that decade plodded ahead with projects, such as the Henry Horner Homes and later the Robert Taylor Homes, that they knew to be flawed. The weight of these albatrosses, spiraling out of control and draining resources, ultimately brought the authority to its knees.

The CHA was not alone with its burdens. Housing authorities in Boston, Newark, Philadelphia, Atlanta, Detroit, St. Louis, New Orleans, Oakland, and San Francisco, among others, also built misguided projects and then ran them into the ground, as concentrated poverty, deferred maintenance, and crime left residents in dispirited conditions. Chicago's failures were more spectacular than most, however, and a congressionally mandated test in 1996 found that fewer than 4,000 of its 29,000 apartments for families were "viable" on a cost and sustainability basis, the smallest proportion of any major housing authority in the country.[9] The significant exception to these outcomes was the New York City Housing Authority, which went in a different direction on major policies and weathered storms that crushed most U.S. cities.

* * *

Other broader ideological and historical contexts guided—and circum-scribed—public housing decision-making in crucial ways. The first in-volved the concept of "market failure" in the New Deal state. Various New Deal programs during Franklin Roosevelt's administration introduced the federal government into realms previously reserved to private actors in the belief that the private market had failed to yield desired outcomes. Some interventions "primed the pump" with government spending to spur lagging demand, while others set up the state as a broker between capital and labor or between producers and consumers to manage the economy. Still others, such as the Social Security Act, helped those dis-carded by capitalism by redistributing income to the aged, disabled, and other "worthy" poor. In housing, reformers argued that the private hous-ing market had failed at providing reasonable housing at affordable rents for at least the bottom third of the income scale. This market failure war-ranted state intervention, but only to the limits of that failure, so that public housing would not "compete" with legitimate private enterprise.[10] These limits—defined by reformers, accepted by them as first principles, and closely adhered to by administrators—set boundaries time and again to restrain program eligibility and project design.

A second context involved the housing market itself. The extent of mar-ket failure described by reformers in the 1930s was hardly fixed. Shortages actually worsened in the 1940s in most cities, as wartime migration by both southern blacks and rural whites to the nation's industrial centers sent de-mand for decent housing soaring. After World War II, however, nearly three decades of real economic growth and a building boom (spurred in part by federal housing initiatives) transformed conditions. Most working-class families could afford respectable shelter in the late 1960s, and levels of sub-standard housing—overcrowded, inadequately plumbed, and dilapidated—shrunk considerably.[11] Demand among the working classes for public hous-ing was not unlimited, as it had been during the shortages of the war years.

In order to understand public housing's demise in Chicago, then, it is essential to remove the arbitrary divide between "public" and "private" housing and place the output and policies of housing authorities in the context of a local housing market. Public housing changed from working-class housing to welfare housing by the early 1970s because it could not match the offerings of private housing, even for African Americans facing a discriminatory housing market. While admission limits excluded some, most working-class families left public housing or refused to enter despite low rents because they perceived that better options lay elsewhere. This may seem obvious, but the point gets lost in the analytic walling off of public housing from the rest of the market.

The slums themselves—and what to do about them—were a related context to the housing market. While progressives had long documented the health and social problems of bad housing in the nation's poorest districts, social scientists, beginning with the Chicago school of sociology in the 1920s, theorized the slums as an urban ecological problem, with decaying structures and unplanned landscapes acting as a cancerous "blight." Land-use surveys in the 1930s allowed planners to map definitions of blight with precision, giving the city what anthropologist James C. Scott calls "legibility." Once planners could "read" the city through fine-grained social and physical maps, governments could systematically reorder it, in this case by clearing and rebuilding slums on a grand scale.[12] Progressive planners believed slums were irredeemable and that new housing would uplift the lives of the poor. However, both this top-down, state-centered planning and the environmental determinism behind it were discredited by the late 1960s—in large part by the experiences of public housing.

A final context involves the deep-seated antipathy of Chicago whites to residential racial integration, as described by Arnold Hirsch's 1983 book, *Making the Second Ghetto: Race and Housing in Chicago, 1940–1960*. Beginning in the late nineteenth century, the city's white residents organized the housing market in ways that barred growing numbers of people of color from white neighborhoods. The confining of African Americans into ghettoes produced rampant overcrowding and rapid deterioration of the housing stock. When the Second Great Migration brought tens of thousands of southern blacks to Chicago after 1940, a new crisis over race and space gripped the city. Hirsch relates how neighborhood whites responded violently to attempts by African Americans to escape the ghetto, while white political and business interests mobilized governmental tools in a racial containment strategy. Neighborhood racial violence and government power combined to define and reinforce a new ghetto on the ground of the old one.[13]

One of the government tools for containment, Hirsch argues, was public housing. After the city's aldermen, fearful of the liberal integrationists running the CHA, subdued the housing authority in the late 1940s, they pressed it into service to clear the original black ghetto and raise a second one in its place. *Making the Second Ghetto* is not a full-length treatment of public housing in the city, nor does it intend to explain the later decline of the CHA, but the book implies that public housing's failure in Chicago was largely the result of its racially determined location. By forcing the construction of public housing almost exclusively in existing black neighborhoods, Hirsch charges, Chicago's racist white leaders sealed its fate. The alternative path not taken—racially integrated projects constructed in white areas—offered a chance to break up the ghetto, alleviate Chicago's deep racial divisions, and presumably sustain healthy projects. The causal link between location and project demise is not described in detail, though Hirsch mentions that slum locations demanded high-density, high-rise forms and that African American public housing residents, resentful at the perpetuation of segregation, lashed out at their surroundings in frustration. Hirsch's book has been influential among urban historians, and a "second ghetto" school has built upon his work to explore racial containment efforts in other cities.[14]

While Hirsch's story still resonates, I depart from the "second ghetto" school in small and large ways. Chief among these departures is my contention that racially liberal housing reformers had longstanding desires to clear and rebuild slums, especially urban black ghettos. Under the progressive leadership of Mayor Edward Kelly (1933–47), Robert Taylor, the CHA's first African American board chairman (1942–50), and Elizabeth Wood, CHA executive secretary (1937–54), Chicago embraced a massive slum clearance agenda, beginning with the city's black belt, where residents faced appalling conditions. Rebuilding black areas required a humane place to relocate African American slum dwellers, and Taylor and Wood proposed large, racially integrated projects on vacant land near the edges of the city, where whites lived. These projects had strong social justice value in challenging segregation, but their main purpose was to assist the primary slum clearance mission of the CHA. The choice in Chicago, then, was never between building vacant land projects in white areas and building enormous slum clearance projects in the black community. Taylor and Wood wanted to do both. The progressive-led CHA of the late 1940s—trusting in the efficacy of public housing, wanting to serve the city's African American residents, and striving for liberal objectives—had every intention of replacing black slum neighborhoods with public housing. It was Taylor and Wood who planned several of the CHA's largest complexes of public housing, including Cabrini-Green, the ABLA group (Addams, Brooks, Loomis, Abbott), and the Wells group, each emblematic of the "second ghetto."

Race and racism, though, are not the only lenses through which to view public housing history. Class is equally vital. Public housers framed their program in class terms, with income, family composition, and housing condition defining eligibility. When class-based policies and market forces led to concentrations of poverty, local housing authorities lost the resources needed to manage and maintain their properties. Removing race from the equation, then, would not have addressed these deeper systemic problems related to class and poverty. Indeed, Chicago's projects that housed only whites were the first to concentrate the poor, fall into deficit, and suffer from maintenance neglect. Race is obviously a key element of public housing's history in Chicago, but class-based policies are also material to its downfall.

Similarly, applying social disorder theories to public housing history reveals the extent to which planning choices matter as much as race and class. Sociologists and architects have long sought to explain the reasons behind social disorder in poor communities and why vandalism, crime, and violence strike in some neighborhoods more than others. They have formulated ideas on how neighbors defend public areas, enforce agreed-upon social norms, and amicably settle disputes. Pragmatic observers such as Jane Jacobs in 1961 and Oscar Newman in 1972 began to rethink how cities function from the street level up rather than from the bird's eye down, as midcentury planners had done for decades. Social order, they asserted, depends upon the daily interactions of neighbors to police their shared space, and the design and planning choices that shape that space make the job harder or easier. Later, sociologists such as Robert Sampson maintained that a neighborhood's capacity to effectively exert order—a community's "collective efficacy"—was a function of its income levels, its residential stability, and its governmental support in the form of services and policing, among other variables.[15]

In chapter 6, I contribute to this literature by arguing that the devastating social disorder in the CHA's high-rises was greatly exacerbated by planning and policy choices that located unprecedented proportions of youths in public housing. Public housing's exceptional youth demographics made exertion of collective efficacy by its adult residents, project managers, and police an insurmountable problem. To invert the title of Alex Kotlowitz's book, the CHA's projects failed in part because there were too many children there.

* * *

Most historians have tended to view public housing as a good program sabotaged in its initial phases by real estate interests, next hijacked by local politicians for racist purposes, and then neglected by government because it housed the black poor. This book challenges these views. It considers real estate interests less powerful than assumed, suggests racial hijacking only partly explains public housing locations, and finds neglect to be more systemic than racist in origin. At its core, public housing, as conceived by reformers in 1937, was a blueprint for disaster and could not have survived the postwar housing boom without fundamental changes. The need for these changes was actually recognized early on, but they were never seriously pursued. The crime was therefore not the effort to better house the poor but the failure by those in power to alter course and to fix evident mistakes. Leadership at all governmental levels abandoned its poverty-stricken residents in public housing—nowhere more than in Chicago.

Finally, the CHA's history speaks to its ongoing saga in the twenty-first century. In 1998, the CHA initiated its bold, ten-year "Plan for Transformation." A decade later, nearly all of its high-rise buildings have been torn down, and its residents dispersed, many haphazardly. Private developers are building "mixed-income" communities with only a portion of new dwellings dedicated to former public housing families. This wrenching dismantlement of public housing has fractured both residents and Chicago's liberal community. Some rage at the human costs of displacement, the loss of affordable housing, and the city's gentrification agenda; others contend that only dramatic action can rebuild urban space, remove stigmas, provide hope, and end the social isolation of the poor. These are not mutually exclusive views, and both sides have legitimate arguments.

But the overriding concern, as indicated by public housing's failed past in Chicago, must be one of sustainability. The history of public housing demonstrates that it is not enough to build attractive new developments that adhere to the latest planning ideas. Without a realistic financial plan, without community capacity to exert collective efficacy, and without substantial resident input, even the best-built public housing will succumb to social disorder, mismanagement, and market forces—once again dooming well-meaning efforts.

The 1937 Housing Act Revisited

Understanding the demise of Chicago's public housing requires a close look at the U.S. Housing Act of 1937, which governed the public housing program with few changes for over thirty years. A coalition of reformers, including progressives concerned with alleviating slum conditions and planners devoted to European modern housing ideas, wrote the act and lobbied for its passage. They faced an uphill battle to convince Congress to break with laissez-faire traditions and to have the state enter directly into housing production and management with public goals in mind. But the reformers successfully communicated a rationale for government intervention, fought off external threats, and won enactment in a remarkable legislative victory. At the time, the act was a triumph of New Deal policymaking, praised by its supporters as a major expansion of state responsibility for the welfare of its citizens. Catherine Bauer, a student of European modernist housing and a driving force behind the act, called it a "radical step," explaining that "there is now unqualified recognition of the fact that families who cannot afford safe and sanitary housing must be relieved—not by attempt[s] to unload on them speculative, jerry-built shacks which they cannot afford, not by fanciful dreams about prefabricated Utopias, not by euphemisms about higher wages—but by direct governmental aid, responsibility, and initiative, here and now."[1]

Beginning in the late 1960s, critics seeking to explain public housing's disappointing outcomes read the 1937 Housing Act's legislative history differently. They argued that conservative amendments crushed original liberal intentions and forced public housing to become a residual program limited to the urban dispossessed.[2] But this is a selective reading. While the law's authors did not win on every point, and a more expansive state-sector housing program was rejected, the core progressive agenda survived intact, allowing deeply subsidized, locally managed public housing for those poorly served by the private market. A close look at the legislative and implementation history of the act shows that the handful of conservative amendments were mitigated in the law's final version, circumvented in implementation, or, more perversely, overzealously embraced by progressive administrators seeking to prove their frugality.

Rather than being subverted by conservative amendments, the 1937 Housing Act's constraints emanated from two sources. First, tensions within the coalition of progressive slum reformers and modern housing planners over the direction of policy were never resolved. Progressive reformers wanted an antipoverty program that would rebuild slums for the benefit of those who lived in them, while modern planners pressed for a nonprofit building program on vacant land for the working classes. The coalition proposed both missions, but Congress—and Chicago reformers—were mostly interested in slum clearance. Second, the market-failure justification for public housing limited its reach. Most reformers conceded that public housing should not "compete" with good-quality housing in the private sector. As will be seen in later chapters, public housing administrators measured their outcomes against the private sector and sought to avoid competition by imposing restrictive policies on cost, design, and tenant selection. Their motives included bureaucratic self-preservation but also a sincere belief in the idea that the state should intervene only where private industry could not meet needs. Yet these limits would relentlessly undermine the long-term sustainability of public housing in Chicago and other American cities.

★   ★   ★

The 1937 Housing Act was the product of more than a half-century of work by progressive reformers—public health officials, settlement house leaders, and other activists—to shape public opinions about urban slums. After the Civil War, the new field of public health amassed data on the worst housing districts in U.S. cities, connecting infant mortality and disease with inadequate plumbing, windowless rooms, and improper ventilation. They convinced cities to pay for public health inspectors to police tenement conditions and force improvements, though the problem vastly exceeded available resources. Similarly, settlement house leaders, like Jane Addams in Chicago, drew on British responses to wretched conditions in London and launched a crusade for better housing. They wrote stinging critiques of the indecent living conditions of unskilled immigrants and demanded state action. Jacob Riis, the reform photographer, added to the urgency of the mission by using new flash technology to illuminate the dark corners of alleyways, tenements, and shelters, creating a sensation among the elite with a visual record of deprivation, especially among children. Motivated by concern for both social justice and social order, progressives by the end of the nineteenth century were asserting the environmental argument that poor housing not only bred disease but also fostered juvenile delinquency and illicit behavior, which in turn led to greater crimes and social disorder that threatened the world of the middle class. Thus, progressives argued, the immigrant poor needed good housing not only for reasons of public health but for the social stability of the city.[3]

Progressive reformers attempted a variety of approaches to alleviate urban conditions, but their efforts proved disappointing. New York reformers led the way by pushing through a housing code in 1879 that regulated new construction, forbidding windowless rooms, for example. They also pursued clearance of whole "lung" blocks on Manhattan's densely packed Lower East Side to let city residents "breathe," though progress on that front was expensive and painfully slow. Reformers in Chicago won a housing code in 1889 and strengthened it 1902, a year after the publication of a detailed investigation of overcrowding and unsanitary conditions in three immigrant neighborhoods by Robert Hunter, a member of Jane Addams's Hull House settlement. Hunter's report expressed moral outrage at housing inequalities and conditions and stirred Chicagoans to action. But in both Chicago and New York, enacting restrictive regulations on private housing proved easier than enforcing them. The immigrant poor, fearing rent increases, did not seek code enforcement, much to the chagrin of reformers, nor did city politicians want to antagonize property owners.[4] As a result, cities had little incentive to enforce their own codes. Reformers tried design competitions to produce inexpensive "model housing," but few were built. Slum dwellers had their own methods for resisting unscrupulous landlords, especially ad hoc rent strikes to demand repairs. Overall, progressive efforts and tenant resistance managed little headway against the avalanche of demand for even derelict housing among the waves of impoverished immigrants of the late nineteenth and the early twentieth century.[5]

Documenting the evils of the slums and the limited effectiveness of restrictive laws, Edith Abbott at the University of Chicago collected two decades of work by her graduate students into a comprehensive and detailed indictment of the city's poorest areas. *The Tenements of Chicago, 1908–1935* reflects Abbott's deep progressive sensibilities. Abbott and her colleagues found copious examples of dreadful living conditions in selected areas of the city and little enforcement of its housing code. Faulty planning and few parks produced neighborhoods dangerous for children, leaving many to play in unpaved streets or in open sewers. "Unsightly" wood-frame buildings with "gloomy" rooms and no flush toilets or baths were condemned as unsuitable for healthy family life. Black Chicagoans faced the worst conditions among the city's ethnic and racial groups because of racial discrimination that severely limited housing and job opportunities, and they paid higher rents for worse housing than their white counterparts. "It is difficult to exaggerate the wretchedness of the housing accommodations which the poor Negroes endure," Abbott concluded. Her researchers found only 26 percent of buildings in black districts to be in "good repair," a far lower figure than white slums. Escaping the black ghetto was a dangerous proposition, as racial boundaries in the city were well defined; the city's traumatic 1919 race riot had been touched off when whites stoned a black swimmer for drifting across a racial line at a divided city beach. Although conditions in the black belt were exceptionally dismal, Abbott's report downplayed physical improvements in other communities between 1908 and 1920, especially in terms of sanitation. A construction boom in the 1920s further improved general housing conditions, but like most reformers, Abbott viewed private builders as hopelessly unable to improve conditions of the poor. She framed the slum problem as intractable without government intervention.[6]

Precisely how to intervene remained a point of contention among progressive reformers. Lawrence Vieller, the dean of nineteenth-century New

York City reformers and the founder of the National Housing Association, rejected public construction of housing and insisted that only restrictive regulation of the private market could solve the problems of the slums. Others challenged Vieller's thinking and, by extension, his leadership. They looked across the Atlantic to European housing initiatives, especially in Britain and Germany, where governments had embraced state-sponsored housing after World War I as the solution to housing the working class. The most prominent reformer advocating direct state intervention was Edith Elmer Wood, a progressive with a Ph.D. in economics from Columbia University. Wood reasoned that if European-style programs were to have a chance at enactment, reformers must do more than just describe the appalling conditions of the slums in graphic detail. They needed to overcome the country's devotion to the private market and show that the current system of privately owned housing rented on a market basis was incapable—now, and in the future—of providing reasonable housing (by progressive definitions) for all Americans.[7]

In 1931 Wood developed her case against the market in her third book on housing, which surveyed housing data and reports from the 1920s. Her conclusion is announced in the first paragraph: the housing problem "is insoluble . . . under the ordinary laws of supply and demand" and "is not a local or transitory phenomenon. It is universal and permanent. . . . The distribution of income is such that a substantial portion of the population cannot pay a commercial rent, much less a commercial purchase price, for a home fulfilling the minimum health and decency requirements." Using progressive standards for plumbing, light, occupancy, and affordability (no more than 20 percent of a family's income spent on rent), Wood calculated that market failure encompassed a wide expanse of America, with at least the bottom third of households not served adequately by the private market. This assessment was the likely source for Franklin Roosevelt's second inaugural statement that he saw "one-third of a nation ill-housed." The private housing market could not address this problem, Wood argued; new housing was affordable only to the top third of income earners, while the "filtering" down of old housing through market mechanisms only offered substandard housing to the poor. Assuming these conditions to be "permanent," she demanded government intervention.[8]

The market-failure argument established the rationale for government to act, but it also placed specific limits on its intervention. Wood and most slum reformers believed that the state should not compete with good, standard housing and that public housing should be limited to serving only those whom the private market could not. Of course, public housing would compete against existing slum housing, but that was the point: slum housing represented a glaring market failure. Reformers had no intention of displacing legitimate private landlords and good-quality buildings; they supported public housing as a public utility, but one that extended only to the boundaries of market failure. Where to draw the line between public and private would be a challenge in future years, but the idea behind the divide was both sincere and pragmatic. Threatening builders and conscientious landlords with government-subsidized competition would have been politically unwise, and most housing reformers—and even most liberal members of Congress—were ideologically predisposed to a capitalist economic system tempered by progressive regulation. The main thrust of New Deal liberalism was to maintain social order by restraining the worst in capitalism, not by replacing it.[9]

The Great Depression and Wood's book reinvigorated a housing reform movement that had lost traction during the housing boom of the 1920s. Job losses, housing foreclosures, and a plummet in new housing construction created an undeniable crisis in housing markets and threatened the social fabric of the nation. In this political moment, New York City settlement house workers Mary Simkovitch and Helen Alfred, along with the Reverend John O'Grady, organized the National Public Housing Conference (NPHC) in 1931 to rally reformers behind direct government action. They combined decades of progressive rhetoric about the evils of the slums with Wood's market-failure ideology to make the case that slums needed to be torn down and replaced with state-sponsored, state-subsidized housing for those whom the market failed. As Simkovitch later explained, "From the beginning it was made plain by advocates of public housing that two basic ideas were to be observed: one, that decent shelter and the abolition of slums are essential for maintenance of the American Standard of living, and two, that public housing is not intended to compete with private enterprise wherever and whenever it can produce shelter within the means of low-income families." Simkovitch emphasized that "it is essential to repeat this statement over and over until people understand it."[10]

Progressive slum reformers had taken decades to reach this consensus, but in the early 1930s a handful of liberal planning intellectuals emerged with a challenge to the direction of housing reform.[11] The most remarkable of these modern housing planners was Catherine Bauer, a charismatic young woman who offered a fresh look at "the housing question," using European precedents and modernist paradigms. After what she called "graduate school" from 1929 to 1934 as the protégée of urban critic Lewis

Mumford and a member in the short-lived but influential Regional Planning Association of America (RPAA), Bauer published *Modern Housing* in 1934, a comparative analysis of housing policy in Europe and the United States. Her book began with the environmental determinist assumptions of slum reformers that bad housing produced social ills, but she went further than Wood in arguing that nearly two-thirds of the nation was ill served by the private market. While she shared the progressive revulsion of the slums, she radically proposed letting them "rot," rather than clearing and rebuilding them immediately. She viewed slum clearance as a gift to disreputable slum owners, who would receive excessive condemnation awards under U.S. property laws. In a 1933 article in the *Nation*, Bauer wrote: "Who knows—if we let the slum rot a while longer, and build decent places for their tenants to live elsewhere, perhaps we may yet be able to plow them under, plant trees over them, and let a little air and light into Megalopolis."[12]

Rather than slum clearance, Bauer's *Modern Housing* proposed that U.S. policy emulate European experiments in community building on vacant land, especially the large-scale, state-sponsored, avant-garde projects designed on the outskirts of German cities by modernist Bauhaus architects in the 1920s. Such apartment complexes, with their carefully planned arrangement of buildings and design efficiencies, offered better housing standards at lower cost with greater community amenities. With an expansive definition of market failure, Bauer argued for dispensing low-interest loans to a range of entities, including not only municipal agencies but also noncommercial groups such as limited-dividend corporations, labor unions, cooperatives, and housing societies. These organizations would then build rental communities that would be "permanently removed from the speculative market" and run as a "public utility" for "use" rather than "profit," targeted not at the very poor (who wouldn't be able to afford the rents) but at the working classes. She hoped that a demonstration of the benefits of European-style development on the urban fringes would ignite a political movement to demand even more state-sponsored housing. Slum clearance, in this formulation, would be postponed until the slums could be acquired at a reasonable cost.[13]

The differences between progressive slum reformers and modern housing planners were both substantive and generational. The NPHC leadership came from well-organized public health and settlement networks and were committed to aiding the urban poor. Abandonment of slum clearance in favor of suburban-style development appeared unconscionable given the immediate ills that would remain if slums were left standing.

Bauer and her handful of supporters, meanwhile, were intellectuals, architects, and professional planners far removed from the grit of the slums. They were enthralled by the Bauhaus movement and other modernist influences, and they viewed housing and planning as opportunities to enhance communitarian values among the working classes. Vacant land was where the future of urban space would be decided, and the problems of urban poverty created more ambivalence than outrage.[14]

★   ★   ★

The New Deal opened up a political space that made possible the enactment of state-sponsored housing aimed at market failure, but who would lead the liberal legislative campaign remained uncertain. Between 1933 and 1937, the progressive slum reformers and modern housing planners engaged in a subtle but unmistakable competition over the control of housing reform. At first the more numerous reformers owned the inside track. NPHC members quietly lobbied liberal Senate giant Robert F. Wagner (D-NY) during the early days of the New Deal for federal intervention. In 1933, he successfully inserted one paragraph into the National Industrial Recovery Act (NIRA) that allowed the newly formed Public Works Administration (PWA) to build "low-cost housing and slum clearance projects." Wagner's amendment offered little policy guidance, but it broke open the door to the nation's first significant public housing experiment.[15]

Yet the new PWA Housing Division had an inauspicious start because, despite decades of reformer attention to the "housing question," no blueprint existed on how to implement a public housing program. The Housing Division began by soliciting applications from limited-dividend corporations for subsidized loans and received widespread interest. But after a year, only seven projects had been approved with hundreds rejected owing to high costs and a lack of equity capital among applicants. The frustrated interior secretary, Harold Ickes, brought in new leadership and ordered the Housing Division to undertake public housing development directly, mostly on slum land. But managing the development of numerous projects from Washington led to interminable delays and elevated costs. Stinging criticism descended on the PWA. Modern housers were angered by the abandonment of the limited-dividend approach on vacant land, while local slum reformers railed against Ickes's heavy-handed centralization of decision making. After a tour of Chicago's three PWA projects in 1936, even Ickes agreed, confessing to his diary, "From what I saw and heard I was very much disappointed with the progress that has been made. There isn't any doubt that something is wrong in the Housing Division, in fact, [something] has been wrong a long time." By 1937, the PWA had constructed only fifty-one publicly owned low-rent projects, with 22,000 apartment units nationwide. Many of these projects were reluctantly built on vacant land sites after an unfavorable federal court decision involving slum clearance (*U.S. v Certain Lands in the city of Louisville*) blocked the federal government from condemning land for housing purposes. Without the power to compel the numerous owners of a slum site to sell, the PWA had little choice but to turn to easy-to-obtain vacant sites.[16]

Progressive slum reformers and modern housing planners took away similar lessons from the PWA experiment, and those lessons would influence the 1937 Housing Act. First, the PWA's micromanagement—especially in site selection and design choices—led both groups to argue that any future housing program should be as decentralized as possible, a point Ickes conceded in 1936.[17] The *Louisville* decision also made some degree of local control imperative, since courts had ruled that only state and local governments had the power to take land for housing purposes. Second, progressive slum reformers believed that PWA missteps had led to embarrassingly high costs. Even with a substantial subsidy that paid for 45 percent of construction costs, PWA projects had rents that were out of reach for the unskilled and semi-employed poor. This outcome was another argument for decentralization but also for even deeper subsidies to ensure that public housing could reach the "bottom third" of the housing market.[18]

Since decentralization required a local administrative infrastructure that barely existed in the 1930s, slum reformers devised a new implementing agency—the local housing authority. Combining European precedents with earlier progressive administrative reforms such as municipal water authorities, local housing authorities in the United States were chartered under state law and required to adhere to state civil service rules and other state-level oversight. Progressives were confident that state charters would distance local housing authorities from the perceived corrupting influences of local government, especially the crooked contracting and patronage hiring that permeated many municipal agencies. Reformers wanted housing experts and civic-minded citizens like themselves, not local ward bosses, to guide development. Still, the new entities would not be entirely independent of urban politics; most states allowed mayors to appoint the members of the local housing authority board, subject to state approval. The local housing authority would be the primary conduit for subsidies and would work in partnership with federal officials to develop and manage public housing projects. Ohio passed the first enabling legislation in

1933, and New York City chartered the first local housing authority in 1934. By the end of the decade, most large cities, including Chicago, and many small ones had created their own.[19]

In 1935, reformers in the NPHC convinced Senator Wagner to introduce legislation to rework the PWA experiment into a permanent program of federally funded but locally controlled public housing. Meanwhile, Catherine Bauer and her modern housing allies were struggling to catch up. After publication of *Modern Housing*, Bauer accepted the invitation of the American Federation of Labor (AFL) to become the executive director of the new Labor Housing Conference (LHC), and, with no staff and few resources, she tirelessly toured the country in 1934 and 1935 presenting her vision of housing to AFL leaders. But advancing her agenda into legislative action was another matter. In a belated effort to respond to the Wagner-NPHC effort, Bauer and two labor allies hastily crafted competing legislation, introduced in the House of Representatives by Henry Ellenbogen (D-PA). The 1935 Ellenbogen bill sidestepped the evils of the slums and instead highlighted the failures of the private market. Rather than reform the PWA Housing Division, Bauer wanted to start over with a new independent agency that would facilitate or directly construct large-scale projects, preferably on vacant land.[20] While Bauer shared the slum reformers' desire to decentralize the housing effort, she was less interested in clearing slums than in empowering a broad range of noncommercial groups to build housing anywhere. Ellenbogen's bill, however, went nowhere. As an unnaturalized Hungarian immigrant, he could not vote in the House, and he could not prevent his bill from referral to the inhospitable House Banking Committee, where it was ignored.[21]

In 1935, it was hardly clear that either the Wagner slum reform bill or the less prominent Ellenbogen modern housing bill could win a majority vote in Congress, or even elicit the president's approval. Yet, through persuasive argument, adept political maneuvering, and some compromises, Bauer emerged by 1936 as the driving force behind public housing legislation and, in the process, relegated the NPHC to a supporting role. The shift in power began in Senate hearings in June 1935 when Bauer testified on behalf of Ellenbogen's bill and sharply critiqued Wagner's bill. The senator, in the audience during Bauer's testimony, was genuinely impressed by her arguments. After she won the full backing for her program at the AFL's national convention in October, Wagner brought Bauer into his fold as his top housing advisor.[22]

When Wagner introduced a new housing bill in April 1936, the legislation was an improved version of Bauer's 1935 Ellenbogen text, with the

NPHC's priorities demoted but not banished. The 1936 Wagner housing bill combined the coalition's priorities, allowing shallow subsidies to non-commercial groups and deep subsidies to local housing authorities. The housing would be for "families of low-income" defined in market-failure terms as "those who cannot afford to pay enough to induce the ordinary and usual channels of private enterprise to build adequate, safe, and sanitary housing for their use."[23] While Wagner's proposed legislation bore her firm imprint, Bauer did not have the political power, even with the AFL behind her, to reject decades of reformer rhetoric and prohibit slum clearance. The bill allowed for both slum clearance and vacant land projects, but she hoped by force of reason to convince local housing authorities that vacant sites were best. Despite the legislation's agnostic stance on the issue of slum clearance, the NPHC remained loyal to Wagner and accepted a supporting role. In a delicate balancing act, Bauer had deftly written Wagner's 1936 bill to favor her worldview while still accommodating the progressive slum reformers.

The uneasy alliance of Wagner, Bauer, and the NPHC was a marriage of convenience. Bauer, with few friends in the Roosevelt administration, needed Wagner's stature in the Senate to move her ideas through Congress. The NPHC and its large New York City membership were tied to Wagner and his power as well. For his part, Wagner knew from his experience enacting the National Labor Relations Act and the Social Security Act that he needed both the backing of labor and the NPHC's moral voice to push monumental housing legislation through a reluctant administration and a skeptical Congress. Still, he left crucial details of policy to Bauer and her close circle of allies. Her irrepressible energy and keen analytical mind made her the dominant force in writing the legislation that would pass the Senate in 1936 but fail to be considered in the House, and then, a year later, pass both houses and be signed into law as the 1937 Housing Act.[24]

As Wagner's 1936 housing bill progressed through Congress, the greatest threats to its inner workings and ultimate passage emanated not from conservatives or the real estate lobby, but from powerful institutions within the Roosevelt administration. For the most part, Bauer's group successfully fought them off. The fledgling Federal Housing Administration (FHA), created in 1934 to guarantee private housing loans and prop up homebuilders, had the most to lose by having a competitor in the field of housing policy, so it sought to derail Wagner's bill by criticizing public ownership of housing and by offering to expand its own mortgage insurance program into low-income markets. But Bauer, who disapproved of the FHA's subsidization of private speculative builders, convinced the

AFL to threaten the FHA with legislation requiring the use of union labor on all FHA-insured housing, a change that would have drastically reduced participation in its programs. The tactic worked, and the FHA quietly folded its opposition and formally endorsed Wagner's bill.[25] A second threat came from Harold Ickes and the PWA, which wanted to continue its Housing Division activities, albeit with more local control. After Wagner and Bauer deflected a PWA bill from President Roosevelt's favor, Ickes agreed to support Wagner's bill, but with one amendment: the new United States Housing Authority (USHA) would be placed under his authority at the Department of the Interior. Slum reformers backed Ickes in recognition of his earlier support for slum clearance, but at Bauer's insistence, Wagner resisted giving the USHA to the Department of the Interior. The issue was decided on the Senate floor in 1937, and Ickes won. Bauer took the defeat hard, but once the public housing program was up and running, Ickes showed little interest in it, and the USHA in practice operated as an independent agency.[26]

Throughout these battles President Roosevelt proved a wild card and source of angst for housing reformers. Because he entertained numerous housing ideas from various sources, Bauer worried about his whims. Roosevelt remained noncommittal on Wagner's bill until June 1936, when he belatedly endorsed it with the demand that first-year authorizations be reduced from $50 million to $10 million. This cut angered Bauer, but she was relieved that Roosevelt had not damaged the "mechanics" of the bill.[27]

The most important of these "mechanics" involved the subsidy provisions, which were flexible, generous, complex—and often misunderstood. Bauer and left-leaning economist Warren Vinton devised two separate subsidies.[28] The first involved a construction loan (financed by Treasury-backed bonds) at favorable rates to local housing authorities and noncommercial groups alike. The loans would cover 90 percent of total project costs—including any slum clearance and site preparation costs—with the remaining 10 percent borrowed locally. But a low-interest construction loan was a shallow subsidy and could not produce rents that reached the poor. Vinton and Bauer therefore crafted a second and far deeper subsidy, known as the "annual contribution," available only to local housing authorities. The annual contribution involved a contract where the federal government agreed to yearly cash payments to local housing authorities in order to reduce rents to affordable levels. In practical terms the bill set the maximum annual contribution at the project's yearly debt service— the amount owed on its federal and local construction loans. In essence, at maximum subsidy the federal government would pay for the entire capital cost of housing built by local housing authorities. Taken together, the two subsidies in the Wagner bill were far more generous than any similar housing program in Europe at the time.[29]

This subsidy system had crucial implications. First, it gave cities public housing projects for free: no cash outlay on the part of cities was required. Second, it allowed rents to be set with social goals in mind. In privately owned housing, rents were set by market forces, but, at a minimum, rents needed to cover total operating costs, including debt service, management, maintenance, and property taxes. Owners also expected a profit. In public housing, many of these demands went away. Debt service was covered by the federal annual contribution, property taxes, as will be seen, were later exempted, and local housing authorities were nonprofit entities. This meant that public housing rents needed to cover only management, maintenance, and a reserve, roughly one-half of total operating expenses in a typical privately owned building.[30] As a result, housing authorities would have the freedom to run public housing in Bauer's vision as a public utility rather than a commercial enterprise.

A third implication was also important to the long-term health of projects. Once Congress approved an initial authorization for public housing, the annual contribution subsidy would be well protected in subsequent years during the federal budget process. The bill's financing mechanism created this privileged budgetary position. Bauer and Vinton's language allowed the new USHA to loan money to local housing authorities from one pocket (the proceeds from Treasury-backed bond sales) and then to contractually guarantee the repayment of these loans using funds from a second pocket (the congressionally appropriated annual contributions). The contract made the Treasury bonds attractive to investors, but it also meant that Congress would have little choice each year but to appropriate sufficient subsidy. Otherwise, Congress risked defaulting on federal debt and creating calamity in markets for Treasury bonds. Of course, Congress and federal administrators would exert influence over public housing in other ways, with conflicts centering on the size of the program and oversight of local housing authority efficiency. But for all intents and purposes, Bauer and Vinton astutely insulated completed projects from federal budget pressures, and Washington's annual contributions for existing projects were never at risk in the history of the program.[31] However, as we shall see in chapter 7, once housing authorities had drawn their maximum annual contribution and had to return to Congress for more funds, as occurred beginning in the in the 1960s, the budget picture changed entirely.

The implications of these subsidies escaped most members of Congress, and even at the Treasury, Henry Morgenthau misunderstood them. But Secretary Morgenthau's staff recognized the overall thrust: Congress would be on the hook for the long-term costs of public housing. Much like a home mortgage, Bauer and Vinton's formula spread the capital cost of public housing over many years, making it appear more affordable to Congress in its first year. Instead, Morgenthau wanted more budgetary transparency and argued for an up-front, one-time "capital grant" subsidy appropriated by Congress to pay for only 45 percent of construction costs (as with the PWA program). No federal loan would be provided, and local authorities would have to borrow and repay 55 percent of capital costs themselves—far less generous than Bauer's plan. Morgenthau's objections triggered months of debate between Bauer's camp and the Treasury Department, culminating in a White House confrontation between Morgenthau and Wagner in March 1937. Afterward, Roosevelt sided with Morgenthau and gave him the go-ahead to draft new subsidy provisions for the 1937 version of the Wagner housing bill. But three months later, Wagner convinced Roosevelt to reverse himself and restore Bauer and Vinton's subsidy provisions. After what Bauer called "continuous struggle" with the Treasury, the Bauer and Vinton formula, and hence protected subsidies and low rents, survived.[32]

★   ★   ★

The Wagner housing bill weathered internal battles among progressives and within the Roosevelt administration in 1936 and 1937, but it did not emerge from congressional consideration unscathed. Several significant amendments deserve careful examination, as they were later blamed for contributing to public housing's decline. Most amendments emanated not from public housing's most visible opponent, the real estate lobby, but instead reflected the lingering tension between progressive slum reformers and modern housing planners over who should benefit from public expenditure on housing.

Three important amendments came from David I. Walsh, a Massachusetts Democrat who wielded substantial power as chairman of the Senate Education and Labor Committee. In the spectrum of Senate Democrats during the New Deal, Walsh was a moderate who held mildly progressive views on social welfare legislation but who opposed Roosevelt's court-packing plan and interventionist foreign policy.[33] On housing, Walsh's field of vision was narrow. While Bauer felt Walsh was "fairly sympathetic" to public housing, he knew little about European housing precedents. But neither was he in the pocket of real estate interests. Instead, Walsh was keenly aware of Ickes's PWA public housing experiment, especially in Boston, and he did not like what he saw. The PWA projects, with their high costs and less generous subsidies, had rents that were too high for the poor. Initial tenants had secure working-class and white-collar jobs. As the son of Irish immigrants who had experienced poverty firsthand, Walsh wanted federal spending on housing to benefit the very poor. He told the Senate in 1937: "The first tenant to get into one of these subsidized tenements . . . will be the poor washerwoman of New York City with her children. . . . I insist its benefits reach the lowest-income group." Bauer characterized Walsh's view as limiting public housing to "the bottom 5 percent," but his view was hardly a reactionary one. He reflected the sensibilities of many slum reformers, and his concerns raised real dilemmas about how to distribute a scarce public benefit fairly.[34]

Walsh's first amendment placed limits on the incomes of tenants. Bauer had defined eligibility for public housing in market-failure terms, but Walsh wanted more concrete measures, and in his Senate committee in 1936, he added a clause requiring that a tenant's monthly income not exceed five times the rent. Bauer's circle was not thrilled with the amendment, objecting to any numerical limits out of a need for administrative flexibility but suggesting that if the Walsh provision were retained, the ratio should be set at six to one. Later, in final negotiations over the bill in August 1937, Wagner succeeded in setting the law's limits at five times the rent for families of four or less, and six times the rent for larger families. Bauer and her allies considered this compromise one they could live with.[35]

A second Walsh amendment intended to settle the submerged debate between progressive slum reformers and modern housing planners over whether public housing should clear slums or build on vacant land. Since he believed slums were the root cause of social evils, as reformers had long argued, Walsh wanted the bill to ensure their removal. He added an "equivalent elimination" provision demanding the clearance of one slum unit for each new public housing unit built. Later critics cited the provision as a gift to real estate interests, since equivalent elimination meant no net addition to the housing supply.[36] Yet Walsh's support of equivalent elimination had little to do with placating the real estate industry and more to do with clearing the slums and their attendant public health and social welfare problems. He could not imagine spending public dollars to build new housing on vacant land while leaving slums standing. In final negotiations, however, Bauer and Wagner again mitigated a potentially restrictive amendment. They wrote a loophole into Walsh's language by defining the word "elimination" generously and by giving administrators the power to defer equivalent elimination in the event of a housing shortage in a locality.[37] While flexibility had been saved, the episode showed the uphill battle facing Bauer in her effort to convince progressives that housing policy should ignore the slums and instead build on vacant land.

Walsh's third amendment removed the Wagner bill's section allowing for reduced-interest loans to noncommercial groups, such as labor unions and housing societies. Bauer had championed the participation of such alternative groups based on her knowledge of Europe, where the practice was widespread. But support for the idea was thin, and Walsh struck them from the bill in his committee in 1936 and on the Senate floor in 1937 without opposition. He believed that alternative groups were best financed by the FHA, which already had a loan program intended for nonprofit and limited-dividend organizations, while the new public housing program should focus on the poor. Wagner, for his part, conceded Walsh's point and never mustered the energy to fight for Bauer's view.[38] While she knew that keeping loans to noncommercial groups in the bill had been a long shot, Bauer still was stung by the loss. It crushed her hope that an expansive USHA might spark a housing movement among the working classes that, in turn, could displace the FHA as the prime agency planning and subsidizing suburban development. Bauer's vision faced major hurdles, including the long-standing cultural preference for single-family home ownership. But the loss did remove the ability of modern housing planners to push cooperatives and other nonprofit developers into building large amounts of affordable housing.[39]

Two other important amendments to the Wagner housing bill came not from Walsh but from conservatives who had little sympathy for public housing. First, Senator Harry Byrd, a conservative Democrat from Virginia, led an effort to impose limits on construction costs. He had long railed at what he considered the profligacy of the New Deal, especially in its efforts to aid the poor. Byrd asked Wagner for recent figures on PWA construction costs per apartment and then proceeded on the Senate floor in 1937 to amend the Wagner bill by setting a maximum limit on costs per apartment at the average figure for the PWA's experimental projects, a potentially restrictive move if applied in a blanket fashion across the country. But again Bauer's team mitigated the amendment's reach in final negotiations over the bill. Wagner successfully inserted higher cost limits and an additional allowance for large cities into the law's final language. Still, the congressional debate made it clear that lawmakers did not want public housing to be costlier than middle-class housing. But neither did the progressive slum reformers or the modern housing planners, who both viewed the PWA projects as overbuilt. For Bauer, modernist designs could offer better housing at lower costs, a key selling point for state-sponsored housing.[40]

The second conservative amendment sought to shift more of the costs of public housing to local government. Under the Wagner bill, projects would cost cities nothing. When the House Banking Committee, run by conservative Alabama Democrat Henry Steagall, finally considered the legislation in the summer of 1937, it added an amendment requiring local governments to contribute 20 percent of the total subsidy for each project. The amendment originated with real estate interests, who hoped that a 20 percent contribution would be impossible for cash-strapped cities to meet.[41] But the amendment allowed either cash or property tax exemption to count toward the local contribution. For most cities, tax exemption was the obvious choice; it easily satisfied the 20 percent contribution requirement as cities received credit for the amount public housing would have been taxed had it been privately owned. Further, the loss of property tax revenue was softened by two factors. First, local housing authorities paid uncollected back taxes on property they condemned (a substantial sum in the case of many slums). Second, they could grant cities "payments in lieu of taxes" (PILOT), usually set as a percentage of rents, to offset the cost of city services. In most instances, the PILOT exceeded the site's actual preclearance tax collection.[42] From a municipal finance perspective, then, public housing remained an extraordinarily good deal even with tax exemption.

Only Bauer seriously objected to the amendment. While progressive slum reformers had long championed tax exemption as an appropriate way to reduce rents, Bauer disagreed. She argued in internal debates that tax exemption was "the worst form of subsidy" because it made potential enemies out of small property owners.[43] She had written the Wagner bill to be neutral on the issue, neither requiring nor prohibiting tax exemption, but the House amendment requiring a 20 percent local contribution indirectly undid her intentions. Bauer's shrewd understanding of urban politics would prove prophetic, as tax exemption offered a wedge for local governments to exert leverage over independent housing authorities, especially in Chicago.

*   *   *

Shortly after President Roosevelt signed the Wagner-Steagall 1937 Housing
Act into law, Catherine Bauer assessed her work in the *New Republic*. She
began by injudiciously settling political scores, taking a slap at Roosevelt
(who "did nothing for this bill") and at the Treasury and the FHA (which
"tried to sabotage it"). But then the normally acerbic Bauer provided an
upbeat review of the final law. She called it "a radical piece of legislation—
perhaps the most clear-cut and uncompromising adopted under the New
Deal." She identified the act not as a piece of special interest legislation
but instead as "a popular measure" that "found democracy functioning
better than usual in America," a reference to the vigorous lobbying campaign for the bill orchestrated by labor and other progressive organizations. Although she admitted that "a series of half-baked" amendments
had taken a toll, leaving the act "battle-scarred," she concluded it was "still
in fairly workable shape" with a "solid foundation definitely intact." She
called the loss of her favored noncommercial implementation groups
"definitely bad." Nevertheless, she continued, "if there is a really strong
demand for this type of housing, it can probably be added later." Although
she cited the equivalent elimination clause as the "most potentially dangerous" provision, she frankly acknowledged the loophole she helped
write into the final bill. Similarly, she predicted that construction cost limits would need upward revision in the future. Her overall enthusiasm for
the new program, however, far exceeded her criticism. Among the new
law's key components, she cited its subsidy provisions: "Generally, liberal
legislation is systematically pared down in the course of passage. But in
the one all-important matter of public subsidy allowed per dwelling unit,
which determines whether the housing will be really low-rental or not,
the Housing Act is just as good as the day it was introduced—and much
better than the housing proposals introduced in 1935 and 1936."[44]

Historians generally have not shared Bauer's view. Relying upon the
only substantial legislative history of the 1937 Housing Act, written by
Timothy McDonnell in 1957, scholars have asserted that conservative
amendments eviscerated progressive intentions and left the program
handicapped from the start. Historian James Patterson, among the first to
make this argument, wrote in 1969 that public housing opponents "emas-
culated" the 1937 Housing Act in Congress by striking Bauer's alternative
agencies and imposing equivalent elimination. Political scientist Eugene
Meehan labeled public housing "programmed to fail" because of its sub-

sidy provisions and cost restrictions, and Daniel Rogers, in his 1998 trans-atlantic study of progressive reformers, argued that "[r]eal estate lobbies, building and loan associations, and chambers of commerce" controlled the legislative "endgame" in public housing and "quickly whittled down the [public housing] bill to its least common denominator: cheap housing for the poor."[45] A progressive vision of public housing, these scholars con-clude, never had a chance to prove itself, let alone succeed.

This evaluation, however, is far too pessimistic and shifts responsibility for policy away from the 1937 Housing Act's primary authors. Rather than a hopelessly narrow piece of legislation, the act represented a compro-mise between progressive slum reformers and modern housing planners, with the result favoring the former more than the latter despite Bauer's best efforts. She did not win a more expansive law to allow alternative implementing agencies, though that loss had more do with weak support among progressives than aggressive opposition from real estate interests. Moreover, she did not abandon the legislation, and she proceeded to help administer the new law. Real estate interests did try to kill Wagner's bill, but their efforts were ineffectual and did not tamper with the important "mechanics" of its most important provisions. Senator Walsh proved a key player, and on most issues he showed progressive, if somewhat narrow, motives for wanting the act to serve the poor. If the act's authors were unhappy with the law, they did not express it until the mid-1950s, and in subsequent years, they proposed few changes to its basic formula, which remained largely intact until important amendments in 1969.[46]

★   ★   ★

The 1937 Housing Act established three overarching principles that de-fined the program for decades. The first created a federal-local implemen-tation partnership, with deference to local officials on important decisions such as site selection and tenant selection. Federal officials still had sig-nificant oversight and even policy control through the annual contribu-tion contract, but the federal-local relationship over time would evolve and become strained, as each side sought to exert control. The second involved the law's deep subsidies, which allowed local housing authori-ties to set policies with social goals in mind. However, these policies—especially on rent and tenant selection—would differentiate public hous-ing in often negative ways, as will be seen. Third and most important was the market-failure ideology that justified state intervention. The extent of private market failure not only limited whom the program could serve but affected design and construction cost decisions, as comparisons with the private market would be made. Public housing had to outperform the private market—in terms of cost and quality—in order to survive.

Each of these broad parameters still left thorny, practical details to be worked out. Where should projects be located—in slums or on vacant land? What designs and site plans should be used? How should rents be set? How selective should projects be in picking tenants? Future administrators in Washington and Chicago wrestled with these details in the late 1930s and early 1940s, but many of their choices would eventually undermine the long-term sustainability of the very projects they built and thus subvert the progressive, idealistic vision behind the 1937 Housing Act.

Building the Chicago Housing Authority

The reformers who wrote the 1937 Housing Act soon took the helm of the new United States Housing Authority to implement their handiwork. Catherine Bauer and Warren Vinton accepted senior positions, and Senator Wagner's top aide, Leon Keyserling, became chief counsel. Robert C. Weaver, an African American and Harvard Ph.D., came from the Department of the Interior to serve as racial relations advisor. For the top job, President Roosevelt accepted Wagner's suggestion and chose Nathan Straus, a wealthy New York City philanthropist, a major contributor to Bauer's cause, and a housing reformer who built one of the PWA's few limited-dividend projects. Straus had the blessing of Bauer and the National Public Housing Conference, though Harold Ickes privately detested Straus as a "dilettante" and wanted nothing to do with him or the USHA.[1] Together, Straus, Bauer, Vinton, and Keyserling spent 1938 and 1939 contending with knotty implementation issues that were only vaguely addressed in the new law.

Meanwhile, in Chicago, Edward Kelly established the Chicago Housing Authority in January 1937. The agency quickly grew to be one of the city's most progressive governmental organizations, first championing housing reform and, after a few years, the rights of African Americans. On the advice of Chicago liberals, Mayor Kelly appointed a slate of nonpartisan experts to the board, including Coleman Woodbury, an economist at Northwestern University and executive director of the National Association of Housing Officials (NAHO), who had worked closely with Catherine Bauer in Washington to pass the 1937 Housing Act. Others selected by the mayor included architect John Fugard, chairman of the Metropolitan Housing Council (MHC), the city's progressive housing reform organization, and, in 1938, at the prodding of Weaver, Robert R. Taylor, the CHA's first African American representative.[2] From this period through the early 1970s, Chicago mayors followed an unwritten rule and maintained a board membership that included one housing reformer, one labor leader, one African American representative, one Jewish member, and one business executive. Under Kelly, this pattern created a reliably progressive board.

Robert Taylor became chairman in 1942, a position he held until 1950. While not a "race man" by the definitions of the day, he keenly understood that African Americans looked to him to tackle the injustices that created both the poor quality and the acute shortages of housing available to black residents. Raised in Alabama, Taylor had studied architecture at Howard University but left and graduated from the University of Illinois with a degree in business. In Chicago, he helped form the Illinois Federal Savings and Loan Association, one of the black belt's leading lending institutions, and also managed the Michigan Boulevard Garden Apartments, a philanthropic, limited-dividend project built by Julius Rosenwald that housed middle-class African Americans. In 1932, Taylor served on Herbert Hoover's Conference on Home Building and Home Ownership, adding to his expertise on housing. While conflict averse, he actively involved himself in the CHA's work and exerted a confident presence as its head.[3]

For the important role of day-to-day manager, the board selected Elizabeth Wood, who ventured into housing reform through an unusual route. Born in Japan in 1899 to missionary parents, she taught poetry at Vassar for four years before moving to Chicago, where she briefly sold books door-to-door. In 1929 she took a job as a social worker and witnessed the human costs of the city's slums during the Depression. This contact led to an interest in housing reform, and in 1934 she became the executive

Figure 5. Elizabeth Wood, no date. Courtesy of the CHA.

secretary of the MHC. A year later she served as executive secretary of the Illinois State Housing Board and consulted for the PWA Housing Division. As executive secretary of the CHA from 1937 until 1954, Wood was its progressive heart. She worked indefatigably to develop, manage, and promote the authority, and she hired a highly educated staff committed to public housing's mission. At the CHA, unlike other city agencies, Wood had full power to hire and fire senior staff and prided herself on running a "clean" agency, free from political influence.

Thus, in both Chicago and Washington, progressive administrators were in charge of the crucial implementation phase of public housing, and they directed the public housing program toward rescuing poor families from slum conditions. By aggressively, even overzealously, setting policies to ensure the poor would benefit, progressives planned to demonstrate that their program would not compete with private housing but would be an efficient and effective tool that would transform cities. But public housing's critics also influenced policy, especially in Chicago where the city

Figure 6. Robert R. Taylor, 1941. Courtesy of the CHA.

council resented the independence of the CHA. As the fledgling housing authority sought to find its way, it negotiated with federal officials, local politicians, and neighborhood residents over the extent of its power. Issues surrounding race, unaddressed in the 1937 Housing Act, were only one of several flash points that emerged to shape the program's early years.

★   ★   ★

The 1937 Housing Act said little about selecting sites for public housing, but the PWA Housing Division's experiment had already revealed many of the challenges involved. In Chicago, the PWA had planned to build three large slum clearance projects ranging from 1,000 to 3,000 units in densely packed areas occupied by Italian Americans, Polish Americans, and African Americans. The ethnically balanced sites were recommended by the PWA's planning consultants, Coleman Woodbury and Jacob Crane (who later became a top USHA administrator), as a good "beginning" point, with each site proposed for "possibilities of future expansion."[4] But land speculation and political entreaties surrounding the locations enraged Ickes, a Chicagoan who had long battled corruption, and as a consequence the Department of the Interior suspended land acquisition activity at the Italian and Polish sites in early 1935. At the African American site in the city's Bronzeville neighborhood, lakefront whites and the Chicago Real Estate Board objected vociferously, arguing the area should be "reclaimed" for "higher use than low-cost housing for Negroes" (meaning housing for whites). The PWA resisted these claims, however, and allowed the project to proceed until the 1935 *Louisville* decision stopped the federal government from using eminent domain to condemn land for housing purposes.[5] Blocked from wholesale slum clearance, the PWA negotiated with individual owners to purchase smaller sites for two projects, Julia Lathrop Homes (960 units) on the North Side and, on the South Side, Trumbull Park Homes (450 units). For a third project, settlement house leader Jane Addams and Chicago slum reformers salvaged a fraction of Woodbury and Crane's Italian American slum site on the West Side, originally planned for 3,000 units. Just before her death, Addams encouraged the Jewish People's Home to sell a twenty-six-acre tract to the PWA, which proceeded to build the 1,027-unit Jane Addams Homes.[6] But legal harassment, both large and small, had forced the PWA to reluctantly abandon most of its slum clearance plans.

Moreover, the three projects were in white areas of the city and left the PWA with nothing to offer the city's African American community. The inability to complete a project for African Americans embarrassed Ickes, the former head of the Chicago NAACP, who recognized that they experienced the worst housing conditions because of segregation and discrimination. As a politician, he also recognized that urban blacks in the North were shifting to the Democratic Party at the polls, so in 1936 he directed the PWA to resurrect the South Side Bronzeville site by renewing negotiations with property owners, this time backed by the condemnation powers of the Illinois State Housing Board. By the summer, purchase, relocation, and demolition were underway, but work halted in the fall when the PWA ran out of funds.[7] Soon after its founding in 1937, the CHA made finishing the Bronzeville project its first priority, but further agonizing holdups ensued. The bureaucratic shift from the PWA Housing Division to the new USHA halted progress, a dispute between the architects and the board over the project's density and architect's fees took months to resolve, recalcitrant aldermen held up the project over tax exemption and work permits, and finally, a labor dispute between the city's unions and the project's contractor led to work stoppages. South Side African Americans, exasperated at what the *Chicago Defender* called "suspicious delays," held protest rallies demanding completion of the project.[8] Belatedly, but with much fanfare, the Ida B. Wells Homes opened in January 1941.

Of all the CHA setbacks, opposition to tax exemption had the greatest consequences, just as Catherine Bauer had predicted. The property tax had long been a politically powerful issue in Chicago, especially during the 1930s. Following a disastrous reassessment of property in 1929, rebellious owners went on "tax strikes" and left the city's finances in a shambles by 1932. City services and education were hit hard, bailed out only by New Deal federal aid. As late as 1938, one-third of Chicago's property tax payers still owed taxes levied in 1932, and in 1940, the city had the highest percentage of uncollected levy (25.9 percent) of any U.S. city. By the time fiscal order was restored by Mayor Kelly, property tax rates had risen substantially.[9] In this climate, tax exemption was a red flag to real estate interests and aldermen alike. The CHA softened the blow by offering the city 3 percent of its gross rental revenue as a payment in lieu of taxes to offset the cost of city services to the project. Elizabeth Wood argued this amount would exceed previous property tax collections from the Bronzeville site, and the new project would replace blighted neighborhoods with their costly fire, police, and welfare services. "The city's tax subsidy to public housing is actually not a subsidy at all but merely municipal good housekeeping," she explained. Yet the CHA was forced to admit that the PILOT was less than one-tenth of what would be collected if the new project were privately owned. Tax exemption amounted to roughly a third of the total public subsidy and kept rents low, but aldermen from working-class neighborhoods, demoralized by foreclosure in the 1930s, saw only an unfair shifting of the tax burden to property owners.[10]

From 1938 to 1940, the CHA and the city council battled over the size of the PILOT payments, and, by extension, the CHA's independence from city government. In theory, the CHA operated with a high degree of autonomy as a state-chartered institution. But USHA regulations required that local housing authorities and city governments enter into a "cooperation agreement," covering the city's responsibility for providing municipal services, street closings, necessary zoning changes, and tax exemption. USHA officials had expected that the cooperation agreement would help local housing authorities by smoothing the hurdles to slum clearance and redevelopment.[11] Instead, the Chicago City Council employed the cooperation agreement as leverage to win a larger PILOT and, more important, to gain a greater say in site selection.

The first cooperation agreement, over the Ida B. Wells Homes, took months to hammer out, but a second agreement, sought in 1939 for two more projects, faced even stiffer aldermanic resistance. The council wanted a 5 percent PILOT and demanded to know where the new projects would be built. The CHA understandably hoped to keep sites secret to prevent corrupt land speculation and to ensure that planning criteria, rather than politics, guided site selection. But Arthur Lindell, chairman of the City Council Committee on Housing, objected to the lack of consultation on sites, informing the *Chicago Tribune*, "I doubt the Council will ever pass such a 'cooperation ordinance' unless it knows where these low-cost houses will be erected." After seven months of delay, Mayor Kelly told the CHA he could no longer protect it from the city council on these issues, and the CHA reluctantly agreed to a higher PILOT and revealed its sites.[12] Alderman Lindell then moved to make the CHA's concessions permanent. In 1940, the council unanimously passed a resolution asking Springfield to amend state housing law to require a 5 percent PILOT and specific site boundaries in all future cooperation agreements. Lindell explained that his change would "make it necessary for the CHA to come to the City Council for permission to locate a project." In July 1941, the state legislature obliged and passed into law Lindell's desired changes.[13]

Thus by 1941, the city council had won significant veto power over public housing site selection.[14] Mayor Kelly, known for his rigid control over the city council and his strong support of the CHA's policies, was unable to prevent the aldermen from overpowering an independent agency that tried to develop large-scale, tax-exempt projects without aldermanic input. Kelly was the CHA's chief political protector in its first ten years, but he had his limits. Racial considerations may well have been in the back of the minds of the aldermen in the prewar period, but if so, they were still submerged. The city council and other organizations proposed sites in white areas between 1937 and 1941 under the assumption that the CHA's tenant selection procedures would not disturb segregated housing patterns.[15] None of these proposals were selected, though the CHA did choose two small, mostly vacant sites in 1941 in the Irish American neighborhood of Bridgeport, home to Chicago mayors for decades, with the blessing of the Chicago Plan Commission (CPC) and without aldermanic opposition. The first site was developed as Bridgeport Homes, replacing an abandoned factory with 128 row houses. The CHA completed land acquisition for the second site but lacked the funds to build the project, leaving the Father Dorney Homes (planned for 108 units) on hold until after the war.[16]

While race remained a latent issue, the central concern in the council involved raw power over development in the city's neighborhoods. A "good government" organization like the CHA lacked the influence to prevail in a battle with machine politicians protecting their parochial interests. Building any project required numerous interactions with local government as the cooperation agreement, with its attendant clauses on building permits, zoning variances, and municipal services, explicitly recognized. A recalcitrant city council or even a single alderman could hold up any of these items and find leverage in the cooperation agreement to sway decisions. Chicago was not alone in this respect, as Philadelphia's city council used similar powers to harass its local housing authority.[17] Public housing's creators had hoped that housing authorities could somehow remain above petty political influence and operate independently, guided by objective criteria and expert thinking. But local politicians were often unwilling to defer to planners and believed they should have ultimate say over development in their wards.

★ ★ ★

Despite these political setbacks, the CHA moved forward with slum clearance in the early 1940s. But its experiences in clearing two densely settled areas would have a lasting influence on future site choices. The first site, eventually the Frances Cabrini Homes, lay in a predominantly Italian neighborhood on the Near North Side known as "Little Hell," though a recent influx of African Americans had increased the black population to 20 percent. The CHA overestimated the extent of substandard conditions in the area and underestimated the number of resident owners, many of whom rebuffed the CHA's purchase offers and hired lawyers. The CHA admitted that the Italian immigrants who owned these homes had "a very strong community spirit, supported by ties of kinship and common language—all resulting in an attitude on the part of the owners which rendered the conduct of negotiations extremely difficult." Homeownership rates among Italian Americans in Chicago were higher than those of native-born whites, and the prospect of renting in a public project offered little appeal. Speaking of his Italian parishioners, Father Louis Giambastini observed that the proposed project "will not be their own. To own the home, to own the land and house—that is the dream of every Italian." The CHA mostly ignored the Italian community's concerns, but it did face competition for the Cabrini site from the highway department and the sanitation department, both of which wanted portions of the area.

By 1941, after expensive and frustrating delays, the costly Cabrini site was whittled down to less than half of its original size.[18]

In sharp contrast, most residents of the second site, eventually the Robert Brooks Homes, were renters, predominantly African American, but also German, Jewish, and Mexican. Most lived in dilapidated structures erected hastily after the Chicago fire of 1871. According to an internal CHA report, community cohesion was low, with "the majority of property owned by non-residents who have no connection with each other." At the Brooks site, absentee landlords were willing to negotiate a quick sale of their substandard properties, and site acquisition and removal of tenants was uneventful—at least from the CHA's perspective.[19]

The disparity between the difficulty in acquiring the well-defended Italian American Cabrini site and the relative ease in obtaining the mostly African American Brooks site influenced the CHA's approach to slum clearance. Never again did the CHA propose large-scale clearance of a white neighborhood. In the 1940s, Chicago had numerous areas labeled as slums by progressives, which housed Polish, Italian, and Irish immigrants in substandard conditions. Cost was not the decisive factor in determining which sites to acquire; a 1948 estimate by the CHA showed that black and white slum tracts were comparable in cost (though not in condition), with numerous large white tracts available for less than $1.50 a square foot, a USHA standard for cost. But the prospect of active opposition from owner-occupied sites made clearing white neighborhoods a time-consuming and politically perilous task. While fears of neighborhood racial change had not been voiced in 1939, they would come to the forefront after the war and make white sites even more problematic. Given such obstacles, the CHA after 1939 proposed slum clearance almost exclusively in relatively easy-to-acquire black neighborhoods where conditions were the worst. Some African American homeowners resisted clearance and voiced protest, especially in the 1940s and 1950s, when slum clearance threatened wide swaths of the black belt. But their relatively limited access to property ownership and political power made it difficult for black residents to defend neighborhoods with the same force that whites could.[20]

The CHA's decision to center its prewar efforts on clearing slums was also driven by its strong belief in the benefits of such clearance, despite calls from the USHA to consider vacant land sites. Catherine Bauer delivered speeches and wrote USHA policy bulletins that explained the superiority of vacant land, and she drafted generous regulations to exploit the loopholes in the law's equivalent elimination provision. The USHA

allowed broad criteria for deferring the requirement and counted as "eliminated" any housing that was repaired, demolished, or cleared in a city
over a five-year period. Typical housing stock attrition, then, would satisfy
the Housing Act.[21] As a result, many local housing authorities around the
country chose a mix of slum clearance and vacant land sites. Between
1938 and 1945, the USHA reported funding 165,000 new permanent public
housing units (excluding temporary projects built during the war for war
worker use) and counted only 54,000 units as eliminated, hardly equivalent elimination by Senator Walsh's standards.[22] Little evidence suggests
that the equivalent elimination clause blocked the plans of local housing
authorities who wanted to build on vacant land.[23]

In Chicago, however, the long history of progressive slum reform predisposed the board to clearance. Beyond the reports of Jane Addams's
Hull House and the work of Edith Abbott at the University of Chicago,
the MHC, with Elizabeth Wood as its secretary, was already engaged in
slum clearance. It used state funds in 1934 and 1935 to demolish 8,597
dilapidated and abandoned housing units, especially in the city's black
neighborhoods. The MHC pushed for the Works Progress Administration
(WPA) to fund a land use survey as a tool to make the city decipherable
to planners who could then identify larger areas needing clearance. When
mapped using progressive standards for housing conditions, these surveys
labeled vast areas surrounding the central business district as slums. With
a board and staff dominated by progressive reformers, the CHA elected to
build 92 percent of all its prewar apartments on dense slum sites.[24]

★   ★   ★

While coaxing housing authorities on site selection, Washington elected
to use the power embedded in the annual contributions contract to wield
greater influence over project design. Nathan Straus set the tone early in
his administration and went far beyond congressional intent in his zeal to
slice costs. In a 1938 speech, he admonished that "building construction
[be] as simple as possible," and despite local control over project design,
the USHA would scrutinize plans. "There will be no frills in any housing
projects," Straus told an assembly of architects. "All unnecessary features
will be eliminated from any plans submitted." By 1940, USHA regulations
stated that projects would not be approved unless construction budgets
were "substantially below statutory cost restrictions" in the 1937 Housing
Act. Vinton and Bauer concurred with Straus's cost-cutting spirit, suggesting in a 1938 memo that the USHA urge locals to use "less desirable sites"
and "smaller living spaces" as an economy move. That same year, Bauer

wrote in *Shelter* magazine that "wasteful ornamentation has been ruthlessly eliminated from their construction plans."[25]

Straus had engineers in Washington build a "housing laboratory," consisting of a full-size apartment with moveable walls, which were closed in, "inch-by-inch, to determine the minimum space necessary to accommodate equipment and furnishings." From this research, the USHA issued size regulations for rooms that resulted in spaces smaller than in the PWA projects, private FHA housing, and even British council housing. Similarly, the USHA recommended omitting doors from closets and supplying curtain rods instead—a savings of $40 per unit. Straus later confessed that the choice was "not arrived at lightly nor did it prove popular. I am not sure that the policy was sound. It certainly evoked bitter criticisms from people who felt that the economy imposed unwarranted hardships on tenant families."[26]

Site planning ideas also helped the USHA cut costs. Borrowing heavily from Bauer's *Modern Housing* work, the USHA in 1939 distributed planning manuals that presented large, European-style "superblock" projects as the most rational and cost-effective. Superblocks eliminated interior streets and removed traffic in order to reclaim land for more housing and green space. Further, building layouts could save money; long, parallel rows of buildings minimized land usage and reduced costs for end walls, utilities, and walkways (fig. 7). Squeezing Bauer's European examples through the wringer of cost reductions, however, produced rigid site plans. Critics such as Lewis Mumford and the dean of Harvard's Graduate School of Design, Joseph Hudnut, deplored the barracks-like look of early USHA projects. "Their dreary repetitions seem to go on endlessly," Hudnut wrote, adding that the "monotony is as unnecessary as it is fatal to good design. . . . [The housing projects] will never become integral with the city, so opposed as they are to its prevailing lines and scale."[27]

The outcomes of Straus's cost containment were plainly visible in Chicago's housing projects. The Ida B. Wells Homes, designed before Straus's guidelines took effect, included more "frills" than later CHA projects, including brick ornamentation, copper awnings over doorways, pitched roofs, and nonessential balconies. The result was housing that more closely resembled nearby middle-class African American neighborhoods. But Cabrini and Brooks Homes, designed two years later with USHA economy measures well established, were regimented and austere by comparison. All three projects were built on slum clearance sites, and the CHA used high densities of thirty to forty units per acre to offset the considerable fixed costs of clearance and thereby meet Straus's cost rules.

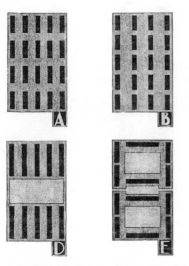
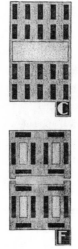

Diagram 4
Pooling of Open Space

Schematic diagrams showing various distributions of space and buildings. In all cases, the number of linear feet of buildings is the same.

A *shows liberal spacing between the ends of the buildings. This tends to increase development costs (roads, walks, utilities) without much increase in livability.*

In B *the buildings are close together in the rows, thus permitting the same number of dwellings in only four rows which are set farther apart. Development cost is decreased, and there is a gain in air, light, and privacy. All the land can be tenant-maintained if it is a row-house layout.*

C *returns to five rows of buildings, but the spacing is reduced,* the land thus saved being thrown together in a usable public area.

In D *this area is increased still further and the construction and development costs (assuming the site to be level) are still further reduced by using longer buildings.*

E *and* F *are court plans which introduce secondary open areas for parking purposes.*

E *shows economical use of long buildings along the perimeter. Of the six plans,* D *would probably show the lowest site-development cost.*

Figure 7. United States Housing Authority, "Diagram 4: Pooling of Open Space," from *Planning the Site: Design of Low-Rent Housing Projects*, Bulletin no. 11, May 1939. The diagram explains, "Of the six plans, D would probably show the lowest site-development cost."

Bauer had feared high densities resulting from slum clearance, and in *Modern Housing*, she suggested twelve units per acre as the ideal for row-house projects. But the higher densities at Wells, Cabrini, and Brooks created narrower public spaces and a cramped site plan.[28] Modernist principles were trimmed to minimalist designs under the pressures of density and cost considerations, resulting in a readily identifiable "government housing" aesthetic.

Why had Straus and the USHA so zealously pursued lower costs and pressured local housing authorities? Both bureaucratic impulses and Straus's personality were involved. Lower construction costs would allow the USHA to build more housing within its fixed loan authorization of $800 million allotted by Congress. But both Straus's ego and public housing's market-failure justification were ever-important in his relentless drive to cut costs. Straus wanted to prove potential critics wrong by building public housing at a lower cost than the private sector, thereby negating the usual

Figure 8. Robert Brooks Homes, October 11, 1950. Courtesy of the CHA.

arguments about the government's inherent inefficiency. If state-sponsored construction could be shown to be more efficient than private builders, then market-failure intervention would be justified. On this point, Straus demonstrated that the government could directly build decent housing for less, at least before the war. The average construction cost of USHA projects nationwide (excluding land costs) was $2,720 per unit by 1941, far below the mandated cost limits in the 1937 Housing Act, which proved irrelevant. The earlier PWA projects cost $4,975 per unit, while FHA-insured, privately owned housing built in the late 1930s averaged $3,601. In speeches and in print, Straus again and again made market-failure arguments and trumpeted the USHA's low costs. "Public housing," he wrote in *The Seven Myths of Housing*, an extended defense of his administration published in 1944, "has been constructed at lower costs than have been achieved by private enterprise. This is the truth and nothing but the truth."[29]

Straus's obsessions with cost won him a rhetorical victory but represented a strategic defeat. The savings wrung from USHA design standards resulted in bare-bones structures arrayed in rigid patterns and at relatively high densities, delineating projects like Cabrini and Brooks Homes as separate institutions divorced from the surrounding urban space. The modern housing movement led by Bauer wanted to build affordable and livable communities using European design ideas, with costs savings achieved through carefully studied functional design choices and avoidance of superfluous ornamentation. The USHA, however, put costs first in a self-defeating effort that produced a stripped-down aesthetic easily legible to outsiders in terms of class and, later, of race.[30]

* * *

While designs certainly mattered, the aesthetics of a project was a secondary consideration to the low-income families living in slums, who desperately sought to gain admission to the CHA's new multi-bedroom apartments with refrigerators, private baths, and low rents. How to select tenants and distribute this scarce benefit absorbed administrators at the local and the federal level. As with construction cost limits, Straus and Vinton viewed eligibility policies in the 1937 Housing Act as "generous" and established regulations that went well beyond the law's requirements. The USHA advised housing authorities that tenants should come from demonstrably substandard housing and have incomes not exceeding USHA-approved numerical limits. Such limits for admission (and later for continued occupancy) should be based on the extent of market failure, as determined by housing surveys. But Straus refused to approve income limits unless they were set well below the level where the private market failed.[31] He wanted to avoid the mistakes of the PWA program and to benefit low-income families, certainly for obvious progressive reasons but also to highlight public housing's market-failure mission.[32]

The CHA shared the USHA's progressive sensibilities. It went to considerable lengths to target admissions to the working poor and, after 1940, the dependent poor as well. While many housing authorities, including Boston, Baltimore, and New York, rewarded the "submerged" middle class within limits, the CHA actively prioritized its applicant pool based on need. In choosing initial tenants for the PWA projects (the CHA assumed their management in 1938), Elizabeth Wood developed a weighted scoring system that favored those who lived in substandard conditions and who paid large portions of income for rent. Tenant selection investigators, recruited from the ranks of the city's social workers, performed "home visits" and assigned numerical scores to an applicant's objective housing conditions as well as to social factors with implicit moral judgments, such as "general thrift" and "good employment record." Investigators frowned upon unmarried women with children from multiple fathers and anyone with substance abuse problems. The USHA was pleased with the system and recommended it to all local housing authorities in 1938.[33]

The CHA initially rejected applicants receiving public welfare on the basis that Chicago Relief Administration payments were "unreliable" and noted that "if relief status were entirely disregarded in the selection process, a housing project might well be more than half occupied by relief families." But the USHA in 1940 encouraged housing authorities to "include a portion of those on relief," though it counseled that "steps be taken to avoid filling any project with relief tenants." After working out bureaucratic problems with Chicago relief officials, the CHA began admitting public and private aid families in 1940 at a time when many housing authorities continued to shun them.[34]

The tenant selection process was staff-intensive and time-consuming, resulting in embarrassing delays in filling newly opened projects, but the system ensured that tenants had "the lowest possible incomes which would still permit them to pay rent," as the CHA proudly announced. While the system allowed it to "screen" its applicants, the CHA claimed that it did not "cream" its lists.[35] As Oscar Brown, the first manager of the Wells Homes, explained: "We didn't use the highest income [among] the poor. We had 18,000 applicants for 1,600 units, and we took the poorest of those." Yet because of their improved living conditions, these families were "the envy of the entire South Side," according to black sociologists St. Clair Drake and Horace Cayton, who lumped Ida B. Wells residents into the "lower middle-class."[36]

By focusing on objective measures of income and housing condition, the CHA removed forces that had long shaped neighborhoods for better and for worse, including familial connections, religion, and ethnicity, much to the annoyance of local communities and their representatives. The scoring system gave no preference to those in the surrounding neighborhood, nor did it give any say to Chicago aldermen. In Boston, public housing spaces were used by politicians as rewards to voters, but Chicago progressives wanted no hint of political favoritism. In 1938, Tenth Ward alderman William Rowan claimed he had supported the PWA's efforts to build the Trumbull Park Homes project in his ward, believing "that consideration would be given to the people in this area and that the authorities would not 'split hairs' in the selection of tenants." But after learning that applicants from his "workingman's district" were being denied, he grew disillusioned: "Civic leaders, school teachers, and most of the nationalistic groups, and labor leaders, have complained about the 'remote control' at the Trumbull Park Housing Project. They feel that someone in sympathy with this community . . . should have some voice in the selection of tenants."[37] Rowan held hearings on the matter and demanded details on the CHA's tenant selection process. The independent administration of the CHA rarely earned the city council's respect and more often its censure.

But aldermanic criticisms had little influence, as both the USHA and CHA acted to further restrict eligibility, believing the average income of its initial tenants was still too high. The USHA encouraged local housing authorities to curtail operating costs at the PWA-built projects they now managed; this would allow lower rents and make projects affordable to even lower income groups while simultaneously making higher-income tenants no longer eligible (since families could earn no more than five or six times the rent under the 1937 Housing Act). Wood squeezed savings out of operating budgets and lowered rents in 1940, making one out of four existing tenants ineligible. All those forced out had annual incomes over $1,400, just above the $1,365 estimate of the top end of the "bottom third" of Chicago's native-born white families. The mass removal of a quarter of the CHA's families, all of whom were white, did not proceed smoothly. They petitioned for delays and filed suits in federal court to block eviction. While it appeared sympathetic to the plight of the evicted, the CHA stuck to its low-income mission, telling one neighborhood group that another extension could not be granted because "the CHA is deeply aware of the thousands of families whose [annual] incomes are less than $1,100 who are in need of decent, safe, and sanitary housing and are unable to secure it at a rent within their income, and who are therefore, undergoing great hardships." Removals of "over-income" tenants were completed by the end of 1940.[38]

The next year Elizabeth Wood reported to the mayor, "It appears that under the present rent schedules public housing in Chicago has achieved its primary objective—the re-housing of the city's poorest families, coming from its worst slums." Further, she noted, "not a single family has been rejected for tenancy in the Chicago housing projects because its income was too low. Families with incomes as low as $305 a year are now living in the projects."[39] Real estate interests had not pushed for this policy. Progressive arguments had led the CHA to distribute its scarce benefit to those most in need.

These relentless efforts to serve the deeply poor raised concerns with housing experts. A senior New York City Housing Authority administrator critically reacted to the CHA's scoring system: "The [CHA] scheme . . . will encourage the selection of those applicants least able to keep up their rent payments. If worked to its logical conclusion, this system will mean 100 percent relief or sub-relief tenantry. . . . I am afraid they [CHA] are not looking far enough ahead." In Washington, Edith Elmer Wood expressed a general concern that the "USHA has gone too far in cutting rents and [average tenant] incomes in many, if not most places, and is in fact very often catering to families who are either lying or living below subsistence level. I don't deny that a large section of Congress demanded just that, but it is not a firm foundation to build on." Elizabeth Wood was not oblivious to the dangers to public housing—fiscally, socially, and politically—if too many of its tenants depended on public aid. In 1940 she wrote that "it would be very unwholesome to have projects become glorified poorhouses whose sole occupants were recipients of charity." But the CHA and the USHA thought the potential problem of concentrating poverty could be managed, especially given the large demand for public housing.[40] So long as working-class families were clamoring to get in, the projects would never become welfare-dependent "poorhouses."

* * *

A final implementation policy from the early years had far-reaching consequences by radically altering rents and fundamentally changing the fiscal calculus in public housing. The 1937 Housing Act said nothing about how rents should be set, except that the sizeable annual contribution subsidy allowed flexibility in order to make rents affordable to the poor. Initially federal and local officials wanted to avoid setting rents too low for fear of appearing excessively generous. Searching for a rental policy in 1939, the USHA encouraged local housing authorities to use "fixed rents" that varied by apartment size (as in the private sector) but arbitrarily set at a level to "duplicate the rents now being paid in substandard housing," since this would involve "no upset in family living patterns." But fixed rents often left very poor families paying more than 20 percent of their income for rent, an amount seen as excessive by housing reformers. To address the problem of families with high rent burdens, Nathan Straus asked the opinion of Edith Elmer Wood, then serving as a consultant to the USHA, about the merits of "income-based" rent, whereby rents were set as a percentage of tenant income. As a tenant's income (and, later, family size) rose or fell, rent would adjust as well, keeping the rent burden constant.[41]

But Edith Elmer Wood emphatically condemned the idea in 1940. Income-based rents, she explained, were used only sparingly in Great Britain and met considerable opposition from working-class tenants who despised rent hikes with each pay increase. Instead, most council housing in England operated with rents based on square footage, amenities, and location, as in private housing. Second, she asserted that while the poor would benefit from lower rents under income-based rent schemes, they would be seen as "dependent" and "forced to live in a segment of sovietized society, separated by an ideological wall from the rest of us who live under a capitalist economy." Wood was hardly a free-market conservative; she had devoted her career in the 1930s to describing market failure and justifying state-sponsored public housing. But her memo to Straus ended with the pronouncement that an income-based rent system would "damage the character of the next generation of American wage earners more than the improved physical conditions could possibly help their bodies. In other words, I would rather see no public housing than public housing so administered."[42]

Despite Edith Elmer Wood's adamant rejection of income-based rents, Warren Vinton and Straus welcomed the idea. "It seems perfectly obvious," Vinton wrote, "that good social policy would demand that families in the lowest income grade pay a lower rent in order to have some decent amount left for food and clothing. The families in the highest income grade might reasonably be expected to pay a higher rent." As well, income-based rent had advantages for large families, who, if they wanted to avoid overcrowding, faced high rent burdens in order to obtain multiple-bedroom apartments in the private market. Not least, the policy also fit the larger progressive vision of those like Catherine Bauer who wanted to decommodify housing and distribute this essential need on a social basis rather than an economic one. In December 1940, the USHA rewrote its policies and urged local housing authorities to switch to income-based rents.[43]

The new policy was only a recommendation, and it did not catch on until the war years. Beginning in 1941, USHA projects nearing completion were pressed into service as housing for defense workers in critical industries such as steel and shipbuilding. Income limits for admission were raised, defense workers were given priority for admission to new projects, and other federal agencies embarked on a crash program in defense housing construction. Rather than charge higher fixed rents, local housing authorities switched to income-based rents to capture the swelling incomes of better-paid defense workers and give these tenants an incentive to find private housing. With low operating expenses to maintain a young housing stock and soaring rental revenues as wages rose during the war, local housing authorities began running large surpluses. Under the terms of the federal annual contribution contract, the difference between expenses (including a reserve set-aside) and rents had to be rebated to Washington to reduce overall subsidies. In 1948, with wartime restrictions still in place, public housing tenants nationwide paid an average of 77 percent of the total cost of their housing, and subsidies were far below maximums.[44]

The CHA switched to income-based rents in mid-1942, but it resisted serving defense workers as much as possible to protect its main mission of rehousing low-income slum dwellers. While four CHA projects under construction in 1941 were enlisted in the war effort and were rented to war workers earning up to $2,100, the CHA board insisted on serving the poor and maintained its five prewar projects exclusively for non–war worker families with incomes below $1,200—a limit that did not change for three years despite rising wages. As a result, the CHA reported that new tenants at the prewar projects had incomes that "ranged among the lowest selected for public housing projects in large cities." By 1943, Elizabeth Wood had misgivings about the policy, noting that the CHA "did not have enough [eligible] applicants to offset the increasing number of units vacated" because of rising incomes. She recommended increasing income limits to $1,500 in the prewar projects, but for one of the few times in this period, the commissioners rebuffed her, finding it "difficult to believe that there were no more families in Chicago with incomes under $1,200." Between 1942 and 1945, relief families comprised more than half of admissions, and by the end of the war the rock-bottom income limit excluded most regularly employed workers from the prewar projects. Despite these trends, the average income of all CHA tenants rose steadily during wartime prosperity, especially after federal officials intervened at the end of 1943 (over the CHA's objections) to prohibit evictions of tenants who earned more than income limits allowed.[45] Rising wartime incomes dismayed Wood and the board; after the war, as will be seen, they aggressively removed tenants who exceeded income limits so that public housing could return to its mission of serving where the market failed.

The shift to income-based rents had crucial implications, some predicted by Edith Elmer Wood at the time, and others unperceived. Wood had foretold tenant dissatisfaction at rents that increased with each pay raise and at intrusive income checks. A federal study from the 1950s, seeking to defend the policy, concluded that, "on balance, families like [income-based rents] in principle, but they do not like the way in which they are personally affected." The policy, as devised by Vinton and Strauss, was intended both to gently push the upwardly mobile out of public housing to make way for those most in need and to cushion the rent burden of the very poor. But federal regulations and large-scale operations resulted in a heavy-handed administration of the basic interaction between tenant and landlord. Especially unpopular were retroactive rents charged to the date of a pay raise and counting the earnings of children toward family income. Tenants resisted by hiding income from housing authority inspectors, a violation that, if caught, often resulted in eviction. Instead of harmonious tenant-landlord relations, income-based rents generated low-level conflict and sharp resentment.[46]

Equally important, administrators rarely acknowledged a flip side to income-based rents. The policy created an incentive for the very poor to

apply to public housing and, once admitted, to stay. The only way housing authorities could avoid concentrating poverty in the long term was
to strategically manage their overall tenant base by admitting enough
working-class residents (paying higher rents but generally having shorter
stays) to offset the long-term poor (paying lower rents and having longer
stays on average). The sustainability of public housing was at stake since
housing authorities relied upon rental income to pay for maintenance expenses. Without sufficient numbers of working-class tenants, project revenues would rapidly erode. During the war years, this balancing act was
not difficult since the war-induced housing shortage created sufficient demand from steadily employed, wage-earning families. But after the war,
income-based rents became a major force in undermining the working-
class tenancy essential to public housing's fiscal health.

*   *   *

Policies surrounding tenant selection and rents were devised using objective measures of economic class, but policymakers could not long avoid
issues of race. Harold Ickes first dealt with the issue of racial integration
in PWA housing projects by issuing the "neighborhood composition rule,"
stating that occupants of completed projects should conform to the "prevailing composition of the surrounding neighborhood" that existed before
its redevelopment. The policy was essentially a defensive one, intended
to prevent the "reclaiming" of black slum areas for whites through discriminatory tenant selection practices, as the Chicago Real Estate Board
had suggested for the PWA's Bronzeville site in 1935. But the policy also
avoided clashes with segregationists and reassured whites that the federal government would not demand racial integration or color-blind tenant selection in its projects. With "separate but equal" the prevailing law
and with powerful southerners controlling Congress, Ickes had limited
room to maneuver.[47] Still, the rule left enough ambiguity in the definition
of "surrounding neighborhood" that integration was possible. Chicago
progressives, however, moved cautiously, even haltingly, toward a liberal
policy, in part because deliberate residential integration simply had no
precedent in urban life.[48]

The CHA conservatively implemented the neighborhood composition rule at the PWA projects that opened in 1938. Julia Lathrop Homes
and Trumbull Park Homes were in white neighborhoods far from any
presence of African Americans, so the board deemed integration outside the scope of the rule. Nine black families who applied to Lathrop
were rejected for initial tenancy after the board heard aldermanic oppo-

sition. Similarly, Trumbull Park whites feared the CHA would integrate the project with African Americans after three Mexican American families were admitted in 1940. But Elizabeth Wood wrote to a neighborhood organization to explain that the CHA "would not permit a housing project to change the racial make-up of the neighborhood in which it is located" and that the CHA "has not, and does not intend to accept Negro families in the Trumbull Park Homes."[49]

The best possibility for integration existed at the third PWA project, the Jane Addams Homes, located in a diverse neighborhood that clearly included African Americans. But the CHA, despite pleas from black leaders and settlement house workers, interpreted the word "neighborhood" narrowly. It used Urban League data showing that thirty-five black families lived on the site before its clearance as justification for admitting only thirty black families to the 1,027 apartments. Fearing a race riot like the one that engulfed Chicago in 1919 and feeling herself in completely uncharted territory, Elizabeth Wood went to great lengths to avoid conflict. She invited the thirty black families, along with several white families, to select apartments in two recently completed buildings in a far corner of the project, close to a neighboring black community. Wood reported that "the Negro applicants chose to be on the stairwell with their race" and that "whites and Negroes do not use the same building entrance." With much relief, she concluded: "We have so far not had one bit of trouble from white families, either within or without the project." The CHA's cautious, circumscribed policy was actually relatively progressive; most housing authorities, even in the North, strictly segregated their PWA projects.[50]

But the strict admissions quotas and segregated stairwells at Addams did not sit well with black residents or African American leaders. In the summer of 1939, Wood admitted that "we had a very serious racial situation" when "we began to accept white families for a turn-over and refused Negro applications." Black sociologist Horace Cayton and Chicago Urban League head Frederick Lane publicly criticized the CHA for its discriminatory quotas, while the USHA's Robert Weaver and new board member Robert Taylor prodded the CHA in a more progressive direction. The board agreed to Wood's recommendation in early 1939 to admit twenty more black families at Addams, to house them in "mixed" buildings, and to remove separate application procedures for blacks and whites. Still, an informal quota remained on black occupancy at Addams, and African Americans were not free to live in any stairwell in the project.[51]

While integration would continue to be micromanaged at Addams, and a more liberal policy would not arrive until after the war, the experience marked a turning point in the evolution of Elizabeth Wood's thinking about race and housing. In 1938 she was relieved that segregating by stairwell had avoided violence. But by 1940, she privately wrote that more integration, not less, was necessary: "If you open a housing project with all the Negroes in one building you are in for trouble, because it is impossible in a governmental project in any northern city to maintain that status." African Americans, she implied, would not accept intra-project segregation for long, nor should they. By 1942 her views had evolved further. In a letter to a colleague in Vallejo, California (whose wartime projects were soon to be integrated), Wood wrote: "I believe, in matters like [racial integration], it is absolutely essential to adopt the most liberal attitude possible and uphold it with the most patriotic talk that can be summoned up, but that at the same time one must not make the housing field the battleground for the equalization of mankind, etc., etc."[52] While still somewhat ambivalent about how far to impose racial integration, Wood and the rest of the CHA board had shifted to a more liberal sense of social justice for African Americans.

This change was apparent in the fall of 1942 when Wood and Taylor moved to substantially integrate the CHA's newest project, Cabrini Homes. Since the largely Italian "Little Hell" area had seen an influx of African Americans just before its clearance, blacks lobbied the City Council Committee on Housing in 1940 for priority in this new project. The aldermen responded vaguely with a nonbinding recommendation that the CHA grant priority to "those people who are now residents of the area affected," dodging the question of racial integration. By 1942, public housing had been drafted into the war effort, and priority went to workers in essential war industries. The surrounding Italian community bitterly resented the CHA's eligibility changes and, even more, its integration policies. Wood proposed distributing 20 percent of apartments to African Americans and scattering them throughout the project. While plenty of black applicants clamored to get in, the CHA struggled to find enough eligible white applicants willing to live in an integrated environment, despite the wartime shortage and the quota on black occupancy. Racial tensions, including a significant clash between whites and blacks at the project in April 1943, contributed to the dearth of white applicants. Belatedly, Wood undertook an extensive publicity campaign to generate white interest, distributed 125,000 preliminary application cards, and convinced the board to raise income limits for war workers. By August 1943, a year after it opened, the project was finally fully occupied, but the threat of violence had led the CHA to maintain "solid white sections" in the project.[53]

The Cabrini experience revealed key problems in pursuing integration. First, attracting and retaining whites in projects with black families proved troublesome, as whites resisted more than token integration. Moreover, at projects where African Americans were in the majority, finding sufficient numbers of whites willing to stay was nearly impossible. At the Robert Brooks Homes on the West Side, opened in 1943, Wood hoped for occupancy to be 80 percent black and 20 percent white, along the lines of the neighborhood before its redevelopment, but she confessed, "I doubt very much if I will secure any white applicants for this project." While some white tenants initially moved in, they quickly left, leaving the project all black within a year.[54] African Americans were willing to be "pioneers" in largely white projects, but whites would not stay long in black-majority projects, even when located close to white neighborhoods (as at Brooks).

★ ★ ★

Achieving racially integrated projects was never the CHA's primary goal. During the 1930s, the mission was to clear and rebuild slums in the progressive mold. But during the war years, Robert Taylor shifted direction and pushed the CHA to come to the aid of African Americans. Conditions in Chicago's black belt had deteriorated rapidly in the 1940s, as migrating African Americans arrived in accelerating numbers, escaping the harsh conditions of the Jim Crow South and looking to find employment in war industries. The beginning of the Second Great Migration caused the city's African American population to jump by almost 80 percent in the 1940s, yet racial transition added only marginally to the boundaries of the black belt. Instead, black migrants strained available housing to its limits as families "doubled up" and took shelter in barely hospitable spaces. Overcrowding reached epidemic levels. Robert Taylor compared Chicago's black neighborhoods to Calcutta, calling them "the most densely populated in the world."[55] Landlords carved up large apartments into "kitchenette" units—usually one room with an electric hot plate and shared bathrooms. Novelist Richard Wright interpreted the psychological effects of such conditions on migrants, writing that the kitchenette "throws desperate and unhappy people into an unbearable closeness of association, thereby increasing latent friction, giving birth to never ending quarrels of recrimination, accusation, and vindictiveness, producing warped personalities. . . . The kitchenette is the funnel through which our pulverized lives flow to ruin and death on the city pavement, at a profit."[56]

To address the immediate problem, Taylor determined that slum clearance had to be put on hold and that black families "would have to expand

and to move further out." With racial transition and integration of white neighborhoods blocked, Taylor offered a new strategy: position new projects for African American occupancy on vacant land away from the ghetto but adjacent to the handful of black homeowner enclaves established in outlying regions between 1910 and 1940. The approach was neither a scattered-site dispersion of the ghetto nor an effort at integration. Instead, Taylor steered a middle course, hoping projects in these areas might meet only limited resistance from whites and serve as nuclei for expanding black residential opportunity.[57]

Taylor had partial success with this agenda, winning three wartime projects totaling 2,172 units, all intended for African American occupancy. The first of these was Altgeld Gardens, a sprawling 1,500-unit project built on an isolated tract on the city's southern edge, far from any residential development, white or black, but within reasonable distance of the Pullman factories and the Calumet River's steel and shipbuilding works, open to black workers.[58] From the CHA's perspective, Altgeld's remoteness had the advantage of limiting potential antagonism from whites while opening up a new area to blacks. In its September 1943 report, the CHA declared that the new site "will permit the natural expansion for the Negro population in the overcrowded South Side."[59] Federal officials at first proposed a temporary project, but Taylor and Wood fought for a permanent one. The isolated site required the planning of an entirely new and self-contained community, complete with a co-op for shopping, a branch of the Chicago Public Library, and a new park for residents. A school, however, took several years to complete. Despite its isolation, Altgeld proved to be a popular project with residents eager to escape the overcrowded black belt.[60]

While white aldermen were caught off guard by this bold foray of public housing into the Far South Side, the next effort to expand black housing opportunities drew a more concerted negative response. With more wartime housing funds, Taylor again advanced a site that would "make a contribution towards expanding the area now open to Negro occupancy."[61] The CHA proposed building near Lilydale and West Chesterfield, two enclaves of middle-class black homeowners developed in the 1920s. The Lilydale proposal drew an immediate angry response from Arthur Lindell, the alderman who had led the charge in 1941 to restrict the site selection powers of the CHA. "The proposal to erect 250 housing units in [Lilydale] will only create a new and more violent outbreak in this and adjoining communities," Lindell wrote to Robert Taylor. Referencing the Altgeld Gardens site, Lindell blamed the CHA for "persisting in creating strained racial relations in so much of the south side." But unlike the earlier USHA projects, expedited war housing did not require a co-operation agreement, and the City council did not have veto power over site selection. Nonetheless, Lindell threatened further amendments to the state housing act, and Taylor quietly withdrew the Lilydale site.[62] Taylor, however, did lobby federal officials to allocate scarce building materials for 900 townhomes in Lilydale, the only private housing built for African Americans during the war.[63]

Even after Lindell's response to Lilydale, Taylor persisted in moving forward with a site in West Chesterfield, a neighborhood of seventy-one single-family homes owned by middle-class African Americans who had escaped the black belt. Lindell's reaction does not survive, but black West Chesterfield owners vigorously voiced their opposition to the CHA's plans for a 250-unit temporary war housing project and sued to block it. The controversy received extensive coverage in the *Pittsburgh Courier*, though far less in the *Chicago Defender*, reflecting the embarrassment of some black leaders that class had infected racial solidarity. West Chesterfield residents claimed a temporary project would create "a potential slum district in the heart of the finest community Colored Americans have built for them-selves anywhere." To overcome neighborhood resistance, the CHA again successfully lobbied federal officials to allow construction of a permanent rather than a temporary project, and it agreed to put the units up for sale after the war. With these concessions, the community relented, and the row houses of the 250-unit West Chesterfield Homes, completed in 1946, proved highly desirable. When put on the market in 1949, the modest, yet solid and attractive duplexes had 800 prospective black buyers.[64] But West Chesterfield was an anomaly; the CHA never again proposed developing public housing intended for sale.

Following the strains at West Chesterfield, Taylor and the CHA board shied away from controversy and no longer proposed sites during the war to expand areas of black housing opportunity. When Wood presented the board six additional sites in 1944, the board avoided the four vacant tracts near black enclaves such as West Chesterfield and Lilydale and instead se-lected the two in the black ghetto.[65] One of these locations had been pro-posed by Wood nine years earlier when she served as a consultant to the PWA; at the time, the site lay outside the black belt, but by 1944, racial transition had swept a few blocks west and placed the site just inside racial boundaries.[66] When Wentworth Gardens opened in 1947 with 422 units, Wood hoped for racial integration, but on the day the project opened to take applications, only African Americans lined up around the block.

Figure 9. West Chesterfield Homes, May 4, 1949. Middle-class African Americans lining up to register for the chance to purchase homes at the CHA's West Chesterfield development. Courtesy of the CHA.

Whites arrived but left without applying, and as a result, tenancy was entirely black. "Based on the Wentworth experience," a CHA staff member wrote, "unless a public relations job is done in advance of the actual selection of tenants, the project will become uni-racial as a result of the overwhelming need among Negro families."[67]

★ ★ ★

Beyond constructing projects and selecting tenants, the early CHA made considerable efforts to develop a middle-class standard of community in its projects. Like other housing authorities, it embraced the ideas of both progressive slum reformers and modern housing planners by offering an extensive array of community services unheard of in most poor neighborhoods. CHA projects included nursery schools to provide educational experiences for the young, parks and swimming pools to offer middle-class leisure opportunities, and public meeting spaces to foster tenant-inspired organizations, including project newspapers, drama clubs, cooperative buying clubs, and sports teams. Wood claimed to avoid "paternalism," telling a reporter, "our idea is to build a community that is raw, unfinished, and let it ripen and mature as people live in it."[68] She called the CHA's tenants "poor but proud" families with "middle-class aspirations," who blossomed when transplanted from slums "into a setting of apartments attractively planned and well-maintained." Following the environmental determinism of progressive reformers, she suggested that "underprivileged families moving into spic-and-span houses really do seem to experience a kind of social rebirth."[69] Moreover, she credited the "middle-class aspirations" of early tenants for this success.

But not all of this activity "ripened" organically or took place without "paternalism." Wood cultivated relationships with settlement houses, welfare agencies, and local government to provide services for residents, and the CHA served as the primary conduit for community building. She encouraged the Infant Welfare Society and the Chicago Health Department to set up clinics in the early projects, and the CHA funded childcare centers during the war. She recruited the YMCA, the Red Cross, the Boy and Girl Scouts, and the Boys' Clubs of Chicago to run programs for youth; settlement houses expanded so that nearly every project had an associated social work organization. She pushed the Chicago Park District to provide recreation and the school board to build new schools.[70]

Finally, Wood was enamored with grounds beautification, especially the planting of flowers. In a CHA pamphlet, she contrasted the "oppressive air, the smells, [the] raucous voices of children playing in the streets" in the slums with the environment of public housing projects, where "it is like stepping into a different world. Everywhere you see green—green of lawns, green of shrubbery. . . . Everywhere you see gardens and overhead stretches of sky that somehow looks bluer and sunnier than it did in the slums." The gardens at CHA projects "have a significance more important than even the beauty of flowers or the food value of vegetables. They symbolize a deep and fundamental change that has taken place in the lives of the people who work in them." Hyperbole aside, tenants remembered with pride the CHA's annual flower contests and saw the care of grounds as reflective of community pride. "We never looked at Altgeld Gardens as public housing," tenant Maude Davis recalled, because "we would do our little yards and the flowers, and we just thought that was the way people lived."[71]

Paternalism also came in the form of extensive rules that circumscribed tenant life. Project managers and staff inspected apartments to maintain standards of housekeeping and required tenants to help with maintenance by cleaning stairwells in walk-up apartments and cutting grass. Residents were told not to hang pictures by themselves lest they damage plaster walls. "Ask the management office to send a service man to put in hooks for you," the 1945 tenant handbook stated. Controlling children was a prime concern. The handbook continued: "The children must be taught to protect public and other people's property and to respect the rights of adults, other children, and the community." In practice, this meant fining tenants for breaking rules. Doris Smith, an early resident of Dearborn Homes, recollected: "The CHA enforced their rules. No playing on the grass. If they caught your kids playing on the grass, then you got a $3 fine." Such rules generated some grumbling among tenants, but most recognized the need for order and the importance of collective enforcement of community standards. As Arnold Weddington remembered at Ida B. Wells, "People planted flowers, they shined floors, and kept the windows clean. Everybody worked at it. They kept it beautiful."[72]

Other tenants tell a similar story, describing their communities in glowing terms. Leon Hamilton recalled his childhood in the Ida B. Wells Homes:

> Here we were, poor families, but we didn't know we were poor because we were in this little development. We had new facilities! Central heat! The apartments were new and clean! Everything! . . . We had Madden Park. We had a swimming pool. We had a center there that we could go to with activities. So we were like little rich kids. We wanted for practically nothing, and we didn't think of ourselves as poor.[73]

By quantitative income standards, the first residents of Wells were decidedly poor, but by social standing among African Americans, their tenancy in public housing marked a step up and planted many on a path out of poverty. Bertrand Ellis, later vice president of a bank, discussed public housing in class terms: "I think Ida B. Wells was probably as close as you could get in those days to a middle-class black community." Early residents credited efficient project management and a strong sense of community for this rise in status. "The managers of these projects were out among the people," former Chicago firefighter Benjamin Crane related. "They were out encouraging tenant organizations and the planting of flowers . . . complaints were answered and addressed. Our janitors took care of the organizations and the block clubs. It was a solid sense of community, right from the manager to the newest tenant." Altgeld Gardens elicited similar devotion from former residents in its early years. "When we moved to Altgeld Gardens [in 1945], it was almost like I died and went to heaven. There was a feeling of family throughout the entire development . . . you had pride in your home," William Shaw, later a deputy chief of the Chicago Police Department, recalled.[74] Living at Wells and Altgeld amounted to a special status in the African American community, not a stigma.

A sense of pride and purpose permeated the CHA staff as well. Wood encouraged a "family" mentality at the CHA, and in the early years she regularly gathered the entire organization—managers, central office staff, and maintenance employees—for social events. Most who worked for Wood admired her personal strength and combative spirit, and her devoted colleagues remained fiercely loyal. Emil Hirsch, a public relations director under Wood, remembered that housing to her "was not [just] a brick and mortar thing" and that "she was very determined to try to get any kind of resource into a project to help the family life and help these people who were living there." John Ducey, one of her two top aides for much of the 1940s, recalled Wood as "a superb manager" who "inspired people all the way down the line." Former research director Jim Fuerst said years later, "Working for Elizabeth Wood was like being at Camelot—you never forget it."[75]

★ ★ ★

Despite the obvious success of the CHA's early projects, Elizabeth Wood had serious doubts about the direction of public housing by the end of the war. In a speech at the 1945 annual convention of the American Public Works Association, she distanced herself from the environmental determinism of progressives and raised alarms about the rising problems of the long-term poor in her projects. Despite her best efforts, some tenants did not "blossom" when planted in a positive project environment. She conceded that "public housers in many cases have had to fight hard to keep their projects from becoming slums because of the living habits of so many ex-slum-dwellers." She admonished her audience to recognize the urgency of this problem and to begin "a head-on facing of the problem of the cultural level of the slum dweller." She rejected, however, greater selectivity of tenants or any changes in rents, the two policies that could most directly affect the social makeup of public housing. Instead, she argued for "an educational program for slum dwellers through every available medium in relation to their living habits." Wood's new tone was among the earliest cracks in the assumption that a changed environment alone was sufficient to rehabilitate impoverished families.[76]

Catherine Bauer also expressed disappointment at public housing's outcomes in the 1940s, questioning even further the program's fundamental direction. In a letter to Washington officials during the war, Bauer set out a fundamental question: "Is public housing really as popular (with the people who need housing, that is) as it ought to be?" She answered, "No," explaining that most public housing projects "lack something in fundamental health and vitality." She assailed the physical appearance of most projects as "dull and undistinguished," and in reporting on projects in San Francisco, she found nothing but fault: "Wrong location, rather grim appearance, inadequate community facilities, particularly shops and transportation, too rigid rules of eligibility, paternalistic company-town atmosphere." While not directly attacking the 1937 Housing Act, her solution involved "getting rid of as much of the red tape on 'eligibility' as possible. . . . We probably must have income limitations, but I would favor getting rid of the rest of it as soon as legally and politically feasible."[77] Bauer's frustration with the early results also signaled her recognition that despite her strong hand in writing and implementing the 1937 Housing Act, her modern housing ideas had largely been displaced by the values of progressive slum reformers. In another letter in 1948, Bauer lamented, "Our worst obstacle all along to getting popular support for public housing has been the social-work, crime-and-disease smell which we couldn't help when we got started in the 1930s." Instead of a program with broad-based support, Bauer saw public housing slipping inexorably into welfare housing, an ominous trend that Elizabeth Wood recognized as well.[78]

While she remained friendly with Nathan Straus, Bauer's disappointment undoubtedly centered on his misguided leadership. Straus's overzealous cost consciousness and insistence on serving the deeply poor won the program few friends. Congress gave Straus little credit for his efficiency at the USHA, and his abrasive personality produced enemies on Capitol Hill. In 1939, during a House Banking Committee hearing to present the case for more public housing, Straus admonished Albert Gore, Sr., the Democratic representative from Tennessee, for his probing questions and then had the audacity to contribute openly to the campaign of Gore's opponent. Although still a first-term congressman in 1939, Gore then led the House in blocking additional authorizations for public housing, effectively shutting off the pipeline for more projects until the need for housing for war workers revived and redirected the program.[79] A general turn against the New Deal following the 1938 elections did not help matters, but the USHA's legislative weakness was largely self-inflicted. The strain of political failure made Straus even more belligerent, and soon his staff grew alienated as well. Bauer left the USHA in October 1940, unhappy with Straus and unable, by her own admission, to make the transition from activist to bureaucrat. While Vinton soldiered on, his personal notes reveal that Straus "avoided real problems," "issued conflicting orders," and was "obsessed with publicity." Robert Weaver left in 1940 after a speech favoring residential integration in public housing drew criticism from Capitol Hill. Finally, Straus resigned under pressure in January 1942 when Roosevelt reorganized the USHA into an entirely new organization, the Federal Public Housing Authority (FPHA), later the Public Housing Administration (PHA), subordinated to the National Housing Agency.[80] Public housing was shoved into a new bureaucratic shell and ceased to be a valued element of New Deal policy.

★ ★ ★

Under Straus's tenure, the USHA had overseen the production of 165,000 apartments for the poor at a remarkably low cost, but his early implementation policies circumscribed public housing in ways that were ultimately counterproductive. Construction cost restrictions, income limits, and income-based rents proved Straus's enduring legacy. In his desire to prove public housing superior to private builders, Straus helped give USHA projects their distinct, stripped-down aesthetic. Further, income-based rents would eventually concentrate poverty and thereby jeopardize the revenue stream needed for maintenance. The British had explicitly rejected income-based rents, but progressive sensibilities and deep subsidies combined to create an expectation that the very poor would share disproportionately in public housing's scarce benefit. Yet the implications of income-based rent for public housing's long-term health were not well considered by those in charge.

Chicago leaders had also set the CHA on a perilous path. The CHA's tenant selection policies, far more aggressive than those in New York or other cities, prioritized those at the bottom of the income scale and threatened to turn Chicago's prewar projects into poorhouses by 1945. Likewise, the CHA's site selections created imbalances. When it began in 1937, the CHA inherited three PWA projects with 2,400 apartments that catered almost exclusively to whites. But between 1937 and 1945, the CHA's leadership planned nine projects totaling 6,300 apartments, 92 percent of which were occupied by African Americans when completed. At the time blacks comprised only 15 percent of the city's population.[81] The CHA prioritized black housing needs under the leadership of Wood and Taylor because African Americans faced the most desperate conditions in the overcrowded and substandard black belt, and no other city agency had the resources or the inclination to relieve the situation. The CHA's new apartments with modern amenities, low rents, and community benefits were highly sought after by ghetto residents during a wartime housing shortage and represented a form of "paradise' by those fortunate enough to win admission. But the emphasis on addressing the immediate crisis of African Americans placed the CHA in the precarious political position of being perceived as an agency that served *only* the black community.

Thus, the seeds of public housing's future struggles were solidly planted by 1945, identifiable in hindsight but recognized at the time only by Catherine Bauer and, to some degree, by Elizabeth Wood.[82] Future decline was not inevitable, of course, but in the coming years public housing administrators in Washington and Chicago would continue to obsess over costs, insist on limiting the program's eligibility, push for superblock redevelopment, and struggle with a response to residential segregation. The mission would remain wholesale slum clearance and large-scale rebuilding, with the assumption that new projects could attract the working classes indefinitely while positively transforming the lives of the very poor. Much of this blueprint proved misguided or unsustainable over the next two decades—with tragic results.

Clearing Chicago's Slums

3

Between 1945 and 1966, the Chicago Housing Authority built 23,400 apartments for low-income families, nearly all in African American neighborhoods. The city's most problematic projects took shape in this period, as the CHA expanded its initial slum clearance sites and created ever-larger conglomerations of public housing. Cabrini-Green (3,606 units), the ABLA group (3,658 units), and the Wells group (3,329 units) grew in size to dominate entire neighborhoods. Along the "State Street corridor" (8,000 units), a string of five high-rise projects, culminating in the Robert Taylor Homes, paralleled a commuter rail line and a major expressway (see fig. 1). In 1986, the *Chicago Tribune* ran an eleven-part series on the corridor entitled "The Chicago Wall," which outlined the "physical and psychological barriers" erected by "city officials to keep poor blacks isolated from the rest of Chicago." More than any other visible symbol, the wall demonstrated the divide between the city's African American poor and the commuters who zoomed by daily on their way to downtown. Historian Arnold Hirsch argued in 1983 that the CHA was "captured" by the city council in this period and pressed into serving a "containment" agenda intended to keep African Americans out of white neighborhoods. By blocking vacant land sites and demanding clearance in the black belt, the council thus coerced the CHA into "making the second ghetto" on top of the first one. Lost was the opportunity to use public housing to force integration of white neighborhoods and thereby help break down ghetto walls.[1]

But the location of postwar public housing in Chicago was only partly determined by the demonstrably racist actions of whites. A second major context also helped to define its geography: the city's slum clearance agenda, promoted by the progressive leaders of the CHA in the 1940s. During that decade a general consensus formed that the city's worst neighborhoods needed immediate clearance and rebuilding. This consensus was broad and included not only the CHA, but also liberal city planners seeking to advance new ideas about urbanism, real estate interests hoping to profit from redevelopment, and downtown business interests anxious to protect the Loop as the city's central business district. Only those immediately at risk of displacement resisted the progressive impulse to raze whole districts, and their voices received thin support. Slum reformers had long conditioned the public to view poorly maintained nineteenth-century housing as a metaphorical "cancer" that threatened the health of Chicago, and Elizabeth Wood feared the "imminent death" of large cities without large-scale clearance.[2] But while a consensus existed among diverse interests on the need for slum clearance, who should control the effort—and what values would define rebuilding—remained hotly contested. The CHA intended to lead the slum clearance effort, envisioning a tabula rasa on which to remake the city in a modernist landscape, compete with high-rise buildings and spacious parks. Under the leadership of Wood and Robert Taylor, the CHA selected sites in the black slums first, where the most desperate conditions existed, and, on its own initiative, planned many of the projects that would later be associated with "the second ghetto." Public housing's location in Chicago, then, has as much to do with the CHA's own postwar progressive vision as with the undeniably racist efforts of whites to contain blacks.

* * *

Slum reformers and city planners had long defined the city's slum problem in sweeping terms. Like the Burnham Plan of 1909, itself an enormous slum clearance proposal, reformers endeavored to wipe away and rebuild expanses of the city deemed unsalvageable by progressive standards. The Chicago Plan Commission, the city's planning body descended from the Burnham Plan, labeled entire neighborhoods as "blighted" and hence beyond usefulness. ("Blight" was defined at the block level when half of the housing units were built before 1895 and half were "substandard," that is, needed major repairs, lacked private bathroom facilities, or crowded more than 1.5 persons per room).[3] Using citywide housing data collected in 1939, the CPC produced a "Master Plan of Residential Land Use of Chicago" and recommended "the demolition and complete rebuilding" of 9.3 square miles of the city in the near term, mostly in areas surrounding the city's central business district, including 240,000 homes, or roughly one quarter of the city's housing stock. Rehabilitation of these areas was ruled out; clearance and rebuilding "neighborhood by neighborhood" was "the only feasible solution." The CHA concurred with the CPC's assessment and "conservatively" estimated the need for public housing at 109,000 apartments, or 45 percent of the total. "Chicago's slum areas must be rebuilt," the CHA intoned in 1947, and it asked the city for the needed "tools"—in the form of funding and relocation housing—to "get to work."[4] Significantly, the CHA sought to be the lead agency in charge of the overall rebuilding effort, though it would vie for control with downtown business interests that wanted to use redevelopment to preserve land values and commerce in the central business district in the face of outward migration of industry and people to the suburbs, a trend that began before World War II and accelerated after it.[5]

Any clearance and rebuilding of 9.3 square miles of Chicago's worst housing would disproportionately affect African Americans, whose dismal living conditions reflected a long history of entrenched discriminatory housing, employment, and education practices. The 1939 housing data found 59 percent of Chicago's African Americans living in substandard housing but only 17 percent of whites. The CHA highlighted this point in its 1940 annual report, noting, "The areas in the city which are most obviously in need of drastic clearance are, although not exclusively, areas of Negro occupancy."[6] A 1942 map produced by the CPC showed the blighted zones surrounding the downtown business district (fig. 10).

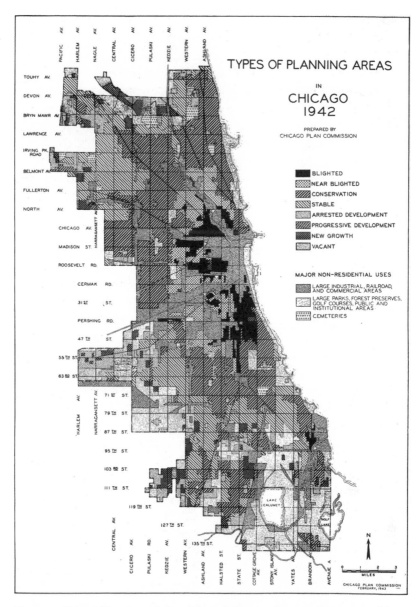

Figure 10. Chicago Plan Commission, "Type of Planning Areas in Chicago, 1942," from
Master Plan of Residential Land Use of Chicago (Chicago, 1943), 68.

The map encompassed nearly every black neighborhood in the city, including all of Bronzeville and the Federal Street slum on the South Side, as well as West Side neighborhoods with sizeable black populations. The 1950 housing census would later confirm the earlier data in the minds of planners: of the 50 census tracts with the most substandard housing conditions, 70 percent had majority African American populations.[7] Rebuilding the slums using progressive criteria, then, could not avoid the razing of black neighborhoods.

The war had delayed slum clearance, but by early 1945 the CHA had revived its clearance mission and outlined ambitious goals: 40,000 units of public housing in five years as the first phase of rebuilding the city, with 20,000 units on slum sites and another 20,000 on vacant land as relocation housing to expedite the emptying of the slums. The CHA expected at least 50 percent of the apartments to house African Americans, but found justification for this lopsided distribution: "The Negro housing situation has become so acute that it overshadows all other social problems in Chicago today." According to census data, between 1940 and 1950, the Second Great Migration swelled the city's nonwhite population from 282,000 to 509,000, an 80 percent increase that resulted in severe overcrowding. The influx drove decision making in the early postwar years, with the CHA resolving that it would be "guilty of dereliction of duty if it failed to utilize every opportunity provided for taking steps towards its relief." It concluded that a total of 52,000 new public housing units were needed for eligible blacks, just to relieve the immediate crisis.[8] Given their desperate situation, the CHA asserted that African Americans had a higher moral claim on scarce housing benefits.

The 40,000-unit plan envisioned a fourfold increase in the CHA's operations in only five years and a massive clearance of the city's slums. To construct 20,000 units on slum sites would mean twelve more projects the size of the 1,660-unit Ida B. Wells Homes, then the CHA's largest project, covering forty-eight acres. If at least half of the sites were in black neighborhoods, as the CHA suggested in 1945, then it would be displacing large numbers of African Americans and remaking the city's black neighborhoods in wholesale fashion. Building 20,000 units on vacant land would be no small task either, because developing fourteen more projects the size of the 1,500-unit Altgeld Gardens would depend on the city council's sensitivity to site selection in outlying white areas.

But the 1945 plan went nowhere, though not because of local opposition. In Chicago the mayor and the city council gave their initial blessing (no sites were specified), but Washington failed to produce new public housing legislation, and a Republican congressional victory in the 1946 elections blocked efforts to revive a housing bill.[9] New public housing and slum clearance, at least at the federal level, were put on hold.

★ ★ ★

While most housing progressives and city planners favored clearance in broad strokes, an alternative—rehabilitation of slum areas by renovating poorly maintained buildings and selectively clearing the worst structures—attracted support in the 1940s from a wide range of community groups, legislators, and property interests. In 1937, state representative Richard J. Daley recommended the creation of a nonprofit housing corporation for purchasing, repairing, and reselling existing structures; legislation, however, stalled in Springfield. Three years later, the Chicago City Council's "Housing Program for the City of Chicago" focused on proposals for neighborhood "conservation" through renovation and limited demolition. Further support on the city council came from Earl Dickerson, a black liberal, University of Chicago law graduate, and later wartime head of the Federal Employment Practices Commission. While not opposed to public housing, Dickerson argued in 1941 that the CHA and the FHA should turn its efforts to "acquiring properties for the purpose of rehabilitation and operation." Groups ranging from the civic-minded Chicago Women's City Club to the more conservative Chicago Real Estate Board also endorsed alternative methods for improving slums.[10]

But public housing supporters rejected the idea. During debate over the 1937 Housing Act, progressives were critical of repairing the slums, and Elizabeth Wood repeated these arguments to the CHA board. Rehabilitation, she concluded in a 1941 report, "is a far too costly method of eliminating areas of dense blight and providing houses for low-income families." Further, Wood objected to efforts to "save" slum neighborhoods with their "worn-out" buildings: "To repair the best structures in a badly deteriorated neighborhood tends merely to prolong the slum character of the neighborhood and postpone the availability of the rest of the area for rebuilding."[11] The city council, however, continued to press the issue and, in 1944, it granted the CHA funds for a more thorough study.

The CHA took this second examination of the issue seriously, but ultimately it stacked the cost analysis to return the desired result. Funding was sufficient to study only one block in depth, and the CHA chose an overcrowded portion of Vernon Avenue with 323 dwellings near the Ida B. Wells homes. The site was "not the worst block in our slums, nor the best," the CHA's 1946 report maintained. It had been a "fashionable resi-

Figure 11. Slum housing on the Near West Side, future site of Brooks Homes, no date. The cropping marks indicate how the CHA used this photograph in its publications; it cropped out the two well-built masonry buildings, leaving only the wood-frame tenement and derelict cottage. The entire area was cleared for the Robert Brooks Homes, completed in 1942. Courtesy of the CHA.

dential district in the 1870s . . . originally designed for large, well-to-do families" who built stone and brick houses at the turn of the century. In the 1920s, the area had housed members of the black elite, but during World War II these structures were carved up into small apartments lacking private baths. For comparison purposes, the report proposed the complete renovation of all but the worst buildings, with new kitchens and baths, appropriate room sizes, and new heating, plumbing, and electrical systems. This full rehabilitation would produce 220 apartments at an estimated renovation cost of $2,500 per unit, while clearing the site and constructing new public housing would produce 270 apartments at a cost of $5,000 per unit.[12] In a surprisingly deceptive move, the CHA buried this unfavorable cost comparison in a table near the end of the report and shifted the focus to a different measure: "lowest achievable rent." The report assumed (without explanation) that a greater federal subsidy could be obtained if the site were cleared and rebuilt as public housing and therefore concluded that slum clearance could build 23 percent more apartments at rents averaging $3 per month lower than under rehabilitation.[13] The

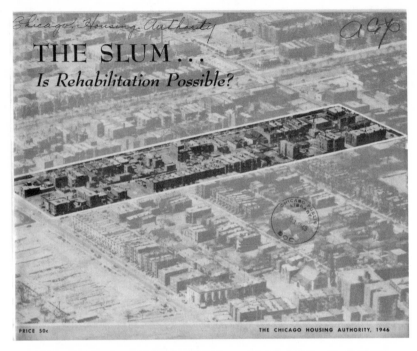

Figure 12. Cover from CHA report, *The Slum . . . Is Rehabilitation Possible?* 1946.
Courtesy of the CHA.

report never considered the more obvious conclusion that federal dollars could be stretched twice as far under the rehabilitation alternative at only slightly higher rents.

Ultimately Elizabeth Wood and most public housers had little interest in rehabilitation of slum neighborhoods. At best, they saw the idea as a quaint proposal by uninformed amateurs; at worst, they perceived it as an effort by opponents to derail the main public housing program and its vision of an improved city. The rehabilitation study went to great lengths to disparage the Vernon Avenue block, noting its "bad land use pattern," "narrow lots," and "alleys strewn with garbage." Clearance would allow planners to "rationalize" the site into modern housing in a completely new neighborhood.[14] Saving the well-built structures—and the often tightly knit communities they contained—was certainly a viable proposition, as the CHA's data showed. But effective resistance to the progressive postwar slum clearance consensus did not emerge in Chicago or nationally until the early 1960s.[15] From the CHA's vantage point, the city had been cleared (often by fire) and rebuilt numerous times in its history; now decaying neighborhoods built in the nineteenth century cried out for the same treatment. Public housing was tried and tested and was ready to tackle the mammoth job. By contrast, rehabilitation required new methods and a house-by-house approach, an entirely different challenge than mass-producing public housing projects.

★　★　★

While it rejected rehabilitation, the CHA never expected to rebuild over nine square miles of the city on its own. Instead, it intended to lead a coordinated slum clearance effort that combined public housing with large-scale, privately owned projects aimed at the "middle third" of the housing market. This private slum clearance component, known as "urban redevelopment," still required public involvement; site acquisition and land costs were prohibitive without state support. Beginning in the late 1930s, the CHA tangled with real estate interests over who would control a future urban redevelopment program. Chicago realtors, picking up on proposals emanating from Washington, favored a state law allowing the creation of quasi-public corporations with the power of eminent domain to assemble land, which would then be sold to private interests for clearance and redevelopment as they saw fit. Daley introduced the proposal in Springfield in 1938, but the CHA criticized the lack of controls in the bill. Instead, the CHA reasoned that it should be the agency allowed to clear slums for lease to private interests, with multiple public strings attached, especially the power to regulate rents. The Chicago City Council, likely pressured by Mayor Kelly, endorsed the CHA's plan and rebuffed Daley's, killing his bill, though the CHA plan lacked sufficient support in Springfield to win passage.[16] During the war, real estate interests and progressives, including Catherine Bauer, offered competing plans for a federally funded urban redevelopment program, and in 1945, Senator Wagner incorporated ideas from both groups into a bill allowing public entities to assemble and convey land at reduced rates to private developers, with stipulations on its usage. But Wagner's bill, too, faltered in Congress in 1945 and would not be enacted until four years later as Title I of the 1949 Housing Act.[17]

With federal urban redevelopment legislation still uncertain in 1945, many states and cities, including Illinois and Chicago, moved forward with their own proposals. Mayor Kelly convinced Republican governor Dwight Green to support a state urban redevelopment program, and under a law enacted in 1945, one of the first of its kind in the nation, the CHA received $4.3 million to acquire slums for clearance and private redevelopment.

That same year, Chicago voters approved a Kelly-backed $5 million bond issue for a similar city-funded program to be run by the CHA.[18] Although Elizabeth Wood recognized that slum clearance without an adequate relocation plan for displaced residents would be "perilous" given the immediate housing shortage, the CHA eagerly accepted its new power as the city's urban redevelopment agency and planned to use privately built slum clearance projects to complement its own public housing efforts.[19]

In a fateful decision, the CHA's progressive leadership used the new state and city urban redevelopment funds to clear areas occupied almost exclusively by African Americans. Five sites adjacent to existing public housing projects on the South and West Sides and a sixth in the heart of the black belt were selected. Only the smallest of the six sites—next to the Jane Addams Homes—contained any white residents. The CHA also began working with Michael Reese Hospital on plans to clear several nearby blocks of housing occupied by African Americans with funds provided by the hospital. Elizabeth Wood justified these choices as a way to protect the authority's earlier public housing investments: "The [state and city redevelopment] funds shall not be spent in driblets creating little islands scattered throughout the blighted area," she wrote to one alderman. "They must be used as part of an extensive plan for rebuilding a large area of the slum that ultimately will contain all types of housing." In December 1945, Wood explained in the CHA's annual report the importance of adding state-assisted private housing near existing public housing projects: "The [private] redevelopment of new areas, when added to the good [public] housing which has already been put down, will amount to a truly sizable start on reclaiming an entire neighborhood."[20]

This coordinated vision became clearer in 1947 when the CHA partnered with the South Side Planning Board (SSPB) to develop an ambitious plan for rebuilding a vast three-square-mile section of the black belt. The SSPB had been founded the year before as a private planning organization funded by Michael Reese Hospital and the Illinois Institute of Technology (IIT). The interracial board and its liberal staff wanted to remove the perceived blight surrounding these South Side institutions and create room for their expansion. The broad strokes of the plan were spelled out in a sixty-two-page color publication depicting a vast array of high-rise towers, park space, and low-rise housing on planned superblocks (fig. 13).[21] Bauhaus architect Walter Gropius and Detroit planner Walter Blucher, head of the American Society of Planning Officials, the nation's most preeminent men in their fields, served as consultants and proposed wiping away the old community and replacing it with an entirely modernist landscape of large private urban redevelopment projects and large public housing projects. Who, exactly, would live in this modern new world was not explained; the SSPB had liberal intentions, but it did not publicize an integration agenda. As the first SSPB project got underway in 1948, Third Ward alderman Archibald Carey sponsored an ordinance to demand nondiscrimination in tenant selection at urban redevelopment projects supported by public funds, but it was defeated after a lengthy debate in the press and on the city council floor, fueling fears among African American leaders that urban redevelopment amounted to a land grab by white institutions.[22]

While it was coy on both its nondiscrimination goal and on public housing's overall role for the area, saying only that "a substantial portion of the dwelling units to be furnished should be built for low-income families, with rentals to fit their means," the SSPB report put the CHA at the center of implementation: "[It] will bear a major responsibility in this redevelopment program." (In 1949, the SSPB planned for 15,000 units of public housing in the area, about half the number eventually built). With Ida B. Wells already in place, land for the Dearborn Homes in acquisition, a Michael Reese partnership in the works, and three of the six 1945 state and city urban redevelopment sites located in the area, the CHA had a head start on the plan's execution. Further, its private redevelopment powers would make it the main government agency overseeing the effort. "The Housing Authority's public interest approach to redevelopment problems will guard against piecemeal and irresponsible proposals," the report noted. In scale and scope, the SSPB plan represented exactly the kind of dramatic vision that Elizabeth Wood desired in rebuilding the slums. "Planning," Wood had written in 1945, "must be bold and comprehensive—or it is useless and wasted."[23]

But the SSPB initiative said little about relocating the tens of thousands of black families living on the site, a crucial issue that extended beyond the plan to the entire slum clearance effort. Solutions demanded citywide action. The most obvious answer involved ending decades of legal and de facto housing segregation practices and allowing blacks to move into vacancies in white neighborhoods. But this reform was beyond the CHA's power, and perhaps beyond the reach of any democratically elected governmental organization in the 1940s given the deep-seated white antipathy to racial integration. More immediate possibilities lay in building new public housing on vacant land to relocate as many slum dwellers as possible. This required only more public funds and accommodation from whites to allow public housing sites on the vast and undeveloped outskirts

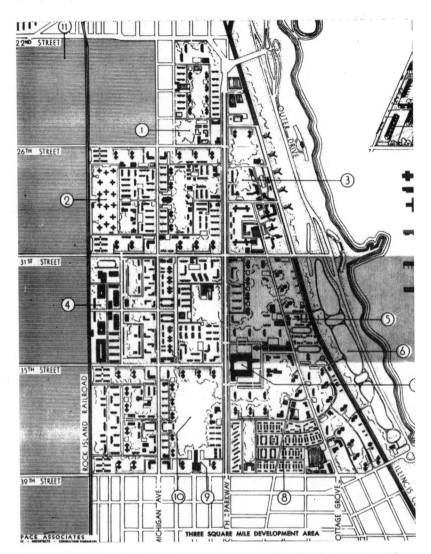

Figure 13. South Side Planning Board, "Three Square Mile Redevelopment Area," from *An Opportunity for Private and Public Investment in Rebuilding Chicago* (Chicago, 1947), 30. Courtesy of the Near South Planning Board.

of the city. The CHA, then, pushed for vacant land relocation housing, in part because of its social justice value in expanding black housing opportunities at a time when continuing migration had stretched the overcrowded black belt to the cracking point, but mostly because such projects were essential for expediting the main slum clearance effort. Without relocation housing, slum clearance would be delayed or only cause further overcrowding within the black belt and hasten racial transition on ghetto margins.

But relocation was a more convoluted problem than this simple formulation suggested. Low-income families from neighborhoods slated for clearance could easily be moved into vacancies in existing public housing projects around the city (though this would crowd out other eligible applicants). But given the limited housing opportunities for African Americans in the 1940s, relocating the far more numerous ineligible families from slum sites—those earning incomes above CHA limits, families without children, and single individuals—proved onerous. Vacant land projects could not directly help such people. The CHA had faced this quandary during its first postwar slum clearance project at Dearborn Homes in the black belt in 1948. Despite raising income limits that year, it determined that fewer than half the 190 families on the Dearborn site were eligible for public housing; the majority had incomes over the CHA's limit of $2,150 and 30 percent had middle-class incomes of over $3,000 a year. Further, the 123 adult couples without children and the 130 single men were ineligible at any income; only those with children were eligible. When the community learned of its imminent clearance, black residents, particularly homeowners, refused to budge and organized in protest. Families were "uncooperative, belligerent, and unbelieving," according to CHA staff. Fearing a public relations disaster, Wood threw additional resources into the relocation effort. The CHA combed its normal waiting lists to find families who could be moved into public housing so that their current private units could be immediately re-rented to ineligible Dearborn site families. Income limits were further eased to aid the effort, and managers at other projects were compelled to take families without screening, "violating a fundamental Authority policy of maintaining . . . freedom for managers to select their own tenants within regulations." While sufficient space for eligible families existed, the relocation of ineligible families required extra time and expense.[24] In 1952, the CHA petitioned the Illinois State Housing Board to exempt residents of slum sites from public housing income limits, but its pleas fell on deaf ears in Springfield. Most ineligible displaced families ended up pushing into racially transitioning neighborhoods of the city, including Woodlawn, Roseland, and East Garfield Park.[25]

★   ★   ★

Even when they could be built, vacant land projects drew a visceral response from whites that permanently circumscribed the CHA's site selections and eventually reigned in its liberalism. The racial backlash first took shape in the fall of 1946, after the CHA had erected a handful of temporary projects on vacant land under the Emergency Veterans Re-Use Housing Program passed by Congress in 1945. In order to accommodate returning veterans, the federal law authorized the movement of temporary war housing—used trailers, Quonset huts, and other barracks-like housing—from various wartime facilities to cities facing immediate shortages. Demand after the war was overwhelming; the Chicago Housing Center received more than 175,000 applications from veterans and sent 25,000 of them to the CHA in 1946. The CHA agreed to acquire 3,000 temporary units and quietly leased twenty-one publicly owned vacant sites from various city agencies, including the Chicago Park District, the Chicago School Board, and the Cook County Forest Preserve. Most sites were scattered on the far reaches of the city near white residential areas, though some were near black enclaves like Lilydale. Unlike permanent projects, the temporary veterans' projects were intended to be in place only until July 1949 and did not require a cooperation agreement with the city council, and, therefore, sites technically could be chosen without council approval. Still, the CHA consulted with the council, and aldermen on two occasions asked it to "reconsider" sites, which were quickly dropped as a consequence.[26]

Unknown to the council, however, was the CHA's intention to integrate its temporary veterans' projects. The war and the fight against fascism had invigorated civil rights activism in the mid-1940s, and black veterans in particular now challenged the country to live up to its wartime rhetoric about freedom. Elizabeth Wood absorbed this spirit in the decision to pursue integration: "We felt that the veterans' projects represented a new era and there could not be the same adherence to the neighborhood composition rule that there had been in the old program."[27]

While the opening of the first integrated veterans' project on an isolated North Side site proceeded smoothly, the second, located near Midway Airport, proved disastrous. Airport Homes lay adjacent to a well-established, white working-class neighborhood with high homeownership rates; its residents reacted violently to the introduction of African Americans. Upon hearing rumors of integration in the fall of 1946, neighborhood whites smashed the project's windows and circulated petitions ordering the CHA to reserve the apartments for neighborhood white veterans living in "doubled-up" arrangements. Then several white "squatters" stole keys from the office of the project manager, moved into newly finished apartments, and admitted they intended to block black occupancy. The CHA allowed a handful of eligible squatters to stay, evicted the rest, and then moved in a black veteran family on November 16. The CHA, the police, and local church leaders were warned of the neighborhood tension, but they could not prevent an ugly mob from descending on Airport Homes, spewing hatred and rocks. The family asked to leave; it took a full complement of police to escort them to safety.[28]

Edward Kelly defended the CHA's nondiscrimination policy, stating the veterans' projects would be made available on the basis of need and "without regard to race, creed, or color" and that "all law-abiding citizens may be assured of their right to live peaceably anywhere in Chicago." But Mayor Kelly's forceful stand did little to calm the neighborhood. After the events of November 16, local alderman Michael Hogan led a protest of two hundred whites to City Hall and demanded that "the CHA be brought under the authority of the Mayor and City Council." The council meeting devolved into chaos as the protesters in the chamber gallery erupted into loud shouts and ugly chants of opposition to integration. Numerous CHA allies condemned the violence, including the American Civil Liberties Union (ACLU), the National Association for the Advancement of Colored People (NAACP), and the Chicago Council against Racial and Religious Discrimination (CCARD). The city council did not immediately bend to the will of the mob and did not attempt to reverse the CHA's nondiscrimination policy—a reflection of Kelly's control. But nor did aldermen come to the CHA's defense. Soon after the protest, the CHA tried to move two more black veteran families into Airport Homes, and several hundred white men and women harassed the policemen protecting the moving truck as well as the civic leaders who had shown up to support integration. Police reinforcements arrived, and the black families stayed. But in early 1947, following several nighttime gunshots directed at the black veterans' homes, the families opted to leave.[29] Mob violence had won—no more black veterans moved into the project.

The Airport Homes "disturbances" in December 1946 were a turning point in the history of the CHA. The riots spotlighted for the first time the CHA's hopes to integrate projects in white areas, and the resulting hostility from whites had major implications for the upcoming mayoral elections in April 1947. Mayor Kelly was by far the CHA's most important protector; he appointed liberal board members, secured urban redevelopment powers from the state, and generally minimized aldermanic influence (except in 1941 when the council asserted veto power over site selection). But Kelly's defense of the CHA's racial liberalism inflamed the Democratic Party machine. Highly publicized instances of mismanagement in other city agencies compounded the mayor's woes. Ironically, Kelly the public housing liberal was also Kelly the machine boss, who tolerated corruption everywhere but the CHA. Machine politicians, fearing he would lead them to defeat, pushed for Kelly's ouster, especially after the Airport Homes debacle made him appear too "soft" on race. Cook County Democratic Party chairman Jacob Arvey reluctantly pressured the mayor to "retire" in early 1947 and in his place selected Martin Kennelly as the "reform" candidate, whose main attribute was his general pliancy and unsullied reputation in the business world.[30]

Without Kelly to protect it, the CHA's political standing entered a free fall. The first loss was its power over private urban redevelopment granted in 1945. Even before Airport Homes, the CHA's management of the state and city urban redevelopment programs did not sit well with Springfield or Chicago. Governor Green and Illinois State Housing Board chairman Temple McFayden were annoyed at Kelly for handing state and city redevelopment funds to the CHA, instead of creating a separate Chicago Land Clearance Commission. Real estate interests grumbled that the sites chosen by the CHA in the black belt were only good for more public housing, not private redevelopment. For its part, the city council feared the CHA might keep the city-funded sites for public housing rather than turn them over to private hands.[31] In the minds of many, the CHA chose sites to meet its own needs, and indeed, two years after receiving funds, it had yet to put in motion any private redevelopment projects.

With Kelly gone and enemies circling, the CHA's days in charge of the redevelopment program were numbered. Downtown business interests were ambivalent on the CHA; they wanted more state funds for urban redevelopment and for CHA-built "relocation" housing to expedite clearance, but not racial integration. Governor Green agreed to their requests, but he went further and demanded that the CHA be cut out from managing future redevelopment. Instead, he wanted only land clearance commissions to be the implementing agencies. Mayor Kennelly, no friend of the CHA, went along with the plan, and the governor maneuvered the program through the state legislature in May.[32] On the surface, the new Blighted Areas Redevelopment Act of 1947 appeared to be a victory for slum clearance, but it amounted to a strategic defeat for the CHA. Stripped of its urban redevelopment powers, the CHA was no longer in a position to harmonize public and private projects in a comprehensive plan, and the Kennelly-appointed Chicago Land Clearance Commission and the CHA never warmed to each other. Other cities merged their urban renewal and public housing operations into one agency, but Chicago divided these functions, producing little coordination between the two most important governmental organizations remaking the city.

Figure 14. Fernwood Veterans Temporary Homes, July 1948. One year after the riots at Fernwood, a constant security presence remained, as seen by the officer seated at rear. The back of this photograph reads: "Not for publicity." Courtesy of the CHA.

Three months later the CHA suffered another setback in the wake of even more rioting at a second temporary veterans' project, the eighty-seven-unit Fernwood Homes in the city's Roseland neighborhood. Over the course of four hot August nights, enraged white mobs battled more than a thousand police after eight black families moved in. City officials feared a general race riot would engulf the city, as in 1919, and only a continued police presence kept a lid on further violence.[33] Unlike his predecessor, Kennelly failed to condemn the violence or come down strongly on the side of the CHA and nondiscrimination. The CHA orchestrated its own campaign of support for integration, amassing hundreds of letters from the city's religious figures, union leaders, and liberal organizations. But neighborhood whites also vented in city papers, with one letter to the *Chicago Daily News* demanding that that the city council "rid the CHA of those misguided liberals who are using a desperate housing situation as a weapon to foster their unworkable ideals of tolerance and the brotherhood of man."[34] Once again, the introduction of African Americans into white neighborhoods had ripped open the city's divides, and the resulting backlash seriously weakened the CHA's political clout and undermined its vision.

The Fernwood Homes riots accorded aldermen the first opportunity to attack the CHA openly since Kelly's forced retirement. Reginald DuBois, whose ward included Roseland, called for an investigation of "corruption" at the CHA and denounced the authority's "ideological theories" on integration. CHA chairman Robert Taylor counterattacked and defended the board's policies, calling DuBois's charges "a smokescreen for a demand the Authority enforce racial segregation." Robert Merriam, a progressive Republican alderman and former director of the Metropolitan Housing Council, chaired the subsequent city council investigation and prevented it from becoming a platform for DuBois's views. But the lukewarm report, completed in March 1948, exposed the CHA's weaknesses at city hall. The report cleared the CHA of any corruption charges, but it only mildly supported the CHA's nondiscrimination policies: "No state-aided housing development should do other than provide housing for all who qualify for it"—hardly a ringing endorsement. Moreover, the report dodged the crucial issue of whether public housing should be built and integrated in white areas. Instead, it censured the CHA's "failure to work closely with the city," emphasizing "the necessity for the CHA to function as a part of the city team." Finally, to close the loophole in site selection opened by the veterans' emergency program, the Merriam report recommended additional state legislation restricting the CHA's independence. Springfield obliged in 1949, effectively guaranteeing the city council's already formidable power to block CHA site proposals.[35]

Meanwhile, deteriorating physical conditions at the veterans' temporary projects further hammered the CHA's reputation. Everyone—residents, neighbors, and the CHA itself—found them deficient. Unlike the permanent prewar projects, the veterans' projects lacked the community facilities and well-built construction that had defined CHA operations. Maintaining the flimsy structures proved costly, leading the CHA in 1947 to default on $2 million in loans provided by the city for their construction, an unavoidable embarrassment. By the time the last veterans' projects were dismantled in 1956, they had become eyesores, blighting neighborhoods on the fringes of the city where the CHA hoped to build vacant land projects.[36] While the 2,600 temporary units provided much needed housing for veterans during the immediate postwar housing crisis, from Elizabeth Wood's perspective they were more a burden than a benefit.

*　*　*

The Merriam report urged the CHA to be part of the city "team," but the difficulties of working with Kennelly, the city council, and other city officials became readily apparent when the CHA tried to find sites for re-location housing funded by the 1947 state law. Instead of prompt action, site selection became a political football, tossed between various agencies before being fumbled by the CHA and then smothered by hostile public opinion. The CHA hoped to build three or four large projects on vacant sites on the south and southwest fringes of the city in rapid fashion. Ken-nelly, however, told the CHA to first get approval from the Chicago Plan Commission, and negotiations stalled in early 1948. The CHA presented a lengthy list of acceptable sites, but the CPC objected to most, claiming they were "suitable for private development" that would expand the city's tax base. Fears of renewed racial violence were also a factor as the CPC rejected several sites because of their proximity to the Airport and Fern-wood Homes. The CHA preferred a handful of large sites, while the CPC suggested a collection of smaller ones. After weeks of discussion, a com-promise list allowed several vacant sites in white areas, as well as vacant sites near the existing black enclaves Morgan Park and Lilydale.

But Kennelly dithered over the list before producing his own slate of sites, all in the black belt on industrial or partially vacant land. Kennelly maintained that relocation housing should be part of the urban redevel-opment effort by rebuilding in blighted areas and that it should allow dis-placed residents to remain near their own neighborhoods. The mayor ap-parently had little stomach for interfering with racial boundaries in ways that might spark another Fernwood Homes crisis. Elizabeth Wood viewed the mayor's plan as a step backward, reporting it would take at least eigh-teen months to acquire and build on his sites. Despite her objections, Tay-lor and the CHA commissioners instructed Wood to meet the mayor's demands as best as possible. In late June, the CHA board and Kennelly finally agreed on a compromise list of four sites for 2,000 units: one from Kennelly's list, two smaller blighted vacant tracts near the Jane Addams Homes (already purchased by the CHA with city urban redevelopment funds), and a CHA proposal to build 1,100 apartments in elevator buildings on one-third of McKinley Park on the Southwest Side.[37]

The four sites were a public relations disaster. The mayor's partially vacant site still contained 118 families who would have to be relocated before the proposed 250 units could be built, angering liberals who ar-gued the site defeated the purpose of the relocation program. Then the alderman representing the Jane Addams area objected to adding to the already high concentration of public housing on the Near West Side. But the McKinley Park site proved to be the most politically damaging. The Chicago Park Commission had given the nod to the CHA's plan, believing the eighty-acre park too large a space, but the surrounding neighborhoods vehemently disagreed.[38] When they arrived at the park on a bus tour, Kennelly, several aldermen, and the CHA staff found an estimated three thousand angry people, including several aldermen who had not been consulted on the site. Signs lined the surrounding streets: "Save the Park" and "Mayor Kennelly, you have no children. If you did you would not want to take this park!" The mayor, spooked by the protest, told the bus driver not to stop. Four hundred protesters followed Kennelly back to city hall, where Richard J. Daley, now deputy county comptroller and Eleventh Ward committeeman, addressed the crowd: "I have talked to several aldermen and they assured me they would abandon the site."[39] Kennelly promptly wrote a letter to the city council and the CHA requesting new site recommendations—thus overturning five months of work.

The CHA had stumbled badly in choosing McKinley Park. The controversy drowned out the importance of vacant land housing to support the slum clearance program and handed opponents an issue that avoided any discussion of race. To public housing planners, McKinley Park made sense: infrastructure was in place, it involved no displacement, and it was close to jobs, transportation, and shopping. By these neutral criteria the park was high on the CHA's list from the start. But politically, the choice made the CHA appear out of touch with the city's aldermen and its neighborhoods, increasingly resentful and suspicious of the housing authority. The divide between Elizabeth Wood and the city council grew as well, with little communication between her and the aldermanic "Big Boys" who ran council business.[40]

After McKinley Park, the CHA had even less leverage in determining relocation sites, and significantly, race, not planning, returned as the central spike of contention. Kennelly again betrayed his racial attitudes when he told the *Sun-Times*: "The problem is should a person who lives in the Negro area be moved out to an area where property value is high?" In July, the mayor, the aldermen, and the CHA produced a final compromise that pleased no one. The new site list included five projects in white areas, three in black areas, and a ninth site in Chinatown. Two of the five white sites were proposed by the CHA and survived despite aldermanic objections, including a large vacant tract on the Southwest Side. The other three white sites, proposed by aldermen, were small and not well located. The three black belt sites were also small, needed to be cleared first, and only one had any relation to existing redevelopment plans. The city's liberal groups railed against the poor planning implicit in the list and the closed-door nature of the site selection. Nor were neighborhood whites happy, especially with the large vacant site on the Southwest Side. The split-the-difference nature of the compromise was reflected in the city's major papers, which offered cautious criticism but general acceptance of the plan. However, the compromise was not as "final" as the CHA expected. In further negotiations, the city council demanded a 10 percent quota on black occupancy at the sites in white areas and scaled back the number of units allowed. The CHA wanted to build between 1,100 and 2,100 units on the largest site; the city council limited it to only 300.[41]

The heavily circumscribed outcome of the 1948 battle revealed the CHA's political weakness and strengthened the hand of aldermen who wanted to restrict public housing to black areas. The CHA urgently needed somewhere to put slum dwellers so it could rapidly rebuild black neighborhoods, but now the relocation projects would be smaller than expected. These 1948 decisions angered Elizabeth Wood and roiled the CHA; two of her closest lieutenants resigned in December out of frustration with the city council.[42] At their farewell event in February 1949, Wood delivered a fiery speech to a room full of CHA friends and supporters—the most passionate of her career—in which she expressed disgust at the compromises and lashed out with rhetorical questions and critical answers:

> What does the city want from this new [relocation] program? The fewest houses it can get away with? Placed on scraps of land that officials can think up no other use for? Destined to remain as symbols of planlessness, of political expediency, and of the repudiation of this city's belief in the dignity of all men— that is what you are in danger of getting.

Even more explicitly, she declared that "Chicago is in a most violent though invisible state of war on the question of race," with aldermen and city officials determined "to sustain a policy of containment" of African Americans. Wood admitted that she was "a controversial figure" for her stands on race and for bucking the aldermen, but she told the audience that she would "fight anybody who stands in the way . . . of getting homes built for the people."[43]

* * *

Wood made good on her promise to fight in the next round of site selections in 1949–50, which involved federal funds and higher stakes. When the 1949 Housing Act belatedly passed Congress and provided federal dollars to build large-scale public housing projects on the same terms as the 1937 Housing Act, the CHA dusted off and modified its 1945 slum clearance plan, proposing 25,000 units on slum sites and 15,000 units on vacant land over six years. In the 1948 conflict, the CHA had tried to work with city officials and aldermen behind closed doors. But now it made its case for sites publicly, hoping to win a better result through open argument and political force, with the city's liberal organizations as allies. The results, however, were even more disappointing than in 1948.[44]

In October 1949, the CHA presented publicly the first phase of its plan: a list of seven sites covering 10,000 units, equally divided between slum clearance and vacant land development. The list included three large clearance sites in African American neighborhoods and three large vacant sites in white areas. These six were "extensions" to existing projects, intended to protect earlier investments and to capitalize on economies of scale by building larger concentrations of public housing (fig. 15). The seventh site was a tiny, four-acre tract south of Bridgeport, the only white slum site on the list, and one already owned by the CHA.[45] Mobilizing a coalition of housing reformers, religious leaders, union activists, and black civil rights organizations, the CHA stirred up a groundswell in support of its 1949 list, and the *Chicago Sun-Times* consistently ran supportive articles and editorials. But property owners and real estate interests organized as well. For several months the city council sat on the proposal until finally, in February 1950, public hearings were held. Hundreds of women from the neighborhoods packed the gallery and taunted pro–public housing speakers, turning the hearings into a raucous event and leading Mayor Kennelly to double the police presence to maintain order. Not surprisingly, the aldermen sided with the representatives of the neighborhoods and rejected all of the sites in white areas and even one in the black belt. Only two slum sites met approval, both supported by the affected black aldermen.[46]

Although the CHA's initial assault failed, neither the aldermen nor the mayor were comfortable rejecting public housing altogether, since that meant forgoing an enormous influx of federal dollars. A special aldermanic subcommittee was appointed to find new locations, and after an informal bus tour, it produced a whimsical list, including a tract containing the University of Chicago tennis courts. Four of the eleven "bus tour" sites were located in the ward of liberal alderman Benjamin Becker, who represented a Jewish area on the Far North Side, a move some saw as anti-Semitic. Ironically, these sites were highly desirable from a planning perspective, but the CHA commissioners dismissed them because they were "actively in the process of high-cost residential development, without government aid, by private enterprise." Privately, the commissioners believed the area to be "too good for public housing," according to CHA planner

Figure 15. The evolution of ABLA (Addams, Brooks, Loomis, Abbott), 1950. This image
shows how the CHA sought to protect its initial housing project using "extensions."
The CHA added to the original PWA-built Jane Addams Homes (1937) with the Brooks
Homes (selected in 1939), Loomis Courts (selected in 1948), and the Addams-Brooks
Extension (selected in 1949, and later renamed Grace Abbott Homes). The image also
shows the evolution in design, from Addams's courtyard apartments built by the PWA,
to Brooks's more regimented forms built by the USHA, and finally to the high-rise
buildings proposed in 1950. Courtesy of the CHA.

Martin Meyerson. Here the CHA, either out of a desire to avoid competing with private interests or to defend Becker, missed an opportunity to
call the council's bluff and win at least one well-located site in a North
Side, middle-class neighborhood. The haphazard bus tour sites, however,
had the effect of strengthening the CHA's hand in the eyes of the press,
which criticized the aldermanic foray into housing planning.[47]

With site selection again stalled, a combative CHA returned to the
council in April 1950 with a modified proposal for 12,000 units, with
a larger proportion on vacant land. The six "extensions" from the 1949
list were still included (three large slum tracts in black neighborhoods,
plus three on vacant land), but the new list added two additional vacant
tracts in the far corner of the city's Southwest Side. These were planned

for sprawling projects of 2,000 apartments each for relocation purposes, similar in scale to Altgeld Gardens, built during the war. The 1950 list fared no better than the 1949 one. The council refused to vote on the new proposal, and instead John Duffy and William Lancaster—two of the city council's "Big Boys"—cobbled together their own list from various proposals and rammed it through the council in May, handing it to the CHA as a "take it or leave it" proposition. The Duffy and Lancaster list accepted all six of the CHA's "extension" sites, including the two in white areas, but the aldermen again sharply scaled back the number of apartments that could be built and rejected altogether the two large vacant sites. To reach the goal of 12,000 units, Duffy and Lancaster added four slum sites—all in African American neighborhoods—and three small vacant tracts (only one of which was in a white area) without consulting Taylor or Wood or even city highway planners, who would later learn that the council's sites would require the rerouting of the south expressway. In all, the CHA's 1950 site list had proposed 4,000 units in the black slums and 8,000 units on vacant land; instead, the Council delivered it 10,250 units in black slums and only 2,100 units on vacant land.[48]

Public housing supporters, including liberal planners and the city's African American organizations, ripped the Duffy-Lancaster list for its obvious racism in limiting the exodus of blacks from overcrowded slums. The Chicago NAACP publicly labeled the sites "improper and vicious in that they seek to maintain and impose a ghetto pattern of segregation." The *Chicago Sun-Times* agreed with critics and accused the city council of creating an "all-Negro" plan. Liberals in the council tried to amend the Duffy-Lancaster list by restoring the vacant land sites, but their motions failed to pass. Importantly, though, the amendments did not strike the council's additional slum sites, and the CHA staff admitted to the *Sun-Times* that they were "good" locations and "suitable" for public housing. The problem with the city council's action was the limited number of vacant land projects to accelerate relocation and slum clearance, combined with the blatant use of race in the site selection process.[49]

In a last ditch effort to win more vacant land sites, the CHA appealed to federal officials, who were well aware of what was happening in Chicago. Staff of the Racial Relations Service at the Housing and Home Finance Agency (HHFA) wrote scathing memos about the Chicago City Council's racial animus, calling the city's combined public housing and urban renewal programs "Negro clearance" that "buttresses up existing patterns of segregation" while doing little for relocation.[50] The Public Housing Administration head John Taylor Egan and his top advisor Warren Vinton required Chicago to modify its plan to achieve "racial equity," meaning more sites in white neighborhoods, and to address the problem of relocation more clearly, but it did not insist on specific sites or numbers of units in white areas. Washington was nervous about pressing too far, fearing the loss of any public housing in Chicago. Duffy and Lancaster placated Washington by choosing a site that was ostensibly white but in the early stages of racial transition and by claiming relocation could be addressed through clearance and rebuilding in stages. These anemic responses passed federal muster, and the CHA's hope for federal muscle evaporated. Robert Taylor, faced with the troublesome choice of building on a flawed site list or not building at all, reluctantly accepted the city council's demands in August 1950. Summarizing the frustrations of CHA supporters, planner Walter Blucher wrote to Vinton: "When we finally succeed in getting a housing authority [the CHA] which is willing to stand for a decent minimum program, it is pretty sad when the Federal officials won't back up that kind of a program." "Political expediency," Blucher continued, "is a very poor rationalization for abject surrender."[51]

Soon the few white sites made available by the Duffy-Lancaster list crumbled under additional pressures. The Chicago Sanitary Board, which owned one of the vacant sites, balked at selling to the CHA after voters in 1950 rearranged the board's membership, ousting several Democrats and installing Republicans. As well, nearby residents filed a nuisance suit and protested at sanitary board meetings to block any project. Since the CHA could not condemn publicly owned land, the site was lost. The CHA-proposed Trumbull Park Extension (already reduced from 1,300 to 300 units by the council) fell through as well. The Chicago and Western Indiana Railroad refused to sell, claiming it needed the site for a switching yard, and the Illinois Commerce Commission sided with the railroad, thereby blocking condemnation. Whether outside pressures or race were involved is unclear, but the CHA twice proposed rearranging the site boundaries, and the railroad still rejected the offers. As a result, the CHA lost two of its four sites in white neighborhoods, along with roughly eight hundred to a thousand potential units of public housing on vacant land.[52]

The CHA had gone to war with the city council in 1949 and 1950 and had largely lost, and the battles left it battered and exhausted. White aldermen had carved up site lists as they saw fit, and race became the deciding factor in public housing's location. Robert Taylor resigned in frustration in 1950, and other liberal commissioners exited or were not reappointed by Kennelly, leaving the board less experienced and decidedly less progressive. Attacks elsewhere also threatened the CHA; in Springfield, only a

veto by Democratic governor Adlai Stevenson saved the CHA from needing a referendum by voters to approve a site. Relations with the city council reached new lows after negative statements made by Elizabeth Wood
about the aldermen appeared in print in June 1950. "They really hate us,"
she told the *Daily News*, adding that the aldermen would "love to have that
gravy," a reference to the patronage potential of the authority.[53]

Chicago was hardly alone in finding its housing authority and elected
city officials at odds over public housing locations. In Detroit, whites
strongly resisted public housing in outlying areas and, in the 1949 mayoral election, defeated a pro–public housing candidate backed by the city's
powerful unions. Public housing was thereafter confined to black neighborhoods. Neighborhood whites jammed a Baltimore City Council meeting in early 1950, clamoring against sites in their neighborhoods, and that
city's aldermen used the cooperation agreement with the local housing
authority to reject racially sensitive locations. In Los Angeles, race was
less important than a general red-baiting campaign to tar public housing
as "socialistic." Pressure compelled the Los Angeles City Council to back
out of a previously approved cooperation agreement with the city's housing authority in 1951. When the PHA in Washington resisted canceling
agreements, some in Congress criticized federal administrators for "shov-
ing public housing down the throat" of the city.[54]

The extent of the damage in the CHA's relationship with the city council became apparent in late 1950 when the CHA applied for planning funds
for another 10,000 public housing units, the second phase of the five-year,
40,000-unit goal. Under federal regulations, the CHA needed a letter of
approval from the city council before it could receive even small amounts
of planning funds from Washington. Previously, the aldermen had readily
given approval; now, the council ignored the request, refusing to give its
assent to any more public housing in Chicago. Throughout 1951 and 1952,
the CHA board, now headed by Wayne McMillan, a liberal University of
Chicago professor of social service administration and a close friend of
Robert Taylor, pleaded with Mayor Kennelly and the city council for the
letter of approval. In July 1952, McMillan scaled back the CHA's application to the city council from 10,000 to 3,500 units, but again received no
response. Desperate to resolve the impasse, the board authorized James
Downs, Kennelly's housing coordinator, to negotiate with the aldermen
on behalf of the CHA . The CHA board approved a list of sites developed
by Downs believed to be "susceptible to City Council approval" and allowed him "to use this group of sites as a working basis for clearing the
way for City Council approval" of additional public housing. He returned

from the council with three slum sites, all in the black belt, accommodating roughly 2,000 units. The CHA board quickly approved these meager offerings.[55]

By 1952, then, Elizabeth Wood and her staff had been entirely cut out of the planning process, and the CHA commissioners had surrendered site selection power to city hall and the city council, letting them choose sites without debate.[56] Any thought of vacant land for relocation, coordination between public housing and urban redevelopment, or building 40,000 units in six years had vanished. By the end of 1954, only 2,513 units were completed; by 1960, when the last of the sites selected in 1950 were finally finished, the figure reached only 9,400. The Korean War and the rationing of building material postponed construction, but the main source of delays in Chicago remained the site selection controversy and the difficulties in relocating slum dwellers ineligible for public housing. While Chicago never completely suspended its program, the city's racial divides crushed the city's liberal slum clearance agenda. The aldermen were willing between 1948 and 1950 to allow the CHA to pursue slum clearance in black neighborhoods, but by the early 1950s, the machine-based aldermen saw little reason to cooperate with the weakened authority. As she later confessed, Wood was "floundering" in the early 1950s, with no hope of achieving her visions of either slum clearance or new vacant land communities.[57]

*　*　*

Although they had a hand in planning much of the clearance of Chicago's black slums, Wood and Taylor were only partly responsible for the CHA's largest complex of public housing, the State Street corridor. This corridor replaced the Federal Street slum (Federal paralleled State), which had long been on reformers' agenda for clearance. Liberal black alderman Earl Dickerson first proposed redevelopment in 1940, and the CHA board under Taylor selected a portion of the area for Dearborn Homes in 1945. Five years later, the city council chose two Federal Street tracts for Harold Ickes Homes and Stateway Gardens.[58] The latter site forced city engineers to move a planned expressway slightly westward, which in turn, opened up more of Federal Street for other uses; by then, vacant lots dotted much of the area, and the CHA viewed it as a promising location with relatively low costs. Between 1955 and 1957, four additional sites along Federal and State Streets were named, three by the CHA after Wood's departure and the last by Second Ward alderman William Harvey, a protégé of the black congressman William Dawson but more re-

Figure 16. Robert Taylor Homes site plan, 1960, Shaw, Metz and Associates.
Photograph by Hedrich-Blessing, HB-23740. Reproduced by permission of the
Chicago History Museum.

cently co-opted by Richard J. Daley, now mayor. In this patchwork way, the remainder of the Federal Street slum fell under CHA control, eventually producing the mammoth Robert Taylor Homes in 1962. The resulting State Street corridor stretched four miles, interrupted only by the besieged Illinois Institute of Technology.[59] In a 1956 interview, Robert Taylor, by then in private business, was not concerned about the selection of the Federal Street sites "because it is a narrow strip" that will eventually create "entirely different communities," and he objected to efforts to "scatter" public housing across the black belt, fearing small projects would be overwhelmed by surrounding blight.[60] But Taylor, who died the next year of heart failure, envisioned neither the massive size of the future Robert Taylor Homes nor the monolithic community that would loom over the South Side of Chicago.

Public housing was not the only force tearing up black slums, as the Chicago Land Clearance Commission's urban redevelopment plans also proceeded apace. It took two decades, but eventually much of the South Side Planning Board's plan for three square miles of Bronzeville came to fruition. Federal funds subsidized a series of clearance projects that pro-

AUTHORITY SHAW METZ & ASSOCIATES   ARCHITECTS-ENGINEERS

duced vast, privately owned, high-rise complexes surrounded by green space—the Corbusian vision come to life. Lake Meadows (2,000 units) and Prairie Shores (1,700 units) were completed in the 1950s, and South Commons (1,700 units in mostly low-rise townhouses) in the mid-1960s. The large scale of both the public and private projects in the area meant they could not easily be meshed into a cohesive community; the fences and inward-focused site plans of the private projects hampered interaction between classes. While the private projects—unlike the public ones—remained economically viable, the modernist environment created by the SSPB was hardly a triumph of urban planning. The old city was wiped away, and a soulless one replaced it.

* * *

For many, the problems suffered by public housing in urban America can be traced to one basic variable—location. The fact that projects sit mostly in African American neighborhoods is evidence that public housing was hijacked by racist forces to impose state-sponsored residential segregation. There is much truth to this assertion, but it cannot entirely explain how

public housing ended up where it did. The Chicago City Council's blatant racism and the backlash against racial integration accounts for why
no more than a handful of projects in Chicago were built in white areas,
but it only partially explains why projects were built in black neighborhoods. A closer analysis shows how the city's long-standing progressive
vision for clearing slums played a major role in location decisions. Several of the projects that are identified as emblematic of Chicago's "second ghetto" were selected under the progressive leadership of Elizabeth
Wood and Robert Taylor with the intention of alleviating the abysmal
housing conditions facing African Americans. These include three of the
CHA's five largest conglomerations: Cabrini-Green, the ABLA group, and
the Ida B. Wells group. The remaining two—the State Street corridor and
the Horner-Rockwell complex—were not chosen under liberal auspices
but by a city council attempting to keep blacks away from white neighborhoods. However, given that the CHA proposed building 25,000 units of
public housing on slum sites in six years and that the Federal Street slum
was among the worst in the city, it is difficult to envision how the CHA
could have avoided rebuilding at least part of the area. Moreover, the enormous size of each project group was not driven by a race- or class-based
agenda to contain the poor; the CHA under Wood and Taylor preferred
large-scale clearance and "extensions" on planning grounds and dismissed
the idea of smaller projects. They never proposed scattering individual
buildings around the city on vacant lots or small tracts; they wanted to
remake the old city in modernist fashion. As a result of these choices, four
out of five CHA apartments planned during this period were envisioned
and built in projects of over 800 units.[61]

The oversimplification of the "second ghetto" thesis by later observers
leaves the impression that a choice existed: either public housing could be
built on vacant land to further integration aims, or it could be built in the
black ghetto as a containment strategy—and a racist city council chose
the latter.[62] But this was not the historical contingency between 1948 and
1952. The CHA wanted both to build large projects on vacant land to expedite slum clearance and to replace a substantial portion of the city's
slums with public housing as part of a comprehensive initiative. Even if
the CHA had won vacant land sites, then, this would not have stopped it
from rebuilding Chicago's black belt with expansive public housing. Taylor and Wood did not intend to "make the second ghetto"; they wanted
housing rights for African Americans, racially integrated projects on vacant land, and a coherent plan for slum clearance that combined large
urban redevelopment and public housing projects. Yet, given the progres-

sive slum clearance agenda of the 1940s, the large-scale thinking of planners, and the challenge of sustaining racial integration (the subject of the next chapter), it is difficult to see how even an unencumbered CHA under liberal leadership could have rebuilt the black belt without erecting projects like those that form the core of what historians today call the "second ghetto."

The End of Integration
and the Taming of the CHA

Had they been approved by the Chicago City Council in the early 1950s, public housing projects on vacant land would have introduced African Americans into white areas and helped in small ways to break up the ghetto. It does not follow, however, that such projects by themselves would have led to long-run residential integration. As the CHA's experience in the 1950s showed, the mixed-race communities sought by progressives such as Elizabeth Wood and Robert Weaver required more than simply moving blacks into new projects in white areas. Given white antipathy to integration and black housing demand, sustaining mixed-race occupancy meant limits on African American admissions, a form of racial planning that conflicted with the civil rights agenda in the postwar period.

In its first ten years, the CHA's approach to racial integration evolved considerably, from a cautious stance to a more outspoken liberalism. Initially, it shied away from the potentially explosive issue and integrated the Jane Addams Homes only reluctantly and in a token fashion in 1938. Then in 1942, in the face of local opposition, the authority successfully implemented the neighborhood composition rule to include 20 percent African American occupancy at Cabrini Homes and created its first truly integrated community. The Cabrini approach preserved the rights of African Americans to space they had previously occupied, but it did not assert their rights to live anywhere in the city. The CHA began supporting these rights after the war at its temporary veterans' housing projects on vacant land, but it used quotas to reassure whites. Even so, the white backlash to any integration was considerable, as witnessed at the Airport and Fernwood Homes in 1946 and 1947. Despite this resistance, the CHA opened its relocation projects in white areas in the 1950s without incident, though again restrictive quotas—this time imposed by the city council—limited black rights. Residential integration, while still a tenuous idea, looked viable in Chicago's projects. All that remained was to lift quotas and open up previously all-white projects so that eligible residents could live in public housing without regard to the color of their skin or the prejudices of their neighbors.

Within a decade, however, residential integration had died a painful death at the CHA, and the rights of African Americans remained unfulfilled. Public housing was a battleground, and renewed racial violence claimed the career of Elizabeth Wood, the city's strongest voice for black housing rights. In her place came men without her progressive values, and Mayor Daley gradually subdued the CHA's liberalism. Meanwhile, existing biracial occupancy evaporated. Still a new and untested idea in the 1940s, planned residential integration proved too fragile to withstand the prejudices, preferences, and mobility of whites. Moreover, integration as a liberal goal was eclipsed by a rights-based, "open occupancy" agenda that demanded freedom for African Americans to choose housing without racial restrictions. But open occupancy and integration were not synonymous. The first involved nondiscrimination in residential transactions; the second required maintaining racial balance in the face of social pressures and economic forces that churned residential neighborhoods. Open occupancy, then, might not lead to integration, and a subtle but unresolved tension existed between the two goals in the 1950s—and, indeed, exists to the present time. By 1960, integration in public housing had fallen victim to white intransigence, African American ambivalence, and the practical dilemmas of social engineering.

*   ★   ★

The rights-based view of housing opportunity developed in the 1930s and 1940s among African American civil rights leaders in response to the blatant racism of restrictive covenants that blocked the sale of property to nonwhites and also often to Jews. Black leaders called for "open occupancy," the idea that African Americans should be free to live anywhere regardless of race. Robert Weaver, the nation's foremost African American housing expert and racial relations advisor at the USHA in the late 1930s, formulated the issue clearly in his 1948 book *The Negro Ghetto*, where he blasted restrictive covenants and laid out the implications of continued segregation in housing. Weaver focused on northern cities such as Chicago, where he believed discrimination could be broken down through new open occupancy laws at the state and local levels, especially for state-subsidized projects. Open occupancy had a decidedly middle-class bent; its main beneficiaries would be black homebuyers shut out of private housing in white neighborhoods. Weaver's main concern was spatial; he wanted both existing property and new developments open to all in order to expand black housing opportunity at time of immense shortage due to the continuing migration of African Americans north. He also viewed segregation as a corrosive force on black life, attributing urban ills to the second-class citizenship it engendered. While he pushed for interracial projects, Weaver was vague on policies for sustaining integration. That potential problem appeared a distant one compared to bringing down the substantial barriers still blocking African Americans from owning or renting property where they pleased.[1]

White liberals supported open occupancy on civil rights grounds, but they viewed it as a means to promote residential integration, which, in turn, would both decrease white racism and improve opportunities for African Americans. "Contact theory," in its infancy among sociologists in the 1940s, suggested that once blacks and whites interacted in work, schools, and residential environments, prejudices would dissipate. Testing these ideas, especially contact theory, was difficult, as intentional residential integration was unknown in the private market and existed at only a small number of public housing projects in a handful of housing authorities across the country. Social scientists began research in the late 1940s, and in 1951 Morton Deutsch published results of a study in an integrated public housing project, finding support for contact theory and gains in reducing prejudice.[2] But black and white activists were united in their pressing quest for open occupancy and left behind practical questions about how to sustain integration.

★　★　★

Stymied on site selection between 1948 and 1952, Elizabeth Wood turned her attention to the cause of African American housing rights and the principle of open occupancy. The CHA, despite the leadership of Wood and Robert Taylor, was far from ideologically pure in its tenant selection policies. At four prewar projects (Trumbull Park, Lathrop, Bridgeport, and Lawndale), the CHA had steered away black applicants for over a decade. In January 1950, Taylor pushed through the board an open occupancy resolution declaring that "[f]amilies shall not be segregated or otherwise discriminated against on grounds of race, color, creed, national origin, or ancestry," but this new policy did not produce immediate action because the board feared antagonizing the city council in the midst of its site selection battles. Foot-dragging continued under the chairmanship of the cautious McMillan, leading a frustrated Wood to conspire with outside liberal groups to apply external pressure on the CHA to integrate. Protests by the Chicago Council against Racial and Religious Discrimination, the Negro Labor Council, and the NAACP led to more CHA board resolutions but again to no action, as the commissioners, concerned about potential violence, instructed Wood not to integrate the four projects without their approval. When she presented the board with carefully selected black families with experience in integrated environments for three of the four all-white projects in 1952, the commissioners rebuffed her request and, as a delaying tactic, asked for an outside study of tenant selection practices.[3]

The behind-the-scenes conflict at the CHA could no longer be contained when the integration issue finally combusted at Trumbull Park Homes in the summer of 1953. Betty Howard, an African American with light skin, had applied for public housing in August and "passed" as white. She was steered to Trumbull Park Homes, where her neighbors immediately identified her husband and children as black, triggering a violent response from the whites in neighboring South Deering. Mobs shattered windows, set off homemade explosives, and harassed the isolated family. The South Deering Improvement Association, a neighborhood group, proclaimed the project for whites only.[4] As civil rights organizations picketed the CHA's meetings demanding integration, Wood urged the commissioners to denounce these racist statements and handed the board fresh legal opinions, which reasoned that the CHA had no choice but to support open occupancy. Led by John Yancey, a labor leader and Robert

Taylor's replacement as the lone black member of the board, the CHA publicly declared: "Public housing must be made available to all eligible citizens purely on the basis of need. There shall be no racial barrier to a home in public housing." But again, obfuscations by the commissioners and other city officials blocked implementation.[5] For two months the Howards remained alone at Trumbull Park, surrounded by racist threats and requiring police escort even to leave their home. Finally, in October, the board moved in three additional black families. Then, after a full year of crisis and with ten black families besieged by whites at Trumbull Park, Mayor Kennelly intervened. He cut a deal with the South Deering Improvement Association to limit black occupancy to no more than twenty-five families, or 6 percent of the project, and ordered the CHA to comply.[6] Token quotas, then, were the mayoral solution to keeping the peace. But even this did not cool tensions, and a constant police presence lasted well into the late 1950s.

Violence again generated seismic change at the CHA. Wood and the board had been in conflict for nearly two years over site selection, hiring powers, and now integration. The fights not only drained her political capital with the commissioners but sapped her health; in mid-1954 she spent six weeks in a hospital recovering from bronchitis. Her absence allowed CHA commissioner John Fugard, reappointed to the board in 1954 by Kennelly after a twelve-year hiatus, to engineer a consultant's report recommending managerial reorganization of the authority, creating a new "high-level executive" position as the top administrative post and demoting Wood to a "social aspects" role, a demeaning and sexist response to her seventeen years running the operation. The board swiftly adopted the idea and hired a retired general as the new executive director.[7] Wood responded with a biting, four-page statement that personally attacked the commissioners and charged that her stand on integration was the real issue behind her demotion: "The Authority has paid lip-service to policies publicly proclaimed while privately issuing instructions thwarting those policies. . . . The long and short of the Authority's racial relations policy is that the commissioners are either unwilling, unable, or afraid to come to grips with it." The next day the commissioners summarily fired her. Wood went down battling for the rights of African Americans, but in the end, the Trumbull Park Homes mob triumphed. Writing in the *Nation*, Robert Gruenberg wrote the post mortem on Wood's tenure at the CHA, recounting how her "integrity, devotion to public service, and belief in the principles upon which the nation was founded, could never be swayed by 'realistic' politicians. This was her undoing."[8]

★   ★   ★

White violence had repeatedly beaten back the CHA's integration efforts, but even when not openly contentious, sustaining integration was at best a tenuous prospect. Beneath the fight at Trumbull Park lay tensions between open occupancy and integration. Open occupancy policies could result in racial transition and resegregation if African Americans flocked to public housing while whites, with far more housing choices, fled. The most straightforward way to ensure integration involved quotas on occupancy, a distasteful remedy to many given that quotas pandered to the racist fears of whites. Elizabeth Wood argued in the early 1950s that limits on black occupancy were "improper . . . a bad policy essentially." The CHA's quota policies at selected projects, required by the city council, meant that whites had far shorter waits than African Americans. At some projects, vacancies were held open until white applicants could be found, while blacks languished on waiting lists. "It is difficult to state policy without revealing the double standard," Wood informed the commissioners in 1952.[9]

In Washington, black civil servants in federal housing agencies shared the dislike of quotas. They pushed white political appointees above them to embrace open occupancy in the changing legal arena of the early 1950s, but white administrators largely ignored court cases that suggested an end to discrimination, including the *Brown v. Board of Education* decision of 1954. The year before, the Racial Relations Service of the Housing and Home Finance Agency released the lengthy report *Open Occupancy in Public Housing*, which laid out the wide range of racial practices of housing authorities that limited the choices of African Americans. Most housing authorities explicitly used race to sort tenants, a practice tolerated by the PHA despite *Shelly v. Kramer* in 1948 and other federal policies, including Truman's announced desegregation of the military, which suggested the time had come for ending federal support for discrimination based on race. Only a few local housing authorities practiced nondiscrimination, and ironically, the federal report listed the CHA among them, despite its practice of keeping several projects restricted to whites. How to resolve the conflict between open occupancy and planned integration, however, was less clear in the report. It encouraged local housing authorities to achieve "balanced" occupancy with "40–60 percent" black tenancy while, at the same time, discouraging quotas. The report acknowledged that "[r]acial minorities, long accustomed to the use of quotas to limit their opportunities, are naturally suspicious of racial designations or other indications of controls based on race." Yet it gave little practical direction on how to achieve a balance, and a later report, intending to provide examples of successful biracial projects, was shelved by Eisenhower housing officials.[10]

But to most African American housing reformers in the 1950s, open occupancy trumped planned residential integration as the primary goal. After the *Brown* decision in 1954, long-time HHFA racial relations advisor Frank Horne demanded a color-blind occupancy policy that would require all federally assisted housing to "be open to eligible families without regard to race," a stance that would cost Horne his job a year later.[11] Further, defining integration as 40–60 percent black made perfect sense to African American administrators and, as revealed by later social scientists, mirrored the desires of black homebuyers and renters in the 1960s. But for whites, integration meant a much lower number, somewhere between 10 and 25 percent black, as their willingness to accept African American neighbors was consistently more limited. With no clear guidance on how to achieve integration or on how to sustain it, and no progress on open occupancy from resistant Eisenhower officials, housing authorities were left to grope for policies on a trial-and-error basis.[12]

White liberals, meanwhile, tried to bridge the dilemmas of open occupancy and planned residential integration. Charles Abrams, a long-time public housing activist and author of the open housing manifesto *Forbidden Neighbors* (1955), called for a color-blind housing world, but he conceded that until the dual housing market for blacks and whites had been dismantled, limits by race were needed in public programs to maintain "workable communities." Abrams bent over backward to distinguish quotas in housing from quotas used to limit the number of Jews, African Americans, and other minorities at universities. Liberals had long fought such policies, but Abrams argued that black housing quotas had an entirely different animus, as they were intended to help break down segregation and to demonstrate the efficacy of integration. If quotas prevented resegregation, then they were a necessary evil. Even so, he suggested that in "most cases, there should be no need for" limits by race and that "if [public housing] tenants are selected on the basis of need without regard to color, the Negro representation should seldom exceed the 32 percent average of Negro admissions throughout the U.S. in 1952."[13]

Abrams's line of reasoning, however, bore little resemblance to the realities of public housing applicant pools in the early 1950s. Without some form of controls on occupancy based on race, differential demand among blacks and whites would mean rapid resegregation in public housing and defeat any integration goals. In Chicago, white demand for public housing eroded in the 1950s as shortages eased in the separate white housing market, while black demand soared with continued migration to the city, discrimination, and overcrowding. At a basic level, neighborhood whites simply did not share the CHA's racial liberalism, and few were interested in integrated housing. One newspaper executive responded to a survey on public housing: "The average Chicagoan thinks the projects were built purely to house Negroes."[14] Between 1952 and 1953 (even before the Trumbull Park Homes riots), white applications for public housing dropped 31 percent, while black applicants increased 37 percent. Sustaining integration grew increasingly strained at the biracial Cabrini Homes, 46 percent black in 1954, where managers held vacancies open for lengthy periods that year while they searched for eligible white applicants in an effort to prevent the project from "tipping" to all black. The director of tenant selection admitted that "all kinds of resistance is met" trying to get "normal white families" into "integrated projects" where African Americans predominated.[15] Without white interest, meaningful integration would wither away.

Elizabeth Wood's replacement cut through these dilemmas without concern for black civil rights or the goals of white liberals. The board hired former brigadier general William B. Kean as the "high-level executive" recommended by consultants; not unexpectedly, his leadership style differed significantly from Wood's. The commissioners touted him as a "liberal," in part to ward off the outcries after Wood's firing, but his record on race was more complex than that label implied. His Korean War command included the Twenty-fourth Infantry Regiment, one of four black regiments in the still largely segregated U.S. Army of 1950. With weak leadership from a mostly white officer corps, the regiment performed poorly in the early setbacks on the Korean peninsula. Exasperated, Kean composed a lengthy memo calling the black unit "untrustworthy and incapable of carrying out missions expected of an infantry regiment" and recommended the unit be dissolved with its men integrated into white units at a 10 percent quota. Kean said that while individual black soldiers performed bravely, segregated units did not work well in combat. Just before his departure from Korea in the spring of 1951, Kean wrote a second memo, this one to Eighth Army commander Matthew Ridgeway, arguing that segregated units were unreliable and that segregation was both inefficient and "improper." Acting on the memo, Ridgeway ordered the immediate desegregation of forces in Korea.[16] Whether a liberal integrationist or battlefield pragmatist, Kean's views were not in the same vein as Elizabeth Wood's. He was not a crusader, nor did he see open occupancy as an unequivocal civil right.

As a result, Kean adopted policies that simultaneously dodged civil rights debates and neglected integration. He quietly terminated the practice of holding open vacancies at most projects: if no white applicants were available, then a black family would be offered the apartment. The change was based on managerial, not ethical grounds; Kean wanted to reduce lost revenue from vacancies. He proudly reported to the board his reduction in the number of days lost to vacancy from thirty-one days per unit in 1954 to four days in 1955. Kean's change was not a true open occupancy policy, as whites still received preference, and he made no effort to publicize the change. Moreover, the policy was still selective. Restrictions remained on sensitive projects in all-white areas such as Trumbull Park. He integrated Lathrop Homes on the North Side with a token presence of fifteen black families, less than 2 percent of the project, while Lawndale and Bridgeport Homes remained barred to African Americans. Bridgeport was in Mayor Daley's backyard and would be the last CHA development to be integrated in the late 1960s, and then only with Latinos.[17]

Kean's selective lifting of quotas resulted in the abandonment of the CHA's experiment with integration at most projects, as urgent black demand soon overwhelmed tepid white interest. The 1948 relocation projects, subject initially to the city council's 10 percent quota requirements, experienced the most rapid turnover. Wood allowed black occupancy to rise above these quotas in the early 1950s while still retaining a commitment to integration. But with restrictions lifted in 1955, projects shot up to between 50 and 90 percent black occupancy within a few years. In less than a decade, all fourteen projects with biracial integration in 1954 underwent resegregation. Projects in black neighborhoods where white tenants were in the minority resegregated first. Prairie Avenue Courts, located in the middle of the South Side Planning Board's three-square-mile redevelopment area, opened in 1955 with fanfare as an intentionally integrated community with 27 percent white occupancy. But by 1962, only 5 percent of its residents were white.[18]

Even integrated projects in white neighborhoods became entirely black once white demand shriveled. Of all the projects lost to resegregation, Leclaire Courts stands out. As the CHA's only large-scale integrated project located on outlying vacant land in a white neighborhood, Leclaire and its extension were exactly the type of project Elizabeth Wood hoped to replicate elsewhere on the city's fringes. The suburban atmosphere attracted whites and blacks alike. Opened in 1951 with a 10 percent black quota, Wood let Leclaire's population rise to 19 percent black by June 1954, and the Leclaire Extension opened with 25 percent black occupancy just before her departure from the CHA. But once Kean's policy removed any restrictions on black admissions, normal turnover meant rapid racial change. In 1956, 26 white families moved into Leclaire, but 136 moved out; conversely, that same year 141 black families moved in while only 35 moved out. By 1964 the project was 90 percent black.[19] Leclaire became an island of African Americans on the city's Far Southwest Side, disconnected from the surrounding—and hostile—white community.

The loss of integration met little resistance. With civil rights leaders struggling to win open occupancy laws at the state and federal levels, and with quotas ethically suspect, no substantial or realistic plan emerged for sustaining integration where it existed. The problem was not limited to public housing, and white communities that felt threatened by racial turnover resorted to crude methods to prevent it. The Hyde Park area avoided racial turnover mostly because the University of Chicago used urban renewal funds to reclaim areas where blacks had moved in and built middle-income housing for whites, a deliberate effort to block an infusion of black residents. The nearby South Shore community took a different path in the early 1960s and aggressively attempted an affirmative marketing campaign to attract new white residents and keep existing ones from fleeing, but the campaign faltered, and the community had tipped by the end of the decade. Garfield Park residents sought a new state university campus and urban renewal funds to thwart turnover, but failed to win either, and the neighborhood changed. In the 1970s, Oak Park sustained integration and avoided resegregation in large part through controversial restrictions that limited black housing freedoms but also fostered integration. Not until the late twentieth century did organic, multiracial communities evolve in sustained ways in U.S. cities without state intervention.[20]

Similarly, new communities created by private urban redevelopment also struggled to sustain integration. Several projects built under the aegis of the SSPB opened with biracial occupancy and sustained it by privileging whites, at least until 1968, when the Fair Housing Act made this "managing" integration untenable. In the 1970s, both Lake Meadows and Prairie Shores lost most of their white residents. At South Commons, which opened with 30 percent black occupancy in the mid-1960s, efforts by whites to create a neighborhood elementary school regulated by quotas on race met with hostility from neighboring African Americans. The Chicago School Board sided with opponents and resisted the efforts of South Commons whites to define the school. When it opened, South Commons whites were disappointed with its quality and soon left; within a decade, South Commons was 90 percent black.[21] Lacking a clear blueprint, integration floundered in both public and private redevelopment.

★   ★   ★

The firing of Elizabeth Wood and the hiring of William Kean thus marked a dramatic change at the CHA. Wood was a product of the New Deal, and her approach to housing issues reflected her social work background and an emerging racial liberalism. Kean was a military man. He turned the CHA away from activism and toward production and bureaucratic standardization, consistent with both his temperament and the recommendations of the CHA's management consultants. While many Wood appointees stayed on and later rose to leadership positions, the former general brought in army colleagues and reshaped the organization's values. Under Kean, the CHA demoted its social goals and measured success by the number of acres cleared, projects completed, and units occupied.[22]

The 1954 and 1956 annual reports—the former completed just after Wood's exit and the latter the first produced under Kean (no 1955 report was published)—symbolized the shift in leadership and mission. Wood's 1954 report, entitled *These Are the Families*, devoted the majority of its pages to the detailed stories of sixteen families—ten white, five African American, and one Puerto Rican. The report presented a sympathetic portrait of families desperately needing improved housing, more space, and lower rents. The narrative described their paths from problematic shelter to a relieved, sometimes blissful life in public housing. The unrepresentative selection of families—62 percent of the CHA's tenants were African American that year—suggested that Wood saw the widely distributed annual report as a tool to attract white applicants and to counter the increasing perception of the CHA as a "black" agency. By contrast, Kean's 1956 annual report was devoid of human interest stories. Proclaiming that "Public Housing is big business," it listed bureaucratic accomplishments and outlined future plans with little reference to social goals. Kean did not entirely dismantle the Wood legacy, but the change in tone highlighted the CHA's massive building program and rapid growth as postwar building tripled the size of the authority's housing stock between 1954 and 1963.[23]

In choosing sites, however, Kean suffered the same frustrations as Wood, and site selection remained fraught until the late 1950s. Initially, Kean offered hope that the animosity between the CHA and city hall might end. He repaired relations with the aldermen with personal visits to their offices—a practice Wood had avoided—and within a month of his arrival, the council permitted the CHA to restart the public housing program with an application to Washington for an additional 3,800 units.[24] Kean's 1955 site list, like the CHA's 1949 list under Elizabeth Wood

and Robert Taylor, offered a balanced plan with 45 percent of units on vacant land and the remainder on slum clearance sites—all but one in black
neighborhoods. Although he made a concerted effort to sell the sites to
the affected communities and the aldermen, Kean's vacant land choices
suffered the same fate as Wood's.[25]

The minutes of the Chicago City Council Committee on Housing and
Planning survive and detail the aldermanic horse-trading that surrounded
any decision involving the CHA. Following a hearing on May 6, 1955,
chairman Thomas Murphy simply scratched off Kean's list three of the
four vacant land sites, leaving only a second extension to Leclaire Courts.
In executive session to decide on the remainder of the list, Murphy allowed a former alderman turned lobbyist into the room to make a case
against a small site in the black belt on behalf of its owner. The lobbyist
gave no substantive argument for removing the site other than its owner
did not want to sell. The site fell in the Second Ward, represented by William Harvey, the only person of color on the committee. Harvey moved
to strike the objectionable site in his ward but also gratuitously proposed
to delete the much larger Leclaire Extension site as well. His motion prevailed.[26] In one fell swoop, Harvey had betrayed the slim hopes of liberals
by giving away the last remaining site in a white neighborhood, effectively
transforming the 1955 site list into a black slum clearance program.

Kean, ever the military man, accepted the orders of his perceived superiors and, unlike Wood, issued no protests. Further, Kean reduced future
conflict and streamlined the site selection process by reaching an agreement with Chairman Murphy and James Downs, the mayor's housing and
redevelopment coordinator, to "pre-clear" sites with a housing subcommittee before their public presentation. In a key passage, the Kean-Murphy
agreement read: "The subcommittee would thus have an opportunity to
clear with Aldermen of the Wards in which proposed sites are located, to
determine community characteristics and attitudes which should be recognized in site selection." The latter phrase signaled that aldermen were
free to strike sites on racial grounds, and it suggested the extent to which
the CHA conceded that public housing fell under the realm of aldermanic
prerogative. The deal was not a secret. The housing committee held a
public hearing, and the next day the CHA commissioners approved it as
well.[27] Where Wood adopted a strong, though futile stand against the city
council, Kean codified the unequal relationship and clarified the chain of
command.

The new "pre-clearance" procedure, however, did not work as planned.
Kean's next site list, presented in January 1956, asked for 4,870 units on

eleven sites, with 30 percent on vacant land. The list was sent to Chairman Murphy's subcommittee, which, surprisingly, approved it in its entirety. When it was made public, however, two Republican aldermen objected that they had not been consulted. The CHA held up its end of the bargain, but council leaders and likely Mayor Daley now elected to play politics with the list; three of the four sites in white areas were in wards represented by Republicans or those who had not supported Daley in his primary election against Kennelly.[28]

These political explanations were missed or overlooked by the South Side press, which instead ignited a resurgence of anti-CHA feeling among neighborhood whites and even some middle-class African Americans. The *Calumet Index*, the *Daily Calumet*, and the *Southtown Economist* editorialized against the CHA and granted extensive coverage to its opponents. The Morgan Park Improvement Association wrote that Kean "gave assurance, via newspapers, 'that there would be no slum relocation public housing units erected in areas where residents took strong exception to it.'" The most moderate South Side paper, the *Southtown Economist*, said Kean had "put sense into CHA operations where nonsense prevailed before," but it advised that the CHA should "confine its program to slum areas only and move quickly to rid the city of these eye-sores." Two long-standing middle-class black enclaves in Morgan Park joined in opposition as well. Their homeowner associations had resisted the introduction of black renters since the early twentieth century, and class trumped race when it came to protecting hard-won gains.[29]

Public hearings in March 1956 brought the battle to the council floor. Republican alderman Reginald DuBois turned the effort to embarrass him with public housing to his advantage. Calling the CHA a "super-government," he marshaled opposition forces to attend the hearing, an effort he described self-servingly as "one of the best organized protest meetings I've seen in my years on the Council." Opponents presented petitions with 4,500 signatures collected by thirty-four South Side neighborhood organizations objecting to the vacant sites, including two African American groups from Morgan Park. Testimony from white women living near Leclaire Courts exposed their racial and class fears. Carol Sestak, a housewife who lived next to Leclaire, reprimanded the aldermen, "Why empty the slums on our doorsteps?" The result was the same as in 1950 and 1955; the full committee rewrote the CHA list to drop six of the eleven sites, leaving only five large sites, all in the South Side black belt.[30] To make up for lost units, the committee added additional sites in the ghetto.

By 1957 site selection was a charade. The CHA presented oversubscribed lists it knew would be pared down, with virtually all of the approved sites in black neighborhoods. The CHA insisted that it had to defer to the city council, and the new CHA executive director Alvin Rose, Mayor Daley's former top welfare official, stated at a City Club meeting in January 1958 that "[e]lected officials will tell us where public housing is wanted." Further, he believed, "too much has been made over this interracial business. . . . We are not going to use public housing as a wedge. . . . Our role must be one of friend of the community." In a private meeting with Kale Williams of the American Friends Service Committee, Rose admitted that rioting at Trumbull Park continued to influence policy. The white backlash there "set public housing back a number of years." To distract from the CHA's deference to community racism, Rose emphasized public housing's slum clearance mission. "We built public housing where there formerly stood the worst slums in the city. It just made sense to us to remove that blight and provide decent shelter for the people who would be there anyway. There is no point in our going out and using vacant property in competition with private enterprise and just leave the slums."[31] Rather than battle for the rights of African Americans, as Elizabeth Wood had, the CHA hid behind the rhetoric of progressive slum reformers and built where its masters allowed.

Throughout this period, the city's three black aldermen never challenged the manipulation of public housing sites by their white colleagues. Resistance would likely have been futile, but black officials openly supported public housing in their own wards. In 1956, Claude B. Holman told CHA opposition leader DuBois, "If the people of the 9th Ward don't want public housing, we'll take all we can get in the 4th Ward." Ralph Metcalfe supported the CHA's plans even as they proposed clearing a large chunk of his Third Ward. William Harvey told the Chicago American, "I favor the two new projects proposed [for the Second Ward]. And they are just a drop in the bucket of what's needed." The only black member of the CHA board, Daley-appointee John Yancey, tried to restrain the enthusiasm, arguing to Metcalfe and Holman in 1956 that the CHA's sites intended to clear the Federal Street slum amounted to "too much public housing in one area and would create more social problems than it alleviates." But Metcalfe disagreed, declaring that more public housing would improve the appearance of the area.[32] By 1956, all three aldermen owed their political position to Mayor Daley, and this undoubtedly circumscribed their freedom to press for black housing rights or sites in white areas.[33] But in their own wards, black aldermen welcomed public housing as a public good and a form of bread-and-butter politics. In the 1950s, experience had yet given little reason to fear more public housing in the CHA's black belt; nearby projects, such as the Ida B. Wells Homes and Wentworth Gardens, were successful, desirable projects with long waiting lists.

Other potential voices of opposition were also muted, arriving either meekly or belatedly. The *Chicago Defender* in 1956 offered mild criticism of the CHA for "substituting expediency for the exercise of sound planning judgment" and "taking the path of least resistance" in its selections, noting that vacant land sites would avoid the "vicious circle" of displacement, overcrowding, and deterioration that accompanied slum clearance. But it acknowledged that "there can be no argument with these [slum] sites" because of their blighted character. In 1958, the *Defender* editorialized that the CHA's site proposals that year amounted to "a studied, though veiled attempt to skirt the highly significant question of 'open occupancy.'"[34] But beyond limited editorializing, civic leaders made little effort to challenge CHA policy after the bruising battles of the early 1950s. The influential Metropolitan Housing and Planning Council (formerly the MHC) did write a letter to Mayor Daley in 1956 objecting to the concentration of public housing along the State Street corridor as a "threat" to private redevelopment of the area, especially the work of the Illinois Institute of Technology to expand its campus.[35] But the letter had no discernible impact, nor did a December 1956 report on public housing site selection from the Welfare Council of Metropolitan Chicago. The Welfare Council concluded that "unless there is a reversal of present trends in site selection, the existing pattern of segregation will be perpetuated" and "the consequences may be tragic."[36] To prevent future site selection problems, the report recommended amending state law to remove the city council's approval power over sites. The CHA dismissed the report as "not the unanimous opinion" of the Welfare Council.[37]

⋆　⋆　⋆

Federal policies surrounding open occupancy were still unsettled in the early 1960s when conflict moved into a new arena—senior housing. Mayor Daley pushed the CHA into building housing for low-income senior citizens soon after taking office in 1955, seeing political gain in addressing this segment of market failure. Chicago pioneered senior projects even before federal law encouraged such efforts, completing Lathrop Elderly housing in 1957 by using leftover 1948 city-state funds. Most of the CHA's senior buildings involved single or paired towers built on small slum tracts located both in white and black neighborhoods. The aldermanic response to senior housing was positive, in large part because the CHA devised a new form of tenant selection that avoided quotas while still ensuring that integration in white areas would be restrained. The "neighborhood proximity rule," developed in 1960 and formalized in December 1962, prioritized eligible applicants residing in the "immediate community" surrounding a project. Highest priority was given to applicants whose current residence was closest to the project, as measured in concentric circles of one-quarter mile that widened to a three-mile limit. To justify the policy, the CHA board claimed that "sociological data established that generally elderly persons do not wish to move from the neighborhoods in which they have established ties of family, friends, religious, recreational, and other associations." More to the point, it noted that such a policy was in the "best interests of the community," code words for the CHA's nod to the aldermen in restricting racial integration. Seventeen sites for senior projects breezed through the city council between 1959 and 1963, with eight sites in white areas and nine in black ones. CHA executive director Alvin Rose (Kean's successor) bragged to the press, "Aldermen keep calling to inquire how soon the projects will be put up in their wards. They can't get enough of them."[38]

The CHA's formal approval of the neighborhood proximity rule arrived only a month after President Kennedy's executive order in November 1962 banning discrimination and requiring open occupancy—but only in future housing subsidized with federal funds. Robert Weaver, now the head of federal housing programs, championed the policy, though he and liberal activists were disappointed that Kennedy officials had watered it down and limited its reach. Still, the executive order prompted long-time CHA housing manager Robert H. Murphy to challenge the neighborhood proximity rule, telling his white bosses that it "will serve to perpetuate, if not intensify, racially segregated housing in Chicago." Senior African American applicants, he said, "are tired of living in Negro ghettos and wish to spend their declining years in more advantaged areas of the city." Finally, he pointed to city council hearings on an open occupancy ordinance as evidence that the CHA should provide "equal opportunity to all elderly housing in any neighborhood." Chicago civil rights groups joined Murphy's objections. The Chicago Urban League and the NAACP called for an open occupancy policy with applicants selected "on the basis of need" and on a "first-come, first-served basis . . . without regard to the location of their prior residence." These objections made their way to Washington, where Weaver's Public Housing Administration ruled in December 1963 against the CHA's policy in an eleven-page legal analysis. The PHA stated that federal regulations, adopted in the wake of the executive order, "prohibit discrimination on account of race . . . in the opportunity to apply for or to be admitted to any housing, wherever located."[39]

The CHA objected to the PHA's ruling and replied with its own twenty-one page legal opinion that denied any intention to segregate. Instead, the CHA argued that the policy actually promoted integration by privileging whites, who otherwise would be swamped by waiting lists. As evidence, it pointed out that in the first six senior projects operating under the policy, completed in late 1963 and early 1964, three were integrated to a substantial degree, as the neighborhood proximity rule did not produce enough eligible applicants. The CHA had turned to its general waiting list to fill the projects without incident. Although the remaining projects opened without integration, including a senior project in Bridgeport that had no black tenants, the CHA claimed that "not a single Negro applicant applied for this location" and that "approximately 15 eligible Negro applicants living within the three-mile limit were offered apartments in the project, but, in every instance, they refused." Elderly black Chicagoans knew that Bridgeport would never welcome them. Still, the CHA claimed its experiences proved "that the potential for the neighborhood policy is *pro*-integration and not segregation." The federal government, however, refused to yield, and CHA officials conceded defeat in April 1964. The proximity rule was removed, and the CHA returned to a "first-come, first-served" policy for those sites approved after November 18, 1962, the date of the Kennedy executive order.[40]

The CHA's claim that it was "pro" integration was disingenuous. The agency did little to sustain integration at existing projects, and the original Bridgeport Homes for families still had no black residents. The neighborhood proximity rule was devised to overcome aldermanic opposition to sites by assuring mostly white occupancy in senior housing without resorting to quotas. It thus fell short of the Kennedy administration's open occupancy policy. But despite the PHA's reversal of the neighborhood proximity rule, the CHA application process still had more subtle means to steer blacks away and prevent the "tipping" of senior projects in white neighborhoods. As the PHA opinion of 1963 made clear, the CHA's other tenant selection policies were legal, at least on paper, including allowing tenants to request one or more specific projects and to reject any offered vacancy without losing their place on the waiting list at other projects. This allowance of choice, federal lawyers noted, would "tend to perpetuate . . . racial segregation," but court cases surrounding school integration had ruled that applicant choice could not be infringed. Unmentioned in the PHA's analysis were the dynamics of waiting lists: given the long waiting lists for senior projects in white neighborhoods, a potential black applicant might have to wait years for an opening while rejecting available apartments in black neighborhoods.[41] As a result, even after the loss of the proximity policy in 1963, the city council continued to approve senior projects in white wards. The record on integration remained modest since senior projects located in white neighborhoods were nearly all white through the 1970s. Of the thirty-four total projects operating in 1969, eleven were substantially integrated, eleven were 97 percent or more white, and twelve were 97 percent or more black.[42] Carefully managing the admissions process, then, could give an appearance of open occupancy while still allowing centralized control.

★   ★   ★

With his power to appoint board members, Richard J. Daley went about draining the CHA of its racial liberalism. His most important appointment to this end was Charles Swibel. During his twenty-six years on the board—including nineteen as chairman—Swibel wielded his outsized personality and relentless ambition to dominate the CHA. Only twenty-nine years of age when appointed in 1956, Swibel was nearly two decades younger than his colleagues. He had the blessing of Jacob Arvey, a long-time Jewish leader, former Twenty-fourth Ward alderman, member of the Cook County Democratic National Committee, and a crucial supporter for Daley's 1955 mayoral run. Born in Poland, Swibel arrived in Chicago at age seven and attended the University of Illinois on a scholarship before joining a real estate firm in Lawndale, the heart of Chicago's prewar Jewish community. A profile in the *Chicago Sun-Times* in 1965 described Swibel in colorful terms as a "a cross between Otto Kerner and Jackie Mason," with a "Yiddish accent and Old World gestures incongruous with his young-executive appearance." Swibel's real estate portfolio included high-profile developments like Marina City, a residential tower along the Chicago River, but also decaying hotels for men, earning Swibel the nickname "Flophouse Charlie" in the 1960s. Swibel viewed himself as an underdog and a reformer who challenged "the Establishment," which he defined as "people who come from the right side of the tracks . . . people who don't like the idea of an upstart making them think, prodding them." He acknowledged to the *Sun-Times*, "I don't want to belong to the Establishment, I want to be the Establishment."[43]

From the day of his arrival, Swibel sparked conflict on the board. By his second meeting, Swibel had antagonized Kean with questions on contracts and votes to abstain, and by his third meeting, he had recruited two

Kennelly-appointed commissioners to form a loose voting majority: Martin J. Dwyer, president of the Elevator Operator Union, and John Yancey, CIO leader and the board's lone African American. The other Kennelly appointees—John Fugard, the architect and former slum reformer, and chairman Joseph Sullivan, a retired DuPont executive—were thereafter isolated. Swibel's faction chafed at Kean's power and demanded more board input, especially on hiring, a power that Wood and then Kean kept from the board. Dwyer announced he was no longer willing to be a "rubber stamp" and that Kean failed "to adapt himself to the civilian method of doing business." Swibel told the *Daily News* that Kean was "packing the Authority with Army men," a reckless comment coming from a non-veteran. Commissioner Fugard complained to a television interviewer that "Swibel's extreme youth is at the root of much of the trouble" on the board and suggested that unless the mayor asked him to step down, he and Sullivan might resign. The general himself soon offered to resign, saying the board divisions hurt "morale" and that he could not be "loyal" to all five commissioners and "loyalty to one's superiors is one of the most important requirements of any organization."[44]

As the *Chicago Tribune* noted, Mayor Daley soon had "one of the biggest official headaches since he took office nearly two years ago." Daley eventually brokered a compromise. Kean would stay on as executive director of the CHA and retain full power to hire and fire his staff, supported by a "unity" statement from the board. Kean could name a deputy director, but the board was under no obligation to accept the deputy as his successor. Yancey would not be reappointed to the board, and in his place Daley selected Theophilus Mann, a conservative African American lawyer, former army colonel, and admirer of Robert E. Lee. He professed little liking of public housing. The appointment was typical of Daley's manner of "plantation politics"—appointing pliant or loyal African Americans to give the appearance of inclusiveness.[45]

The move, however, did not immediately bring the CHA under city hall control. Mann initially sided with Fugard and Sullivan, denying Swibel his majority on the board. Daley attempted to exert more direct power over the CHA by pursuing state legislation in 1957 to permit the mayor's office to name the CHA's chairman (currently elected by the board) and to allow the chairman "to employ and discharge any or all subordinate employees." But Springfield legislators tabled the bill, and Daley eventually backed down.[46] Retired colonel, Kean subordinate, and later CHA executive director Gus Master claimed that "Daley let [senior administrators] run their own shops. He trusted his people. If he didn't they weren't there."[47] Senior administrators adamantly denied that CHA hiring had become a patronage operation in the Daley years, as in other city departments where the mayor personally dispensed thousands of jobs to aldermen for political purposes. Charles McCall, CHA comptroller from 1965 until 1986, remembered "one or two cases where Swibel suggested someone . . . but not for important posts." Without acknowledging the contradiction, Daley wanted "experts" at the helm of city agencies but demanded their loyalty.[48]

Daley did gain greater control over policy when Swibel rose to the chairmanship of the CHA in 1963, though more by default than any city hall plan. Fugard, the 1930s slum reformer and elder statesman, could have won a board majority, but he did not want the chairman's job. Instead, he hoped Mann would take the position "on account of the delicate racial situation in Chicago." Mann, however, also demurred, opening the door for Swibel, who at age thirty-six was still the youngest member of the board. Fugard abstained from voting for Swibel in 1963, but over time he became a strong defender of his former adversary, announcing in 1968, "We have never had such a smooth working organization as we have had now." Mann, too, became a supporter of Swibel, perhaps because the chairman regularly sent a car and driver to take him to board meetings.[49]

If he intended the Swibel appointment to allow the machine greater control over administrative appointments at the CHA, Daley kept it hidden. Instead, the record of senior staff at the CHA suggests Daley was content with Swibel's performance and a defanged CHA. Alvin Rose, Kean's successor and former head of Chicago's welfare agency, had all the trappings of a machine choice, but nevertheless, he butted heads with Swibel and by the early 1960s had little real power.[50] After Rose, top administrative jobs at the CHA fell to career civil servants hired by Wood or Kean and promoted from within. C. E. "Buck" Humphrey, hired by Wood but Kean's choice back in 1957, stayed on as deputy director and succeeded Rose in 1967. Harry Schneider, also appointed by Wood, served as director of management for twelve years before succeeding Humphrey in 1973. Then came former Kean assistant Gus Master, who held the top job from 1975 until 1982. The chief counsel position went to Wood protégée Kathryn "Kay" Kula in 1957, a job she held until her death in 1974. They were each nonpolitical professionals, influenced by previous careers in social work, real estate, and the army. With the exception of Rose, none were "sent" by city hall, though none challenged the mayor, either. Keeping one's job meant deferring to Swibel's power and, by extension, the mayor's office, which had no interest in public housing sites for families outside the ghetto or in residential integration. The liberal crusading and independence of the Wood years were definitely over.[51]

* * *

Even with President Kennedy's limited executive order, open occupancy—repackaged as "fair housing" in the 1960s—struggled to gain traction. Legislative success in California in 1962 was soon reversed by referendum in 1964, and the issue remained hotly debated through the rest of the decade. Martin Luther King marched in Chicago in 1966 against white racism in the North, and housing and open occupancy were among the central issues of his Poor People's Campaign in 1968. His marches aroused the wrath of neighborhood whites, showing how little had changed since Trumbull Park Homes.[52] Still, liberals in Congress shamed their colleagues into passing the Fair Housing Act, by the slimmest of majorities, making housing discrimination based on race illegal. While it offered great hope, the new law provided little enforcement and spurred alternative modes of discrimination to achieve similar results.[53] Much like the parallel in school integration, open occupancy and fair housing, seemingly straightforward propositions in the late 1940s, began a decades-long odyssey in which legal and legislative victories met with massive resistance on the ground from whites unwilling to accept blacks as neighbors.

Fair housing laws, moreover, did not address the tension between freedom of housing choice and residential racial integration. So long as whites could flee, mixed-race neighborhoods remained fragile constructions. After three decades of struggle against a discriminatory white power structure, many African Americans grew ambivalent about the promises of residential integration. The black power movement of the 1960s resented integration goals and sought racial nationalism instead. Others in the African American community wanted nonsegregation in principle but preferred black neighbors, believing that white Americans would never accept them as full citizens. For white liberals, however, racial integration remained the best measure of a just society, as it would end the exclusion and diminished opportunities of black-only neighborhoods. Precisely how to achieve this goal, however, was still unclear, and activists offered various proposals, ranging from further antidiscrimination laws and their rigorous enforcement to more "engineered" approaches that involved public housing and "inclusionary zoning."[54] None were widely embraced, and achieving residential integration remained an unfulfilled dream.

The CHA under Elizabeth Wood had wanted both open occupancy and racial integration but got neither. Instead, the backlash at Trumbull Park

Homes, the culmination of years of racial strife, blocked open occupancy. City politicians granted the CHA only a minimal quota for black residents at Trumbull, a settlement resented by African Americans and white liberals. After Wood's ouster over the issue—and with some irony—racial integration withered away once Kean lifted quotas on blacks at some projects (though not Trumbull Park). Lost were examples of mixed-race communities that worked, at least for a time. Stripped of its liberal leadership, the CHA became more closely aligned with Richard J. Daley's goals, and when it sought to revive white interest in public housing, it did so only through senior projects that fit the mayor's political interests.

The CHA's conflicts over race and space have dominated the historical literature on public housing, but its family projects did not descend into an urban hell in the 1980s merely because they were built on top of existing black slums and segregated African Americans. Many variables contributed to the unsustainability of the CHA's largest projects: design, planning, tenant selection, management, and other policy areas play prominent roles in its demise, and it is to these topics that we now turn.

Designing High-Rise Disasters 5

For many, public housing's failure in Chicago and elsewhere can be blamed on its architecture, especially the stark elevator buildings built from the late 1940s on. Few defended these designs, even in their early years. Catherine Bauer in 1954 privately called early postwar projects "monstrous barracks blocks," while the *Chicago Defender* in 1957 labeled Chicago's first wave of postwar high-rises "prison-like."[1] Criticism mushroomed in later years, especially after St. Louis imploded its 2,700-unit Pruitt-Igoe project in 1972 (after a mere seventeen years of operation). Postmodernists condemned the minimalist, repetitive, concrete towers of Pruitt-Igoe and the Robert Taylor Homes on aesthetic grounds as sterile and unfriendly environments. They heaped criticism on the intellectual forefathers of architectural modernism, including Swiss-born theorist Le Corbusier and his 1932 "Radiant City," which proposed leveling central Paris and replacing it with "Towers in the Park" in an effort to impose rational order on the perceived chaos of that city. Le Corbusier's ideas and the equally influential teachings of Walter Gropius at Harvard's Graduate School of Design elevated high-rise forms to futuristic inevitability and greatly influenced a generation of architects. But once applied to real cities, critics maintained that modernism produced rigid buildings in undifferentiated spaces that lacked "human scale." Modernism was supposed to put functionality and efficiency first, but later observers found the buildings dysfunctional when it came to the essential tasks of creating community and policing social space. Building residents were unable to "defend" their communities because of such misguided designs.[2]

Some contended that factors beyond the architects' control were the source of public housing's dysfunction, including the program's restrictive limitations, urban racism, and the poverty of residents. Architectural historian Dell Upton asserted that projects had to be Spartan "to reinforce the economic principle that only those who can pay should have pleasant physical surroundings: anything more robs the industrious."[3] But many critics pointed to the design professions for public housing's debacle. As Paul Gapp, the *Chicago Tribune*'s architecture critic in the 1980s, declared, "Overall, much of the blame for the Chicago Housing Authority's failures must be attributed to architects. The influence that began with Le Corbusier has persisted, and ugly, oppressive buildings have multiplied."[4]

While Corbusian ideas swayed planners at many housing authorities and while the CHA's high-rises did function poorly because of a host of design choices, blaming architects for public housing's failure exaggerates their importance. Such arguments assume that the complex social problems of families and cities could be solved merely by proper design—a variant of the environmental determinism that plagued the logic of progressive slum reformers. Instead, architects operated within planning assumptions and policy restrictions that tightly constrained design possibilities. As we've seen, progressive planners wanted large-scale projects, and USHA regulations limited room sizes to minimal levels. The continued cost obsessions of Washington administrators—more than any other factor—forced the CHA to build upward. Using the market-failure logic that had justified public housing in the 1930s, administrators in the 1950s believed that public housing projects had to be less expensive to build than private ones. Otherwise, justification for the program—and congressional support—would vanish. Federal officials operated in a fragile political environment in the 1950s, and while blatant McCarthyism played only a small role, public housing was continually attacked on ideological grounds. Thus, bureaucratic anxieties and cost concerns, far more than modernist architecture, led to high-rise construction in large cities, including Chicago. Untangling these concerns tragically reveals avoidable decisions reached with at least some understanding that public housing's high-rise buildings would be unmanageable failures.

★ ★ ★

The CHA began "experimenting," in the words of Elizabeth Wood, with high-rise buildings soon after the war. In 1945, the CHA proposed multistory buildings for its first postwar project, Dearborn Homes, located on a black belt slum site recommended by neighborhood groups and the area's African American state senator. A distinct choice was available for the Dearborn design: the CHA could use three-story walk-ups, as at the earlier Ida B. Wells Homes, or it could venture into new territory and build six-story elevator buildings with roughly the same number of apartments and cost per unit. Elizabeth Wood defended the latter choice by claiming that elevator structures "achieve a more attractive pattern for the use of the land" and "gives us wide-open spaces, larger playgrounds, and a general effect of a park that will not be possible if the land were developed as three-story walk-ups."[5] Following the ideas of Corbusier and Gropius, high-rises offered the best of both worlds—ordered housing and more park space—thereby rationalizing the urban environment.

Corbusian logic, however, was only one element of the CHA's think-

Figure 17. Sketch of Dearborn Homes, 1947. Courtesy of the CHA.

ing; practical concerns influenced choices. Issues of cost weighed heavily on planners, and the CHA carefully studied the experience of the New York City Housing Authority, which had begun rebuilding the Lower East Side of Manhattan in the late 1930s with six- and eleven-story buildings. The CHA considered New York's high-density designs to be the "most economical" at keeping construction costs low. Although it seemed counterintuitive, the CHA recognized that high-rise buildings were less costly on a per-apartment basis than walk-ups, with savings in mechanical systems and other design features outweighing additional costs related to foundations and elevators.[6] Further, elevator buildings offered the flexibility of increasing the number of apartments at a future date without sacrificing green space. When additional funds became available in 1948, for example, the CHA added three extra floors to half of the buildings at Dearborn, creating a density one-third greater than the Chicago Plan Commission's guidelines. Wood dismissed concerns, saying the increased density would "change the picture of the future community little . . . and the present serious overcrowding in the Negro areas indicates the need for an augmented supply of housing for Negroes."[7] This same urgency to address the housing shortage also pressured planners of the 1948 relocation projects. The CHA proposed a "Tower in the Park" plan for the ill-fated McKinley Park site and slated mid-rise buildings for seven of its nine relocation sites, believing higher-density elevator buildings could address the housing shortage with little apparent damage to urban space.

To design the CHA's earliest high-rises, Elizabeth Wood convinced the CHA board to hire prominent and rising Chicago architectural firms with modernist bents, including Skidmore, Owings, and Merrill and Harry Weese. She hoped their reputation and abilities could assuage the nervousness of many regarding the high-rise form. Skidmore produced designs that strongly resembled Mies van der Rohe's 1948 Promontory Point apartment building in Hyde Park, with exposed structural elements, concrete frames, and minimal ornamentation. Promontory Point was designed under strict cost restraints by its developer, and its relatively low cost made it attractive as a prototype for numerous CHA projects, including Ogden Courts and later the Cabrini Extension (figs. 18 and 19).[8]

Weese moved in a different direction at Loomis Courts, using outdoor "galleries" rather than more traditional indoor corridors to provide entryways to apartments. Both Ogden Courts and Loomis Courts earned high praise in a review by architect Julian Whittlesley in the April 1951 issue of *Progressive Architecture*. Calling Weese's galleries "innovative," Whittlesley described them as "sidewalks in the air" (fig. 20) and predicted the design

Figure 18. Model of Promontory Apartments, rear view, designed by Mies van der Rohe, September 1946. Photograph by Hedrich-Blessing, HB-09577-B. Reproduced by permission of the Chicago History Museum.

would "come into its own." He reported that Wood hoped the wide galleries would serve as important play spaces for children and would "humanize" the high-rise form.[9] Weese's gallery style and Skidmore's concrete frames (per Mies van der Rohe) would be key elements in many of the CHA's later high-rise designs.

While Chicago was building cutting-edge modernist structures, the Public Housing Administration's architectural advisory board, of which Whittlesley was a member, observed that good public housing design was "hard to find" and expressed major concerns about the general lack of innovative and interesting work. The board concluded that the problem stemmed from "a combination of architects who take the easy way out and the inevitable sterility that comes from the imposition of too many and too detailed standards."[10] Federal standards had grown more onerous

Figure 19. Model of Ogden Courts, rear view, Skidmore, Owings, and Merrill, 1949.
Courtesy of the CHA.

in 1950 under PHA commissioner John Taylor Egan. An architect by training, Egan was hired by Nathan Straus to be the USHA's chief project planner in 1938, and he rose within the ranks through various public housing
reorganizations before Harry Truman appointed him head of the PHA in
1948. Egan was often blunt and hard-charging in his speeches, but Catherine Bauer regarded him as "weak and third-rate," and said he took the job
"when nobody else in the whole USA wanted it." She feared the "dread-
fully low caliber" of top administrators at the PHA and their "slow, negative, and cautious" approach to running public housing.[11]

During hearings on the 1949 Housing Act, Egan reassured Congress
that the PHA exercised vigilance in containing construction costs. His
word would soon be tested. Estimates for the first wave of proposed
postwar projects around the country soared far higher than expected and
could not be explained by general price inflation, since comparisons with
the private sector were also unfavorable. During the late 1930s, Nathan
Straus had prided himself on keeping public housing costs far below those
of private builders. Now the roles were reversed; private costs were lower
than public ones. Private builders had adapted wartime techniques and

Figure 20. "Sidewalks in the air": Gallery-style design at Loomis Courts, 1952. This image is one of a series taken by Harry Callahan, an internationally renowned modernist photographer. Courtesy of the CHA.

new materials and in 1950 were building new FHA-insured single-family homes with a median value nationally of $8,300. In Chicago, the CHA estimated that the lowest purchase price of a new private home was $10,000 that year. By comparison, the CHA's Altgeld Gardens' Extension, a low-rise project on vacant land and the CHA's first project under the 1949 Housing Act, amounted to $11,090 per unit in construction costs alone (excluding land costs, infrastructure, and overhead). At Loomis Courts, the total development cost (including slum clearance costs) ran to $13,400 per unit in 1952.[12]

Of course, slum clearance was always more expensive than building on vacant land, and comparisons between public and private housing were rarely on a level playing field. FHA developers often used nonunion labor to erect wood-frame homes, while public housing required union labor to build mostly brick and concrete structures. But these caveats failed to shake a basic conclusion that alarmed public housing administrators: by 1950 it was less expensive to purchase a home in Chicago's suburbs than to construct a public housing apartment (let alone clear slums)—a dramatic change from the days of the USHA. As William Bergeron, long-time head of the PHA's Chicago Field Office, construed the problem in 1953, after learning about a developer advertising $6,000 prefabricated houses in Chicago's suburbs: "We in PHA must be prepared to answer the question which could very well be raised by any citizen—'How is it that private enterprise for slightly over $6,000 can sell a 4-bedroom unit which will be insured by FHA for 30 years, and public housing . . . costs about twice that?' (at least in Illinois)."[13] Unless costs could be curtailed, simplistic comparisons by Congress and others could easily jeopardize a program that was founded on the principle of market failure.

Egan's obsessive cost-containment strategy took shape in 1950. In July, he considered placing a fixed cap on total development costs per unit. As with Straus's actions in the 1930s, the proposed cap went well beyond the construction costs limits required by law.[14] Former CHA planner John Ducey, now head of the National Association of Housing Officials (NAHO), objected to the change, writing to Egan that a "fear psychosis" was raging among federal officials.[15] Ducey's protest temporarily staved off an inflexible per-unit cap, but Egan pressed on and announced a series of other restrictions at the annual NAHO convention in October. He warned the assembled housing authority commissioners and their staffs that "runaway costs . . . could well be fatal" to the public housing program, and he blamed his audience for not "designing down to minimum requirements for livability." He urged them to move "a little closer to the attitudes that necessity forces businessmen to adopt" in developing housing. Ultimately, he argued, public housing would be compared to private housing, and housing authorities needed to adjust: "Public housing is justified as an *economical* way to provide decent housing for low-income families. If public housing becomes expensive, this justification will vanish." Egan reminded his audience that "all we do will be watched by many critical eyes. The Congress will be scrutinizing us. . . . There will be watchful eyes, too, in every city, and town."[16] His message was clear. Public housing must be cost conscious above all else; otherwise political support would crumble. As the USHA's former project planner, Egan remembered when government-developed projects had compared favorably to private ones, thanks to Straus's aggressive but ultimately self-defeating cost-cutting. Now Egan would repeat the mistake, but on a grander scale. His draconian, shortsighted approach would haunt public housing design for the next decade.

Although his speech suggests something of the "fear psychosis" identified by Ducey, Egan was hardly paranoid. Opposition to public housing in the early 1950s was stronger than in the previous two decades, as well-organized real estate interests and their allies launched grassroots campaigns to fight the program at every turn. They exploited the non-universal nature of public housing's benefit by distributing flyers asking, "Who will pay *your* rent," a reference to the taxpayer subsidies that produced low rents. (At the same time, real estate interests supported government intervention through the FHA to entice capital into federally organized mortgage markets, an indirect subsidy that lowered the cost of borrowing to homeowners and spurred a postwar housing boom.)[17] Opponents were most successful in California where red-baiting and McCarthyite tactics pushed voters to amend the state's constitution in 1950 to require a local referendum to approve any new public housing project, thereby crushing local housing authority independence. Warren Vinton kept a running tally of referenda across the country intended to damage the program, and he optimistically found public housing winning far more than losing, but the existence of such votes put the program and its leaders on the defensive. The real estate lobby, despite being condemned in congressional hearings in 1947 for its pressure tactics, remained a formidable political presence, with members of the National Association of Real Estate Boards and National Association of Home Builders scattered throughout the country. By contrast, the interest groups in support of public housing had narrowed since 1937. While labor could be counted on, no national voice for low-income tenants existed, and the National Association of Housing and Redevelopment Officials spoke mainly for housing authority boards and executive directors. As a consequence, it struggled to be taken seriously by elected officials.[18]

Orchestrated opposition to public housing from the real estate lobby resonated in Congress. Conservative opponents questioned the program's existence by annually revisiting the 1949 Housing Act's authorizations between 1951 and 1955 and sharply restricting the number of units to be built. The Korean War triggered the first cuts, but in 1953, following a Republican sweep, Congress stopped the pipeline of projects altogether. The program was only salvaged when an Eisenhower advisory committee in early 1954 recommended that public housing continue so it could serve the relocation needs of urban renewal, but only until a new FHA low-rent housing program could be formulated to replace it. Fortunately for public housing officials, the FHA had little interest in such an effort. The main result of congressional action was to limit the program's output substantially: instead of 135,000 units per year as expected under the 1949 act, public housing starts ranged from 35,000 to 45,000 between 1951 and 1965. While Congress made few changes to the program's complex subsidies and policies, the recurring battles over public housing authorizations took their toll on those running it. As Catherine Bauer lamented in 1956, the public housing program had not "taken off": "Public housing officials, federal and local, have been kept continuously on the defensive, and the neuroses that come from chronic fright and insecurity are translated into excessive caution, administrative rigidity, and lack of creative initiative. Everybody tends to sit tight, clinging desperately to the beleaguered formula, instead of trying to improve it in the light of experience and public attitudes."[19]

The debates over public housing in the 1950s were largely ideological, but the reach of McCarthyism was relatively limited, especially given the flirtation with radicalism of many public housers in the 1930s. Despite the program's innate liberalism and Senator McCarthy's intimate knowledge of housing programs from his work chairing the Joint Housing Committee in 1947 and 1948, McCarthyite committees in Washington fingered only four people connected to the program: Catherine Bauer and her architect husband, William Wurster (both teaching at the University of California, Berkeley), Leon Keyserling (then chairman of Truman's Council of Economic Advisors), and Jesse Epstein, former executive director of the Seattle Housing Authority and then a regional PHA director. Each was charged with membership in "subversive" organizations in the 1930s, but all were cleared after the indignity of board loyalty hearings. Public housers had long been accused of "socialism," a charge not entirely farfetched, but the leap to "communism," as some opposition groups claimed, was classic red-baiting.[20]

Whether driven by an intimidating Congress or, less likely, anti-communism, Egan obsessed over the details of his program and generated incalculable damage. He codified his demands for frugality in a contradictory ninety-three-page policy bulletin: *Low-Rent Public Housing: Planning, Design, and Construction for Economy*.[21] Some of his changes were subtle but unmistakable steps backward. Room dimensions were shrunk, a move that infuriated the CHA's planners, who had recently completed a "livability" study suggesting that larger room sizes were needed. CHA chairman Wayne McMillan expressed the authority's dismay at the PHA's heavy-handed interference: "The CHA does not wish to be responsible for building housing that is inferior to present developments, of which the city can be proud. It has no intention of building new 'slums.'" After studying the new rules, the CHA circumvented limits by shrinking its one- and two-bedroom apartments and "borrowing" the space for its multi-bedroom units, a sleight of hand acceptable to the PHA as long as total space did not exceed maximums. Still, these modifications resulted in the CHA's projects of the 1950s having roughly 12 percent less space per room than the 1948 relocation projects.[22]

But the most crucial PHA change involved Egan's density requirements. The new standard of fifty units per acre for high-cost slum land implicitly mandated the use of multistory designs. Decently spaced row houses, or even walk-ups, could not be accommodated at this density, leaving local housing authorities in major cities no choice but to build high-rises on their slum sites. The rationale for greater density related to cost and output; more units per acre would spread fixed land costs and keep per-unit total development costs within politically acceptable bounds. Yet, ironically, even as it required high densities and elevator buildings, the bulletin also called high-rises the "least desirable" among designs, explaining that the "grave and serious problems incident to the rearing of children in such housing are too well known to warrant any comment." Further, the "disadvantages are so great and so thoroughly understood" that high rises should only be used "where the cost of land would make other types prohibitive in total development cost."[23] Thus, the PHA condemned high-rises while at the same time describing them as the "only solution" on slum clearance sites in large cities.

★ ★ ★

How the PHA bulletin could claim that the problems with high-rises were "well-known" and "thoroughly understood" is unclear, as the issue was far from settled among architects or public housers in 1950. Although she had objected to the trend in the early postwar years, Catherine Bauer limited her criticisms to private correspondence. After a trip through Chicago in 1948, where she met with leading planners Walter Blucher, Reginald Isaacs, and Martin Meyerson, Bauer wrote to Elizabeth Wood that she was "more prejudiced than ever against the romantic–aesthetic–Le Corbusier-ism that dominates all our brightest young planners and architects. . . . It's all very well that the intellectuals do not personally like to look at the 'sprawl' made by row-houses, but if dwellings at ground level just *are* the best homes for families with small children, then it's up to the architects to find a way to design them so they won't be dreary." Her thinking, however, was in the minority. Local housing authorities in twenty-three cities, ranging from Syracuse to Omaha to San Francisco, had been pulled by Corbusian logic and pushed by Egan's cost strictures into planning 53,000 units in elevator buildings by mid-1951, amounting to roughly 25–30 percent of new public housing construction.[24]

Not until January 1952 did high-rise design in public housing receive a more thorough discussion, when *Architectural Forum* devoted eighteen pages to the subject. The editors featured Elizabeth Wood as the only voice favoring low-rise over high-rise apartments. In a reversal of her earlier thinking, Wood acknowledged that her "experiment" with high-rises in Chicago was a mistake, and she argued for the superiority of low-rise designs on gendered grounds. She began with the premise that "the design of a dwelling unit must make possible the fulfillment of other than mere shelter needs." A child, she explained, has a "need for nearness to his mother." These assumptions led Wood to call the row house "simple and natural. The indoor-outdoor activity takes place close to where the mother is at work. The child can keep in touch with her. She can hear him if he cries or gets into a fight." By contrast, in high-rises the "playgrounds are carefully arranged at some distance, vertical as well as horizontal, from the family supper table," resulting in "much less parent-child play." Further, she had changed her views on the green space created by Corbusian layouts and was no longer convinced of their utility:

> It is argued that by piling families up in the air you have much more ground available 'for use.' . . . But it is also interesting that when architects and planners lay out a low coverage high-rise project, they almost immediately will lay out a large and beautiful mall and other fenced and grassed areas, all of which will promptly be labeled with 'keep off the grass signs.' . . . No matter how many uses the landscaper and planner allot to the usable areas, they are essentially less personal, less capable of creative use by man and child, than are row-house areas.

Wood added that she had attempted to re-create the benefits of low-rises by using gallery designs but admitted they were a "poor substitute" for low-rise grounds.[25]

The modernist *Architectural Forum* framed the debate between low and high designs as one between the "sociologists," represented by Wood, and the "architects," represented by Douglas Haskell, the journal's editor.

Haskell used his editorial power to shape the issue to his liking. Whereas Wood began with gendered observations of family living patterns and the desires of tenants, Haskell presented the architect as master of spatial realities to which tenants must conform. Working from the premise that "increased density of population and building" was an urban fact, Haskell declared the preference of tenants was "unimportant" and that "a public not used to elevators or play corridors must learn to use them, just as new car owners must be taught to drive." Haskell criticized "idealists" like Wood who cherished private play space, and he championed Corbusian thought. Disparaging a New Orleans walk-up project for producing only "useless shreds and patches" of grass, he concluded that high-rises "yielded acres [of grass] in big sweeps." While conceding Wood's point that these open spaces needed to be available for play, he reasoned that competent management could make "imagined perils disappear" and "new advantages learned until they become natural." To prove the point that with a little "imagination" high-rise forms could be perfectly functional—and to undercut Wood's argument—Haskell then devoted three pages to the CHA's relocation projects, using them against her by deeming them a success.[26] Next to Haskell's vision of architects as practical problem solvers in the "real" world of high density and high urban costs, Wood's "idealist" and gender-based defense of the low apartment appeared quaint and weak.

The *Architectural Forum* series exasperated Catherine Bauer, and she belatedly entered the fray in opposition to her "old friend" Haskell in the May 1952 issue of *Progressive Architecture*, a competing publication. Bauer raged against the high-rise form and the architects who pushed "Le Corbusierism" and "showy structures and slick technocratic 'solutions'" to urban problems. She objected to high-rises on a host of grounds, including Elizabeth Wood's child-rearing concerns as well as their high density. But her main objection was that families with children did not want to live in such buildings. "When every survey ever made in the United States to my knowledge, from the crudest market study to the most refined piece of intensive field research, seems to indicate an overwhelming preference for ground-level living, this fact can hardly be tossed aside with contempt," she wrote in a slap at Haskell. Retreating from some of her collectivist impulses of the 1930s, Bauer maintained that high-rises were rigid and "impersonal"; they failed to allow the necessary privacy and personal freedoms that families craved, often in the form of an enclosed backyard. High-rises could work for certain groups, namely, the rich, the old, or single individuals, but they were "least suitable" for those on "whom we are now foisting it wholesale: families with very low incomes, from slums, mostly with children." As an alternative, she returned to her theme from the 1930s that slum clearance should be abandoned for the time being and low-density vacant land projects should be developed instead.[27]

But Bauer's ideas met a cold reception from the architects most involved in designing public housing. In a speech to public housers shortly after the appearance of Bauer's article in May 1952, Minoru Yamasaki, a leading modernist and the architect of St. Louis's Pruitt-Igoe project (and later of the World Trade Center), disparaged her views and offered a blend of slum reformer and Corbusian logic in response. Yamaski asked, "How can anyone say—as one eminent low-riser did recently—that we should put off building in slum areas until a better time? Now is the time, today, not tomorrow; for every year until we have eliminated all the slum areas from all our cities. Slums are the cancers of our cities, and the only time to stop a cancer is now." He renounced vacant land construction, stating that "building large projects on the outskirts further overextends our already inadequate transportation systems and by-passes our major problem—that of eliminating slums." Yamasaki insisted that high-rises were the future of the city and defended his designs for Pruitt-Igoe, regretting only that Egan's Public Housing Administration had required a density of fifty-five units per acre, "almost double the thirty-five per acre which we were trying to attain and which we believed desirable."[28]

The PHA's regulations also forced the CHA back to the drawing board on its federally funded projects. In a compromise between cost and design, Wood had hoped to build a mix of two-story row houses, mid-rise buildings, and high-rise buildings on the CHA's 1950 slum sites, but the new rules on density and total development cost meant scrapping the row houses and using only elevator buildings. Federal officials then compelled multiple redesigns of several projects. The Cabrini Extension rose from a collection of seven-, nine-, and sixteen-story buildings to its completed form of seven-, ten-, and nineteen-story structures. Density increased only slightly, from fifty-one units per acre to fifty-four, but cost savings were found by deleting one entire building while adding floors to the remaining buildings at a relatively low marginal cost, driving down the all-important total development cost per unit to acceptable levels. The CHA's original plans for the Cabrini Extension easily met the per-room construction cost limits in law; row houses and high-rise apartments both cost close to $2,000 per room to build, well within the statutory limit of $2,500. But clearance expenses added another $2,000 to $3,000 per unit, depending on density, pushing plans beyond Egan's arbitrary total development cost guidelines. The easiest way to reduce total development cost, then, was to build higher. Years later, Elizabeth Wood recalled, "We hated the federal agency with a passion since it was so absolutely inflexible in every aspect of design."[29]

However, provisions in the 1949 Housing Act championed by Catherine Bauer offered a way around the high cost of slum land. Federal Title I urban redevelopment funds could be used to purchase and clear land that could then be sold to public housing authorities at their write-down cost on the same terms that might go to private builders. This, in essence, would dramatically lower the cost of slum land to public housing authorities and allow for lower-density row houses and walk-up projects.[30] Philadelphia was the first city to use Title I money to support its public housing program, but few cities followed its lead. Warren Vinton pushed the Urban Redevelopment Administration and the PHA to cooperate more, but incentives in the 1949 law, unforeseen and left uncorrected, worked against coordination. Slum clearance using Title I funds required a direct cash contribution from cities (equal to one-third the federal contribution). If Title I slum clearance was used for private projects, this cash contribution would be recaptured in the form of property taxes on the new privately owned structures. But if Title I money was devoted to public housing, then cities would still have to lay out a direct cash contribution and would recapture only a modest PILOT payment. Moreover, the public housing program had long absorbed its own slum clearance costs under Vinton's generous 1937 formula with no cash subsidy from the city (only tax exemption). Given the choice of spending its cash for urban redevelopment for public or private ends, cities rationally chose to devote urban redevelopment money exclusively to private projects. This meant the public housing program had to absorb slum clearance costs within its total development expenses, thereby forcing higher densities and hence high-rise buildings.[31]

* * *

By 1954, the CHA had sufficient experience to confirm Wood and Bauer's thinking that high-rises were detrimental for public housing. Families with children preferred row houses, as the two women understood, and, overshadowing everything, the CHA's early high-rises had become managerial headaches. Trash chutes, heating plants, and elevator systems proved difficult to maintain. As we shall see, even more than the preferences of families, ballooning social disorder, serious security concerns, and escalating maintenance costs at the new high-rises drove the CHA to seek ways to build low-rise, walk-up buildings within acceptable costs.[32]

Figure 21. Five-story, "row-on-row" design for public housing, 1958. Courtesy of the CHA.

After considerable research, CHA planners in 1955 proposed a "row-on-row" design to replace high-rises in future projects. The first iteration of the design involved a four-story building that stacked one layer of two-story row houses on another, with external stairwells connecting the two layers; a later version in 1958 added single-level ground floor apartments, intending to reduce costs per unit but raising the building to five stories in height. In this later design, family members living in the top layer of row houses would walk up three flights of stairs to reach the entrance of their unit on the fourth floor, then use an internal staircase to reach the bedrooms on the fifth floor.[33] This row-on-row approach did not use elevators, and two-thirds of the families would reside at or near ground level.

CHA executive director William Kean traveled to Washington in April 1955 to present this new concept and received the PHA's blessing, provided that total development costs per unit did not exceed the CHA's estimate of $16,000. But a year later, with plans ready to move forward, the PHA's technical staff reversed itself and objected to what it called the inefficiency of the row-on-row approach, with its use of internal staircases within each unit to reach the upper floor. They argued that single-level apartments (or "flats") were more cost-effective. Another year of discussion and negotiation followed until finally, in July 1957, the PHA granted a waiver from its regulations to permit the CHA to attempt its row-on-row idea.[34] But by this time costs had risen as a result of general price inflation, and now CHA estimates exceeded the PHA's acceptable limits. Again, statutory cost limits were not at issue; the CHA's designs cleared this hurdle. Instead, PHA commissioner Charles Slusser, an Eisenhower appointee, insisted that the CHA not exceed a total development cost (including slum clearance expenses) of $17,000 per unit, an administrative cap similar to the one Egan had favored in 1950. The CHA pleaded for a lifting of this cost cap but to no avail. In 1958, the CHA was compelled to set aside its low-rise, row-on-row approach and to proceed almost entirely with high-rises in its future projects. But even high-rise costs had ballooned. The first bids on the high-rise designs at the Washington Park Homes came in at $20,585 per unit—way over Slusser's cap. Stunned, the CHA had no choice but to reject the bids, and public housing in Chicago was again on hold.[35]

The PHA, reluctant in 1950 to intervene during the CHA's site selection battles for fear of congressional retribution, would micromanage the CHA's design choices throughout the decade, lest it build embarrassingly expensive projects. Frustrated and angry, executive director Alvin Rose wrote to Slusser in early 1959 about the dilemma the CHA faced:

> [Your cost limits] left this authority and the city administration with one of the following decisions to make: (1) Should sound and sensible planning concepts be ignored and site densities increased so that the reduction in land costs per dwelling could absorb the rise in construction costs, or (2) should low-income families living in unsafe and unsanitary buildings be left in this environment, and should the city's urban renewal and highway programs be delayed.[36]

There was some hyperbole in Rose's letter; the city's urban renewal and highway programs were never threatened with delay, as the CHA easily accommodated eligible families needing relocation. Further, the entire conflict might have been avoided had the CHA abandoned its long-held slum clearance mission and convinced the city council to turn exclusively to vacant land development. But a fundamental reversal of direction was not politically possible. Instead, CHA administrators saw their choice as either building flawed housing or not building at all. The pressure to move ahead was substantial: most sites were already cleared in early 1959, plans publicized, and thousands of jobs were at stake.[37]

Even with these pressures, the CHA pressed its case for low-rise housing and enlisted Mayor Daley in the effort. Daley was informed of the delays and the design controversy, and in February 1958, he traveled to

Washington to lobby Slusser, unsuccessfully, for the CHA's low-rise proposal. He returned again in July 1959 and appeared before a Senate committee to sharply criticize the PHA's policies. In previous testimony before Congress, Daley blandly read from prepared statements on topics ranging from water diversions to juvenile delinquency. But on July 23, he engaged in an extemporaneous, lengthy dialogue with several senators, blasting the PHA's "time-consuming practices," its earlier about-face on the CHA's row-on-row design, and the PHA's $17,000 cost limit. He told senators that the CHA wanted to avoid using only high-rise designs but was stymied by the PHA's bureaucracy. "We have constant harassment and difference of opinion on architectural plans in the desire to try to improve what is now public housing, in the desire to make it not only high-risers [sic] but also walkup and row houses," Daley testified in uncharacteristically candid fashion. He explained that the CHA needed to build four- and five-bedroom apartments to accommodate the large families on the CHA's waiting list, but "everyone who has studied the building code knows that we cannot put up a four-bedroom house in the city for $17,000, including the cost of the land." Senator Paul Douglas of Illinois, a liberal economist from the University of Chicago, praised Daley and suggested that the PHA was essentially forcing the CHA into building high-rises. Daley agreed and later acknowledged a fundamental policy difference between the CHA and the PHA:

> There is no dereliction of duty on the Federal level . . . I say there is a difference of opinion as to how we can get these 10,000 units constructed. Where the difference of opinion is that if we are limited to $17,000, including the land, we cannot put up much public housing, other than high-rise. . . . I know they [the PHA] are considerate; I know they are apprehensive about it; and I know they realize it.

Prescott Bush, Connecticut's Republican senator, sounded genuinely surprised by this discovery of problems at the PHA. He asked Daley if the problem was with the law or the administration of it, and Daley responded, "I would say in the administration of the law." Daley's exasperation was palpable, and the senators were sympathetic. Daley wanted to rebuild the slums, but he also sided with the CHA in its desire to avoid high-rise buildings if at all possible.[38]

The PHA, however, had a ready response to Daley's charges. Publicly, the housing administration admitted that large, low-income families were best served by row houses but said flat out that the ideal was not possible: "[It] cannot be done on expensive slum sites within approvable cost limits." The PHA was not criticizing slum sites or endorsing vacant land development. Instead, it fashioned itself as the defender of the public purse and appropriate design. In an internal PHA staff memo, likely leaked to Congress, administrators rebuked the row-on-row concept and even described the CHA's proposed mix of high-rises and a handful of row houses at Washington Park Homes as an "excessive" plan. In a comparison between New York's latest project and Washington Park, the PHA found the CHA's plans to be 25 percent more expensive per unit, after adjustments. Site costs could not account for these differences; both projects used slum land and Chicago's per unit land costs were similar to New York's. Indeed, the PHA maintained that "land costs were relatively low" at Washington Park and then blamed the CHA's use of gallery high-rise designs for the discrepancy in cost.[39] The gallery design had been used by Harry Weese at Loomis Courts in 1950 to architectural acclaim, but the PHA's technical staff found the idea to be an "exorbitant design concept," criticizing the use of thin buildings with two exterior walls per unit and expensive cantilevers to create the galleries. The PHA held that traditional center corridor buildings seen in the New York City Housing Authority, with access to apartments through an interior hallway, were the most cost-efficient design.[40]

With Senate hearings unable to resolve the CHA-PHA bickering, the CHA established a special committee of architects and contractors to report on the design controversy. In August 1959, the committee offered an unflattering portrait of both agencies, blaming "confusing, wastefully expensive, and arbitrary" public housing procedures for high costs. By contrast, the report clamed that "effective and economically normal procedures of the long established operations of private enterprise" were superior. Further, the report assailed the PHA's $17,000 cost limit per unit, noting that it "does not furnish a basis for a fair evaluation of construction costs and is an invitation to widespread misunderstanding and misconceptions." Instead, the report proposed a cubic foot cost guideline, as used in the private sector. Although the bias for private approaches was clear, the committee revealed compelling evidence that the multiple layers of authority governing all aspects of public housing design and construction had created an unwillingness among contractors to bid. Those bids that were submitted often included extra sums to cover expected delays and unanticipated change orders demanded by "inexperienced" CHA and

PHA inspectors. The report, however, offered only long-term reforms for public housing's bureaucracy and could not break the immediate deadlock between Chicago and Washington over costs and design.[41]

Finally, in September 1959, the CHA commissioners and the PHA ended their four-year feud. The commissioners traveled to Washington for a climactic conference with Charles Slusser to convince the PHA to lift its $17,000 cap so that the four-story, row-on-row design might be used. Slusser, however, yielded little ground. He did agree to refrain from meddling directly in the CHA's design choices, but his refusal to remove the per-unit cap determined that the projects built would be almost entirely high-rises. The CHA-PHA agreement covered a total of 9,000 units in what may be called the "1959 projects," including the mammoth 4,400-unit Robert Taylor Homes, the 1,400-unit Washington Park Homes, the 1,000-unit William Green Homes addition to Cabrini, and the 800-unit Henry Horner Extension.[42] After four years of disappointment, the CHA surrendered its hopes for low-rise designs, bowing to the PHA's cost obsessions in an effort to end the deadlock and start building.

The 1959 agreement, however, still left the CHA's architects with the challenge of designing high-rise buildings on expensive slum land for less than $17,000 per unit. Several months later, the CHA presented the PHA with high-rise gallery plans and bids that conveniently, in the case of the Robert Taylor Homes, came in at $16,905 per unit. Crucial sacrifices were made, however, including the use of untested heating and trash systems that later proved costly to replace. Moreover, the designs called for only two elevators to move roughly nine hundred residents across sixteen floors. After PHA reviewers questioned this decision, PHA regional head Bergeron said he would approve additional spending of $25,000 per building (roughly $166 per unit) to add a third elevator. But the CHA inexplicably refused the offer, pessimistically claiming that a third elevator would cost $37,000 more per building. Instead, the CHA said that two modern, electronically controlled elevators would move the same number of people as three, providing "service equal or superior to all high-rise buildings currently owned by the Authority and many luxury apartments on Lake Shore Drive." The Otis Elevator Company backed the CHA's design plans, and the PHA reluctantly demurred. Frustration, inertia, and perhaps exhaustion had led the CHA to poor choices. Ironically, contractor Gus Newberg found economies of scale in construction at the Robert Taylor Homes that brought the actual cost to $15,950 per unit.[43] Much of the bureaucratic wrangling, then, proved illusionary, chasing after numbers rather than striving for quality.

FILE PRINT NUMBER

SUBJECT

PHOTOGRAPH BY HEDRICH-BLESSING
DELEWARE 7-1500

SHAW, METZ AND ASSOCIATES

Figure 22. Robert Taylor Homes, 1963. Photograph by Bill Engdahl, Hedrich-Blessing, HB-26129-B. Reproduced by permission of the Chicago History Museum.

★   ★   ★

Within a decade, the CHA's high-rise projects were seen by most observers as completely misguided. They produced imposing, institutional environments that were easily stigmatized and readily identifiable as second-class housing. Especially painful in these outcomes was the knowledge that planners and administrators at both the local and federal level understood that they were building problematic developments, yet for a host of bureaucratic reasons plodded forward. They knew from experience that lower density row-house designs provided a more manageable environment, especially for families with children. But the CHA's slum clearance agenda required costly sites, and Truman and Eisenhower officials obsessed about total development costs. The fundamental problem, however, was that no one creatively pursued a way out of the planning box that compelled high-rise construction. The CHA might have abandoned slum clearance and pushed the city council to find alternative sites. Federal officials might have relented on costs and then patiently described the problem of high-rises to Congress. Or the urban renewal program might have stepped in and subsidized the public housing program. Any of these were possible in the 1950s. But pursuing these more difficult roads required strong leadership on various levels that simply did not exist. The CHA made a concerted effort to avoid high-rises, yet then surrendered to the federal officials of the PHA, who styled themselves as the defenders of the public purse but who, at times, behaved more like petty bureaucrats, less concerned with outcomes than with protecting their program from the perceived excesses of local authorities and the potential wrath of Congress.

The story of Cabrini-Green, the Robert Taylor Homes, or the Henry Horner Homes, then, lacks a conspiracy to "warehouse" the low-income poor in unattractive "vertical ghettos," though this was certainly the end result. Instead, administrators followed a progressive slum clearance agenda, adhered to modernist design ideas, and clung to their own perceived self-interests to produce a flawed outcome. Only after the first binge of building was complete did Chicagoans realize the damage, rendered in concrete, to the city's fabric. As Monsignor John Egan, the director of the Chicago archdiocesan office of urban affairs in the 1950s, observed in an interview in 1985 on Cabrini-Green:

> When [Cabrini Extension] was being planned in the 1950s, it seemed like a good idea. The people who planned it were high-minded people who wanted to put up decent housing, and, for a number of reasons, high-rises seemed to be the way to go. The problem is, we didn't learn from our mistakes. We should have stopped the massive high-rise developments as soon as we saw what was going wrong in Cabrini. But we didn't. We kept doing it over and over again. The city has paid a price for that, and it will continue to pay a price for all the social, psychological, familial and human problems that come with packing a very large number of very poor people into one small space.[44]

Given the excessive constraints on public housing design, its projects can hardly be considered evidence of modernism's true possibilities. Elizabeth Wood and Catherine Bauer correctly pointed out that families with children were better served by low-rise designs, but this does not mean that high-rises were completely inhospitable for such families. Many modernist high-rise buildings—even ones with a similar aesthetic to public housing—house low-income families and function reasonably well in cities across America and around the globe. Similarly, public housing for low-income seniors in Chicago, most of it in high-rise form, never descended into chaos like the CHA's family buildings. This last example suggests that the main issue is not low versus high, as the debate was framed, or whether children can live in high-rise buildings—they can. Instead, the urgent question should have been this: How *many* children can successfully live in a high-rise building?

Planning a Social Disaster 6

During the protracted battle between the Chicago Housing Authority and Washington over designs in the 1950s, officials rarely offered precise rationales for their objections to high-rises as a form for housing families with children. Elizabeth Wood stated that low-rises were more "natural," while Catherine Bauer pointed to surveys of tenant desires. CHA administrators found it difficult to manage elevator buildings but offered no clear explanation why. "Experience," vaguely defined, indicated that high-rises were a bad idea, though knowledge was intuitive or anecdotal at best. But no one at the time questioned a planning choice that would lead to public housing's demise in Chicago and elsewhere. During the 1950s, the CHA programmed its high-rise projects to accommodate large families with many children; by the time the 1959 projects were planned, 80 percent of apartments had three, four, and even five bedrooms. This choice created an unprecedented ratio of youths to adults in public housing communities—with devastating implications.

Placing enormous numbers of children and relatively few adults in high-rise buildings resulted in widespread "social disorder," defined by Wesley Skogan as a breakdown in civil community and social control as evidenced by rampant vandalism, blatant vice, and "sundry problems relating to congregating bands of youth."[1] Sociologists, such as Skogan and Robert J. Sampson, theorized social disorder in the 1980s and 1990s, seeking to explain its prevalence in poor communities. They moved away from explanations centered on individual pathology and instead focused on the importance of "neighborhood effects" in controlling crime. They argued that safer communities resisted social disorder and enforced agreed-upon norms through collective efforts. Residents band together, informally policing shared space, especially from the potentially destructive impulses of youth, through social networks and local organizations, with formal police in support. Where the capacity of residents is weakened—by poverty, changing populations, governmental neglect, and other factors—then communities struggle to restrain youths, resolve disputes, expel disruptive outsiders, and identify criminals. Sociologists labeled this capacity "collective efficacy," a measure of the ability of neighbors to work together and in cooperation with the police to maintain social order and limit crime. Sampson and his colleagues suggested that the variables most likely to influence collective efficacy, and hence social disorder and crime, involved community cohesion, concentrated poverty, residential turnover, and family disruption.[2]

Youth-adult ratios are an overlooked factor in collective efficacy and are essential to understanding the history of public housing's decline.[3] In project communities where youths far outnumbered adults, those seeking to enforce order faced a daunting, and perhaps insurmountable, demographic burden. Undoubtedly other structural variables like poverty influenced collective efficacy, but the timing of social disorder in public housing is material. Widespread social disorder emerged in Chicago's high-rise projects shortly after they opened in the 1950s and early 1960s, before poverty became entrenched, before jobs disappeared in black ghettos, before the CHA's finances collapsed, before deferred maintenance meant physical disorder, and before the drug scourge ravaged tenants. These structural forces later deepened problems in the 1970s, but social disorder was present in high-rises with large numbers of children right from the start. Design also mattered, as high-rise forms made collective efficacy more onerous. But many people live successfully in high-rise designs, including families with children; it is the relative number of children in high-rise buildings that counts. When coupled with high-rise building forms, public housing's youth-adult demographics undermined the collective efficacy of adults, caused extensive social disorder, overwhelmed community partners, and eventually sent the buildings themselves into a death spiral from which the CHA never recovered.

★　★　★

The unique magnitude of the CHA's youth demographics becomes astonishingly clear in youth-adult ratio comparisons.[4] During the twentieth century, the typical Chicago neighborhood, as defined by census tracts, averaged roughly one youth (defined as under age twenty-one) for every two adults; in 1960, the average youth-adult ratio for Chicago tracts was 0.53. Only a handful of tracts had more youths than adults (i.e. a youth-adult ratio greater than 1.0)—except those containing public housing. Most neighborhoods included not only families with children but also single men and women and childless couples of all ages, resulting in a predominance of adults. Even in the nation's postwar, baby-boom suburbs, such as Park Forest, Illinois, and Levittown, New York, youth-adult ratios never exceeded 1.0. Robert Hunter's 1901 survey of Chicago's worst tenement districts found desperate poverty and overcrowding, but youths were still outnumbered by adults. More contemporaneously, other high-rise, urban redevelopment projects with middle-class residents, such as Lake Meadows in Chicago or Stuyvesant Town in New York, had low average youth-adult ratios, as seen in table 1.[5]

By contrast, Chicago's public housing projects inverted the ratios found in the rest of the city. The CHA's ratio grew from 1.42 youths per adult in 1951 to a peak of 2.39 in 1970, as more and more large, multi-bedroom apartments were completed. At the Robert Taylor Homes, a community with more residents than many Chicago suburbs, youths outnumbered adults nearly three to one (youth-adult ratio: 2.86). The youth-adult ratios in Chicago census tracts containing mostly public housing were 1.9 to 6.3 standard deviations away from the mean in 1960, showing the "off-the-charts" nature of the CHA's youth demographics.[6] In short, CHA planners produced communities with youth-adult ratios several magnitudes greater than any previously seen in the urban experience.

Changing family structure played some role in youth-adult ratios, especially after 1965, but such effects should not be overstated. CHA projects before the late 1960s housed predominantly two-parent and working-class families, not that far from city norms. An analysis of census data

Table 1. Ratios of youths to adults in various communities and jurisdictions, 1880–1975

	Year	Population	Ratio of youths (under 21) to adults
Large jurisdictions			
City of Chicago	1970	3,366,957	0.58
	1960	3,550,404	0.53
	1890	1,099,850	0.75
Chicago metropolitan area	1970	6,978,947	0.65
Chicago slum tenement districts	1901	45,634	0.97
New York's Lower East Side	1910	408,985	0.84
United States	1970	203,211,926	0.66
	1930	122,775,046	0.68
	1880	50,155,783	1.01
Suburbs			
Park Forest, IL	1960	29,993	0.97
Levittown, NY	1960	65,276	0.85
Urban renewal, moderate income high-rise housing			
Lake Meadows, Chicago	1960	5,022	0.35
Stuyvesant Town, New York City	1960	22,405	0.40
Public housing in Chicago			
Chicago Housing Authority,	1951	33,375	1.42
family public housing	1960	79,838	1.77
	1965	131,454	2.11
	1970	137,271	2.39
	1975	131,513	2.25
Cabrini-Green Homes	1965	17,750	2.09
ABLA	1965	13,600	1.67
Robert Taylor Homes	1965	27,000	2.86

for 1960 shows that if public housing families were "average" in terms of both family size and rates of single-family households (compared to the Chicago metropolitan area), then the youth-adult ratio in CHA projects would have dropped slightly that year from 1.77 to roughly 1.5. Using 1970 census data, the corresponding drop is from 2.39 to roughly 1.6, as a rapid increase in the number of single-parent households in the late 1960s swelled the CHA's youth-adult ratio.[7]

But blaming families for having many children, or parents for separating, or even youth for exhibiting destructive behavior would miss the point. Policy choices, not the situation of individual families and youth, created a communitywide collective efficacy problem. The CHA's extraordinary youth-adult ratios were the result of intentional decisions to build projects specifically to accommodate large families. Although Elizabeth Wood and others wrestled with questions about the appropriateness of high-rises for families with children in the early 1950s, the implications of concentrations of youth for community life were simply not understood.

Progressive logic led public housing leaders across the country to choices that swelled the number of children in the projects. Reformers had long proclaimed with both sentiment and social science that public housing's main beneficiaries would be children saved from the evils of the slums. The CHA justified the exclusion of most childless families from its projects on the grounds that "the greatest possible social return from the public subsidies . . . would be realized from the better citizenship of children, rescued from the slums to grow to maturity in a decent environment." Elizabeth Wood proudly touted the CHA's "Children's Cities" in the 1940s: "The Authority has built its program around the children. . . . Already thousands of children have left the slums and had their first chance through Children's Cities at health, at normal family living, at happiness." The 1945 annual report noted with satisfaction that at Altgeld Gardens, "citizens under 19 made up 61 percent of the population. . . . [In] the rest of the city, those under 19 account for a mere 27 percent of the total population!"[8]

Market-failure concerns were also behind the effort to house families with many children. Such families struggled to find apartments of sufficient size at affordable rents, and even those who could afford such spaces were often rejected by landlords as undesirable. Public housing waiting lists across the country testified to the extent of the problem. From the first days of the USHA, reports surfaced that projects did not have enough three- and four-bedroom apartments to accommodate the numerous large families who applied. In 1944, top-level administrators and public housing supporters encouraged a policy shift to build more multi-bedroom apartments, and PHA head John Egan told Congress in 1949, "I think we should . . . put emphasis on the serving of families with a substantial number of children, rather than smaller families which need only one bedroom."[9] Egan later warned local housing authorities not to "attempt to make up the entire deficiency [in large apartments] in the first project . . . since this may produce a project devoted to unusually large families." But the PHA's voluminous regulations never set limits on the proportion of multi-bedroom apartments in a project. Federal planning documents include virtually no discussion of the implications of the change in policy toward favoring large families, and no studies followed up on the social impact of the change.[10] Nor did the CHA consider the potential problems of high youth-adult ratios. Led by its market-failure logic and with astonishing little forethought, public housing drifted into building communities comprising enormous numbers of children.

Early CHA projects, while tenanted largely by families with children, had small apartments, with only one or two bedrooms, producing youth-adult ratios near 1.0. Nathan Straus's cost obsessions contributed to these small apartments, but CHA planners also imitated community norms in working-class neighborhoods. In the late 1940s and early 1950s, planners steadily increased the number of multi-bedroom apartments in projects, though not without restraint. In early elevator buildings, for example, they resisted high proportions of multi-bedroom apartments, reflecting Elizabeth Wood's intuitive understanding by the 1950s that the low-rise was the best form for families with children. Of the 9,000 units in elevator buildings designed during Wood's tenure, 29 percent had three bedrooms and only 3 percent had four or more bedrooms.[11] Federal officials pushed the CHA to find ways to add more large apartments. In mid-1954, during the planning of Stateway Gardens, the PHA regional office charged the CHA with "ignoring the very urgent needs . . . of large families" and contended that 40 four-bedroom, row-house units (a form they acknowledged to be better for children) could be shoehorned into Stateway within acceptable cost limits if another high-rise building were added to the plan as well. But the CHA rejected the idea of increasing overall density at the project just to secure a handful of large units.[12] Even so, federal high-rise projects planned in the Wood years had youth-adult ratios ranging from 1.5 to 2.0, or three to four times the city norm.

Wood's successors went even farther. They built projects that were top heavy with large apartments: of 10,500 units (nearly all in high-rises) designed between 1954 and 1964, over 39 percent had three bedrooms, and another 33 percent had four or more. Again, waiting lists pushed the CHA in this direction. A monthly report in 1955 noted that "the supply of large [public housing] dwellings has lagged far behind the demand. . . . A study of applications from eligible families on CHA waiting lists indicates that families requiring three-bedroom apartments usually wait a minimum of two or three years. . . . Many families with seven or more persons have been on CHA lists for five years or more."[13] Where the private market could not provide, the CHA intervened.

While applicants begged for large apartments, the CHA by the mid-1950s was challenged to find tenants for its existing one- and two-bedroom units. In one three-month period in 1957, the CHA reported that 1,400 families rejected offers of two-bedroom units at various projects (though the CHA specified neither the race of the applicants nor which projects they were rejecting). These trends showed a surprisingly weak demand among small families for the CHA's housing product, as applicants preferred to remain on waiting lists and in private housing until an apartment in the most desirable projects (usually low-rise) became available. Even with subsidized rents and continued housing discrimination, smaller African American families had become more selective by the late 1950s about whether to accept a CHA unit, once akin to a winning lottery ticket. Meanwhile, large apartments were desperately sought after, making the choice to build a greater proportion of multi-bedroom apartments an obvious one for the CHA.[14] No analyses, either in Chicago or Washington, wrestled with the ramifications of this choice. Despite two decades of research on topics of space, design, site planning, population density, and construction cost, public housing planners never considered the youth density of their projects a concern. No one asked, in essence, "Are we are housing too many children here?"

Other cities also built high-rises with many large apartments, though Chicago stood out. Even before Chicago built its 1959 projects, St. Louis planned Pruitt-Igoe to handle large families, and in 1968 the project had a youth-adult ratio of 2.63, similar to Chicago levels. After experiencing massive social disorder, St. Louis demolished the project in 1973. Available data on average number of minors per unit—a reasonable proxy for youth-adult ratios—shows that Chicago in 1968 had the fourth-highest average among a selection of twenty-three large housing authorities (exceeded only by authorities without high-rises); Chicago had 3.1 minors per unit, while New York had only 1.8, a sizeable difference.[15]

★ ★ ★

Figure 23. First tenants at Henry Horner Extension, 1961. One of the "1959 projects," 71 percent of Horner Extension apartments had three or more bedrooms.
Courtesy of the CHA.

Architects, community planners, and sociologists in the 1940s and 1950s had limited understanding of how adults informally police social space. While juvenile delinquency was frequently studied by urban reformers and sociologists, a street-level view of how neighborhoods contain the impulses of youth was not offered until social critic Jane Jacobs wrote *The Death and Life of Great American Cities* in 1961. Jacobs is best known for attacking modernist planning ideas and defending the organic messiness of the nineteenth-century streetscape. Instead of seeing the typical city street as dangerous and wasteful, as reformers and superblock advocates did, Jacobs celebrated street-level social interaction as an essential mechanism for community control and cohesion. A recurring theme in her book is the importance of neighborhood policing—not by uniformed officers, but by resident adults. Social order and viable neighborhoods require "natural proprietors," such as shopkeepers, homeowners, and long-time residents, to be "eyes on the street," demanding that children and outsiders adhere to community values. Jacobs was among the first to explain collective efficacy, well before sociologists invented the term.

In a telling and neglected passage, Jacobs maintains that "planners do not seem to realize how high a ratio of adults is needed to rear children at incidental play . . . only people rear children and assimilate them into civilized society." Jacobs's use of the words "ratios" and "people" is significant: the daily interactions between children and adults who are nonparents are an important force in creating the boundaries of expected social behavior: "In real life, only from the ordinary adults of the city sidewalks do children learn—if they learn it at all—the first fundamental of successful city life: People must take a modicum of public responsibility for each other even if they have no ties to each other. This is a lesson nobody learns by being told. It is learned from the experience of having *other people without ties of kinship or close friendship or formal responsibility to you* take a modicum of public responsibility for you."[16]

Early CHA residents referred to this dynamic in concrete terms. "If somebody else's mom saw you doing something," recalled former Ida B. Wells resident Bertrand Ellis, "she just picked up the phone, and when you got home, you had to answer to that. And that was very important; it was a community raising children." When Ellis left Ida B. Wells in 1952, the low-rise project had a youth-adult ratio of 1.24—higher than any non–public housing neighborhood yet still low by CHA standards. But in larger projects full of children, this informal policing by neighbors broke down. Jerry Butler, later a Cook County commissioner, described his brand-new, twenty-two-story tower at Cabrini Extension (youth-adult ratio: 1.83) as "a very large building . . . I didn't know anybody that even lived on my floor. I might know the kids—you know, what they looked like—but I didn't know their names. There were lots of kids. . . . It wasn't like the Cabrini Homes [row houses] where you walk out in the street, and the guy next door is sitting in the front yard and says, 'Hey, how ya doin'? It wasn't that. No, you can't develop a feeling of community in a tall building."[17] The scale of Butler's high-rise project and the large number of children created more anonymity than community.

At the same time that Jane Jacobs was writing about social control, Elizabeth Wood was also engaged in the topic. After her dismissal in 1954 from the CHA, she was hired as a consultant by the Citizens' Housing and Planning Council of New York. In a 1961 study entitled *Housing Design: A Social Theory*, one of a series of reports she wrote for the council, Wood wrestled with how to design public housing projects in New York City that could create a strong sense of community. She encouraged planners to design buildings that "richly fulfill people's needs and desires" and that allow residents to "create their own social controls and do their own self-policing." Wood understood the social problems of public housing emerging in the 1950s—what she called the "loitering" of teenagers, the "hostile and indifferent" tenants, and the "absence of commercial recreation." Design should counter these trends by fostering greater social interaction. If high-rises had to be built, as she assumed was unavoidable in New York City, then she suggested wide outdoor galleries (as at the CHA's Loomis Courts), lobbies with glass walls to encourage community policing, and greater recreation space. "Design," she wrote, echoing Jacobs, should include "the planned presence of people" and "should help the aggregation of strangers become less strange." But beneath this discussion loomed the core question of how to achieve a stable social environment in public housing that residents could informally police and easily control. As Wood admitted, public housing design was well studied, but "completely lacking is a study of design based on a theory of what kind of social structure is desirable in a project and how to design to get it."[18]

Not until the early 1970s did architects begin to evaluate how design influences social control and collective efficacy. In 1972, Oscar Newman published *Defensible Space*, an influential study on how design choices affect the ability of community residents to "defend" their homes and their shared public space. While Newman acknowledged debts to both Jane Jacobs and Elizabeth Wood, his work was more empirical than their qualitative approach, involving analysis of reams of crime reports from the New York City Housing Authority to determine exactly where incidents occurred and whether architectural choices made crime easier or harder. In a seminal comparison, Newman examined two neighboring public housing projects, one consisting mainly of fourteen-story high-rise slabs and the other a combination of three- and six-story walk-ups and midrises. Economic and social characteristics were similar in the two projects, but perceptions of safety differed dramatically. The "indefensible" high-rise project had open lobbies, long internal corridors, and emergency stairwells, which made it all but impossible for tenants and even security guards, when present, to monitor who entered and left buildings. Each high-rise building was shared by at least 112 families, so recognizing neighbors was difficult. By contrast, the walk-up project had entryways that served only 9 to 13 families, and site planning had created other zones of exterior space that tenants could control. Crime and vandalism were serious problems at both projects, but the walk-up design had comparatively less crime, less vandalism, and higher morale. In Newman's terms, the walk-up project exhibited far better "defensible space" than the high-rise one. The height of the project in Newman's view was less important than the ability of tenants to police their own space and monitor comings and goings outside their doors.

Newman's work shifted attention to public space, but like other analysts, he did not thoroughly investigate the possibility that youth-adult ratios might play a role in the ability of a community to defend itself. Buried in the regression tables at the back of *Defensible Space* are data that suggest average family size (an imperfect proxy for youth-adult ratios) is more closely correlated with higher crime rates in public housing than the physical design that received most of Newman's attention.[19] Criminologists since the 1940s have suggested that youth and poverty are strong correlates with criminal activity, but Newman shied away from drawing conclusions from his social data and instead clung to the idea that design mattered most.[20] The social characteristics of public housing were a given, but design could be altered to create more ordered space and reduce crime.

*   *   *

When enormous densities of youth resided in the "indefensible space" of Chicago's high-rise public housing, the result was social disorder on a staggering scale. Vandalism in the CHA's large high-rise projects was endemic within months of occupancy, directly affecting tenant quality of life. While quantifying vandalism is difficult, tenant complaints and managers' reports are filled with evidence that youths had the upper hand in the new projects. Within a year of the opening of Cabrini Extension, destruction of tenant mailboxes made mail delivery insecure, damaged laundry machines compelled tenants to wash clothes in their apartments, and profanity-laced graffiti in stairwells demoralized residents. Light-bulb breakage kept buildings fearfully in the dark; in 1958, the CHA reported replacing 18,000 light bulbs *a month* systemwide, mostly as a result of theft and because boys ran through hallways smashing fixtures with baseball bats. Within three years of the opening of the Harold Ickes Homes, every wooden front door had to be replaced with steel; because of excessive damage, glass in many public areas was removed as well. At Stateway Gardens, thieves systematically stripped several hundred pounds of brass from CHA fire equipment and, at one building in 1961, turned the hoses on, flooding nine floors. After one year of operation at the Robert Taylor Homes, manager Robert H. Murphy conceded that "we have had problems—some very serious problems—with children playing on and abusing elevators" and that "unsupervised" youth "are continually breaking light bulbs, scribbling and drawing obscene pictures on stairwell walls, throwing toys and other objects over gallery railings, using the stairwells for toilet purposes, climbing trees and pulling flowers, [and] throwing rocks at passing trains."[21] In these new projects with high youth-adult ratios, constant disruptive vandalism marred project life.

Elevators were the Achilles' heel of public housing. With only two elevators serving most high-rise buildings, the loss of one caused irritation, but the loss of both—a frequent occurrence according to tenant complaints—created immediate and obvious hardship on residents on upper floors. Breakdowns were most often caused by youths, who routinely pried open doors, damaged electrical controls, or climbed on top of elevator cabs. At Grace Abbott Homes, a collection of seventeen-story buildings opened in 1955, managers complained of making elevator repair calls "almost daily" by 1957. Elevators became instruments of death for children as well. In 1956 at the new Henry Horner Homes, a nine-year-old boy died when an elevator crushed him during a game of "elevator tag." The *Sun-Times* reported that the game was played by "as many as 50 children at a time," a figure that, even if exaggerated, suggests the extent to which youths swarmed over the key mechanical system in high-rises. Other stories are equally tragic. In 1963, an elevator breakdown was blamed for the death of three children when firefighters had to walk up fourteen stories to reach a burning apartment at the new Robert Taylor Homes. During the 1970s, the only decade for which records survive, the CHA recorded 417 injuries and 15 deaths related to elevators. In 1980, the CHA's chief of maintenance lamented, "With so many kids, the elevators are just $80,000 playtoys."[22]

Press accounts blamed much of the destruction on youth "gangs." In 1958, a *Chicago American* reporter toured Dearborn Homes (completed in 1950) and charged "'teen-age gangs' who roam the CHA projects at night" with vandalism resulting in "torn window screens, mutilated storm doors, yards littered with garbage, . . . walls, doors, and casings marked by knife slashes and crayon marks; holes gouged in plaster; obscenities scrawled on the stairway walls." *Chicago Sun-Times* reporter Ruth Moore, an astute observer who covered the CHA from 1956 to 1970, surveyed the CHA's Grace Abbott Homes two years after it opened and recognized a link between design, social disorder, and vandalism, though she missed the projects' high youth densities. "A project like Abbott is a magnet for teen-age gangs in the vicinity," she wrote in 1957. "The spacious grounds and the public lobbies are natural hangouts, and the neighborhood toughs converge. When the lights in the stairwells are smashed, as they are night after night, the dark makes a fine place to hide or meet a girl." Echoing

Moore's reports from the late 1950s, the *Chicago Daily News* ran a five-part series in 1965 calling the CHA's Robert Taylor Homes "a human ant heap" and a "jungle" where "teenage terror and adult chaos" reign.[23] Media reports were, at best, only partial glimpses into project life, and they lumped any congregation of youth under the label of "gang activity." Organized gangs with criminal bents, such as Chicago's Vice Lords and the Cobras, did infiltrate Chicago's projects in the 1960s, and undoubtedly they found high youth densities conducive to gang organizing. But the press left the impression that widespread chaos was linked only to the presence of organized gangs or, more subtly and unfairly, to white notions of African American urban culture.[24]

Vandalism and criminal activity, of course, had complex causes. African American social critics pointed to the pernicious effects of segregation and the dispiriting aesthetics of public housing as the source of problems. James Baldwin in 1962 called public housing "hideous" and "colorless, bleak, high, and revolting . . . cheerless as a prison." Writing about projects in New York City, he argued, "The projects in Harlem are hated. They are hated almost as much as policemen, and this is saying a great deal . . . both reveal, unbearably, the real attitude of the white world, no matter how many liberal speeches are made, no matter how many lofty editorials are written, no matter how many civil rights commissions are set up." This hatred led to "the most violent bitterness of sprit" directed at their physical surroundings. "Scarcely had they moved in," Baldwin wrote of tenants in an urban renewal development in Harlem, "before they began smashing windows, defacing walls, urinating in the elevators, and fornicating in the playgrounds." African Americans understood segregation and lashed out at it. "The people of Harlem know they are living there because white people do not think they are good enough to live anywhere else," he concluded. Years later, Baldwin admitted that residents of Harlem's projects were "much embittered by this description," but he wrote that those who deny the "common pain, demoralization, and danger" of segregation are "self-deluded."[25]

Baldwin's work resonated with Robert Murphy, who used it to explain the disorder at the Robert Taylor Homes. After an article appeared in the *New Republic* sourcing Murphy in reporting that rapes occurred in elevators, that stairwells were used as "convenient abodes for all kinds of mischief" and "serve as toilets for small children," Murphy was asked by his superiors to respond. "I'm afraid there are some people living at Taylor Homes today who do harbor deep-felt resentments, hostilities and bitterness, and are overly distrustful of management and the Housing Authority. And I don't doubt that some project youngsters vent their hostilities and resentments by destroying CHA property."[26] Similarly, sociologist Lee Rainwater studied St. Louis's chaotic Pruitt-Igoe project in the late 1960s and formulated a theory regarding the destructive behaviors he saw. The nation's racial caste system, he argued, denied opportunity based on race to which African Americans adapted with "social and personal responses," including aggression, which "results in suffering directly inflicted by Negroes on themselves and others." He summarized: "In short, whites, by their greater power have created situations in which Negroes do the dirty work of caste victimization for them."[27]

Murphy's experiences, Baldwin's anger, and Rainwater's theory all help explain why youths lashed out against their homes in response to their victimization. But vandalism is also a crime of opportunity, and public housing's youth-adult ratios were involved. If segregation and discrimination amplified vandalism and violence in the black community, then public housing's demographics made restraining destructive acts that much more difficult. Residents, security guards, and formal police authorities were handicapped by the odds facing them as they struggled to contain the impulses of youth.

★ ★ ★

From the early days of public housing, managers sought to channel youthful energy into nondestructive pursuits. But over time, growing youth-adult ratios, disagreements over the proper role of housing authorities in providing social resources, and limited staff capacity at the CHA and social service agencies hampered such efforts. In the end, the CHA and other city agencies were simply unprepared for the onslaught of youths in public housing communities.

During its experiment in the mid-1930s, the PWA allowed local housing authorities to spend rental income for direct provision of nursery schools, health clinics, summer recreation, and adult literacy. But USHA administrators changed this approach, arguing that public housing should not be isolated from existing community social services. Instead, projects were expected to include community space that would then be leased to local agencies with specialized expertise, such as the YMCA or a settlement house. At the CHA's early projects, Elizabeth Wood achieved considerable success in recruiting private agencies and public entities such as the Chicago Park District to serve public housing residents. Ida B. Wells included a city-run health clinic, and settlement houses were active at both Cabrini and Brooks Homes.[28]

But maintaining relationships with such agencies and ensuring they provided sufficient programs for youth met obstacles large and small. For example, the Chicago Park District built a small indoor field house to serve residents of Ida B. Wells, but by the early 1950s it had deteriorated under heavy usage. The park district proposed building a new, larger field house to meet recreational needs not only for Wells, but for the Wells Extension, scheduled to open in 1955. For its part, the CHA also planned to build a small community center at Wells Extension, which would be leased to the park district and other agencies for youth programs. But the park district dropped its plans for the new field house and elected to cram its programming into the CHA's small community center, a completely inadequate space for indoor recreation. At the same time it closed the old field house; neighborhood youths, enraged at the turn of events, vandalized the old building. As a result, Wells both grew in size and shrunk its indoor facilities. Similarly, outdoor programs for youths fell short. A review by federal officials in 1958 found that summer programs at the CHA were "lacking in quality and in the number of leaders necessary for the proper conduct of a program of activities." But rather than propose the direct provision of a CHA summer program, Washington told the authority to "work more closely" with the park officials who had already slighted them.[29]

At low-rise projects with fewer youths, strong management overcame the anarchic tendencies of youth. The Jane Addams Homes had a relatively low youth-adult ratio by CHA standards (1.0 youths per adult, still double the city norm), but in the early 1950s Addams teenagers battled over project space. Managers believed two Italian-American youth gangs within the project were relentlessly destroying the buildings and demoralizing tenants, management, and social service agencies. "Vandalism was the catchword that explained everything," observed Mary Bolton Wirth, a CHA community and tenant relations staff member.[30] Wirth counted over four hundred broken windows in the 1,000-unit project shortly after she arrived in 1952, with windows broken as fast as maintenance crews could replace them. Community rooms used by the Boys Club, a Jewish school, and the Near West Side Community Council were repeatedly wrecked. Wirth undertook extensive efforts to control the projects' youths with both sticks and carrots. She recruited gang leadership into various youth organizations and pressed management to threaten eviction of those families who did not cooperate. Her efforts had some success, at least through the late 1950s: the broken-window problem at Addams diminished and morale improved.[31]

Wirth, the widow of University of Chicago sociologist Louis Wirth, who himself had been a strong supporter of public housing, was promptly promoted to head of tenant and community relations. She began a long battle to keep park programs running and to find settlement houses willing to take on the CHA's large new projects.[32] At her suggestion, the CHA doubled the community relations staff and partnered with over forty organizations to provide services ranging from recreation to mental health care for residents. Community space, underestimated by project planners, was expanded by converting 171 apartments for agency uses.[33] In 1961, executive director Alvin Rose proposed using the CHA's plentiful reserve funds for expanded social programs for teenagers, but the board rejected the idea on the grounds that Washington would not approve such a move.[34] A year later, he recommended using surplus CHA development funds to construct an indoor swimming pool at the Henry Horner Homes, an idea allowed under PHA rules, but only board member Charles Swibel backed the proposal. The rest of the board wanted the Chicago Park District to construct pools, which they belatedly did at several projects in the late 1960s, supplemented in part by CHA funds. Most of the pools, however, were far too small, were immediately swamped by youths, and were never properly maintained.[35]

Rose also threw his energy into a crusade to expand scouting programs as a way to deal with the crushing numbers of youths in public housing. He proposed using a piece of land at the Robert Taylor Homes for a Boy Scout "headquarters or capital" in the form of a log cabin built by the boys themselves. (The Girl Scouts were left out.) Rose passionately detailed the possibilities at a CHA board meeting, suggesting overnight camping, cookouts, and hikes from the site "to all points of the city." He hoped "to change the bad image surrounding" Robert Taylor so that the project "referred to as a jungle" could become "the Boy Scout Capital of the World." But the board opposed the plan, as it had done with Rose's other scouting initiatives over the previous four years, and then the debate turned personal. The minutes record that Theophilus Mann, the only African American commissioner, told Rose to "stay out of Boy Scouting, the Board of Education, and the Chicago Park District and run the CHA the way it should be run"—condemning the entire scope of Rose's community-building efforts. Rose jumped up and stated furiously, "I refuse!"[36] On a final vote, the board rejected Rose's proposal and, critically, expressed their lack of confidence in his ability to lead day-to-day operations. But rather than fire him, Swibel—now chairman—allowed Rose to remain as executive director for three more years (until he had turned sixty-five and could retire), though in the final year, the two men never

Figure 24. Alvin Rose with a Boy Scout Troop at the Robert Taylor Homes, 1967.
Courtesy of the CHA.

spoke face-to-face.[37] Of all the issues debated by the board in the 1960s, none generated more fervor than Rose's quixotic scouting crusade.

Indeed, many residents responded to Rose's campaign and formed scout troops, often against great odds. A 1964 news story profiled the heroics of CHA janitor and scout master Clarence Phillips, who had successfully organized 25 percent of the boys in one Stateway Gardens building—132 boys in all—including "former Cobras and Vice Lords Juniors." The effort won him few accolades, however. Gang members warned Phillips to quit his activities and then smashed his car windows and slashed his tires. Several scouts had their uniforms torn off while selling candy door-to-door to raise money to attend a summer camp. But Phillips still told a reporter, "I could start five more troops down here if I could find some brave parents."[38]

While numerous groups made serious efforts to address the situation, the CHA and the city were unprepared to provide the resources needed for environments with so many youths and so few adults. In 1962, during final construction of the 1959 projects, the CHA's management department (in charge of running the future developments) asked its colleagues in the development department (in charge of design and construction) to provide more play areas for children, even to the extent of exceeding federal limitations. At existing projects the management department had already paved over large areas of grass in an effort to accommodate the overflow from small playgrounds by children "seeking legitimate pursuit of their recreation."[39] Despite clear knowledge of the need for playgrounds, the CHA and federal officials failed to include adequate space in the 1959 projects; inevitably, children overran the equipment provided. A year after the projects were fully occupied, the CHA wrote to the PHA seeking funds for more playgrounds. "Children line up seven and eight deep just waiting to use a piece of play equipment" at the Robert Taylor Homes, the CHA complained, and "upwards of 2,000 children may be cramped into one or two relatively small play areas."[40] Without sufficient recreational space at the massive project, children turned stairwells and elevators into playgrounds—with the inevitable consequences for social disorder.

Nor did other social service agencies or city organizations have the capacity to serve the 90,000 young people concentrated in CHA projects, and Herculean efforts made little headway. Firman House, a settlement organization serving the Robert Taylor Homes, used a federal War on Poverty grant in 1965 to launch an ambitious preschool program for 425 children, but at least 3,000 children at the project were eligible.[41] Similarly, 46 separate tutoring projects organized 800 volunteers to work with 2,000 school-age students at CHA projects in 1965. This major educational accomplishment, however, reached only 3 percent of the CHA's school-age population, numbering some 70,000.[42] The Chicago Public Library opened branches using converted apartments at Ickes Homes, Robert Taylor, and Rockwell Gardens in late 1968. Each library was besieged by children clamoring to use its limited facilities.[43]

In contrast, the Chicago School Board neglected its obligations to public housing residents, often willfully.[44] In early 1960, the CHA informed the school board to expect 10,583 new elementary school children in the Robert Taylor Homes area by 1963. School superintendent Benjamin Willis planned three new schools but failed to acknowledge that the proposed facilities would accommodate only 7,765 students, even assuming 35 children per room. Frustrated CHA staff members tipped off Noel Naisbitt, an Urban League researcher and citywide PTA member, who confronted the school board about the obvious discrepancies in its numbers. She exposed how Willis had plainly underestimated space needs while at the same time refusing to integrate nearby half-empty classrooms. Chicago

School Board staff responded that the CHA had overestimated the number of students, that 40 students could be placed in each classroom, and that trailers—dubbed "Willis Wagons" by opponents—could be set up in any event. Naisbitt appealed to federal officials, noting that the CHA "is under a great deal of pressure from (School Board head) Dr. Willis to lay off, not to fuss about this situation." Willis then proposed to convert ground-floor apartments into classrooms (ready-made Willis Wagons), a plan that CHA commissioner Mann decried as "dynamite."[45] But with few immediate options and with no interest in a public confrontation that might embarrass the mayor over the explosive issue of school integration, in 1962 the CHA leased to the school board a total of seventy-eight apartments for use as classrooms at the Robert Taylor Homes, Washington Park Homes, and Lake Michigan Homes, three 1959 projects. Despite their supposed "temporary" nature, and despite numerous protests and even boycotts from public housing tenants, the leases were renewed annually until 1972.[46]

* * *

CHA managers often blamed tenants for their inability to assert collective efficacy in their projects. CHA director of management Harry Schneider (later the executive director) encouraged managers in 1962 to do more to foster resident organizations, believing that "tenants take a greater pride in their home and surroundings if they are encouraged to assume responsibility for making their project a better place in which to live."[47] But as problems continued, Schneider's responses to tenants took on a patronizing tone. His reply to a 1966 letter from a resident about constant mailbox vandalism was characteristically acerbic:

> One of the things that concerns us is that these mailboxes were vandalized at a time when there was considerable activity around your building yet we have received no reports or assistance from the families in your building or any other building regarding the parties responsible for this damage. It is likely that the families in your building will continue to experience these inconveniences unless some individual or collective action is taken to eliminate these kinds of problems.[48]

Of course there was "considerable activity" around the building—it was swarming with youths, and the relatively few adults undoubtedly felt powerless to stop the destruction or report the perpetrators for fear of reprisal. Schneider's successor, Gus Master (also later the executive director), responded to a tenant's concern over debris thrown from galleries at

Robert Taylor Homes with similar disregard: "Our experience is that these kind of incidents seldom occur in buildings where there is a real interest and concern on the part of the residents to keep it from happening."[49] Master and Schneider placed responsibility on the tenants and censured them for a perceived lack of community effort, never acknowledging that high youth-adult ratios made "interest and concern" among responsible adults an extraordinary challenge.

But residents in CHA high-rises tried desperately to impose order on their chaotic environment. They wanted to build a successful community as residents at early CHA projects like the Ida B. Wells Homes had done, and they recognized the threat and challenge posed by large numbers of young people. By the late 1950s, tenant councils at many high-rise projects had organized volunteers to supervise elevators and lobbies. At Stateway Gardens, tenants patrolled their building during "rush hours," defined as before school, noon, and after school—when children were most present. Other residents formed laundry co-ops to defend their laundry rooms and, in the 1970s, "vertical tenant patrols" to attack the problems of vandalism. To provide positive outlets for youth, tenants organized drum corps troops, Junior Cadet organizations, and youth choirs; they sponsored sports teams, dances, and field trips for youths; they clamored for park district programs, more playground equipment, and community centers at their projects. They worked with churches, settlement houses, and universities to produce plays, offer tutoring, provide job training, and encourage entrepreneurship. They held elaborate debutante cotillions at expensive downtown hotels, a southern tradition brought north that suggested the desire to socialize teenage girls into upper-middle-class norms. They met with CHA staff to demand more from management.[50] Tenants were hardly passive in expecting others to come to their rescue and understood that community had to be built from the ground up. But they still faced the daunting proposition of keeping the enormous number of youths in their midst occupied.

At times, residents' efforts did contain youths, and not every building was chaotic. Measuring the level of order in projects in the past is not possible, and interviews with tenants reveal only perceptions of relative conditions that changed over time. Some buildings were more out-of-control than others, former tenants say, and strong-willed mothers were often able to maintain stability. Dorothea Washington remembered that her mother, a building president at Dearborn Homes in the early 1960s, acted as a discipline enforcer. "My mother's mere presence was enough" to restrain other children, she recalled. Residents banded together to manage

Figure 25. Henry Horner mothers manning elevators, 1967. Courtesy of the CHA.

youths: "There was a relationship that intertwined and everyone was co-operating [in her building]. You'd always get one person who wants to act crazy every now and then, and my mother would have a private conversation . . . which corrected the problem."[51] Sociologist Sudhir Venkatesh argues that tenants created "personal networks" to conduct "indigenous law enforcement" at the Robert Taylor Homes. Women in some buildings patrolled public spaces and, with the help of male enforcers, would perform vigilante justice in the absence of official police response.[52]

But perceptions of order were relative and varied from individual to individual and within a project, making assessment of resident satisfaction difficult, as Mary Wirth found after field visits and interviews with tenants at several CHA high-rises: "It is impossible to make a definite statement about the attitudes and feelings of the tenants of public housing based on random interviewing and visits. . . . There are letters of complaint from tenants describing life as unbearable and there are thank-you letters and congratulations to CHA from others." She was at a loss on how to evaluate tenant complaints. "It has been said that a lack of complaints from tenants at the complaint desk in management offices is an indication of happy tenants. On the other hand, there are tenants who say that they have 'complained' so many times that they no longer bother to do so."[53]

Still, in late 1963, social disorder sparked a full-scale tenant revolt at Robert Taylor, the CHA project with the highest youth-adult ratio. Despite Murphy's efforts to organize floor clubs and building councils, residents were alarmed by their conditions and organized a "law and order committee" to secure more police protection. In a letter published in the *Chicago Defender* in December 1963, an anonymous Taylor tenant council member charged that youths had begun terrorizing the project the previous summer, shortly after its completion: "It was unsafe for women and men to be out after dark and even sometimes during daylight hours. The stairways and laundry rooms were being used for card playing, dice shooting, and sex parties by teenagers. . . . [Youths] tie up our elevators, throw bottles over the galleries, pick pockets, and steal groceries from people using the elevators. They abuse children coming to and from school. . . . There have been robberies, beatings, killings, and shootings from the galleries." The author vaguely blamed nearby DuSable High School students for these acts, but like most complaints, it was unclear whether the instigators lived in the building, came from other nearby project buildings, or lived in the surrounding neighborhood. In all likelihood, they came from all three locations, as high youth-adult ratios created an environment that attracted even more youth to the relative anarchy of its public space. The Robert Taylor Homes was a "blackboard jungle," the tenant council member accused, and "the people are about to give up in disgust." The author concluded with a rhetorical question: "Are we forgotten citizens of Chicago?"[54]

Instead of giving up, however, residents organized that winter in a protest the *Chicago Defender* called "the Battle of the Robert Taylor Homes." In late 1963, tenant groups briefly convinced the CHA to pay welfare recipients to serve as elevator operators. In January 1964, following the stabbing murder of a seventy-year-old resident by a seventeen-year-old neighbor, fifty women picketed the management office, winning a hearing with project manager Murphy. Fearing the "hoodlums" that prowled the project, the "Taylor Tenants Association to Improve Community Conditions" made three demands: twenty-four-hour police protection, twenty-four-hour elevator attendants, and faster elevator repairs. At first Murphy simply referred much of the problem to his superiors and to city police officials, but over time, he won the confidence of the protestors, who saw him as an ally against higher authorities. Still, little action took place. CHA officials asked Washington for more funds for resident janitors, but were rebuffed. The Taylor women then met with alderman Ralph Metcalfe, who tried unsuccessfully to reassign police to the area, as commanders insisted they did not have the manpower. In February, a thirteen-year-old boy died when an eighth floor railing gave way, triggering the tenant group to add more responsive maintenance to their list of demands and to threaten a rent strike. The CHA added a handful of guards and paid more attention to elevator maintenance, but the underlying problems of security—derived from youth-adult ratios and indefensible space—could not be solved without a solid security presence. Moreover, the guards that had been provided earned little respect from tenants. As Earline White, a tenant leader put it, "We were told the guards' duty was to protect the property and not the people who live here." An eighteen-year-old living in Robert Taylor wrote a letter to the *Chicago Defender* explaining that guards routinely beat youths up and "look so phony most of the teenagers just don't respect them."

Resident organizing at Taylor continued through 1964 and beyond. Leaders had specific demands for their community and resisted offers of alliance with more militant civil rights groups, though they did meet with Jesse W. Gray, the leader of a widely publicized rent strike in Harlem in 1963–64. In April 1964, according to the *Chicago Defender*, the tenant group again threatened a rent strike, impelled by the death of ten-year-old Richard Davis, struck by a nine-pound drain lid dropped eight stories by a fourteen-year-old boy with "a history of throwing things from the galleries." But despite anger over the tragedy, the strike never materialized, undoubtedly because residents feared losing their apartments. A cycle of angry complaints followed by minimal response and limited accountability exposed the powerlessness of tenants. "We have had so many meetings with officials of the CHA," complained tenant leader Blanche Greer, "that we are beginning to think that we are getting the runaround."[55] Managers and tenant activists alike faced long odds in fighting social disorder in an environment overwhelmed by hordes of young people.

In 1968, after hearing from tenants across the system through a crude survey, the CHA grudgingly agreed to fence in the galleries at most high-rises. The move created a stultifying, prison atmosphere, though it did put an end to the problem of objects being thrown from above and injuring or killing those below. But now, instead of Elizabeth Wood's "sidewalks in the air," the CHA projects looked like cages, a devastating aesthetic that defined perceptions of Chicago's projects thereafter.[56]

* * *

As social disorder in projects became more and more evident by the mid-1950s, public housing administrators did not revisit planning choices but instead attributed disorder to recalcitrant but isolated "problem families," who needed intensive social work. Elizabeth Wood was among the first to express concern with the "cultural level of the slum dweller" in 1945, and by the mid-1950s she was a leader in the field of the problem family, which she defined as those with a "hard core" dependency on public aid and "more than one really serious behavioral, mental, or physical disorder" such as "children born out of wedlock, husbands or sons in jail for assault, problems of rape, narcotics, alcoholism, vandalism, [and] the most serious physical and mental illnesses." As part of her consulting work for the Citizens' Housing and Planning Council of New York, she began an investigation of the issue, and, in a widely reprinted speech in 1956, expressed dismay at the "fact that housing authority projects are gathering to themselves a group of families . . . who represent the consolidated failures of social agencies." Further, "normal families" increasingly shunned public housing. "As proof of a changed era," she told housers, "we are now saying to one another that there *are* some slum dwellers who can and do help make slums."[57]

In startling and frank terms, Wood had taken a key mantra of 1930s progressivism—the environmentalist argument that slums make bad families—and turned it on its head. Slums were not simply a "housing question" solved with improved surroundings, but a social question involving the entire gamut of poverty, delinquency, and health issues that had long bedeviled efforts of reformers. While new surroundings, by themselves, would help most families, they could not change everyone. But she dismissed the idea of denying admission to problem families, calling this option inappropriate for a "public servant" like public housing. The way out, she submitted, was for a "reorientation of the public housing program," with a greatly expanded corps of social workers promoting a new "family casework" concept for the most troubled families. Paternalistic as this was, she concluded, there was no other choice: "[The problem family has] put us in a different kind of business whether we like it or not" and housing authorities "are not meeting the situation as it is, head on. The way we handle this new situation will determine whether or not public housing will ultimately represent a net gain to the community."[58]

Wood's successor at the CHA, former general William B. Kean, took her concerns seriously, especially after he learned that 5 percent of the apartments in the new mid-rise Ida B. Wells Extension (opened in 1955) had experienced "substantial destruction" within the first year of operation. While the project had high youth-adult ratios, Kean blamed problem families, which he equated with the welfare dependent, and he asked the progressive Welfare Council of Metropolitan Chicago for advice. The council, however, replied that only 31 percent of damaged apartments at Wells Extension housed those on state aid, the same percentage as at all CHA projects. In other words, welfare families were no more likely to be destructive than other tenants.[59] Instead, the council cited "poor housekeeping habits, family disorganization, teen-age gangs, and alcohol and narcotics addiction" amid a general "unfamiliarity with urban living" for the serious damage and strife at newly opened developments. The council suggested that the CHA increase its community relations staff, train tenants in housekeeping, and police tenant behavior more carefully. But Kean balked at additional staff and insisted that the CHA should not become a social welfare agency. Instead, he wanted the settlement houses and additional private and public agencies to do more. The CHA's primary responsibility, he stated, was housing, and further expansion of social work would have to be assumed by outside groups.[60]

Not until 1960 would the CHA and city officials begin the kind of aggressive social work on problem families advocated by Wood. The Cook County Department of Public Aid initiated a pilot program at Rockwell Gardens, a newly opened project on Chicago's West Side, where county welfare workers integrated intensive casework and community services into project life, including health care, child care, and church-based support. The goal was to "re-educate and rehabilitate" clients, a progressive approach espoused by social work reformers in the late 1950s as a move away from the more bureaucratic and punitive methods that had developed during that decade. By providing comprehensive casework, the demonstration program sought to "help people become self-supporting and more constructively self-directed, and to break what may be an increasing pattern of dependency carried from one generation to another." After several months, an interim assessment decided that the frequent contact and supportive approach employed by the carefully selected caseworkers indicated the "possible success" of the new approach: 20 percent of participants had left the welfare rolls. But the report emphasized that the program required "interested, motivated public assistance workers" with manageable caseloads of roughly 60 clients, one-third the normal load.[61] Both the CHA and the public aid department followed up on the Rockwell demonstration program and found the resources to implement the approach on a broad scale during the 1960s. Ground-floor apartments in projects were leased to welfare officials to create substations, allowing caseworkers to be near clients, an important element of the Rockwell demonstration. At the Robert Taylor Homes in 1965, caseloads averaged 60 clients, and Firman House, the area settlement house, worked in conjunction with city officials to serve an average of 4,800 people a month.[62] But while intensive casework undoubtedly helped recipients, it made little apparent dent in the social disorder undermining life in the CHA's projects and missed the underlying demographics that drove it.

★   ★   ★

Managers and tenants alike had limited patience for problem families, and many wanted to screen them from admission or evict them once they became disruptive. But the extent of screening and its effectiveness is hard to gauge from surviving evidence. In the 1930s, the CHA conducted "home visits" to applicants to measure their worthiness, but as the CHA rapidly expanded in the 1950s, this practice fell by the wayside. In 1956, Kean initiated a new procedure in response to the problem-family issue whereby questionable applications were passed on to a social worker who made deeper inquiries into a family's history. That year, out of a total of 6,048 applications, 147 applicants received the second level of evaluation, with 79 approved, 47 rejected, and 21 deferred. "Patterns of illegitimacy" proved the most common red flag, though more than half of such applicants were admitted. On the other hand, all six cases of alcoholism or addiction were rejected or deferred. Roberta Coffee, a social worker in the tenant selection department from 1960 to 1968, recalled that of the cases handed to her requiring further evaluation, roughly one in five were ultimately rejected. The main reasons for denial of these "Coffee cases," as they came to be known within the CHA, included family disorganization (mostly multiple children out of wedlock), bad housekeeping, prior negative rent record, criminal record, and drug addiction.[63] Whether Coffee's practices represented a strong standard of screening or a weak one is difficult to assess. Her boss, Gus Master, who started his twenty-six-year career at the CHA in 1955 as head of tenant selection and who later rose to executive director, said about screening in the 1960s: "Hell, we didn't screen anybody. If the applicant wasn't in jail, or found ineligible for income or specific reasons, they were admitted."[64] It seems unlikely, then, that a weakening of screening policy was the main cause of the CHA's widespread social disorder in the 1950s, as screening had not been restrictive since the 1930s.

Evictions offered another tool to enforce social control. During the 1950s, the CHA evicted roughly 1 percent of its tenants each year for "general undesirability" without explanation, a power similar to that wielded by private landlords and upheld by Illinois state courts in 1950. Eviction threats were equally important and were often made in blunt fashion. In 1966, the CHA threatened to throw out fifty-eight Robert Taylor families unless they could "cooperate" and "control their youngsters who have caused so much trouble as street gang leaders." The exasperated *Chicago Defender* applauded the move, writing in an editorial that the CHA had "no other defensible alternative" to dealing with "parents who are unwilling to discipline their children and keep them from transforming the community into a jungle of lawlessness. . . . They and their brats have no place among civilized people. An overwhelming number of these wild youngsters come from families who live in the housing projects." But the CHA's tactics drew a different response from community activists and lawyers for the poor in the 1960s, who argued that housing authorities acted capriciously in their evictions and failed to provide due process to tenants. Legal aid lawyers began challenging CHA eviction procedures in 1968, seeking to undo decades of jurisprudence that treated housing authorities as private landlords, rather than state agencies administering public benefits. Local courts, however, continued to side with the CHA and viewed its leases as private contracts subject to state law.[65]

But other cases around the country eventually forced a change in eviction and tenant selection policies, altering the balance of power between tenant and public housing landlord. In January 1969, the U.S. Supreme Court ruled in *Thorpe v. Housing Authority of the City of Durham* that a housing authority had to give prior written notification and an opportunity to reply to any tenant facing eviction. Two years later, a U.S. district court ruled that a record of previous unpaid rent was not a good reason for rejecting an applicant without a fair hearing. In the wake of these decisions, the Department of Housing and Urban Development (HUD) issued new regulations in 1971 requiring administrative hearings in all cases of eviction and denial of application. The courts, which in the 1950s had treated housing authorities as privileged landlords, now held them to standards higher than the private sector.[66]

If some of the reforms eliminated the worst abuses, their combined effect demoralized the CHA and weakened its ability to deny admission and evict for cause in the 1970s. The new HUD rules created administrative hurdles and time-consuming delays in selection and eviction, burdening managers, who now felt powerless to enforce disciplinary polices. Muriel Chadwick, originally hired by Elizabeth Wood in 1952 and promoted to assistant manager at Ickes Homes in 1961, vividly recalled the policy changes:

> [In 1961] we were still inspecting apartments, putting people out for bad house-keeping. . . . And then you started getting these legal aid and these community groups blocking evictions and complaining about the rules, and that's when the CHA started going down. This was in the '60s. The do-gooders came in say-ing, "Oh this poor, poor woman, she came from a rural area in the South, and hasn't had the opportunity and so forth." They didn't seem to take into consid-eration that we'd had people like that in the developments years ago, but you worked with those families. But if they couldn't learn, they were evicted.[67]

Another project manager, Daisy Brumfield, found the change in rules equally distressing:

> By the time I became manager at Stateway [in 1977] we had to lease to all these crooks and criminals without really having the ability to look into their back-ground. HUD was telling us that you've got to be very careful that you don't infringe on a person's civil rights. It got so that you couldn't even ask them if they'd been in jail. Before, depending on what a person had been jailed for, we just automatically didn't house them.[68]

Brumfield and Chadwick are both strong-willed African American women who resented what they perceived to be the courts' lack of understanding of public housing management. For their part, community activists found the CHA to be arrogant and disdainful of tenants, nearly indistinguishable from slumlords in the private sector.[69]

"Problem" families were undoubtedly detrimental to project life. As the head of the CHA's community and tenant relations department noted in 1956: "the effect [of problem tenants on a project] is far greater than their number."[70] But the formulation of the problem-family concept was too narrow to explain the social disorder experienced by newly opened high-rises. Administrators assumed that most antisocial qualities devel-oped before the family entered public housing and failed to ask whether the enormous numbers of youth exacerbated or even fostered juvenile delinquency. Moreover, and more important, problems of social control in public housing high-rises were too widespread to be pinned entirely on screening policy or on the relatively small number of "problem" families in the 1950s and early 1960s. The CHA's problems were systemic and demographic, and no amount of social work could overcome its planning mistakes.

★   ★   ★

While the CHA, tenants, and outside agencies struggled to resist disorder and enhance the collective efficacy of the community, the obvious answer for many residents and managers was to expand formal policing, either by CHA security guards or, better yet, by the Chicago Police Department. But neither the Chicago Police Department nor the CHA's senior leadership were willing to spend resources beyond ordinary levels to increase formal policing. Chicago officers patrolled in cars and responded to police calls, as they did in other neighborhoods, but they were reluctant to go beyond these policing basics. Foot patrols of public housing superblocks were rare, and "vertical patrols" inside buildings were nonexistent. With elevators problematic, officers often asked tenants to come to lobbies to relay grievances so that they did not have to climb stairs. In 1960, the *Chicago Defender* reported that "delegations of residents" asked CHA officials for added police protection, but the CHA refused to ask the Chicago Police Department for more help. A year earlier, the militant black newspaper *New Crusader* reported that public housing residents "live in fear" and condemned the CHA for not hiring black-owned security firms to impose order. During the early 1960s, the CHA did enlarge its guard force, but only from thirty to fifty men—a tiny number to serve 30,000 units of family housing. With so little protection, the *Defender* announced, "constant fear is a part of everyday living in Chicago's jungle of high-rise, low-income projects."[71]

Crime rates rose nationwide in the 1960s for numerous reasons, including rising numbers of baby-boom teenagers, increasing availability of handguns, and deteriorating relations between police and minority communities. Chicago's general crime trends mirrored those of the rest of the country, but in public housing, crime rates were devastatingly high, especially as poverty grew more concentrated in the 1970s. The earliest project-specific report on crime showed that at Cabrini-Green's four largest high-rises in 1972, residents were five times more likely to be raped, three times more likely to be robbed, four times more likely to be victims of aggravated assault, and six times more likely to be murdered. With the exception of homicide, these figures likely underreport actual crimes, as public housing residents feared retaliation and distrusted the largely white police force. Many of the crimes occurred in public spaces—hallways, elevators, and project grounds—adding to the fear of residents, many of whom became reluctant to leave the confines of their apartments after dark.[72]

Not until the summer of 1966 did security receive focused attention. Following Martin Luther King's nonviolent marches through the city demanding fair housing (which received an ugly response from neighborhood whites), King's allies sat down with city officials—including CHA chairman Charles Swibel—for a "summit" negotiation. Of the many demands, three involved public housing: establishment of sites in white areas, an end to high-rise construction, and increased guard protection for residents. Swibel deflected the first, agreed to the second, and offered to increase the CHA's meager security force from 60 men to "somewhere between 300 and 400 men," with CHA residents the first hired. He also offered elevator operators for the high-rises and a buzzer system for walk-up buildings.[73]

But Swibel's promises dissolved. He had assured Mayor Daley that funds for the security officers could come out of the CHA's budget, but in 1967, finances were strained, and the CHA only found funds for an additional 55 guards. The CHA appealed directly to HUD in late 1966 for new federal resources to hire 160 additional Chicago police officers at an annual cost of $1.4 million to perform "vertical patrols" inside the buildings at Cabrini and Horner, two of its most troubled projects. Regional HUD officials approved only $700,000 for a scaled-back initiative, but Washington refused to go along, contending that the funds should come from the CHA's budget and that the city's police force should protect public housing residents as it did its other citizens. The idea of increasing security languished, but the issue remained high on the CHA's agenda. Richard Wade, a University of Chicago history professor and stalwart Kennedy Democrat, told an audience at a CHA meeting in 1970 that security was the authority's primary concern: "Since I've been on the board, it's fair to say that the thing we have talked about most . . . [has been] the whole question of security." Yet surprisingly little progress was made. When Wade asked earlier that year for "two guards at each building, 24 hours a day," the CHA's executive director curtly responded, "We can't afford it."[74]

In August 1970, just weeks after Wade's request for more guards, two white Chicago police officers were gunned down by rifle fire from a Cabrini high-rise, jolting the city into action. The CHA and the police department agreed to split the cost of a fifty-five-man police detail, and vertical patrols began in January 1971, but only at Cabrini. Officers received training for their new mission in public housing, but many resented their selection and wanted transfers. The program soon faltered. As one assigned officer testified: "After four or five months, this program became a tragic joke to the people in public housing. . . . We were told to be out there, [to] be visible but not to get into any kind of incidents. 'Let the people see you in the daytime' but as soon as it became dark, it was all right to disappear."[75]

Tenant cries for more formal policing were met with belated and ineffectual efforts. A "comprehensive security program" in 1972 for Cabrini offered an environmental approach based on the "defensible space" ideas of Oscar Newman. Phase 1 proposed enclosing four lobbies at Cabrini to limit entrance to buildings, with protection provided by new guard stations that would be staffed twenty-four-hours a day. Video cameras and additional fencing would be used to "create zones of influence" so that project grounds would "become an extension of a particular building rather than of the 'public' street." But this initial effort, estimated at $2.6 million but costing more than twice that, was not completed until 1977, and the effectiveness of the intervention at the four buildings was mixed. One reporter suggested that the grounds were in better shape and vandalism was down, quoting a resident: "Things seem to be different around here now. The kids aren't as bad as they used to be. They don't bother me or my garden at all. They are beginning to seem human—almost." A 1980 evaluation by the Chicago Department of Planning found that crime had decreased overall in the four buildings, but it had also decreased at a control group at another project. One building actually became worse, a situation blamed on "special problems with certain tenants." The report indicated that the crime drop probably had less to do with CHA efforts than with the changing demographics of Cabrini, where the number of eleven- to fifteen-year-olds decreased by 18 percent and the number of sixteen- to twenty-year-olds by 35 percent. These demographic changes remain unexplained in the report but were likely caused by move-outs (as reflected by rising vacancies), perhaps by families seeking to protect their children from the dangers of Cabrini.[76] Phase 2 of the comprehensive plan, covering the remaining buildings, never got off the ground.

All the attention focused on Cabrini meant other projects received little consideration and had to settle for the CHA's easily corrupted and inadequate privately hired guard services. Stateway Gardens, for example, experienced a rash of crime in early 1973, with gang- and drug-related shootings and murders terrifying residents. Individual residents complained to management, asking for an increase in the two daytime and six nighttime guards to patrol eight high-rise buildings with 1,600 apartments. Nancy

Brown, a tenant leader who survived a shooting herself, told a *Chicago Defender* reporter, "We can't expect the police to stop this [violence], but the CHA can be forced to provide better security if only we can get the tenants organized." But CHA staff and police officers were more pessimistic and had nearly given up on the project. "Even when we catch people (committing crimes), we can't do anything to punish them because no one will come forth to testify," said the project's manager. "There's no way more patrols will prevent the tenants from shooting each other," a homicide detective claimed. "It would take an armed guard in every apartment, stairway, and laundry room at Stateway Gardens." In 1979, the CHA beseeched HUD for funds to address security and enclose lobbies at Stateway. Again, the agency was rebuffed.[77]

The CHA understood that enhancing the collective efficacy of tenants to combat social disorder was central to regaining control of developments. In 1974 correspondence regarding HUD's new "Target Projects Program," which directed funds to the most troubled projects around the country, the CHA wrote: "We sincerely believe that while the 'hardware' types of improvement have value, it is the involvement of the residents that ultimately will bring about a change in the conditions which exist." Public housing residents did band together for protection, but this meant an uneasy truce with gang members, who not only wielded the threat of retaliation but were also a part of the community—the sons, brothers, cousins, and boyfriends of residents. These tangled relationships made the usual forms of policing—especially witness cooperation—exceedingly difficult. Moreover, low-income African Americans often distrusted the police, having experienced or heard of abuse and corruption. Without a working relationship with law enforcement, order suffered.[78]

Crime at Cabrini-Green returned to epidemic levels after the initial and incomplete efforts of the 1970s. By then, poverty was intensely concentrated and deferred maintenance had produced grim physical conditions, and neither vertical patrols nor attempts to create defensible space made much difference. In the first two months of 1981, nine homicides and thirty-four woundings by gunfire were recorded. "There is shooting there every night," the Chicago Police Department's gang crimes commander told the *Chicago Sun-Times*. The vertical patrol had shrunk to thirty officers, and a spot check by then mayor Jane Byrne showed a 40 percent absentee rate. In a dramatic gesture in mid-March, Byrne moved into a fourth-floor Cabrini high-rise with a security detail of sixteen, operating in two shifts, and told reporters, "The Mayor of the City of Chicago has a lot of power and it's time for Cabrini-Green residents to get that power personally." The night she arrived the elevators were broken, and her apartment was full of roaches. In her first impressions, she noted the "tremendous number of children on the loose" and that "too many families were too large for their assigned apartments. There was certainly not enough room for so many children to study or play in their own homes." When reporters quizzed her on project life, she commented on the small size of elevators and the demands on their use: "Have you ever looked at them? Do you know how many kids use them?" During her stay she noted that "city agencies were falling all over themselves to provide extra services" at Cabrini. Some residents, though, were less than impressed. "Things are about the same," a mother of three told a reporter. "There are more police. But the elevators still don't run." Reports showed Byrne's arrival resulted in immediate crime reduction, as her presence amounted to an instant burst of resources, with only 104 major crimes and 2 homicides that quarter, compared to 217 major crimes and 11 homicides in the first quarter of 1981. But Byrne only stayed full-time for three weeks, and sporadically after that, moving out permanently from her "in-town" home at Cabrini in December 1981.[79] Improvements, then, were transitory, and solutions to the security problem in public housing remained elusive.

★ ★ ★

While precisely quantifying the CHA's social disorder is not possible given the scope of available data, evidence suggests that high-rise projects with high youth-adult ratios suffered far more than others.[80] Projects with the most children experienced the greatest turnover, the highest vacancy rates, and the severest problems with security. Following the King summit in 1966, CHA staff recommended that the additional security guards be placed at five projects; each had high-rise buildings and large youth-adult ratios, and four of the five were 1959 projects, either in their entirety or as extensions. At the same time, older CHA projects with relatively lower youth-adult ratios (closer to 1.0)—both low-rise and high-rise—had lower turnover rates despite higher incidences of welfare dependency and lower average income.[81] Assuming turnover reflects social disorder (at least in part), youth-adult ratios, coupled with design, are a better predictor of disorder in the CHA's projects in the 1960s than are poverty levels or rates of single-parenthood. Low-rise projects, despite having lower average incomes and more single-parent families, were viewed as more stable by residents and applicants. Low-rise projects were never immune from the problems of youth, but conditions were less debilitating than in high-rises, where the infrastructure of daily life—elevators, stairwells, trash chutes, laundries, and mailboxes—was vulnerable.

Waiting list figures by project from 1970 to 1976, the only years for which data survive, give further insight into project reputations and the perception of social disorder. Prospective tenants could apply to specific projects and could reject offers at undesirable projects, often waiting years for admission to the project of their choice. Through the early 1970s, the most popular projects were older row-house and walk-up developments, such as the Ida B. Wells Homes (1941; youth-adult ratio, 1.2) and the Jane Addams Homes (1937; youth-adult ratio, 1.0), which had "long" or "very long" waits despite having few large apartments. Similarly, Leclaire Courts, with its amply spaced row houses, remained popular. Leclaire had a relatively high youth-adult ratio of 2.0, but its low site density and semi-suburban setting created more "defensible space" that mitigated youth-inspired disorder. Meanwhile, Cabrini-Green, Taylor-Stateway, and Grace Abbott had "immediate housing" available for all applicants in 1970 and widespread vacancies throughout the decade.[82]

A final comparison drives home the significance of youth-adult ratios. Between 1958 and 1984, the CHA opened forty-nine high-rise buildings for the elderly poor. Senior projects had exceptionally low average incomes yet had few vandalism, maintenance, and, hence, quality of life problems in the 1960s and 1970s. While only half of the senior projects were located in the black ghetto, even those adjacent to the CHA's worst family projects had good reputations, in large part because life within the buildings was secure.[83] Single entrances and the absence of youth meant they experienced little social disorder. Senior projects underscore that tall buildings and design were not the sole cause of public housing's problems—the determining difference was the presence of large numbers of youths.

* * *

The lack of understanding of youth densities has led critics of public housing to point fingers in various directions, but especially at tenants. In a 1979 *Chicago Defender* column that expressed the frustration of middle-class blacks and whites alike, Louis Fitzgerald directly blamed Robert Taylor residents for the social disorder that permeated their community. Fitzgerald rejected the idea that architecture was the problem: "High-rise buildings do not commit crimes—people do! . . . There are people 'stacked up' along Lake Shore Drive and they do not have the problems of the Robert Taylor Homes. So what is the problem? The problem is people!" He argued that public housing residents "would have the same problem in high rise buildings such as Lake Meadows, Prairie Shores, and South Commons." Commenting on elevator service, Fitzgerald attacked the residents: "If in fact the elevators are not working, who the hell is to blame? You can't destroy elevators and expect them to work!" He concluded that public housing residents needed to be taught "not to destroy elevators" and taught to "clean up rather than to mark up."[84]

Fitzgerald's criticisms assumed that tenants did not try to control their environment or were somehow incapable of "cleaning up." But this was unfair. Tenants tried desperately to exert collective efficacy in their public housing communities. Blaming the victims, as Fitzgerald did, ignores how CHA projects designed between 1951 and 1959 were entirely new demographic worlds. No one had ever constructed a community with two youths for every adult in a vertical space, and no one—not Elizabeth Wood, not project managers, not city agencies, and not the tenants themselves—had the social resources to confront the problems caused by overwhelming populations of youths.

Of course, most youths were not delinquent or destructive, nor were all adults responsible. The preceding discussion does not argue that high-rise public housing and high youth-adult ratios determined individual outcomes. Many parents disciplined their children appropriately to keep them from involvement in antisocial acts, and other youths learned to avoid the temptations of anarchy. Many who grew up in high-rise public housing joined the middle and upper classes. In conversations, they resent the broad strokes that paint all public housing residents as an "underclass." Further, they explain that the extent of disorder varied from building to building and over time within high-rise projects, and some residents successfully exerted collective efficacy to achieve relative order. Such success stories have been well told by others and need to be acknowledged if we are to avoid easy stereotypes.[85]

That said, the planning choices of the CHA raised the bar for achieving collective efficacy to daunting heights and made residents' efforts to control the chaos of the projects incredibly arduous. Other communities with far more adults could absorb and contain their youth problem, but Chicago's public housing projects opened with an enormous demographic burden—well before poverty and other social ills engulfed them. In its overall scope and scale, public housing design created a *community* problem of social control. Blaming the tenants or even "problem" families avoids the central policy decision that produced buildings with unheard of youth-adult ratios, resulting in environments where opportunity for destruction multiplied, where gang cultures thrived, and where responsible adult tenants suffered. Passing judgment on either wayward youths or irresponsible adults would see social control as a problem of the individual, not a collective concern. Like any other urban dwellers, public housing residents searched for order in their neighborhoods, at times valiantly, and they pleaded for help from public officials. But the structural demographics created by policy decisions, coupled with indefensible high-rise designs, made both informal social control by residents and formal control by management or the police an extraordinary challenge.[86] High-rise projects for families like the Robert Taylor Homes and others conceived in the 1950s were doomed from the day they opened.

The choice to build multiple-bedroom apartments and fill them with large families was the CHA's alone, made in a well-intentioned effort to address the greatest needs on its waiting lists. By their oversight of funds, federal officials were complicit in this decision and at times actively encouraged it. How could the CHA have made these choices with so little forethought and so little evaluation? While Elizabeth Wood's thinking about high-rises was not ignored by the mostly male CHA planners who followed her, larger imperatives to clear slums and build vast quantities of housing overshadowed all. The need to address market failure and to respond to the migration of African Americans to Chicago left little room for assessing high-rise designs or evaluating how "community" formed in such buildings. Community facilities were included in all projects in a perfunctory way, but exactly how successful communities worked—beyond design, but also in social and demographic terms—was simply poorly understood.

Nor have sociologists, historians, or other observers of public housing analyzed the unique age demographics of Chicago's projects. Most have seen social disorder as a function of poverty, racism, and societal neglect.[87] Vandalism, crime, and loss of community have complex causes that social scientists have been debating for decades, and income, race, and policing all play important roles.[88] But the preponderance of youth is the crucial factor that set in motion the downward spiral of physical and other social conditions in public housing. High youth-adult ratios had a catalytic effect on social disorder and made informal policing unmanageable, which then drove out those with other options, which then concentrated poverty, which then diminished the CHA's financial resources—a vicious cycle. Had the CHA built more low-rise, low-density row-house communities with limited numbers of youth, the combination of community self-policing, tenant organizing, and defensible designs might have made the problems less intractable. Instead, tenants in high-rises were on their own, living in large buildings overrun with youth and hardly protected by ineffectual guards. With demographics stacked against it, the CHA's large projects proved ungovernable. Their failure dragged the rest of the operation down with them.

The Loss of the Working Class

In the decades following World War II, the Chicago Housing Authority underwent a dramatic reversal in its tenant population. In 1948 it housed predominantly working-class, two-parent families, and three-quarters of its 7,600 families had at least one wage earner. The average CHA family had an income equal to 60 percent of Chicago median income— low income, but not desperately poor. Only 22 percent of households relied on public assistance, and only 27 percent were headed by a single parent (both roughly double the figures for the city as a whole). African American tenants (six out of ten residents) had incomes nearly as high as white tenants on average, and, in an indication of the class status of the CHA's black families, their incomes equaled the median for African American families in the city as a whole.[1]

But by 1984 everything had changed. Only the city's

poorest families lived in the CHA's 30,000 family apartments, with just 10 percent reporting employment and 73 percent relying on the meager benefits of the federal program Aid to Families with Dependent Children (AFDC). Ninety-five percent of families were African American, and only 7 percent of families with children were recorded as having two parents. The CHA's projects were some of the poorest communities in the nation; some social scientists labeled its residents an "underclass," a description intended to describe their social and economic isolation from the American mainstream.[2] More than design, more than location, critics pointed to deep concentrations of poverty as the defining characteristic of public housing in Chicago and in much of the nation.

The transformation of the CHA's tenant base was not a smooth declension. Instead, major change took place during time periods when policy, as well as exogenous forces, influenced both eligibility and demand for public housing. In figure 26, we can trace median family income of CHA tenants from 1948 to 1984 by two measures. The first measure (indicated by the solid line) tallies the median income of CHA families in inflation-adjusted dollars. The second measure (indicated by the dotted line) describes the relative position of public housing residents, plotting median

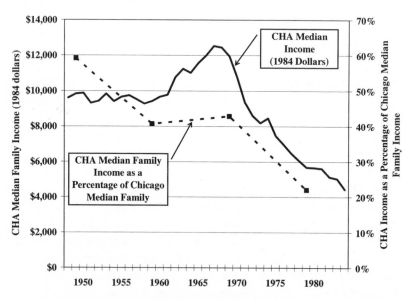

Figure 26. Median incomes for CHA families, 1948–84 (in 1984 dollars). From CHA, *Annual Statistical Report*, 1948–84. The report for 1950 is not available, and data for that year is extrapolated. City of Chicago median family income data for 1949, 1959, 1969, and 1979 from the U.S. Bureau of the Census, *Population*, 1950–80.

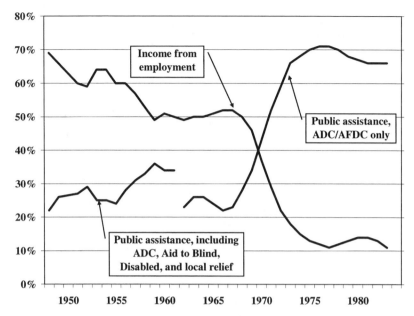

Figure 27. Sources of income for CHA families, 1948–83. From CHA, *Annual Statistical Report*, 1948–84.

CHA incomes as a percentage of Chicago family incomes (using decennial census data for the latter). Several periods of change are evident. During the 1950s, CHA tenants lost ground compared to others in Chicago, with average family incomes dropping from 60 percent to 40 percent of the city median. But this relative decline was arrested by 1959 and a period of real income growth among tenants took place, with public housing incomes slightly outpacing the gains made by the rest of the city. However, after 1967, tenant incomes suffered a sharp reversal, plunging thereafter until concentrated poverty became the norm in most CHA projects after 1975.

The dramatic post-1967 plummet in median tenant incomes, both in real terms and relative to the city, can be seen even more clearly in figure 27, which charts the sources of income for CHA families. From 1967 to 1974, income from wage employment dropped precipitously while the proportion of families receiving public aid skyrocketed. As late as 1967, only 23 percent of CHA tenants relied on AFDC. Six years later, more than two-thirds of CHA households received AFDC funding. In a surprisingly short period of time, Chicago's projects went from housing the African American working class to sheltering predominantly female-headed households dependent upon a penurious welfare state.

All this being so, the data in figures 26 and 27 need to be viewed with some caution. Since rent was set as a function of earnings, with the exception of the period from 1966 to 1970, public housing tenants had an incentive to hide their income from CHA examiners. This incentive extended to hiding the presence of a man in the household, especially if the woman of the household received AFDC benefits. Similarly, families on public assistance often relied on outside sources to supplement their meager benefits in order to survive. Therefore, figures 26 and 27 likely underreport income and understate the proportion of families receiving income from employment.[3]

Still, the erosion of the collective class standing of CHA tenants in the 1950s and, beginning after 1967, the wholesale exodus of the black working class from Chicago's projects were real. No single policy caused these swings, nor is it possible to designate a tipping point from existing data. Instead numerous policy choices and external forces converged to both push and pull the working class out of public housing—and kept others from entering altogether—until a new equilibrium was reached in the mid-1970s, with a radically transformed public housing population.

Because of the CHA's income-based rents, this impoverishment of its population had critical implications for the authority's financial health. At a basic level, the CHA, like private landlords, could not escape the market forces that drove the demand for housing. Once African American working-class families no longer perceived the CHA's product as a desirable good, and its tenant base became inordinately poor, then the CHA lacked the rental income to maintain its buildings. Decay and social isolation followed. These trends were readily understood by public housing insiders as early as the 1950s, and reform was still possible in the mid-1960s. Avoiding the tailspin, however, would have required a fundamental rethinking of public housing's mission, orienting it toward the working class and away from the very poor, a reform not contemplated by those in charge in Chicago. Congress compounded the downward descent with top-down policies that offered only feeble incentives and little accountability while effectively making local housing authorities financial dependencies of the federal government—with ruinous results.

★   ★   ★

The first erosion of the CHA's tenant base occurred from the late 1940s through the mid-1950s as a direct result of the concerted effort by progressives to return public housing to its low-income roots. During World War II, the CHA's board under chairman Robert Taylor reluctantly rented

its newest projects to war workers with higher incomes, but it successfully fought to keep the prewar projects strictly low income. Yet by 1947,
more than one-third of its tenants had incomes exceeding commissioner-
approved "continued occupancy" limits and were labeled "excess income."
Shortly after officials in Washington lifted wartime regulations blocking
evictions that year, the CHA formulated a plan for removing these tenants. But in July, Congress, responding to an outcry from tenants nationwide, passed an amendment blocking evictions unless "no undue hardship" was caused or unless "other housing facilities" were available. The
CHA spearheaded a legal challenge to the amendment by filing a test case
against seventeen tenants earning more than $5,000 a year, easily a middle-
class salary. Its suit was dismissed in January 1948, and the excess-income
tenants remained. In August, however, Congress reversed itself and gave
local authorities the discretion to remove excess-income families, though
it did not mandate such action. Taylor and the board "resolved to proceed
immediately with evictions." By December 1949, Wood had worked out
a procedure with the circuit court to simplify and accelerate eviction proceedings, and excess-income families were given six months to find new
housing.[4]

Disgruntled tenants again resisted eviction, as they had in 1940, in part
because they liked their apartments and in part because the housing shortage made it difficult to find housing elsewhere. Aldermen called on the
authority to ease its policies, but the commissioners defended their actions by reminding critics of the CHA's low-income mission, noting that
the average excess-income family earned an unacceptably high $3,400, or
"$65 a week, which is $10 below the mid-point for all Chicago families."
The CHA did not want families near the city median; it wanted to serve
a far needier population. By 1953 thousands of middle-income and skilled
working-class families were forced out of public housing, often against
their wishes.[5]

The CHA also kept income limits low during the early postwar period,
squeezing out unionized workers—even unskilled ones. The wartime
$1,200 income limit for admission remained in effect until early 1947, by
which point Elizabeth Wood had labeled the figure "entirely unrealistic."
After raising the limit to $2,100 for a family of four (larger families had
higher income limits), the CHA still found that 60 percent of new tenants in 1948 reported no full-time wage earner.[6] Prodding from the city
council motivated the CHA commissioners to raise the limit again in late
1950, when it reached $3,000 for a family of four, a level equaling roughly
75 percent of Chicago's median family income that year. Still, the CHA's

income limits remained lower than that of other cities, including Cleveland, Peoria, and New York. During the mid-1950s, the commissioners did adjust income limits upward faster than the rate of inflation but not as fast as rising real incomes in Chicago. In 1957, CHA leaders expressed surprise at a survey showing that two-thirds of blue-collar workers in Chicago industries were ineligible for public housing. That year, a unionized janitor's helper—the lowest-paid maintenance job at the CHA—earned $4,320 in base pay. But for a family of six, the income limit for admission to public housing was $4,000 per year.[7] Unionized workers with their healthy wages could no longer be admitted.

While real estate interests certainly supported low income limits to avoid competition with the private market, public housing officials in Washington and Chicago also shared these sensibilities and took their market-failure mandate seriously.[8] In an effort to return to their prewar mission of serving low-income families and to prove that public housing did not compete with the market, federal administrators, in consultation with public housing progressives, proposed a requirement in 1945 that income limits be set at levels to ensure a 20 percent "gap" between public housing rents and those "substantially available" for "standard" housing in the private sector. In essence, the policy created a buffer between the private and public sectors of the housing market. The idea, first devised by Nathan Straus in 1939 and refined by Warren Vinton during the war, utilized a market-failure logic: by leaving a gap, private industry would have an incentive to find ways to serve this untapped market and thereby reduce the extent of market failure. Senator Robert Wagner wrote the policy into 1945 draft legislation, and it was later included in the 1949 Housing Act.[9] The provision was intended to appease congressional opponents and real estate interests but was not a concession, since in practice public housing authorities already maintained a 30–40 percent gap by choice in an effort to target their scarce benefit. At the CHA, the gap was actually 40 percent in 1948, a chasm that continued well into the 1970s.[10]

Years later, Elizabeth Wood called the eviction of excess-income tenants in the late 1940s and early 1950s "the Great Purge" and pointed to income limits as the reason for the loss of "leadership" families. She blamed Washington for these policies, failing to acknowledge the complicity of local housing authorities in setting income limits. She did admit, however, "with shame," that she, too, had "smirked" when excess-income families complained. "Your incomes have risen, that's just what we wanted to have happen," she told those about to be evicted. "And now you have learned how to use good housing. You should, therefore, be proud to move out, so that a lower-income family can have the advantage that you have had."[11] Wood articulated a midcentury progressive impulse that combined a faith in social engineering with a tinge of class condescension. In fairness, few predicted in the late 1940s that income-limit policies would later contribute to concentrated poverty in public housing. Instead, environmental determinism suggested that the poor, once admitted to good, affordable housing, would see their fortunes rise and would then leave for greener pastures, making way for more potential beneficiaries in an endless cycle of social improvement.

But by the mid-1950s, optimism had waned, and Elizabeth Wood had changed as well. She was among the first to sound an alarm that public housing, through its own policies and market mechanisms, might no longer be transitory housing for the upwardly mobile working class, as it had been during the housing shortages of the 1940s, and instead might filter downward to become housing of last resort, largely for those dependent on welfare. In her 1956 speech on the "problem" family, she observed, "So long as public housing is the *temporary* home of the capable, the honest, the ambitious—a home such people would rather not accept, if possible—but is the *permanent* home of the damaged, the non-normal, the deceitful—public housing will not produce good neighborhoods." She proposed "setting free" the program so it could admit higher-income families and let them stay, and she argued for "conceiving of public housing as a community where people can live as they can live anywhere—where they can put down roots, where leadership is wanted and rewarded."[12] Wood wanted public housing to act more like private housing and less like a public utility, though she never went so far as to say rents should be fixed or the very poor should be rejected. She was still wrestling with an element of public housing's mission unresolved since the legislative debates of 1937: Who should the program serve? Should it be an arm of the welfare state serving those most in need, as Wood initially believed but now doubted? Or should policies favor the least problematic families, the "deserving," "normal," and "upwardly mobile"? The New York City Housing Authority (NYCHA) answered these questions with careful screening and by keeping the proportion of welfare families low. As late as 1968, only 15 percent of NYCHA residents relied upon AFDC funding, though external pressures would soon force it to take more. But in Chicago, officials were on a fast path toward making the CHA almost entirely welfare housing.[13]

The net effect of the Great Purge and postwar income-limit policies was to remove the skilled working class from public housing and make the unionized working class ineligible. Ironically, however, Chicago's projects housing African Americans remained largely working class because of the racial discrimination that permeated the city's housing and job markets. The CHA's income limit in 1959 of $3,800 was only 52 percent of the median family income for whites in Chicago, but it was 80 percent of median nonwhite income, as recorded by the Census Bureau that year.[14] Further, the rise in the proportion of African American residents from 60 percent in 1951 to 90 percent by 1964 (because of the opening of projects in the ghetto and the end of managed integration) actually helped preserve the working-class nature of CHA projects through the mid-1960s. The non-unionized black working class continued to be eligible for and actively wanted public housing because of entrenched housing discrimination, which, along with continued migration from the South, created a housing shortage. While the proportion of single-parent and welfare-dependent families edged upward in the mid-1950s, public housing's tenant base was still solidly working class and predominantly two parent. Only now its residents were almost exclusively African American.

Indeed, the four projects protected for white occupancy through racial steering were the first to lose the working class and concentrate poverty. By 1958 median incomes at Trumbull, Bridgeport, Lawndale, and Lathrop were the lowest among the CHA's family projects. These older, low-rise projects (two built by the PWA) had drifted downward after the war as upwardly mobile white tenants were either forced out by the "purge" or left voluntarily. In their place came white applicants with far lower average incomes than their African American counterparts.[15] But the easing of the housing shortage for whites by the early 1950s, their strong wage gains, the CHA's restrictive limits relative to white incomes, and the popular association of public housing with African Americans—each contributed to the erosion of interest and eligibility among whites in public housing.

★ ★ ★

The relative decline in tenant incomes during the 1950s had serious consequences for the CHA's fiscal health. Under the generous subsidy structure created by the 1937 Housing Act, Washington paid for construction costs while housing authorities agreed to charge enough rent to manage and maintain projects for sixty years. From 1938 through the early 1950s, income-based rents swelled housing authority coffers. After provision for a healthy reserve, federal administrators required that any surpluses or "residual receipts" (rental income minus expenses) be returned to Washington to offset annual contribution spending. In 1947, tenant rents nationwide covered not only maintenance but offset 85 percent of annual

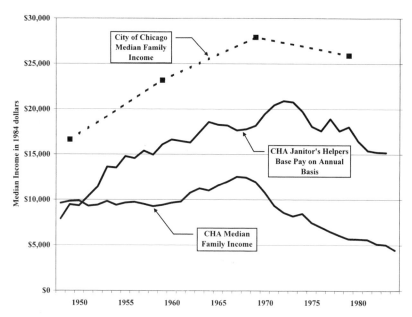

Figure 28. CHA tenant incomes compared to CHA janitor's helpers base pay and City of Chicago median family incomes, 1948–84 (1984 dollars). From CHA, *Annual Statistical Report*, 1948–84. CHA janitor's helpers base pay from "Labor Contracts" folder, CHA Subject files. Data for 1963 is not available and is extrapolated for that year; data from 1948–52 is adjusted to reflect a forty-hour work week, established in 1953.

contributions. Tenants, in effect were paying nearly the entire federal cost of the program. But by the late 1950s, declining rental income meant declining residual receipts, and annual contribution subsidies began to approach maximums.[16]

Public housing budgets could be sustained so long as tenant incomes— and hence income-based rents—kept pace with rising expenses. Roughly half of management and maintenance expenses involved utilities, materials, and insurance, which changed little in real terms between 1950 and 1970; utilities on a per-unit-month basis were actually cheaper in 1970 than two decades earlier. But the other half of expenses involved salaries to administrative and maintenance employees. Aided by federal "prevailing wage" requirements and represented by strong unions, public housing employees across the country shared in the real wage gains experienced by most Americans in the postwar period. As figure 28 shows, between 1950 and 1960, the annual base pay for a CHA janitor's helper rose (in 1984 dollars) from $9,336 to $16,622, a 78 percent real increase that roughly matched city trends. Meanwhile, median tenant incomes stagnated.[17]

Thus, rising labor costs outstripped the rent-paying ability of tenants in public housing in the 1950s.

CHA administrators were not blind to these trends, and executive director William Kean issued several orders in the mid-1950s to bolster income. As we have seen, he reduced vacancy losses by ending Elizabeth Wood's integration policy of holding open apartments for potential white tenants. In 1956 he negotiated with federal officials for additional funds for the PWA projects (as well as for two black projects built during the war) to begin much-needed upgrades and replacements.[18] The next year he raised rents for families on public assistance, which were not income-based but instead were negotiated with county welfare officials. Income limits were steadily increased, rising 23 percent in real terms between 1955 and 1962 and nearly keeping pace with wage growth. Kean also eased the CHA's policy on excess-income tenants: evictions were no longer standard procedure and these families were only "encouraged" to leave.[19]

In line with these changes, the board approved a new tenant selection policy in late 1957: no longer would tenants be selected on a first-come, first-served basis (with exceptions for emergency cases, disabled applicants, relocation families, and, unstated, racial steering). Instead, economic and social characteristics would be considered so that a more "representative" cross-section of the low-income population would be selected. Priority would be given to eligible two-parent families and applicants with higher incomes. The board, now dominated by appointees of Mayor Daley, said it wanted "more tenants with qualities of leadership . . . to improve the social and moral conditions in CHA buildings."[20] These were code words for two-parent, working-class households—what the CHA had defined as "normal" families since the 1930s.

Federal Public Housing Administration officials concurred with the CHA's new selectivity, warning in an audit that "the current trends as to the characteristics of project populations place a serious strain on the hopes and aims of the low-rent housing program as first it was conceived and developed. . . . In the interest of the families themselves, public housing projects should not become ghettos inhabited only by broken families and those on public relief." The word "ghetto" in the audit likely refers more to class than race. Eisenhower administration officials had no comment about site selection, the loss of integration, or the predominance of African Americans in CHA projects. They worried that stagnating income and rising expenses would leave the CHA "insolvent by the end of Fiscal Year 1960."[21]

Chicago's fiscal trends were typical of large housing authorities across the country. In a 1960 internal report, the PHA argued that short-term reforms, like the ones implemented by the CHA in late 1957, had "kept the wolf from coming through the door" at most housing authorities but had not "chased him away. . . . In other words, we have managed to keep the program solvent but haven't been able to keep it from getting closer to insolvency."[22] By 1960, then, administrators in Washington understood that public housing's fiscal condition was fundamentally unhealthy, with expenses set to overtake rental income in the near future. But they kept this concern hidden from public view.

The PHA's 1958 prediction of insolvency at the CHA proved premature by several years. Median tenant income rose in real terms between 1960 and 1966 and thus kept pace with incomes of janitor's helpers and city residents, as seen above in figure 28. The proportion of single-parent and welfare households remained low as well, helped by the new tenant selection policies put in place in 1957. But most of the rise in income can be attributed to the opening of a string of projects between 1958 and 1963 totaling 14,844 units, nearly doubling the size of the CHA. The new apartments, even in high-rise developments in the ghetto, initially attracted a majority of working-class, two-parent African American families. Since income limits were set significantly higher for larger families and since such families tended to have more employed members, filling the multi-bedroom units had the effect of boosting median income figures.[23] As a result, most new projects ran surpluses in their early years, amounting to a sizeable windfall for the CHA between 1958 and 1965. This phenomenon was not unanticipated; both the CHA and the PHA understood that the new projects would, as the PHA put it, have "the temporary effect of propping up the sagging finances of the older projects."[24]

The illusory nature of these surpluses was readily apparent in CHA budget documents. In the early 1960s, the commissioners approved initial budgets at the start of each fiscal year projecting overall deficits, burdened by high costs at older projects. But these preliminary budgets did not include estimates for the opening of new developments. The 1963 budget, for example, did not include a line for the 4,400-unit Robert Taylor Homes, which became fully operational that fiscal year. By the end of 1963, the projected deficit had turned into a substantial surplus.[25] While the budgets were not intended to deceive, the reliance on the opening of new projects placed the CHA in a precarious position. Continued construction was hardly assured, and the new high-rises with their tremendous youth densities soon became costly to maintain.

Yet the budget turnaround after 1958 and the stabilization of the CHA's tenant base lulled the commissioners into complacency. Although executive director Alvin Rose told the board in a 1961 meeting that "if it were not for the newer projects the Authority would not have any surplus funds," the commissioners expressed little concern and rarely took a hard look at expenses or income trends. Shortly after becoming CHA chairman in 1964, Charles Swibel confessed that "the review [of budgets] in the past has been perfunctory. . . . [I]n the last six or seven years, every time I saw the budgets, everything was already done."[26] Swibel claimed he wanted the board to be more involved, but the minutes of meetings in the following years show limited discussion on the subject. Apathy was fueled by the CHA's largest surplus ever in 1964, and the authority's reserve account held $7 million, the maximum allowed under federal regulations.[27] Director of management Harry Schneider reported on the budget to the board in October of 1964 with only the briefest of comments: "We are moving along and in good shape."[28] If the looming structural problem with the CHA budget was understood, no one discussed it publicly.

One other important policy change in this period also helped retain the working class and drive up median tenant income in the 1960s. Beginning in 1962, the CHA shifted away from income-based rents, starting at its two newest projects, the Robert Taylor Homes and the Washington Park Homes. The drawbacks to income-based rents had been apparent since their inauguration during the war. Intrusive income checks and rent increases with each pay raise created resentment among working-class tenants and a disincentive to stay. Fixed rents, based on apartment size, removed these tensions and were easier to administer. Federal officials, however, feared "hardship cases" among the working poor, who would see their rents increase under the new policy, so they blocked the CHA from implementing it across the board. Tenant groups wrote to the CHA both opposing and supporting fixed rents, and this apparent ambivalence eventually convinced Washington to relent. When the new policy was fully implemented in 1966, every three-bedroom apartment, whether in a high-rise or row house, whether in a desirable or undesirable neighborhood, rented for $75 a month. Excess-income families, however, still paid more. A family of six earning more than $6,600 paid $100 a month for the same unit. Welfare rents were set at $65 for a three-bedroom unit, a figure unchanged from 1960 to 1968. The CHA was the first housing authority in the nation to switch to fixed rents, but few followed its lead, fearing the impact on the working poor.[29] Fixed rents offered administrative simplicity, but it cut against the grain of two decades of progressive sensibilities.

★　★　★

While the CHA succeeded in increasing rental income, controlling management and maintenance expenses was far more troublesome. The problem went beyond costs associated with social disorder, which, while substantial, were less debilitating than the CHA's considerable inefficiencies. Ever since the mid-1940s, the CHA's maintenance operation had been woefully unproductive. While Elizabeth Wood and later executive directors kept a tight rein on the non-unionized administrative staff at the CHA (department heads, planners, project managers, clerical workers), its maintenance staff was another matter. Maintenance positions were controlled by the city's powerful unions, which had nearly complete power to hire and fire the CHA's carpenters, electricians, engineers, janitors, exterminators, glaziers, and plumbers, among others. The labor movement in the United States helped the working class achieve middle-class wages and secure valuable workplace protections, but the specific practices of Chicago unions also resulted in sizeable inefficiencies when compared to the unionized maintenance employees of other housing authorities. Inefficiency did not mean poor service for tenants, at least not until the 1970s. But it did bloat maintenance expenses—a budgetary burden that would eventually cripple the CHA.

Evidence of the high price of union control in Chicago first appeared in a confidential 1946 study by the Federal Public Housing Authority (FPHA). Investigators reported that labor costs at the CHA were 40 percent higher than those of comparative authorities as a result of "overstaffing" in maintenance areas. Particular criticism was directed at the CHA's Central Maintenance Section (CMS), which operated as a centralized clearinghouse for work orders and maintenance personnel. Foremen for each craft ran the CMS, determining who got hired and fired and how maintenance work was divided among the various crafts. The FPHA report called for eliminating the CMS and replacing it with a more decentralized approach in order to reduce the "excessively high cost" and "extreme amount of unproductive man hours" in the current system. Federal officials further recommended that the CHA take a strong stance with its unions. The commissioners, Washington said, needed to "establish the supervisory rights" of management to override union "jurisdictional claims on minor or intermediate maintenance work." Union leaders, the report warned, had to "recognize the 'non-profit' character of the CHA" and cooperate with needed reforms.[30]

The report triggered a major behind-the-scenes clash between the CHA and its unions. Elizabeth Wood had long been reluctant to take on the unions, given their political power in Chicago and given that labor was a major supporter of public housing in the campaigns for the 1937 and 1949 Housing Acts.[31] The CHA, by tacit understanding since its founding, always had at least one representative from organized labor on its board watching out for union interests. But the federal report demanded action. In August 1946, the CHA board passed a resolution disbanding the CMS, but less than a year later, in June 1947, it backpedaled, rescinding the resolution and claiming that the federal proposals "could not be successfully accomplished due to local factors." A series of internal negotiations between chairman Robert Taylor and commissioner Patrick Sullivan, the union representative on the board, lasted into early January 1948. As one CHA staff member at the time recalled, Sullivan "would go back to the Chicago Federation of Labor and ask 'Can't we do this or that [differently]?' and they'd turn him down. They'd say, 'Well, if we open the door here then we'll open it up everyplace else.' They were completely resistant." Sullivan did achieve minor workplace concessions, but the CMS, with its highly paid foremen, survived.[32] A CHA study in the spring of 1948 confirmed that little had changed, as it still had the highest number of maintenance workers per unit among comparable housing authorities. In contrast, the CHA's administrative operation was quite lean and near the median in terms of number of employees.[33] Following a brief strike in May by CHA maintenance workers over the layoff of two glaziers, Taylor propelled a resolution through the board, with Sullivan absent, which asserted authority over the CHA's labor policies and stated the "principle that the Authority and not the union has the right to determine the amount and kind of work to be done at the projects."[34] Policy statements, however, resolved little on the ground. The CMS remained, and union foremen still controlled hiring, the pace of work, and jurisdictional lines. The CHA board was assertive, but in the end, union control proved more powerful. Throughout the next three decades, the CHA board granted steady real wage increases (required to match the pay of city employees under "prevailing wage" regulations) but received few operative gains in return.

Ten years later, a second federal investigation showed how little had changed. A 1958 Public Housing Administration audit labeled excessive maintenance costs as "the outstanding characteristic of the CHA operation." General repair, maintenance, and replacement expenses were 51 percent higher in Chicago than in Detroit, the second closest city, and 84 percent higher than in New York. Labor practices accounted for nearly the entire discrepancy. Differences between housing authorities "cannot be accounted for by qualitative standards or by significant variations in wages and salaries," the PHA concluded. Instead, it blamed an "overemphasized, un-natural preoccupation with 'jurisdiction'" that resulted in "absurd" and "hair-splitting" work rules with "no thought of efficiency and economy." The craft foremen who continued to run the Central Maintenance Section, the report stated, were accountable more to their unions than to senior management.[35]

Concrete examples of waste in the report revealed the heart of the CHA's inefficiencies. Glaziers earning $3.92 an hour in 1957 replaced an average of 6.5 panes of glass per day while unionized Detroit Housing Authority glaziers replaced almost 18. To repair an oven cost $3.49 in labor in Chicago, $1.35 in Detroit, and $0.89 in Milwaukee. Other tasks were equally wasteful because of jurisdictional rules and the use of high-wage, skilled labor for basic tasks. A pipefitter and an electrician were required to disconnect an oven and a refrigerator before a painter could repaint a kitchen. At other housing authorities, janitorial staff handled these jobs. Even without such responsibilities, janitorial expenses in Chicago were higher than any other city, with the CHA employing "an excessively large hierarchy of head janitors and assistant head janitors." Finally, despite the retention of high-cost foremen, supervision over repairs was "not only inadequate, but sometimes completely lacking," according to the PHA. The conservative *Chicago Tribune* had a less friendly assessment, accusing union leaders of "milking the [CHA] since its early days" by using "political influence" to make the authority the "private property of the bosses of the building trades unions."[36]

Career PHA auditors prepared the Chicago report confidentially under the direction of regional director William Bergeron, a public housing administrator since the PWA days. Their motive was largely fiscal; the PHA was under pressure from Eisenhower budget officials to find savings, and every dollar not spent on maintenance meant more "residual receipts" and less annual contributions. When the report was leaked to the press two months after completion, federal officials expressed alarm and blamed CHA staff for the breach. An anonymous CHA staff member confessed to the press that the authority "has always been at the mercy of the unions," and the CHA board admitted that the report was "perhaps long over due."[37]

Echoing the 1946 report, the PHA in 1958 called for jurisdictional reforms and the disbanding of the Central Maintenance Section. But union leaders again successfully resisted change through a series of delaying tactics that blocked reform. CHA commissioner Martin Dwyer, the board's union representative at the time, and former CHA commissioner Patrick Sullivan, then president of the Chicago Building Trades Council, made veiled strike threats after the report's leak, demanding that the affected unions "be consulted so that there will be no conflicts with Labor Organizations." In May, union leaders met with the CHA board and expressed a willingness to cooperate with management in "correcting any practices that produce less than a full day's work for a full day's pay." But they opposed the firing of the six $10,000-a-year CMS foremen. A month later, Dwyer steered through the board a resolution putting off immediate action and calling for more study, concluding "it is determined to be in the best interests of the CHA to maintain the status quo" and postponing "taking any action until the Authority has had a reasonable time to work out a solution." Alvin Rose asked for six months to study the matter, and Bergeron granted a three-month reprieve on firing the foremen but demanded specific operational changes and spending cuts totaling $901,672 from the CHA's proposed $12 million budget for the upcoming fiscal year. The cuts covered all areas of maintenance and would require laying off 127 employees, the CHA claimed. The move outraged the board and added to the general hostility between the PHA and the CHA that had been simmering since 1955 with the long dispute over high-rise designs. While the commissioners prepared for a legal challenge to the PHA's authority, Rose continued the war of words in the media, labeling the PHA's demands "unrealistic, unreasonable, and arbitrary." He proclaimed with much hyperbole that the CHA intended to issue a "Declaration of Independence" from the overly intrusive PHA authorities.[38]

Rose and the board had two reasons to be confident in their challenge to the PHA. First, the CHA's overall budget picture had brightened since the PHA report had been completed in January. The opening of new projects had turned the PHA's projection of a $560,000 deficit for 1958 into what looked like a potential $400,000 surplus. Cuts were no longer needed, the CHA argued. Second, and significantly, the PHA had antagonized other local housing authorities with its criticisms and micromanagement of local operations. With the help of their national organization, the National Association of Housing and Redevelopment Officials (NAHRO, formerly NAHO), housing authorities petitioned Congress to restrain PHA oversight and grant more local autonomy. A NAHRO-backed bill passed the Senate in July 1958, and the backlash against the PHA gained momentum. A year later the 1959 Housing Act directed the PHA to give far greater freedom to local authority operations.[39]

The Senate vote led Bergeron and Washington PHA officials to back down in their fight over efficiency. PHA chief Charles Slusser sent his top deputy, Abner Silverman (a seventeen-year veteran of the program), to Chicago in early August to conciliate, and after a week of negotiations, the PHA capitulated. Silverman allowed the Central Maintenance Section and its foremen to remain intact and gave up the effort to force cuts in the CHA's 1959 budget. For its part, the CHA did agree to get the "full cooperation" of the building trades unions for "increased efficiency" and to "make more effective use" of the foremen. Four months later, Rose claimed he found $263,000 in efficiency gains from implementing PHA reforms, though only $92,000 came from maintenance improvements with changes in work rules. Non-unionized administrative employees took the brunt of the reductions in a reorganization that mainly involved demotions and a resultant savings in wages.[40]

As in 1946, the battle between the CHA and the PHA over maintenance and management practices in 1958 was won by labor, which gave little in efficiency gains while continuing to saddle the CHA with excessively high maintenance costs. The PHA tried to force reform but withdrew in the face of local and congressional pressure, as it had over site selection in 1950 (though it did not give in on construction cost limits). Unlike in 1946, when Robert Taylor and Elizabeth Wood had at least attempted reform, the CHA in the late 1950s, blinded by resentment of PHA control and captured by the interlocking interests of labor and city hall, equivocated on reform.

★   ★   ★

The unusual conditions that produced budget surpluses in the first half of the 1960s did not last. First, the pipeline of new family projects slowed to a trickle after 1964 as African Americans and city liberals objected to further ghetto sites for public housing. The CHA opened only 1,900 apartments for families between 1964 and 1970, a far cry from the boom years of 1958–63. It did, however, build almost 7,000 units of housing for seniors, but low fixed rents at these mostly high-rise projects did not generate the operating surpluses experienced early in the decade.[41] Second, the family high-rises opened between 1955 and 1963 soon became maintenance headaches and within a few years went into deficits themselves because of youth-inspired social disorder. Excessive wear and tear and vandalism sent total spending on repairs, maintenance, and replacements soaring: between 1960 and 1966, these expenses rose 47 percent in inflation-adjusted, per-unit-month terms, while other expenses declined by 7 percent. Wage gains among maintenance staff do not account for the increase; salaries rose only 9 percent in real terms in this period.[42] Instead, the costs represented more maintenance staff on a per-unit basis. This meant that projects remained reasonably well maintained through the mid-1960s, though at excessive cost. The CHA had the funds for these staff positions because it had not yet reached its maximum annual contribution. Inefficiency, then, had no real cost to the CHA, or, for that matter, to tenants. The CHA merely spent more of the federal annual contribution subsidy and returned fewer "residual receipts" to Washington.

But once maximum subsidy ceilings hit in 1967, the fiscal tables turned. The CHA dipped into its fully funded reserves—intended to pay for major replacements like roofs and windows—to absorb its first deficit. In 1968, it raised fixed rents by $5 a month, but this did not prevent a deficit that year, nor the next.[43] Maintenance costs continued their upward climb, rising another 21 percent in real terms between 1966 and 1970, while rental income plunged 19 percent, as the proportion of welfare-dependent families paying a lower fixed rent spiked. By 1970 the CHA's reserve fund had been drained, and Chairman Swibel acknowledged in July that the CHA was "nearly bankrupt."[44]

Chicago actually hit crisis later than most large cities, owing to its artificial surpluses from opening new projects in the early 1960s and the stable revenue generated by fixed-rent policies in the second half of that decade. Nearly all U.S. housing authorities experienced accelerating operating expenses and stagnating income among tenants. In New York City, while average tenant incomes increased by 65 percent (in nominal dollars) between 1952 and 1967, wages for the unionized maintenance staff rose 165 percent in the same period. A 1969 report by the Urban Institute of twenty-three large housing authorities across the country found only three that were healthy. The report blamed price and wage inflation for the rise in operating costs between 1965 and 1968, and it argued for raising rents, increasing federal subsidies, and, most provocatively, reducing the "number of minors per unit" through "greater emphasis on elderly housing and less on housing large families." A regression analysis predicted that lowering the average number of minors by one would decrease operating costs per unit month by about 9 percent, a measure of the importance of youth-adult ratios on operating costs.[45]

★ ★ ★

The CHA's fiscal crisis coincided with the wholesale exodus of the working class and the influx of the welfare-dependent poor between 1968 and 1974. The sources of this transformation are complex and difficult to unravel. Social disorder and fiscal crisis contributed, but they are only two of several forces that converged to produce the dramatic changes in the CHA's tenant population. Broader social and cultural influences, specific policy shifts, and a changing housing market also contributed. When combined, these trends propelled the CHA toward welfare housing with overwhelming pressure.

Social upheaval gripped Chicago and the nation in the late 1960s, creating an important context for working-class exodus. African Americans, bitter at the slow pace of civil rights reform and the assassination of leaders such as Martin Luther King Jr., expressed their anger in a series of riots between 1966 and 1968, tearing up the city's West Side. Many small businesses and services were lost for decades. The Black Panthers and other African American political activists faced off against the Chicago police, and a strong undercurrent of resistance to state authority, including the CHA, permeated ghetto life by the late 1960s. Increasing levels of crime and violence added to the climate of tension and fear. At Cabrini Homes in 1970, CHA officials attributed the outflow of six hundred families in four months (about one-sixth of the project) to the murder of two police officers by sniper fire.[46] African Americans and whites alike believed Chicago's projects were coming unhinged, and this undoubtedly prompted public housing residents to flee to safer ground.

Shifting welfare policy also underpinned the CHA's changing tenant base. The CHA's trends mirrored the explosive rise in welfare rolls both locally and nationally. While U.S. welfare rolls doubled between 1966 and 1974, Cook County AFDC cases quadrupled, from 38,000 to 151,000, in the same time period. This increase can be attributed largely to the success of the welfare rights movement, itself an amalgam of the civil rights movement and black empowerment activism. In the 1940s and 1950s, state and local welfare agencies discouraged or denied eligible applicants in a deliberate subterfuge to keep welfare rolls low. Beginning in 1966, community activists, legal aid lawyers, and the National Welfare Rights Organization mobilized local chapters of welfare mothers to fight administrative barriers in a state-by-state, county-by-county effort. They succeeded not only in adding millions of eligible families to welfare rolls but also in changing unfair governmental practices. Rolls were also expanded as a result of migration, rising divorce rates, and increasing numbers of single parents, but these trends had been occurring steadily throughout the 1950s and 1960s. It was not until the welfare rights movement, coupled with court cases favoring recipients, that long-eligible families began to receive the benefits they were entitled to. The reforms, however, had a double edge; critics and supporters alike agreed that AFDC incentives discouraged both work and marriage. As one welfare rights activist put it, poor women faced the difficult choice of finding "a man" who might be unreliable, or being dependent on "the Man," represented by the government welfare case worker. Moreover, the erosion of welfare benefits in real terms during the inflationary 1970s helped drive average tenant incomes to new lows.[47]

Changes in employment patterns, however, are not consistent with the timing of the working-class exodus. During the late 1960s, job markets in the nation, including Chicago, were healthy, with manufacturing employment in Chicago holding steady, unemployment reaching an all-time low, and real wage gains continuing, even for African Americans. Work had not yet disappeared from black neighborhoods in Chicago, and the urban crisis was centered more on political grievances, continued discrimination, and second-class citizenship than concern over lost industrial employment. But wrenching economic change took place beginning in the early 1970s and damaged the prospects of unskilled African Americans. Job flight to the suburbs and deindustrialization throughout the 1970s and the 1980s caused painful economic dislocation among both the black and the white working class. But these changes cannot fully explain the exodus that began in 1967 and was nearly complete by 1973.[48]

Instead, we must look to the consequences of specific public housing policies. Between 1965 and 1967, HUD went through several revisions of regulations to comply with Title VI of the Civil Rights Act of 1964 to implement a true open occupancy policy. Up to that time, housing authorities had used a wide range of admission practices, but many prioritized higher-income applicants. Applicants were also given the "freedom of choice" to turn down openings elsewhere but remain on the waiting list at a preferred project. For years, these policies had satisfied federal officials, but in 1967 it became clear that local housing authorities were not desegregating all-white projects and that they were using admissions rules to racially steer applicants. Unwilling to impose quotas or other numerical targets that might have resulted in rapid racial integration, HUD wrote new rules it hoped would indirectly achieve that result. Applicants now would be offered openings on a "first-come, first-served" basis from a housing authority's entire available supply. Applicants could reject up to three offers before moving to the bottom of the waiting list. The CHA unsuccessfully protested HUD's new rules on racial grounds, calling them "a step toward all non-white public housing in Chicago." With overwhelming black demand, the CHA feared HUD's rules would make it difficult to attract white tenants (who would reject offers at black projects) and result in racial transition at four family projects and several senior projects where black occupancy was still restricted by CHA's discriminatory fiat.[49]

Tenant selection policy veered again in Chicago in 1969 during lengthy negotiations between the CHA and lawyers suing the authority over its policies on race, especially in site selection. A federal judge approved new tenant selection rules that combined elements of "first come, first served" and "freedom of choice." Eligible applicants would be offered, "in numerical order," the first appropriate vacancy "irrespective of location." Applicants who turned down the initial offer were required to "designate a public housing project of their choice." If, after one year, no opening in that project was available, applicants would be returned to the top of the "first-come, first-served" list, but they were still free to reject any offer and retain their spot on the waiting list for a specific project. This process could be repeated for a total of three years, at which point tenants would simply remain on the waiting list. Unfazed by the dance over open occupancy and integration, the court addressed the problem of discrimination at the CHA's four mostly white projects by imposing quotas that limited African Americans to 15 percent and total nonwhites to 25 percent of occupancy, though it still left implementation in CHA hands.[50]

But the class implications of the order were to have a greater effect on the CHA's tenant base than the attempt to deal with racial segregation. Taking applications "in numerical order" meant an end to prioritizing higher-income tenants. With waiting lists flooded with poor families, the "first-come, first-served" policy changed the class status of the CHA's residents significantly. Without flexibility to select tenants, the pressures of waiting lists meant the loss of economic integration, just as it had meant the loss of racial integration in the 1950s.

Income limits also undermined working-class tenancy, but this influence should not be overstated. In 1968, income limits jumped 25 percent, and the CHA stopped "encouraging" excess-income families to leave in an effort to preserve the working class. But these changes did little to stop the turnover and the flood of very poor families moving into projects. Income limits were raised again in 1973, though in real terms they declined in the inflationary 1970s, making it increasingly difficult for the working class to apply for public housing. But the median incomes of new residents plunged even faster, suggesting that the CHA's new selection policies were more important influences than income limits in shaping median income trends. In 1979, income limits doubled, but by then it was too late; concentrated poverty meant few working-class families applied.[51]

Later commentators assailed a change in federal policy known as the Brooke Amendments for chasing out the working class, but this policy also had limited influences in Chicago, at least before 1982. In 1969, Edward Brooke (R-MA), the Senate's only African American and one of the few interested in public housing policy, sponsored the first of a series of amendments to housing law, requiring that public housing tenants pay no more than 25 percent of their income toward rent.[52] The policy was intended to protect the working poor from rental increases imposed by housing authorities desperate for revenue. The new law, however, undid the fixed-rent policy that had helped retain working-class tenants in the mid-1960s. As a countermeasure, rather than return to income-based rents for all tenants, the CHA created a hybrid rental structure that granted income-based rents to poor families but capped the rent for working-class families at thresholds designed to shield them from the penalties of income-based rent. Still, even as the CHA tried to hold on to its working-class families with its rent policies, the return to income-based rents renewed the incentive for the very poor to apply for public housing. Moreover, in 1982, the cap on working-class families was lifted. In a misguided effort to enhance CHA revenues, HUD demanded that all CHA tenants, regardless of income, be charged 25 percent of their income for rent (soon increased to 30 percent)—a move that meant skyrocketing rents for the small fraction of remaining working-class families. Few stayed.[53]

Congress belatedly recognized the problem of concentrated poverty in public housing in the early 1970s. During a six-month period in 1973, 89 percent of all families admitted to public housing across the country were reliant on state aid, a figure that alarmed Congress and led to language in the 1974 Housing Act requiring that local housing authorities select tenants to "assure that, within a reasonable period of time, projects will include families with a broad range of incomes" and to "avoid concentrations of low-income and deprived families with serious social problems." However, the law added a caveat that the rules "shall not permit maintenance of vacancies to await higher income tenants where lower income tenants are available." HUD took this vague guidance and produced new rules in August 1975, but an outside study by the General Accounting Office (GAO) in 1979 found that few housing authorities had made much effort to implement changes in tenant selection. Despite the law and HUD regulations, of six large housing authorities surveyed on the eastern seaboard, only New York City had used the new rules to actively admit higher-income families. Local administrators told investigators that few such families applied (though no effort was made to attract them) and that they needed more direction from HUD on exactly how to prioritize applicants. Some were wary of undoing the policies of 1965–67 intended to ensure racial fairness, while others expressed reluctance to make very poor families wait longer than less needy families. Charles Swibel echoed the attitude of many housing authority heads in 1967, when, in responding to criticisms that too many single-parent families had been admitted recently, he commented that these families "are the people who need help most of all. . . . It appears to me that the authority should be seriously castigated if it failed to accommodate them."[54]

But the federal push for economic diversity in projects was short lived. Beginning in 1979, Congress made more and more demands on housing authorities to house the very poor through legislatively mandated "preference" rules. At first, it recommended that those "occupying substandard housing or involuntarily displaced" be given priority. In 1984, those paying more than 50 percent of income were to move to the front of the line. And in 1990, language was added requiring that 70 percent of all vacancies be given to such families, "including the homeless." Any hope of bringing the working class back into public housing had little chance against such preferences, and in most cities public housing continued its slide into welfare housing of last resort.[55]

★   ★   ★

Sorting the many forces that pushed the working class out of projects is complex, but projects did not exist in a market vacuum. Public housing tenants and applicants had agency and were not prisoners. Some were encouraged to leave after breaching income limits and others moved to new cities, but at a fundamental level, the working class left public housing because they were pulled by better options elsewhere. Despite deeply subsidized rents, multi-bedroom apartments, and no heating costs (an important benefit when energy costs spiked across the country), Chicago's projects could not compete with private options for steadily employed working families after 1970. As project reputations eroded under high proportions of welfare tenancy, rising disorder, and poor maintenance, any hope of retaining the working class—or drawing them back in—vanished.

In the 1940s and 1950s, public housing offered the best source of new, decent housing at affordable rent for black Chicagoans. In the private market, African Americans paid higher rents than whites for comparable housing—a racial premium caused by artificial shortages in the discriminatory dual housing market. But by the late 1960s, the black portion of the still divided market had altered considerably. While overt and subtle forms of racial discrimination continued to exist, the boundaries of the black belt had expanded considerably in that decade. A suburban housing boom for whites (fueled in part by FHA programs) combined with racial succession meant that large swaths of the city's housing stock filtered down to the black middle and working classes, improving their housing conditions.[56] Moreover, real wages for the steadily employed rose faster than housing costs during the 1960s, improving affordability. Finally, migration from the South eased in the second half of the decade. The housing shortages of the 1940s and 1950s were a thing of the past for working-class African Americans, and the racial premium in housing evaporated. After an extensive study of 30,000 real estate transactions from 1968 to 1972, Harvard economist Brian J. L. Berry concluded that while housing discrimination remained pervasive, "by 1972, blacks and other minorities were paying less for housing than the white majority" even after controlling for "quality, improvements, incomes, and other neighborhood factors."[57] The filtration pressures were so powerful that widespread abandonment became a problem in black Chicago neighborhoods; the population of Woodlawn and Washington Park shrank by half between 1960 and 1980 as the black working class and middle class moved out of overcrowded and decayed housing and into an expanded black housing market.[58]

This is not to say that the private market had solved the housing problems of low-income African Americans. A discriminatory dual market remained, and slumlords abused tenants, as Martin Luther King's marches in Chicago clearly demonstrated in 1966. The CHA's waiting lists were still clogged with very poor families who paid a high proportion of income for rent. But working-class renters fled public housing—or no longer applied—because the CHA's overall comparative advantage with the private market had dwindled by 1970.

Additional evidence for the CHA's relative decline in the overall housing market can be seen in its waiting list and vacancy data. By the late 1960s, applicants were turning down not only small apartments in undesirable projects but large ones as well. Chronic vacancies at the CHA's high-rises became a constant concern after 1970, even with a lengthy waiting list. African American applicants were specifying individual projects and passing up vacancies under the new admissions rules created in 1967 and amended in

1969. One anonymous, unemployed construction worker, forty-seven years old, with a leg injury and eight children living in a crumbling apartment, turned down vacancies at the Robert Taylor Homes and Cabrini-Green in 1968, observing to the *Chicago Defender*, "There's no point in moving from one slum to another." By 1971, he had spent three years on the waiting list holding out for a low-rise unit in a "good" neighborhood. Apartments on upper floors of the CHA's high-rises went begging while smaller low-rise projects built on vacant land had waiting lists of several years.[59]

Consequently, the CHA resorted to desperate measures to fill its undesirable projects. In 1972, with welfare families already comprising 55 percent of all tenants, it sent letters to 70,000 public-aid recipients in the city in an effort to fill the estimated 750 vacancies at Cabrini and Taylor alone. "Not only lower rents but increased security make public housing more attractive than ever," the CHA mailing read. Caseworkers resented the solicitation, telling a reporter, "We're aware that CHA, especially the high-rises, are pretty detrimental housing."[60] Still, with lower rents and larger apartments, public housing represented the best economic deal for many welfare families. While welfare-dependent families had the fewest options and hence were the most likely to turn to the CHA, working-class African American applicants elected to wait for a handful of desirable projects or to reject public housing altogether, despite its promise of substantially lower rents.

★   ★   ★

The exodus of the working class deepened an already serious fiscal crisis, but the CHA, HUD, and Congress danced around issues more than they confronted them. From the CHA's perspective, options were grim. The Brooke Amendments precluded raising rents, and reducing operating expenses involved laying off employees. But youth-driven vandalism and crime meant housing authorities needed more, not fewer, maintenance, security, and maintenance staff. Further, efforts to redress the CHA's long-recognized maintenance inefficiencies required tackling the CHA's powerful unions, a political nonstarter.

Since raising rents or lowering expenses was onerous, the CHA, like most other housing authorities, petitioned Washington for more funds. Public housing's main lobbying organization, NAHRO, pleaded with members of Congress, beginning in 1964.[61] Congress, however, was preoccupied in the late 1960s with Great Society legislation and the Vietnam War; little oversight of existing programs took place. Instead, the Johnson administration, reflecting the increasing disillusionment with traditional funding of public housing, created new programs that moved away from the local authority model and embraced private builders. Federally subsidized loans were offered to developers through the FHA to build privately owned housing subject to federal rent and income guidelines. The experimental Section 23 leasing program in 1965 gave funds to local housing authorities to subsidize rent in privately owned housing for low-income families, a prelude to the tenant-based programs later enacted as part of Section 8 of the 1974 Housing Act. In the wake of Martin Luther King's assassination and the alarming riots that followed, Congress passed the 1968 Housing Act to authorize vast amounts of new subsidized housing, including additional public housing on the same terms as the 1937 Housing Act, even as that model was on the verge of fiscal disaster. Congress did initiate reforms, including the "turnkey" approach, where private developers built projects and handed over the finished buildings to housing authorities. But housing authorities were still expected to maintain the buildings using income-based rents, an increasing impossibility by 1968. These reforms and alternatives sent construction soaring, and the nation's stock of subsidized housing rose from 891,000 units in 1970 to 1,389,000 by 1973, a 55 percent increase.[62]

Nonetheless, HUD recognized the crisis in existing public housing projects and devised new initiatives. In 1967, the agency's modernization program offered grants to local housing authorities to improve public housing conditions, including upgrades and replacements. Reserves were intended to pay for these improvements, but as these funds were drained to pay for operating deficits, Washington assumed the responsibility. As its first modernization grant, the CHA received $27 million for replacing trash systems, upgrading electrical systems, installing new security measures, and building additional community centers. These funds went mostly to the large, youth-filled, high-rise projects less than a decade old. The amount represented a major infusion of funds at a time when the entire CHA annual budget totaled only $32 million, and it demonstrated HUD's grave concern with social disorder at the CHA. Washington hoped to redeem the CHA's most problematic projects, and over the next fifteen years, modernization funds for the CHA totaled $201 million, most used for community centers and major repairs. An additional "special subsidy" arrived in 1968 when Congress authorized HUD to grant $120 per year for each extremely poor or large family with four or more children, the latter an unstated recognition of the effect of youth density on project life.[63] Neither subsidy, however, arrested the exodus of the working class; if anything, they created further incentives to admit more of the deeply poor.

HUD had sent a strong signal that it would bail out the worst projects and continue to subsidize the poorest tenants.

The modernization program of 1967 and the special subsidy of 1968 represented the first unraveling of the fiscal compact of the 1937 Housing Act, but the Brooke Amendments of 1969–72 cemented a disastrous dependency relationship between local housing authorities and Washington. The Brooke Amendments required housing authorities to use income-based rents set at 25 percent of income, but they also authorized HUD to provide additional operating subsidies to offset any lost rental revenue and to "ensure that housing authorities had sufficient funds."[64] Chicago returned to income-based rents in April 1970 (though with a cap to protect the working class), but the new subsidies were slow in coming. Confusion and disagreement over the amendments' implementation in Washington led to five agonizing years of budget uncertainty for housing authorities. At first the Nixon administration judged that no operating subsidies were needed, leaving local authorities starved of funds. After the 1970 Housing Act reaffirmed Brooke's intent, HUD belatedly developed an "interim" funding formula in 1972 for determining how much additional subsidy each housing authority deserved. The interim formula pleased no one. Local authorities found funding to be too low, while HUD abhorred rewarding inefficiency. As one senior HUD administrator confessed to Congress, "The challenge [was] to develop a method that would provide . . . a reasonable level of funding without . . . bailing out housing authorities which were wasting money through poor management."[65]

This intrinsic tension was never resolved. After more years of study and an intensive survey by the Urban Institute, HUD produced the complex Performance Funding System (PFS) in 1975, which keyed subsidies to the operating costs of "well-managed" and "high-performing" housing authorities. Adjustments were made for a host of variables, including general inflation, energy costs, the average age of projects, their average height, and the average number of bedrooms. This last variable was given a heavy weight in the formula, another hint that youth densities played a major role in operating costs. These adjustment factors in the PFS formula should have favored the CHA, but the use of "high-performing" housing authorities as a baseline hurt Chicago materially. The PFS formula made the assumption that "low-performing" authorities such as the CHA were inefficient and that lower subsidies would force them into line. But these penalties did little to spur reform and instead exacerbated the budgetary crisis and accelerated project decline. In their defense, NAHRO argued that low-performing housing authorities suffered from disproportionately poor

tenants, not weak management ability. In reality, the CHA was both demonstrably inefficient and, by the early 1970s, burdened with impoverished
tenants. Rather than face these facts head on, the CHA persistently complained about the PFS formula and continually resisted internal reform.[66]

Despite tension between housing authorities and Washington over the
PFS formula, operating subsidies exploded. Nationwide, outlays for operating subsidies ballooned from $28 million in 1970 to $535 million in 1976
to $1.3 billion in 1984.[67] Much of this increase was generated by a rapid rise
in energy costs in 1973 and again in 1979.[68] From public housing's earliest
days, tenants had not been charged for utilities, and now operating subsidies were used to cover the spike in energy outlays. By 1973, the operating
subsidy represented 50 percent of the CHA's operating expenses, and by
1980 the figure had risen to 70 percent, vastly greater than the annual contribution subsidy.[69] Modernization money also rose rapidly, with Chicago
consistently receiving large grants, including a $21 million award in 1978
just for upgrades at the deteriorating Robert Taylor Homes. This was an
enormous sum for one project, and had the funds been used for replacements and upgrades at the CHA's still viable low-rise projects, they might
have stabilized that vital portion of its inventory. Instead, Taylor and other
unmanageable projects absorbed a disproportionate share of resources,
leaving smaller projects starved for funds to maintain reasonable conditions.

Modernization money, walled off from the annual contribution subsidy
and the PFS-based operating subsidy, involved a different set of regulations,
and the CHA struggled to spend the money in a timely manner, resulting
in disillusionment among tenants. Early modernization money granted
in 1968 was earmarked for community centers, playgrounds, and day-care
centers, but as late as 1975 only three-quarters of the initial funds had been
spent, with some tenants waiting six years for promised enhancements.
The $21 million for Taylor, announced in September 1978, was expected to
replace elevator cabs, enclose lobbies, replace kitchen tile, upgrade doors
and light fixtures, and remove graffiti around the project. HUD released
the funds in August 1979, but nearly a year later, in July 1980, the CHA sent
a letter to tenants detailing further delays. By March of 1982, with work
only half complete, the CHA said that the remaining balances would be
better spent on upgrades elsewhere. Moreover, the renovations that were
made often did not last; new gallery lighting systems at Taylor, installed in
the spring of 1982, were largely destroyed by vandals by that fall. A GAO
report in 1983 showed that the CHA had been awarded $138 million in
modernization funds since 1968 but had spent only two-thirds of it.[70]

Despite its ever-increasing cash infusions, HUD could not stem the CHA's budgetary bleeding. In 1978, the CHA received a "special assignment" of $10 million as an "advance" on its next-year's PFS operating subsidy. When next year came, the CHA requested and received an even larger advance. HUD officials during the Carter administration were reluctant to stand up to the CHA and embarrass its well-connected leaders, bowing to Chicago's important role in national Democratic Party politics.[71] These actions, moreover, only fed the CHA's addiction to HUD funds. By May of 1981, the CHA had already spent all of its 1981 annual contribution and operating subsidies as well as a $59.5 million advance on its 1982 subsidy; it appealed to HUD for an additional $49 million "administrative loan," just to survive the remainder of the fiscal year.[72] The CHA's finances by this point were out of control. The authority was entirely insolvent and wholly dependent on the generosity of HUD to continue its operations.

★   ★   ★

The exodus of African American working-class tenants between 1968 and 1974 was a crucial loss for the CHA. It cemented public housing's reputation as welfare housing and turned the CHA's large projects—already isolated racially—into reservations where poor, single mothers endured the indignities of second-class citizenship. Once tagged as welfare housing, and without tools to attract the working class, CHA projects lost the possibility for economic integration. The CHA's data does not reveal a tipping point whereby a certain proportion of welfare tenants sent the remaining working class fleeing. Instead, multiple policy, management, social, and market forces collided to make public housing unattractive to the working class.

The transformation to welfare status by the early 1970s represented the death of public housing from the perspective of the program's authors. In a 1948 letter, Catherine Bauer wrote that limiting public housing to welfare-dependent families "would of course be fatal beyond question, and we'd have to disown the [1937 Housing Act], get it put under the Social Security Board if possible, and try to forget all about it. . . . If even half the tenants had to be relief cases, it would be the final blow."[73] Elizabeth Wood shared Bauer's apprehension that public housing nationwide was drifting toward welfare status as working families slowly rejected it. In a 1960 letter solicited by Eisenhower administration officials, she didn't mince words: "If the public housers have not recognized that public housing has been operated like public assistance, the American public has. The reluctance of eligible families that are normal in their economic aspirations and their earning power to accept housing under these terms is well documented. As they have rejected it, it has been turned over in increasing proportions to a veritable welfare constituency. . . . [Public housing] has become in actuality a public welfare program." Under these parameters, she declared that public housing "cannot—perhaps should not—survive as a housing program."[74]

The way out of this quandary, however, was less than clear. Once projects lost the working class, became deeply impoverished, and experienced physical deterioration, reversing decline became exceptionally difficult. Recovering from this disastrous tailspin required a rethinking of public housing's progressive mission and a deliberate turning away from helping those most in need. Administrators made that painful choice in the late 1950s by prioritizing the working class, but by the late 1960s, the political climate, not to mention the political activism of the welfare rights movement, had moved in the direction of greater protection of the rights of the very poor.[75] Moreover, bringing the working class back to public housing required more than new admission policies; underlying problems of social disorder, security, and maintenance efficiency needed solutions before families with options would return.

The loss of the working class steered the CHA into fiscal crisis, and its projects could not survive long without adequate resources. Importantly, the new subsidy structure implemented between 1968 and 1975 did not create the fiscal and managerial discipline needed to keep projects afloat. Despite sending hundreds of millions of dollars, HUD could not revive or make viable the CHA's poorly conceived and inefficiently managed high-rise projects. Their downward spiral mirrored the problems of insolvent buildings everywhere: once income failed to meet expenses, once vacancies piled up, once deferred maintenance rotted buildings, then only radical changes could save them. Demanding such changes, CHA residents sparked a tenant revolt beginning in 1970 and attempted to take control of their housing.

The Tenants Revolt

8

The market-failure ideology that shaped the worldview of public housing advocates in the 1930s encompassed not only the production of rental housing but also its ongoing management. Reformers generally viewed private landlords in low-income neighborhoods as unscrupulous actors who neglected maintenance in order to profit from slum conditions. Public housing would be different, managed with public values and run by trained administrators as a nonprofit, independent, public utility for the benefit of tenants. This direction and public-spiritedness would, reformers expected, allow projects to remain in good shape over their expected sixty-year life span. Enlightened managers would ensure order and careful upkeep, while tenants would participate as dutiful partners in policing social space, creating social activities, and building community in general.

But by 1970 this vision lay in shambles, and tenants were up in arms. At housing authorities across the country, residents revolted in protest against poor maintenance, inadequate security, and the general indifference of aloof housing authority board members, most of them white power brokers with little understanding of poverty. Tenants demanded real control over their communities, and President Johnson's War on Poverty created a bureaucratic outlet for their anger. In Chicago, frustration was directed at CHA chairman Charles Swibel, who continued to be appointed by Mayor Daley despite budgetary and managerial turmoil. Yet protest and activism produced scant gains in the 1970s. Despite intense effort, Chicago tenants won little leverage over resources, and most policy continued to be effected without their input. The CHA remained immune to reform, and its residents were left to struggle in increasingly dangerous and dispiriting conditions.

★   ★   ★

Before 1970, residents' voices in policymaking at the CHA were limited. Tenant councils, originating in the Elizabeth Wood era to build community and help with social control, had declined after her departure. By 1958, only 40 percent of projects had active tenant councils.[1] As seen earlier, women at the Robert Taylor Homes organized in 1964 to confront the project's management, demanding more security and social order. Two years later, a new group, Taylor Residents United, pressed for resident empowerment and insisted on being recognized as the representative of tenant interests, especially in eviction proceedings. Similarly, the Together One Community went door-to-door at the ABLA project in 1965 in an effort to form a tenants' union.[2] Radicalism germinated earlier and more rapidly in other cities, including St. Louis, Baltimore, and Newark, where public housing tenants actively clashed with housing authority management between 1965 and 1970 over conditions and rental policies, culminating in lengthy rent strikes that laid bare their rage at their powerlessness. Out of these actions emerged a national tenants' rights movement that called for transference of control of public housing to its residents.[3]

In Chicago, the tenant movement exploded in 1970, driven by the examples of other cities, the broader radicalization of African American politics, the deterioration of project life, and the CHA's handling of federal modernization funds. The Johnson administration's War on Poverty expected federal officials to include the "maximum feasible participation" of the poor in establishing priorities, and HUD applied the idea to the modernization program, requiring housing authorities to survey tenants before submitting their application for funds. Here was a chance for residents to be heard, but the CHA made only a cursory effort at soliciting tenant input. Even so, the responses to a 1968 survey were indicative of residents' daily fears. Tenants put vandalism, security, and the need for community centers for youth at the top of the list, reflecting the ongoing problems of the CHA's high youth densities. With this input, the CHA authored a $27 million modernization application in 1968 that included $8.3 million for new community buildings and day-care centers at twenty-five of its thirty-four projects. But more than half of the funds were targeted for routine maintenance upgrades and replacements, mostly the kind of work usually funded from the operating budget or the reserve account, and had little immediate bearing on tenant lives. Electrical wiring upgrades accounted for almost $7 million and closet doors—omitted in the 1950s as a PHA cost-cutting measure—were $4.2 million. Had the CHA been more efficient, much of this work could have been accomplished without modernization money.[4]

The lack of real control over modernization funds, as promised by the War on Poverty, spurred African American activists associated with the Committee of United People to join with legal aid lawyers to contest the CHA's leadership and its priorities. They formed the Chicago Housing Tenants Organization (CHTO) in 1970 as a CHA-wide group, though the bulk of members came from the 3,400-unit ABLA complex on the Near West Side. Beginning in the summer, the CHTO initiated a concerted campaign to confront the CHA and HUD and other housing officials in an effort to make their voices heard. In a hard fought, twelve-month campaign, the CHTO nearly succeeded in winning power.

The CHTO began systematic protests in the summer of 1970 with picketing at the CHA's central office to demand security guards for all elevators in high-rise buildings. After two policemen were gunned down at Cabrini, shocking the city and the nation, the Reverend Jesse Jackson and the Peoples Organization of Cabrini Green—a tenant group affiliated with CHTO—met with HUD secretary and former Michigan governor George Romney and requested condominium ownership of the project by tenants, supported with CHA funds, and more social programs. They asked that all high-rises have day-care centers and recreation halls and that "the people of the area will be entrusted with shaping stimulants for employment and other types of economic development proposals." They wanted the hiring of security guards independent of the CHA and demanded guards in every elevator. Much of the focus was on jobs, as Jackson explained in the *Chicago Defender*: "Black men who live in Cabrini-

Green should be able to work in their neighborhood, or just across the river . . . in Montgomery Wards or at National Tea. They should expect to be hired in those billion dollar companies not as stock boys but as truck drivers, fork-lift operators, mechanical craftsman and, yes, as Executives." He asked that the CHA and residents "move in concert to transform this patchquilt of ghettos and canyons of fear into a city of brotherhood and justice." While the CHA instituted more security at Cabrini, using "vertical patrols" of police officers at considerable expense, action on power sharing or employment opportunity never got off the ground.[5]

Jackson's meeting with Romney, however, did make HUD officials more sympathetic to tenants and more distrustful of the CHA, a stance that infuriated Swibel. On August 17, HUD agreed to investigate CHTO complaints that the CHA was not allowing sufficient participation of residents in the allocation of modernization money. Shortly thereafter, the CHTO invaded the CHA boardroom, turning the August 27 board meeting into a "chaotic shouting match." Incensed and belligerent tenants informed the board about appalling conditions and inaction by management on basic maintenance issues. Brooks Homes tenant Louise Brownlow described her exasperation: "We were wearing rubber boots in the basement and water was backing up into our apartments. . . . The only way we got those sewerage pipes [unblocked] was because me and some more of these citizens got a rat and put it in a fruit jar, plus pictures of violations, and carried it down and put it on the Mayor's desk." Continuing, Brownlow demanded the CHTO be given "full control" over $27 million in modernization money, which "will be spent for what we want, not for what CHA wants. . . . If we want wall-to-wall carpeting, we get it." She railed that the CHA could no longer be trusted and did not have the interests of tenants in mind: "The money all down through the years has been spent for what CHA wants and we've been having plaster falling down on us. All last winter we had people with no heat in that sub-zero weather. We got 135 city code violations and brought them right here in this room and laid them on this table."[6] By 1970, a clear disconnect had emerged between reports of millions in modernization funds from HUD and CHA conditions on the ground. As with the American public's loss of faith in the government reporting of the Vietnam War, CHA tenants no longer believed what project managers told them.

Tenants wanted respect but also a share of power. One tenant told Swibel, "I don't know how tall the Sherman Hotel [a hotel frequented by Swibel and city politicians] or any of them are, but I'd like to have the same kind of service they have because I bleed red blood like they do. This is what I want: I want the same type of service, it doesn't make any difference what it costs. I live in the U.S. and I think I have a right to live as well as Mr. Swibel. That's what I want, and we'll go to HUD with you to get this money [to renovate public housing]."[7] But the board had little patience with confrontational tactics, and the chasm between tenants and the commissioners widened. Swibel opened the August board meeting with a condescending speech that claimed credit for winning the modernization money and maintained that tenants had already been consulted on how to use the money, a vague reference to the 1968 tenant survey. The African American members of the board, brought into Swibel's orbit and allied with Daley, betrayed their lack of regard for the protesters. Earlier, CHTO members had ambushed board member Letitia Nevill, a forty-three-year-old mother and tenant appointed to the board by Daley in 1969, at a meeting at ABLA, demanding more security. At the next closed session of the board, Nevill vented that tenants should "leave the television or whatever else they were doing and go so see what their teenagers were doing at night. . . . [I]f they were more involved with their families they could alleviate a lot of their own problems because we didn't create the problems, they created the problems." Theophilus Mann concurred, and the aggressive demands of tenants received a cold response from the board.[8]

Swibel had no intention of being politically outmaneuvered by tenant activists or by HUD. In an obvious effort to co-opt the issue of tenant input, he created the Central Advisory Council (CAC) with thirty-six tenants selected by CHA staff, mostly from surviving tenant councils. In a report in the *Chicago Defender*, the CHTO called the new CAC representatives "lackeys" and charged that they had been "bought" by the CHA, which indeed had given them a modest budget. Most CAC representatives felt differently, having been chosen by their projects, even if in ad hoc tenant council elections, and many on the new council had served in leadership positions for years. In a tactical blunder at the September board meeting, the CHTO's legal aid lawyer, who was white, insulted CAC members, most of whom were black, by publicly telling them they were puppets of the CHA board and were "not that far advanced in thinking" when it came to tenant control in public housing. The remark set off an explosive exchange between the two tenant groups that made reconciliation and a united front impossible. The incident also alienated the CHTO's one potential ally on the board, Richard Wade, the lone liberal voice among the Daley appointees. Still, CAC members acknowledged their lack of clear legitimacy and voted to subject themselves to CHA-wide elections in November of 1970, less than two months away.[9] The CHTO, however, objected to the rapid election timetable and appealed to HUD to intervene. The activists needed time to organize and demanded an agreement that spelled out the potential power of any newly elected body. HUD sided with the activists, arguing that the tight timetable jeopardized a "fair and representative election," and ordered the CHA to negotiate with CHTO representatives. The ruling from Washington aggravated Swibel, who initially intended to ignore it and proceed as planned. He told the *Daily News*: "The tenants' organization will not tell us what to do, and HUD cannot dictate to us." But HUD threatened to withhold the CHA's remaining modernization money—$8.7 million out of the original $27 million— until the CHA agreed to postpone the elections and reached an agreement with the CHTO over the status of any future advisory council.[10]

The modernization funds were sorely needed by a cash-strapped CHA. Reluctantly, Swibel postponed the tenant elections and negotiated a memorandum of accord with the CHTO over the powers of the new advisory council. On April 7, 1971, an agreement was reached that appeared at first to be a stunning victory for tenants. A reconstituted CAC, with representatives chosen in projectwide elections, would be an active participant in the budget process for allocating not only federal modernization money, but the annual operating budget as well. The CAC would be allowed to scrutinize and change any CHA budget proposal and have $25,000 at its disposal to hire outside consultants to aid in their review. HUD made clear it would only approve modernization projects on which both the CHA and the CAC agreed.[11] Other areas of management were also affected. Preference in hiring would go to public housing residents "to the greatest extent possible," minority enterprises would receive preference in contracts, and individual building councils, the smallest jurisdiction of tenant government, could file "charges of mismanagement or incompetence" against CHA employees.[12]

The CHTO was not entirely satisfied since it wanted full control over the CHA budget, the right to hire and fire project managers, and the right to name new members to the board—so it called the agreement a "partial victory for tenants."[13] But the agreement should have marked a substantial shift in power at the CHA. The new structure gave tenants a role in decision making unheard of in private housing management and radical even by War on Poverty standards. In signing the agreement, the CHA won some peace with HUD and the release of much needed funds, but a new layer of oversight was added that had the potential to burden management. The upstart CHTO had challenged Charles Swibel and seemingly

won. Its aggressive, confrontational tactics had resulted in major concessions and brought new hope for change among public housing residents.

But the CHTO overestimated its own support and underestimated
both the political machine and Charles Swibel. Change would hinge on
who won the all-important tenant elections to the CAC, now scheduled
for Sunday, July 11, 1971. The election was a complicated affair, with a total
of 258 "precincts"—generally project buildings—selecting 843 tenant representatives, who, in turn would be organized into nineteen local advisory
councils (LACs)—roughly one for each CHA project. Each LAC would
then select representatives to serve on the sixty-member Central Advisory
Council. The CHTO launched a campaign to win a majority on the new
CAC, holding a "convention" at Malcolm X College to select a slate of
candidates and to adopt forty-eight resolutions calling for even more tenant power in CHA developments. But it struggled to recruit candidates at
the numerous projects, and only 25 percent of elections were contested,
with 9 percent having no candidate at all.[14]

Immediately following the July 11 elections, CHTO leader Jerome Hunt
claimed outright victory in five projects (Lawndale, Stateway, Dearborn,
Hilliard, and ABLA) and said the CHTO had a "good chance" of controlling the CAC. Hunt, however, lost his own bid to be a tenant representative from Dearborn, blaming the "machine being in CHA and doing its
thing." Within a few days, the CHTO's overly optimistic count of its fol-
lowers became apparent. Leaders of the old CAC claimed its candidates
had won 665 of the 732 positions filled. The various councils selected a
new sixty-person CAC that largely reflected the membership of the old
one. Later, the CAC elected as its president Jack Marlow, a precinct worker
for Cook County Democratic Party chairman George Dunne, signifying
the CAC's nonradical, machine-friendly stance. Swibel gloated over the
election results at the next board meeting. Despite all its work and hope,
the tenants rejected the CHTO's leadership, either because of the "machine" or because they clung to old allegiances, or both. After this crushing defeat, the CHTO lost much of its steam. The next year's elections
generated little enthusiasm and had even more uncontested and unfilled
positions.[15]

While group members continued to attend board meetings to make
their voices heard, the CHTO turned to the courts, hoping for a more hospitable venue to win greater rights for tenants. Legal aid lawyers worked
with the CHTO to sue the CHA over a host of policies, including a more
codified hearing process for tenant eviction, a new lease that gave tenants
more rights, more stringent controls on fines, and better maintenance.

In November 1970, in the midst of the fight over the CAC, legal aid lawyers allied with the CHTO sued in federal court to prevent the eviction of families whose teenage children were engaged in destructive behavior, ranging from ripping out eighty mailboxes to creating small explosives that started a fire and severely burned a boy. Judge Julius Hoffman proved surprisingly sympathetic to the tenants. When the CHA argued that its other tenants had a right to live in safety and that eviction is the best discipline for extreme behavior, Hoffman responded, "We are dealing with the lives of people here. I don't mean to be overly sentimental, but I don't want to be a party to throwing all of these women and children on the street because ultimately they are going to have to be taken care of anyhow. . . . Looking at it very practically, you are going to have to take care of these people. You might as well face up to it." The judge blocked the eviction and ordered the CHA to comply with recent HUD grievance procedures on eviction—a victory for the CHTO and a discouraging loss for project managers.[16]

In 1975 the CHTO sued the CHA over the lack of code enforcement in public housing. The case began when CHA tenants at several Stateway Gardens buildings complained to the city that they "were without heat or hot water continually" during the winter of 1974–75. When legal aid lawyers investigated the relationship between the Department of Buildings and the CHA, they found that the department failed to inspect every CHA high-rise building as required, though when inspectors did do their rounds, they found numerous code violations, including exposed wiring, garbage in public areas, pervasive rodent and vermin infestation, defective incinerators, missing banisters, and damaged walls. Yet, despite hundreds of code violations, city lawyers never dragged the CHA into court to demand compliance. Further, when tenants complained to the city or asked for an inspection, the building department ignored the requests or, at times, forwarded the complaints to the CHA, contrary to its own policies intended to protect tenants from landlord retribution. With overwhelming evidence against it, the CHA and the City of Chicago settled the case, caving to nearly all of the CHTO's demands for reform.[17]

Still, change was fleeting, and code enforcement was no substitute for conscientious and effective management. Building department lawyers and Chicago judges rarely threatened to shut down public housing buildings for fear of throwing hundreds of very poor tenants on the street. Even when reprimanded, the CHA only made superficial repairs sufficient to placate housing court judges. In other cities, courts intervened more forcefully. In Boston, a Massachusetts Superior Court judge in 1979 found the Boston Housing Authority guilty of so many code violations that it forced the BHA into receivership, declaring, that "[i]f the BHA were a private landlord, it surely would have been driven out of business long ago or its board jailed or most likely both." But in Chicago, politically minded local courts were an unlikely venue for such a radical step. Belatedly, city inspectors began a more concerted effort in 1991, and the CHA racked up over 50,000 outstanding code violations. A year later, a federal consent decree was reached to consolidate city lawsuits against the CHA so that one housing court judge could supervise cases. The action did help cut through the backlog, but by 1994 roughly 21,000 violations—often the most serious ones—remained.[18]

Reform was still possible through the newly elected CAC and the 1971 agreement to share power. But the CAC offered little resistance and only occasionally prodded and questioned Swibel through the 1970s, infrequently challenging his authority. Not until 1979, with maintenance reaching new lows during a decade-long budget crisis, did the CAC threaten legal action, with its president, Jack Mayberry, telling the *Chicago Defender* that his group would use "the courts and political pressures to overcome oppressive actions" by the CHA and the city and "elect and punish" political candidates accordingly.[19] But the CAC threat fell short. In 1980, despite CAC opposition, Swibel was again elected chairman of the CHA, this time by a close three-to-two vote, with the deciding vote cast by tenant board member Nevill, then employed by the Chicago Department of Human Services. In a classic version of plantation politics, Nevill knew that her job depended upon her voting for Swibel. The hundred spectators who watched the election in the CHA boardroom erupted in a demonstration against Nevill and Swibel, but they could not alter the outcome.[20] From Swibel's perspective, tenant activism was a nuisance to be managed, not negotiated with. While residents continued to raise their voices at CHA board meetings, which often became heated, the mechanisms for turning frustration into real power never materialized. Lawsuits were blunt clubs and had forced some changes, but such weapons did little to shake Swibel or the board from their fundamental complacency. Instead, the 1971 agreement to share power with tenants allowed Swibel to deflate radical resistance and then co-opt tenant government.

While ineffective in changing policy at the board level, the 1971 agreement did shift the balance of power at the project level between management and tenants. Elected tenant representatives to the LACs now had authority to criticize project managers, who in turn had incentives to keep the elected representatives happy. As a result, new patronage networks developed whereby project managers funneled jobs, program funds, and privileges to LAC representatives, who selectively distributed this limited largesse to tenants. Sociologist Sudhir Venkatesh explored the power of the local advisory council in an ethnography of the Robert Taylor Homes, finding LAC leaders in the 1990s using their limited power to dispense favors where they could. LAC members controlled which apartments received repairs and which tenants were disciplined for various licit and illicit income-earning activities. At times, prostitution and drug rings were protected by LAC members in return for payoffs, as neither the police nor the management would investigate without first receiving a complaint from the elected project representatives. At other times, semi-entrepreneurial activities, like in-home day care or catering businesses, might be squashed by an LAC if a tenant was out of favor.[21]

The delicate balance between landlord and tenant now had a new intermediary, but LAC power did not necessarily mean real reform. In many ways the new LAC regime discouraged broader resident activism while undermining the morale and authority of managers, whose jobs hinged in part on satisfying their new tenant boards. The LACs mimicked local patronage networks in Chicago, where precinct captains and ward bosses determined what services were provided and which businesses were allowed to thrive, but with far fewer resources to distribute. Residents remember this early period of LAC activism as "the Glorious Seventies," but the local councils did little to restore social order and only gave an illusion of tenant power. If anything, the doors were opened for further disorder. As Venkatesh reveals, LAC petty corruption gave way to increasing gang activity in the 1980s, with destructive consequences.[22]

Throughout the 1970s, Richard J. Daley and his machine successor, Michael J. Bilandic (1976–79), reappointed a board that was subservient to Swibel and allowed him to consolidate his power. Neither Nevill, the tenant, nor Wade, the liberal from the University of Chicago, questioned Daley, and both provided the mayor with some immunity from criticism. Wade left for New York in 1971, replaced by an assistant dean from the University of Chicago Law School, Nicholas J. Bosen. By 1973, one reporter who had covered the CHA for years described the board in his unpublished notes as "one tottering old man [Theophilus Mann] fond of chastising his fellow coloreds against getting uppity, a woman CHA resident [Nevill] who has spoken ten words in the two years I have watched her, and Bosen, a lawyer and son of a downstate patronage chief now rising on the Regional Transportation Authority board . . . who enters carrying his *New York Times* and talking about playing tennis at the University of

Figure 29. CHA board meeting, no date, likely 1975 or 1976. From left to right: board members Nicholas Bosen, Theophilus Mann, chairman Charles Swibel, executive director Harry Schneider, board member Letitia Nevill, and deputy director Gus Master. Courtesy of the CHA.

Chicago."[23] This harsh assessment suggests how little interest the board had in standing up to Swibel or tackling the deteriorating conditions, especially in the 1970s. Daley made appointments based on loyalty to him, and those he chose knew that Swibel was in charge.

The tenant activism of the early 1970s did turn the spotlight on Charles Swibel's ethics, mostly in unflattering ways. Swibel had been a lightning rod for the city's reformers since the mid-1960s, with his numerous outside interests and his "power broker" status. The CHA chairmanship did not receive a salary, so Swibel continued to manage a real estate firm, whose skid-row men's hotels were cited with recurring code violations. Swibel defended his properties as "the finest fireproof, sprinklered buildings of their kind in the United States." He also viewed his properties as providing a public service, telling the *Sun-Times* in 1965, "Where in hell else are these men going to live?"[24] Two years later, the heirs of the founder of the real estate firm sued Swibel, claiming he had stolen at least $2 million; he settled the case in 1967 for a reported $900,000. Having a slumlord of dubious character at the helm of the CHA was an affront to reformers.[25]

In 1968 Swibel engineered his most lucrative and most troubling development deal. He partnered with two Tennesseans, Wallace Johnson and Kemmons Wilson of the Holiday Inn chain, to bid for a large urban renewal site at Madison and Canal Streets, just west of the Loop. The two granted Swibel $100,000 a year for ten years, plus a 15 percent interest in the proposed $350 million development with no equity required, in return for his influence with the city. Rumors flew that bids were rigged after the city made its decision to award the site to Swibel's group in a mere seventeen days, a fraction of the time taken for less important sites. But Swibel's role as a partner in the Madison-Canal deal was not revealed until a year later in August 1969 by *Daily News* columnist Mike Royko. A lawsuit to halt the sale was dismissed after Swibel produced a legal opinion from the mayor's office, which found no conflict of interest in his activities.[26]

Other investigations produced much smoke but no fire. In the wake of Watergate, investigative journalists began long probes into city corruption, and between 1973 and 1975, Chicago's Better Government Association (BGA) funded two *Sun-Times* reporters to dig into Swibel's conduct at the CHA. Their work uncovered numerous improprieties but few indictable crimes. One red flag involved the Continental Bank, which received favorable terms on CHA short-term deposits while also serving as Swibel's primary banker, providing him loans and hiring his management firm to run the now bankrupt Marina City complex. But neither HUD nor the GAO, both of which investigated, was willing to condemn Swibel or the bank, so the issue failed to stick.[27]

A more obvious breach of ethics involved Swibel's interference in contracting practices, though his intrusions were small by Chicago standards. In 1968 he accepted a Wells Fargo security system for his suburban Winnetka home just months before the firm received a contract for guard service at CHA projects. Swibel claimed the absence of a bill from Wells Fargo was an oversight, and when it came to light in 1974, he promptly paid the $6,000 Wells Fargo invoice. Ironically, burglars robbed "thousands of dollars" worth of jewels from Swibel's home in 1977. Buck Humphrey, now retired as the CHA's executive director, told BGA investigators that Swibel had "gone around him" to help Wells Fargo get the CHA contract. Humphrey then ticked off a handful of other low-value or minor contracts where Swibel had steered business to city hall favorites at the request of the mayor. Swibel also claimed power in 1967 to move names to the top of the waiting list for elderly housing; a BGA investigation found most to have Jewish last names and some had assets over allowable limits. Humphrey and other CHA employees took notes to protect themselves, preparing for what Humphrey called "the day of reckoning" on Swibel's interference. HUD, however, refused to intervene, and although the BGA considered asking for an indictment, it doubted that a court would convict.[28]

Any one of these malfeasances should have been enough to force Swibel's resignation, had Daley demanded it. But the mayor, three months before his death in 1976, accepted Swibel's rebuttals, saying "there was no proof" that Swibel had enriched himself at taxpayer expense and that the BGA should "investigate itself" rather than tarnish the reputation of "good public servants." Given the intensity of the search for evidence against Swibel by the BGA, the *Sun-Times*, and even the U.S. Attorney's Office, the findings were disappointing to reformers. In the context of the mid-1970s, the claims against Swibel were relatively minor, especially when compared to the indictments secured around the same time by U.S. Attorney Jim Thompson, a Republican, against numerous Daley administration officials and contractors for direct payoffs, land sales, and other more dramatic forms of public corruption.[29] Swibel clearly used his position as CHA chairman to leverage connections in city hall, where he enriched himself in non-CHA business in unethical ways, especially in the Madison-Canal deal. He helped out city hall by steering a handful of contracts to cronies, and he moved his elderly friends into CHA senior housing. But he was careful not to dip his hand directly into the CHA cookie jar.

He was also careful not to turn the CHA into a purely patronage operation, like Chicago's Department of Streets and Sanitation, where jobs were dispensed through city hall. Most political pundits in Chicago have assumed that under Swibel the authority operated similarly, but evidence supporting this claim is thin.[30] Most higher administrators rose through the ranks based on seniority and loyalty to Swibel, not political connections. Gauging the extent of political hiring in lesser administrative positions or maintenance jobs—where unions controlled placements—is more difficult. Despite numerous investigations in the Swibel years, no concrete examples of patronage emerged. In interviews, former CHA administrators vehemently denied that hiring was controlled by city hall during the 1960s and 1970s. This does not mean that merit systems or sound personnel practices were followed, however. Some personnel did come from jobs in other city agencies, perhaps as patronage hires, but interviews suggest that seniority, internal promotion, and insider networks were the most important forces shaping hiring and promotion.[31]

While hiring mechanisms may have been less than transparent, unlike other city agencies their outcome largely benefited African Americans. Under Elizabeth Wood, several blacks served as project managers, but senior administrators were almost exclusively white. At the end of

1955, eighteen months into Kean's tenure, a payroll list indicating race showed that slightly more than half of all administrative employees were black, though whites accounted for 83 percent of high-level administrators. Among the maintenance ranks, jobs were evenly divided between blacks and whites, and 40 percent of maintenance foremen were African American that year. Under Swibel, the proportion of blacks continued to grow. In 1975, the next year of available data, African Americans made up 86 percent of administrative employees and 78 percent of the maintenance workforce, though a more detailed 1980 list shows that among the higher-paying professional roles, blacks held 61 percent of slots. Different conclusions can be read into these data: since 88 percent of CHA tenants were African American in 1975, black representation among CHA staff, especially among professionals, remained proportionately low.[32] As well, the long line of white executive directors descending from the Wood and Kean years meant that the CHA did not gain a black chief until 1983. Still, under Swibel, African Americans had a substantial presence throughout the organization.

This hiring record, however, did not mitigate Swibel's reputation, and the increasing decay of CHA projects rankled the city's press. The *Sun-Times* in 1975 called on Daley to fire the "arrogant and unqualified" Swibel, not just on ethical grounds but also for his general stewardship of the CHA. Daley should appoint "a more compassionate, more visionary housing expert—one who does not trade off the needs of the poor for political favors and who does not operate in an atmosphere of secrecy more befitting of the CIA." The *Chicago Defender* wrote that Swibel was "undoubtedly the most unconscionable and insensitive chairman in the history of the CHA." BGA head J. Terrence Brunner told the *Sun-Times*, "They don't come any sleazier than Swibel." Amid a slew of bad press, Swibel professed martyr status: "If I had done one thing wrong, you know they would have nailed me . . . I just try to survive."[33]

Swibel did survive, through stormy tenant conflicts at board meetings, through budget crises, and through the mayoral terms of Daley, Bilandic, and even Jane Byrne (1979–83), though at first she defied him by appointing to the CHA board Renault Robinson, a police officer and head of the Afro-American Patrolmen's League. Robinson, who formed the league in the late 1960s to challenge brutality and racism within the Chicago Police Department, had a reputation as a maverick reformer. It was Robinson who challenged Swibel for the board chairmanship in 1980, although he fell short. But Byrne, who initially ran against the machine in 1979, quickly reversed course and sought to win over elements of the white machine in a desperate attempt to head off the political ambitions of the State's Attorney, Richard M. Daley. Byrne and her husband soon grew close to Swibel, who became a top political advisor and key fundraiser, even accompanying her on a European tour.[34] Thus, Swibel's power actually grew under Byrne, a demonstration of his capacity to charm Chicago politicians.

All the attention directed at Swibel's ethics and his presumed corruption, however, detracted from his real malfeasance—namely, his appalling stewardship of the CHA. During the 1970s, management failures in the form of maintenance inefficiencies, poorly written contracts, and lax oversight plagued the CHA with underperforming and expensive services. Swibel's claim to the CHA chairmanship was that he was an expert in housing and real estate, yet he could not lead the authority on its most necessary tasks.

Nowhere was this truer than with the CHA's contracts with private elevator repair services. Despite being among its most critical responsibilities, the CHA had limited knowledge of the productivity of the crews that kept its elevators working, and its contracts afforded inadequate control over costs. In 1966, "extraordinary" repairs added 40 percent to routine elevator costs, and by 1975, a federal GAO study found that the bulk of payments to Otis Elevators—$2.2 million of $3.1 million in 1975—went for extraordinary repairs. Chicago's elevator maintenance costs that year were $7.59 per unit per month, 58 percent higher than the New York City Housing Authority's and more than three times Newark's costs.

Fraud was rampant. In 1978 the CHA hired private investigators to watch Otis elevator repairmen and discovered at least twenty mechanics (out of roughly eighty) falsely claiming overtime averaging twenty-five hours per week at $26 per hour. Most mechanics were at home or in neighborhood taverns during the hours they claimed to be working, a waste that amounted to $676,000 a year. The CHA terminated the Otis contract and signed a new one with Westinghouse in 1979, but lack of contract oversight allowed the abuses to continue. A BGA study in 1980 found that 80 percent of the new Westinghouse mechanics formerly worked for Otis at CHA buildings. Mechanics regularly waited until 4:30 in the afternoon or until weekends to begin repairs in order to earn double wages. Further, the BGA claimed that mechanics deliberately failed to perform repairs or sabotaged their work to ensure that return calls would be made. The study concluded that problems had gone on for "at least a decade" and that "the rip-offs at CHA by elevator mechanics are universally known. It is amazing how well known this racket is, and how accepted it is by the industry." For their part, mechanics viewed their work environment as hazardous and saw their corruptions as "battle pay." Whether the money was earned or fleeced, the CHA estimated that six mechanics took home over $60,000 a year in 1979, more than twice the salary of the typical CHA project manager. Senior administrators recognized the problem and tried to put mechanics directly under CHA control at several projects in 1973. But Otis threatened to withhold spare parts, and the union refused to cooperate, claiming it could only enter into collective bargaining agreements with elevator maintenance companies. Without access to parts or current mechanics, the CHA had no recourse, and its attempts at reform were stymied.[35]

Despite this excessive expenditure, the CHA's maintenance chief, Virgil Cross, conceded in 1980 that CHA "elevators don't work 30 percent of the time." The figure had to be guessed because reliable records did not exist, but a spot check in 1982 found over half of the elevators inoperative.[36] Faulty elevators and poor repairs had tragic consequences. In 1980, Reginald Taylor, age twenty, fell to the bottom of an elevator shaft after bumping against the twelfth-floor elevator doors at Darrow Homes during a tussle. An investigation by city building inspectors of work tickets revealed that in the previous six months repairmen had made eighty-five visits and billed 600 hours to repair the elevator involved, including six trips and 25 hours of work on the twelfth-floor door. More important, investigators found that a part designed to keep the 12th-floor door shut was missing at the time of the accident, though just when and how the part came to be missing was unclear.[37] Managers had requested the investigation of the Reginald Taylor death because they had little idea about what was happening with their elevator repairs and could not challenge the explanations given for breakdowns and delays. The problem was a general one: by the early 1970s, the CHA's capacity to manage, oversee, and implement an efficient and above-board contracting system had almost completely eroded.

Other decisions were conceived in a triage mode of management that only made things worse. In 1975 and 1976, the CHA decided to remove windows from vacant units on the upper floors of several high-rise projects and use them to replace broken windows elsewhere. This immediately made the vacant units more costly to repair and rent, and the plywood used to cover the now-empty window openings cracked in winter and offered poor protection from the elements. A 1976 study showed that heat loss due to vacancies and boarded up windows at Robert Taylor amounted to "the output of approximately 100 boilers." When the plywood broke off, vacant units were exposed to Chicago winters, resulting in burst pipes, water damage, and costly plumbing replacements. Taylor was particularly vulnerable, as it was heated with a radiant system of pipes inside concrete floors. When these embedded pipes froze and began to leak, floors needed to be torn up at great expense.[38]

To be sure, not all the CHA's management problems could be laid on Swibel's doorstep. As the problems at Taylor demonstrate, the CHA was also dealing with the design mistakes of the past, including misguided engineering. The vulnerable heating system at Taylor had been selected to cut construction costs, but it had been untried in public housing; at the time of its design, only one other heating plant of its type and size had been built. The system heated water to 400 degrees and kept it in a liquid state with 400 pounds of pressure per square inch to provide radiant heat in Taylor's floors. During construction, two workers were killed when a pipe exploded. These pipes failed repeatedly, leaving residents without heat during winter months. In 1974, after four years of discussion, the twelve-year-old central heating plant was scrapped entirely, and individual heating plants were installed in each building at a cost of $14 million. Ironically, HUD found the money for this replacement from unspent funds from the demolition of the Pruitt-Igoe high-rise project in St. Louis.[39]

Similarly, poorly engineered trash incinerators proved incapable of handling the CHA's waste loads. Trash chutes backed up regularly, often resulting in fires—sixty-five "uncontrolled fires" in 1961 alone—that sent soot into apartments. The incinerators also produced unbearable pollution. The City of Chicago Air Pollution Control Department initially rejected the untested design of incinerators at the Robert Taylor Homes in 1962, but an appeals board overturned the ruling and approved the plans. After ten years of service, the incinerators violated tightened air pollution codes, and in early 1974, the Illinois EPA filed a complaint, telling the CHA to remove four hundred incinerators at twenty-one projects at a cost of roughly $8 million. Further, failing trash systems brought vermin into projects, an epidemic problem. The 1958 federal report noted rat, roach, and bed bug (*Cimex lectularius*) infestation was "practically universal" throughout the CHA. At Stateway Gardens a year after opening, investigators found every single apartment infested with bed bugs, including the project's model apartment. Infestation, of course, plagued much of the city, but the CHA had a full-time extermination staff of fifteen in the 1960s and still fought a losing war against bugs.[40] Finally, expensive remediation of asbestos and lead-based paint sapped funds, as did enclosing unheated elevator shafts at gallery high-rises to protect them from severe cold and extreme heat. Fixing each of these engineering and design inadequacies left the CHA with fewer resources for security and other quality-of-life maintenance issues for its demoralized residents.[41]

★ ★ ★

The CHA's declining health in the 1970s, both fiscal and managerial, led to nine separate studies by consultants and auditors between 1978 and 1982. Each study told a familiar story, one that had changed little since the 1958 PHA report. The CHA's labor costs remained the highest in the nation because of the continued inefficient use of skilled craftsmen for basic maintenance. Budget and management controls were weak, purchasing and procurement systems were routinely circumvented, and the elevator repair contract siphoned away funds. And HUD had not fulfilled its review responsibilities. Board member Renault Robinson called the eighth report, by the accounting firm of Ernst and Whinney "a devastating picture of an agency out of control." But each study left the remedy up to the CHA and assumed that the authority would reform itself. Instead, efforts at reform took place haltingly, without strong leadership, and without the follow-through needed to reshape an organization afflicted by bureaucratic indifference.[42]

The last major report, completed at the insistence of HUD in January 1982, was the first comprehensive review by federal officials since 1958. It depicted a culture of staggering mismanagement. HUD paid for the study after the CHA had admitted its towering fiscal crisis and begged for a $49 million administrative loan to survive the 1982 fiscal year. As a condition for a far smaller $16 million loan, the CHA had to cooperate with New York consultant Oscar Newman, the blunt-spoken author of *Defensible Space*. Newman assembled a "study team" of housing experts, spent two months at the CHA, and then painted a grim picture in what became known as the Newman Report. Rejecting outside factors for the CHA's malaise, such as its high-rise designs and its impoverished tenants, Newman pointed directly at senior managers:

> In every area we examined, from finance to maintenance, from administration to outside contracting, from staffing to project management, from purchasing to accounting, the CHA was found to be operating in a state of profound confusion and disarray. No one seems to be minding the store; what's more, no one seems to genuinely care.

Newman also rejected the idea that insufficient budget resources were at the heart of the CHA's problems:

The CHA is not an under-financed, understaffed authority with a lack of funds with which to modernize its aging plant. Quite the contrary: the CHA receives one of the highest per-unit subsidies in the nation; it has one of the highest staff-to-unit ratios; it pays its disproportionately high ratio of skilled craftsmen very handsome wage rates; and it systematically keeps tens of millions of dollars in unused modernization monies earning relatively low interest in local banks.

Newman found that the other studies in the preceding three years had "correctly identified" problems, but, he concluded, "nothing has been done about them to date." The previous studies "assumed that the act of showing the CHA where its problems lay would be enough to prompt the CHA to overhaul its operations and create a more efficient and accountable management." Instead, managerial intransigence and union power explained the inaction. "The problem," Newman stated, "is one of implementation and commitment to the [existing] system."[43]

The CHA's per-unit maintenance costs were double those of Cincinnati, Cleveland, or Milwaukee and were 25 percent higher than New York's. In a comparison, Newman found Chicago used 70 percent more staff to maintain its Horner Homes project than New York did to maintain its similarly designed Vladeck Homes. As in 1946 and 1958, the report blamed jurisdictional issues and the use of high-wage, skilled craftsmen for all work when most repairs required few skills. While other authorities allowed janitors to perform basic maintenance, at the CHA, electricians replaced light bulbs, carpenters fixed doorknobs, and plumbers replaced tap washers. Moreover, repairs were badly backlogged, with the average project having a thousand uncompleted work orders in 1981. Finally, Newman found low morale among maintenance workers, which he identified as an attitude of "who gives a damn, it'll only be broken again tomorrow" among the skilled craftsmen.[44]

In Elizabeth Wood's day, an inefficient maintenance operation was offset by a strong administrative staff. But by 1982, the administrative ranks were anemic. Newman found the problem of hiring qualified personnel had become systemic and debilitating, with "only four or five of CHA's 19 project managers" competent enough to fill their crucial positions. Staff had simply moved up through attrition, "rising through the ranks of the CHA over a 20-year period, without either testing or training." Senior leadership was lacking. The head of management and information systems "has no ledger system, can't do budget or finance adequately, or track any activities under his purview." The chief of maintenance "has no experience in housing management, is a retiree of the Sanitation Department, and . . . is completely unqualified." The CHA's new executive director, Mayor Byrne's twenty-nine-year-old former campaign manager Andrew Mooney, was labeled "smart" but in way over his head. In correspondence, Newman told HUD secretary Samuel Pierce that his team "liked Mooney" and "found him bright and affable." That was hardly enough in the circumstances: "[H]e just doesn't know where to begin and has no experience in assessing whether the remedies being proposed to him are workable—or even whether solutions are actually being implemented." The report found pervasive bureaucratic inertia, lack of ability, and low morale: "The vast majority of staff show no professional quality or are incapable of implementing the changes needed to turn the CHA around." Other factors that might have contributed to the CHA's unsound state—site selection, design, tenant selection, subsidy levels—were all "hindsight" factors or "Monday morning quarterbacking" according to Newman. Instead, the "conscious policies of the present board and senior staff" had created the CHA debacle. Newman concluded that "significant change . . . could not be implemented without the resignation of the current Chairman and the appointment of a new Chairman with independence from the patronage system."[45]

While Newman's claim of "patronage" lacked evidence and was the charge most hotly contested by the CHA, the culpability of Swibel in his organization's gross inefficiency and managerial incompetence was clear. Yet Swibel would not resign the chairmanship; he clung to his power despite intense pressure from Washington. In 1981, even before the Newman Report came out, Reagan appointees at HUD wanted to take a hard line against the CHA and considered the extraordinary step of a federal takeover. But HUD staff deemed the move unrealistic and suggested other options, including a court-appointed receiver, as had been authorized for the Boston Housing Authority in 1979.[46] When the Newman Report came out, even long-time HUD officials were dismayed at the depth of the CHA's management crisis. In January 1982, Philip Winn, HUD's assistant secretary for public housing and a Reagan appointee, traveled to Chicago and met with Mayor Byrne, demanding that she fire the entire board and appoint a blue ribbon commission to oversee a top-to-bottom reorganization of the CHA as outlined in the Newman Report.[47] Moreover, HUD intended to retain Newman as a consultant to ensure compliance with proscribed reforms.

But Swibel and Byrne stalled and mounted a counterattack that soon sent HUD retreating from its demands. The backpedaling began after

Winn exited in February to return to Colorado to run for governor. With his departure, HUD's resolve waned. Regional director Donald Hovde feared a conflict with the CHA might hurt tenants more than it would Swibel. On February 19, after a month of inaction from Byrne, Hovde blinked and reduced HUD's demands to two: the removal of Swibel and the appointment of a "Management Oversight and Review Committee" with less power than the original blue ribbon commission. Byrne at first agreed to the watered-down offer, but then reneged, claiming she lacked the power to fire Swibel. Technically, she was correct. Mayors could not remove commissioners at will under state law; only the ineffectual and barely functioning Illinois State Housing Board had that power. Up until this point, the Newman Report, with its devastating conclusions, was kept private. Seeking new pressure, Hovde released the report on March 18, calling the CHA "a disgrace" in an effort to humiliate Swibel and prompt his resignation.[48]

With the battle now in the open, Swibel and the CHA took a new tack by counterattacking Newman. Mooney called the report "careless and lacking in professional quality" and accused Newman of deliberately overlooking recent CHA reforms in an effort to paint the authority in the worst possible light. Those reforms included payroll cuts, the creation of a new "utility janitor" position for basic maintenance, and improvements in the purchasing operation. Newman, Mooney claimed, wanted "to make the Authority a failure regardless of the situation." Byrne turned up the heat by claiming that the Newman Report was part of a Reagan plot to undermine public housing and end the program. She spent $35,000 in city funds to take out full-page ads in Chicago papers to defend the CHA's performance.[49] Mooney also traveled to Congress to protest the report and received a sympathetic audience in Representative Henry Gonzales, chairman of the House Banking and Housing Committee. Gonzales had been defending housing programs from the Reagan administration's efforts to scale back Great Society programs, and, echoing Byrne, he perceived the Newman Report as one more endeavor to undermine public housing. In a hearing, Gonzalez told Mooney, "I lament very much that you've got a hatchet act in the shape and form of the so-called Newman study." In a change of tune, the *Chicago Tribune* wrote an editorial that expressed mild sympathy with Mooney and the CHA, buying their arguments that Newman had exaggerated the problems. In the "name-calling contest" between Newman and Mooney, the *Tribune* wrote, "both sides are scoring about even, and nobody is looking very good."[50]

In April, still refusing to fire Swibel, Byrne fulfilled Hovde's demand for an oversight committee, to which she named prominent Republicans who also happened to have close ties to city hall. By releasing the list to the press rather than privately to HUD, Byrne made it politically difficult for Hovde to criticize her choices without angering state Republicans. Rather than an oversight committee composed of housing experts, HUD was stuck with a political group with little experience in the details of public housing. Meanwhile, the press grew bewildered as to why Byrne did not simply fire Swibel and name a new chairman. Byrne responded defensively: "If I fire Swibel, who would run the CHA? Do you want an outsider from New York running it? If I let HUD have its way, we would have a New York consultant [Newman] who knows nothing about public housing running it." Further, Byrne felt the media's treatment of Swibel to be "terribly unfair," and Swibel agreed, claiming anti-Semitism was behind the attack on his management.[51]

But Byrne's political position grew more tenuous, as her defense of Swibel won her few friends. She was "getting creamed in the black community," according to Renault Robinson. With an election only a year away, Byrne offered a new compromise to Hovde, who accepted. She would ask the Illinois General Assembly for legislation to make the CHA chairmanship a full-time paid position and to expand the CHA board from five to seven members in an effort to add more experienced members. Swibel, she said, would resign "within 90 days." In return, HUD would end its embargo of CHA funds. The deal offered Swibel the face-saving position of explaining that he could not devote himself to the CHA full-time given the extensive obligations of his real estate business. The claim was surprising, as Swibel had told an interviewer less than a year earlier that public service claimed "99 percent of my time." For HUD, the deal offered an exit from an embarrassing situation, with Byrne and the CHA declaring that HUD's withholding of funds only hurt tenants.[52]

But the final agreement also meant a lost opportunity for real reform. Instead of an outside panel of experts and an overhaul of CHA practices overseen by Newman, HUD won only an inexperienced oversight committee without tenant input and a board still appointed by the mayor. After Swibel's belated exit in July 1982—just within the ninety days promised—Byrne promoted the now thirty-year-old Mooney to the chairmanship and selected two new white commissioners to maintain a white majority. Although she eventually backed down on the board appointments amid outrage among African Americans, the choices earned Byrne further scorn and contributed to her loss in the April 1983 Democratic Party primary to Harold Washington. For his part, Mooney continued to battle HUD officials in 1982 over the Newman Report, refusing to meet with Newman and his team or to accept their recommendations. While Mooney did make a genuine and concerted attempt to implement reforms proposed in earlier studies, the authority continued to be mired in management problems. In November 1982, a nine-month investigation by the FBI determined that six CHA maintenance employees had stolen millions in paint, floor tiles, roofing material, and other supplies for use in their own private painting and remodeling operations.[53] The scandal added yet another black eye to the beleaguered agency.

★   ★   ★

Charles Swibel survived a tenant rebellion, a decade-long budget crisis, and numerous outside investigations, and he fought off a six-month campaign by HUD before finally succumbing. By 1982, his power-broker status, dubious ethics, and inability to improve conditions at the CHA made him a prime media punching bag. During his final crisis, editorial after editorial excoriated his rule. The comment on Chicago's NBC Television was typical: "Charlie Swibel's been disastrous for 20 years, the worst slumlord in the country, lining the pockets of his friends at the expense of the poor." Columnist Mike Royko pointed his readers to a fundamental question about Chicago politics: "With so many thousands of honest and intelligent people around, why does the mayor of Chicago surround herself with characters you wouldn't trust near the everyday silverware?" While he offered no specifics on Swibel's personal gain, Royko observed that "anybody with Swibel's gamey reputation would have to be brilliant just to have remained unconfined this long." WBBM reporter Walter Jacobsen asked why Byrne hadn't fired Swibel in April 1982: "The only answer that I can come up with . . . is the money at the CHA. The $100 million budget that Swibel can control and manipulate for political purposes. It's money that they want to be able to use in the interest of her [upcoming mayoral] campaign."[54] The hyperbole of the charges and the extent to which one man was blamed for bringing down the CHA suggests the depth of frustration in the city.

But the attention focused on Swibel's wheeling and dealing distracted from the real crime at the CHA, and it had little to do with stolen floor tiles or even $6,000 home alarm systems. Swibel tolerated a mediocrity in administration that undermined the CHA's capacity to manage its properties, to deal with the recognizable crises, and to implement reform. He made no effort to address inefficiencies in maintenance, which would have freed up millions of dollars, enhanced the CHA's performance funding score, and improved living conditions for tenants. He never got a handle on the CHA's elevator contracts or its other oversight problems. He put off tenant leaders rather than work with them as partners. He never required systematic recruitment of quality managers and repeatedly dodged consultants' reports of systematic problems. And, as will be seen in the next chapter, he thwarted desegregated scattered-site housing in the city, showing that his true bosses lay in city hall. He had few answers for reversing the CHA's disastrous decline, a leadership failure far more destructive than his ethical lapses.

In turn, focusing too much on the leadership of one man misses the systemic problems of accountability and oversight that plagued the public housing program. As a semi-independent entity, the CHA was removed from political mechanisms that could spur it to respond to its constituents. It could ignore its tenants' complaints without official penalty as it played by different rules, receiving deference from building inspectors and housing court judges. Washington, which held substantial powers given its role in financing the CHA, offered only weak oversight and struggled to effect change from a distance. Timidity, political considerations, and poor leadership trumped effective action. Aggressive tenant organizing offered some hope, but only when coupled with lengthy legal action and HUD pressure to pry reform from a reluctant CHA. Progressives in the 1930s had envisioned autonomous housing authorities staffed by experts and overseen by well-equipped board members appointed by mayors. But by 1980, the CHA's unqualified staff and politically selected commissioners exercised little control and deferred to Swibel. With elections on the line, other city agencies, while patronage-ridden and likely just as inefficient as the CHA, responded to political demands from aldermanic ward bosses for alley paving, new sidewalks, and snow removal. This is not to defend the machine, only to note that a feedback mechanism existed that was absent in the progressive model of a nonpolitical housing authority. Tenants could vote on their LAC representatives in the 1970s, but representatives had little real power beyond petty patronage and lacked the resources to offer significant improvement in project conditions. With tenants unable to elect board members and with HUD unwilling to forcefully step in and demand real reform, accountability withered.

The victims were the CHA's tenants. Broken elevators, noxious trash systems, long waits for basic repairs, and unsafe hallways made project life a struggle, mitigated only by low rents. The CHTO revolt, an attempt to win strong tenant oversight of CHA management, was too weak to overcome the authority of existing tenant leadership as well as Charles

Swibel's political skills. For his part, Swibel oversaw the transformation of the authority's operation from competent if improvident to demonstrably incompetent and extraordinarily inefficient. Progressive reform had come full circle; a program meant to end the unscrupulous landlord instead had became one. Reformers underestimated how political pressures could undermine public values, not only in Chicago but in nearly every major city. Mayors made appointments to housing authority boards based on loyalty rather than expertise, and housing authority bureaucracies grew disconnected from the progressive goals of the program. Federal officials were not immune to pressures, either, so they were reluctant to take aggressive action to restore managerial discipline to the nation's most troubled housing authorities. With diffuse power and little oversight, the CHA was adrift, unwilling to listen to its tenants and unable to come grips with the unraveling of its projects.

The *Gautreaux* Case and the Limits of Judicial Activism

9

Even before Charles Swibel earned the enmity of Chicago reformers in the 1970s, African American activists had joined with public interest lawyers to challenge public housing policy, especially with regard to its location. The CHA's binge of building between 1949 and 1962 cleared acres of the city and produced 18,000 apartments, but the results—mostly monolithic, institutional tower blocks located in black neighborhoods—angered a new generation of liberals, both black and white, who viewed these outcomes as a travesty created by racist public policy. African American–led community groups joined with the American Civil Liberties Union and filed suit in 1966 to block the CHA's site selections, beginning an epic legal battle that guided the course of public housing policy in Chicago and, at times, the nation for the next thirty years.

⋆   ⋆   ⋆

In the 1950s, opposition to the CHA's site selection policies was ineffective, and the relative powerlessness of city liberals continued until 1963, when the CHA returned after a four-year hiatus with a list of projects that again assumed clearance of the black ghetto. One site on the 1963 list was particularly irksome to critics: a small 360-unit project for families at State and Cermak Streets. The site would, in essence, extend the "wall" of public housing along State Street formed by the previous construction of Dearborn Homes (1950), Harold Ickes Homes (1955), Stateway Gardens (1958), and the Robert Taylor Homes (1962). Commissioner Theophilus Mann expressed his disapproval, asking that CHA staff "concentrate on scattered sites. . . . I want no more of these massive developments, like along South State Street. I don't think that is good." To placate Mann, Swibel added a slate of scattered sites within the black belt for 588 units, but he kept the Cermak and State project on his list.

Liberal voices, both black and white, railed against site lists that excluded white areas. Monsignor John J. Egan, the Catholic Church's urban affairs leader, attacked the Cermak and State site as "an extension of the ghetto. . . . To provide safe and sanitary housing is not enough. The County jail does that. We are dealing with families." Even the more pro-growth Metropolitan Housing and Planning Council advised the CHA that it opposed "extending economic and racial segregation in the area," adding that "the effect on the human personality and the quality of living of the entire community is deadly . . . in a program which organizes a community of similar people with similar problems in similar packages, on a large scale."[1]

Amid rising criticism, Swibel delayed action and asked for a report on the State and Cermak site by a handpicked planning firm. A month later, the report called the State Street public housing corridor "unfortunate from many viewpoints, particularly with regard to its sheer mass and overall dominance of the neighborhoods within which it is contained," but it still recommended moving forward with the site. Swibel used the report to override objections and pushed the project through the board. Mann voted no and offered a prediction: "I am not interested in blocking anything, but I was against this project from the beginning, and my first objection still stands. We have extended this ghetto too far, and I think it is going to have repercussions when I am gone. I think someone will come out and spit on my grave because I should have done something." Swibel, however, defended the CHA's ghetto projects. Looking out from CHA

Figure 30. Mayor Daley with a model of Hilliard Homes, 1964. From left to right: Alvin Rose, Bertrand Goldberg, Theophilus Mann, Richard J. Daley, John Fugard, John Masse, Charles Swibel. Courtesy of the CHA.

headquarters, which sat near the site in question, he pointed to the State Street corridor and proclaimed, "What did we see when we looked south ten years ago—the worst slums—but they are not there now."[2]

To placate critics of its oppressive designs, the CHA hired architect Bertrand Goldberg, designer of Swibel's popular Marina City towers, to produce a fresh look for the State and Cermak project, eventually named Hilliard Homes after Cook County's long-time welfare director. Goldberg departed from the rigid Miesian modernism of the 1959 projects and produced rounded forms, though his twenty-two-story family towers still packed large apartments and numerous children into elevator buildings. The CHA had little choice but to build high-rises at the site, as Kennedy administration housing officials had persisted with the Truman and Eisenhower practice of imposing strict limits on total development cost.

Critics lost the battle to block an extension of the "wall," but the effort drew attention to the charade that had played out since the mid-1950s. For its 1965 site proposals, the CHA submitted racially balanced lists to Chicago's new Development and Planning Department where commissioner John Duba, a close Daley ally, reviewed the sites, contacted affected aldermen, and whittled away until only one site for family housing in a white area remained (white sites for senior housing generally survived). The pared-down list then moved to the city council for a hearing, where the remaining white site was quickly struck, leaving the 1965 list, like those of the previous fifteen years, without any locations for family housing in white areas. The practice begun under Kean's directorship of deferring to aldermanic privilege was refined into a scripted play that allowed the authority to claim a clean conscience but in reality made it complicit in the city's racially discriminatory selection practices. In a 1967 interview, Swibel explained his thinking on sites, recalling a meeting with the NAACP a decade earlier, when African American leaders had sought to prevent any more public housing in the ghetto. "I asked the [NAACP] woman, specifically, whether . . . she was not more interested in making sure that the people who needed housing would get decent housing than in worrying about where the sites are. . . . [S]he said she would rather see that we not build any more public housing and let the people stay in the slums. I think that made such an impression on me—that a do-gooder, in my opinion, as I rightfully refer to them, felt that it was more important to worry about integration than to get the people out of basements and rat infested apartments. I just couldn't see it."[3]

The 1965 site list did not sit well with Harold Baron, an Urban League leader and organizer of the West Side Federation, a collection of fifty-three mostly African American community and neighborhood groups. Baron composed a four-page complaint to Robert Weaver, administrator of the Housing and Home Finance Agency, author of *The Negro Ghetto*, and now the top-ranking African American in the U.S. government. The West Side Federation asked that Weaver not approve the CHA's 1965 sites because the obvious racial factors in their selection meant they violated both the Kennedy administration's 1962 executive order forbidding housing discrimination and the 1964 Civil Rights Act, whose Title VI prohibited discrimination in any program receiving federal money.[4] The letter arrived in HHFA offices at a propitious time. Legislation had just passed Congress to transform the HHFA into the Department of Housing and Urban Development and elevate it to cabinet status. Weaver was in line to be the first African American cabinet member, but President Johnson was under pressure from southern senators and the U.S. Conference of Mayors to reject Weaver and appoint a white mayor to head the new department. Richard J. Daley was the conference's inside choice, according to the *Chicago Sun-Times*. On September 9, 1965, Johnson snubbed Weaver at the signing of the bill creating HUD, and five days later, with rumors of Johnson's interest in Daley for the HUD job circulating in Washington, Weaver chose to pursue the West Side Federation's complaint. Washington insiders suggested the decision had been motivated by Weaver's desire to embarrass Daley and head off his appointment.[5]

But this speculation was likely off the mark. Weaver desperately wanted the cabinet position, and he needed Johnson's support and Senate confirmation to get it. Two years earlier Weaver's agency had responded favorably to complaints from activists and blocked the CHA's discriminatory "neighborhood proximity rule" for selecting tenants for senior housing. But this time, the federal government sided with the CHA and against the West Side Federation. Weaver's subordinate, PHA commissioner Marie McGuire, a Kennedy appointee and former executive director of the San Antonio Housing Authority, wrote the response and rejected the argument that CHA policy amounted to discrimination, noting that 93 percent of family applicants on the CHA's waiting list were black and that 94 percent indicated a preference to live on the South Side or the West Side: "It is apparent, then, that the group of sites submitted by the CHA corresponds to the demand for locations expressed by eligible applicants." But McGuire went further and commented that her office had no interest in tackling the city council's racial vetoes: "We are also advised that sites other than in the south or west side, if proposed for regular family housing, invariably encounter sufficient objection in the City Council to preclude Council approval." Unwilling to challenge this political interference, McGuire's letter closed with the argument that half a loaf was better than none: "Disapproval of the sites by the PHA would be tantamount to an arbitrary denial of [public housing] to the thousands of low-income families waiting for it in Chicago." McGuire's view on the "acceptability" of sites reflected the long aversion of career PHA officials (who drafted the letter) to interfering in site selection except on technical grounds. Local control had been a mantra of the program from its earliest days, and blocking sites, it assumed, would only generate congressional antipathy that might also harm Weaver's chances at becoming HUD secretary. Other bureaucratic impulses may have been in play as well: rejecting the CHA's sites would make it difficult for the PHA to use up its 35,000-unit authorization for the year, a goal that it had struggled to attain since the late 1950s because of waning interest from local housing authorities.[6]

McGuire's letter later became crucial evidence in proving the federal government's complicity in the CHA's discriminatory site choices, but, more important, it spurred Urban League leader Baron to seek legal counsel. He was dismayed by the implications of McGuire's logic, which suggested that any decision by a locally elected body could trump Title VI of the Civil Rights Act. Baron was introduced to Alexander Polikoff, a Chicago corporate attorney, who agreed to take on the CHA with a team of ACLU lawyers. On August 9, 1966, Polikoff filed two class action suits, one against the CHA and the other against HUD, on behalf of CHA tenants and those on its waiting lists. Using the logic of the litigation over school desegregation since the *Brown v. Board of Education* decision in 1954, the suits charged that the two agencies had violated the 1964 Civil Rights Act and the Fourteenth Amendment's equal protection clause by limiting public housing sites to the ghetto. The lead plaintiff was Dorothy Gautreaux, a Dearborn Homes resident and African American neighborhood activist who had worked with the Urban League for many years. Polikoff considered suing the Chicago City Council as well but discarded the idea because the aldermen would have to be sued individually. The distinction was material. Throughout the subsequent legal battles, the CHA's lawyers argued that the city council was the institution rejecting sites in white areas, not the CHA board. Polikoff knew he had a strong case for proving that public housing's statistical outcomes had the effect of discrimination but proving intent by the CHA appeared an uphill battle.

Gautreaux v. Chicago Housing Authority (the plaintiff's name was pronounced both *gah-tro'* and *gow'-tro* by various parties) became a thirty-year legal odyssey for Polikoff, the CHA, and the federal judiciary.[7] The case at first seemed tenuous. The randomly assigned federal judge was Richard B. Austin, a former prosecutor, state court judge, and, in 1958, the losing Democratic candidate for Illinois governor. Polikoff was wary of Austin, believing him a friend of Daley's. In their first encounter, Austin remarked to Polikoff, "Where do you want to put 'em [CHA projects]? On Lake Shore Drive?"[8] But Austin in fact had a complicated past with the mayor and the Democratic Party machine. The party put him on the ticket for governor only after its first candidate, Cook County treasurer Herbert Paschen, was caught with a suspicious "flower fund" in his office. Daley dumped Paschen and replaced him with Austin, then a relatively obscure Chicago Superior Court judge. Many believed that Daley "trimmed" party support for Austin and handed the election to incumbent Republican governor Stratton in return for Stratton's continued support of city interests. Chicago insiders then speculated that Austin might use the *Gautreaux* litigation to pay back the machine, especially when he rejected the CHA's attempts to dismiss the case and granted Polikoff's request to comb through the CHA's files for evidence of discriminatory intent in site selection.[9]

A year into the litigation both sides began searching for a settlement. The CHA's long-time chief counsel, Kay Kula, first hired by Elizabeth Wood in 1950, worried that Polikoff had uncovered evidence about the CHA's close contact with city hall in choosing sites that gave the strong appearance of collusion with the aldermen. As well, she knew that Polikoff could expose the CHA's racial steering that kept African Americans out of four all-white family projects, including one in the mayor's neighborhood of Bridgeport. But Polikoff was also unsure of his case, and a trial meant uncertainty. Austin had ruled that he needed to prove intent, not just de facto segregation, to meet the court's discrimination standard. Plenty of evidence indicated that the CHA had proposed sites in white areas throughout the period, only to have the council exclude them.[10] Since Polikoff was suing the CHA and not the aldermen, he had to make the case that the CHA's excessive deference meant it had proposed the white sites in bad faith and had abetted the council's preordained decision to reject them.

In settlement talks in December 1967, Polikoff proposed the outlines of a deal that came close to being accepted by both parties. First, he demanded a formula requiring that at least 50 percent of new projects be built in white neighborhoods, divided equally between the city's North Side and the South and Southwest Sides. Until the CHA won sites in white areas, no public housing would be allowed in black neighborhoods. Surprisingly, the CHA suggested it would accept this basic outline, but sticking points emerged. First, the CHA wanted to exempt sites previously selected in 1965 and 1966, many already under development by late 1967. This would mean another 1,400 units in the ghetto before Polikoff's new accounting would begin. At first Polikoff said no, but later he showed a willingness to allow some room for negotiation on how the 1965 and 1966 sites would be counted.[11]

Second, Polikoff wanted his deal to apply not only to "regular" public housing but to HUD's new Section 23 program as well, the federal demonstration program providing funds to local housing authorities to lease private apartments as low-income housing. The CHA contracted with landlords to guarantee rental payments, with the tenant contributing 25 percent of his or her income and Section 23 funding the balance. For their part, landlords had to provide decent apartments but retained the right to reject prospective tenants, though not on the grounds of race. In its early practice, the CHA did not enforce the antidiscrimination clause in its eagerness to find landlords willing to participate, and it also privileged the elderly: the bulk of the Section 23 apartments—397 out of 463 units in 1967—went to elderly white tenants. That same year, Swibel negotiated with three black neighborhood groups to use 900 Section 23 program units to guarantee rent in rehabilitated buildings on the South and West Sides. But Polikoff saw the move as furthering the ghetto and wanted to include the 900 units in his settlement formula so that half would be forced outside of black areas. Further, and more significantly, he demanded that landlords not be allowed to refuse any applicant. In essence he wanted to use Section 23 to begin introducing low-income black families into white neighborhoods.[12]

The Section 23 program was ready-made for controlled integration. The CHA, however, would not agree to include it in the discussion, nor would it support forcing tenants on landlords. Its response laid bare the CHA's timidity on using its power to open up white neighborhoods to black occupancy. It argued that landlords would never participate without a veto over tenant selection. Swibel wrote to Polikoff:

> The CHA knows that it cannot find and rent anywhere near 900 apartments for families in white neighborhoods. In many of the white neighborhoods there are few multi-family buildings; the program is a voluntary one and only landlords who have a vacancy problem are willing to bring their buildings into the program. . . . [O]wners of standard multi-family buildings which are located in white neighborhoods do not need CHA and will not lease to CHA. This is borne out by all experience to date.[13]

Swibel's letter was disingenuous—Chicago's white neighborhoods, even in the bungalow belts, had plenty of apartment buildings—but landlord intransigence on issues of race were real. Disagreement over the Section 23 program and how to count the 1965 and 1966 sites led the CHA to break off settlement talks on February 6, 1968; both sides placed the case in the hands of Judge Austin.

This early sparring revealed the chasms between Polikoff's worldview and the CHA's. Polikoff, affected by rioting in the 1960s and the subsequent Kerner Commission report of 1968 warning of the nation's profound racial divides, wanted to get African Americans out of the ghetto and into white neighborhoods to reverse the social and economic effects of ghettoization. He did not see any value in clearing more slums; indeed, the entire slum clearance agenda was discredited in his view because it reinforced the ghetto and produced inhuman projects like the Robert Taylor Homes. In many ways, his was a more radical stance than the fair housing agenda of the mid-1960s. Instead of focusing on the rights of middle-class African Americans to become suburban homeowners, Polikoff sought to move the black poor affirmatively into white neighborhoods using both Section 23 units and a reformed public housing program that emphasized "scattered-site" rental apartments and vernacular designs.[14]

For its part, the CHA portrayed itself during the litigation as a powerless enterprise at the mercy of the city council and the federal government. In one of its court briefs, the CHA demurred: "The main point is that while CHA can propose [sites], only the Chicago City Council can dispose." Further, the CHA claimed: "If most, if not all, public housing were in the ghetto, it may be due to a State law which required that CHA's public housing program 'facilitate slum clearance, rehabilitation and redevelopment.'"[15] The CHA had sunk to a spurious logic that equated slums with the ghetto and suggested that council approval and its slum clearance mission justified sites *exclusively* in black neighborhoods. It had little interest in the kind of crusade Polikoff was suggesting, which the board and staff viewed as a self-destructive effort that would likely mean the end of any more public housing.

On February 10, 1969, Austin handed Polikoff a victory, ruling that the CHA had violated the Fourteenth Amendment's equal protection clause and intentionally discriminated in both site selection and tenant selection. He avoided the more subtle legal debates and, siding with Polikoff, saw discriminatory intent in public housing's outcomes:

> It is incredible that this dismal prospect of an all-Negro public housing system in all-Negro areas came about without the persistent application of a deliberate policy to confine public housing to all Negro or immediately adjacent changing areas.

Austin further held that by informally submitting sites in 1965 and 1966, the CHA was complicit in the city council's veto power and "deprived opponents of those policies an opportunity for public debate." Finally, he ruled: "Even if the CHA had not participated in the elimination of white sites, its officials were bound by the Constitution not to exercise CHA's discretion to decide to build upon sites which were chosen by some other agency [City Council] on the basis of race."[16]

From the CHA's perspective, this last element of the ruling was particularly discouraging. It implied that since white sites had been rejected by the city council for racist reasons, the CHA should have refused to build any housing, an opinion that would have essentially shut down new construction after 1949. Though the CHA had made some effort to win vacant sites outside the ghetto during the Kean years, it had lost that battle and believed it had little choice but to proceed with sites made available, despite the council's discriminatory actions. The judge essentially labeled the CHA's entire postwar public housing program a racist violation of the law. The ruling was the first case in the country in which a local housing authority was found guilty of discriminatory site selection practices.[17]

Austin left the remedy for correcting past discrimination to further negotiation. During the next five months, Polikoff and the court solicited views of outside planners, academics, and federal agencies, though not the tenants themselves. Washington provided little help, and the CHA proposed a vague court order, one that merely prohibited it from discriminating without defining any ratios of sites in white and black areas. If a map had to be drawn, the CHA wanted Polikoff's definition of "white" neighborhoods watered down so that sites in racially transitioning areas would be available. Above all, the CHA feared that too stringent an order would create a political backlash that would make future construction impossible. Richard Wade, newly appointed to the CHA board, made the case that forcing public housing into white neighborhoods was "an open invitation to block-busting on a grand scale," since realtors could use proposed sites to pander to white fears and precipitate white flight. With little guidance from the U.S. government or the CHA, Polikoff then ventured into policymaking on his own. He proposed to Austin as a first principle that the court not allow construction in black areas until a significant number of units in white areas were developed.[18]

Austin sided mostly (but not entirely) with Polikoff in July 1969. He allowed the CHA to proceed with the flawed 1965 and 1966 sites, thereby adding another 1,400 units to the ghetto, but the next 700 units had to be built in white areas, using a map that strictly defined permissible locations for both family public housing and Section 23 landlords. The map included a one-mile buffer around the city's black areas to ensure that the CHA would not locate projects in racially transitioning areas. Following this immediate construction in white areas, only one of every four future units could be built in black neighborhoods. Austin allowed that the CHA could satisfy the order by building up to one-third of its new units in suburban Cook County, provided they were made available to CHA residents. On the issue of tenant selection, half the apartments in white areas would go to neighborhood residents, the other half to those on the CHA's wait-

ing list (then 90 percent black), a variation on the "neighborhood proximity rule" shot down by federal officials in 1963. Finally, the court order
prohibited projects of over three stories and greater than 120 units, and it
limited the concentration of projects in any one neighborhood—a repu-
diation of three decades of public housing planning. Polikoff and Austin
hoped that small-scale, scattered-site projects would "break the ice," in
Polikoff's words, in white neighborhoods. The order, later amended and
modified numerous times, restricted the CHA's site selection well into the
next century.[19]

In an unexpected move, the CHA chose not to appeal Austin's decision. After the initial verdict, Kula favored appeal, writing to Swibel that
Polikoff's agenda "would cause a sudden and radical shift in public housing operations and would be largely self-defeating and unworkable. . . .
[It] will impose upon CHA a specific and affirmative role on population
redistribution in Chicago." Kula perfectly understood the issues at stake,
and her pessimistic view of the political climate permeated the CHA's
thinking. But she changed her mind about appealing the case once Austin's order was finalized in July. Austin offered some further leeway, particularly on tenant selection, and Polikoff agreed to exempt some of the
Section 23 units (the ones promised to black community groups). Finally,
Kula feared that an appeal might lose and that HUD would support Austin's order, making future construction uncertain.[20]

* * *

Not appealing Austin's order was one thing; complying with it was another. At first the CHA staff made some effort to find sites in the permissible (white) area, but soon political considerations suffocated any good
intentions. The CHA and the city began eighteen years of bureaucratic
and legalistic delays designed to avoid carrying out the orders of Austin
and two succeeding judges. With the CHA and Mayor Daley rarely giving
an inch, Polikoff trudged his way through what he called the "jungles"
and "bogs" created by the CHA and the court.

The initial delays were the most telling. A year passed before the CHA
found enough scattered sites in white areas for 1,500 units that met HUD's
stringent regulations on cost and planning; then it said it wanted to wait
until it found suburban ones as well before making any site list public.
Kula argued that only the simultaneous selection of sites in the city and
the suburbs could neutralize devastating white flight; white Chicagoans
would not be able to flee the city and find racially exclusive communities if the CHA could somehow win a metropolitan-wide agreement to

scatter public housing. Polikoff did not disagree with the idea of suburban sites but found the CHA's proposal evasive. No suburban sites had even been identified, and only preliminary "discussions" had taken place with a handful of suburban housing authorities. Besides, the suburban authorities faced the same problem as the CHA—namely, local elected officials could easily block plans by refusing to approve the "cooperation agreement" required between the city and local housing authorities under the 1937 Housing Act. The *Sun-Times* called the suburban idea "whistling down a drainpipe," so Polikoff went back to court and asked Austin to force the CHA to submit the HUD-approved sites to the city council.[21]

A new reason for postponement was then advanced: the CHA wanted to hold off on naming its sites for nine months until after city elections in April 1971. Commissioner Wade made the case for further delay in a letter to Austin:

> My judgment is that submission of the sites at the present time would make it the central issue of the upcoming campaign. . . . It would be unfortunate if your historic decision got embroiled in a political contest, where there was not adequate defense of either public housing or your decision. . . . I would not like to see this great opportunity for integrated housing jeopardized by temporary political consideration.[22]

Wade's argument elevated political judgment above justice. Austin spurned Wade's views and once again sided with Polikoff, giving the CHA one month to submit sites to the City Plan Commission, where they would be made public knowledge. Continuing its obstructionist strategy, the CHA appealed the new order all the way to the U.S. Supreme Court, which, on March 4, 1971, refused to hear the case. Swibel and Daley had succeeded in pushing the revelation of sites past the important February Democratic primary but not the April general election.

The next day, the city's newspapers published the entire list, complete with maps. Reaction was fierce. White politicians ranted at Austin, at HUD, and at the CHA, with Frank Kuta, the Democrat incumbent in the Twenty-third Ward, announcing to the *Chicago Tribune* that it would be a "long time before they have any public housing in my ward—I'd rather go to jail first." U.S. representative Roman Pucinski, whose white Northwest Side district received the bulk of the sites, threatened to get Congress to block the Austin plan, declaring the judge was "setting himself up as the housing czar." Pucinski claimed that race was not a factor in his response to Austin's order: "The opposition of residents here . . . is based on the fact that their largest single financial asset is their home. . . . Where public housing comes in, property values go down."[23]

As in the early period of 1948–50, public housing had again moved front and center in Chicago, and whites began beating it back with much the same force as twenty years earlier, albeit with less direct violence. Neither the civil rights movement nor the authority of the courts had weakened white reaction to residential integration; if anything, the events of the 1960s, including King's marches, African American militancy, and court-ordered school integration had intensified the antipathy. As well, the rhetoric from real estate agents, appraisers, and the Federal Housing Administration had trained white Americans to connect housing values with racial homogeneity. Any upsetting of neighborhood social characteristics, whites believed, was sure to be cataclysmic. Soon after the list was released, six hundred people crammed the monthly meeting of the East Side Community Association in the Tenth Ward to hear their alderman and state representative describe the tools at their disposal to resist the CHA in the city council and the courts. "Don't panic . . . fight the proposal intellectually not emotionally," they counseled their constituents. Richard Bonetti, a white South Side homeowner living adjacent to one of the CHA's proposed scattered sites, struggled to contain his temper. He called Mayor Daley and his aldermen to protest the list, and then told a reporter: "We have all our money here [invested in his house]. I could kill for this house."[24]

Mayor Daley's rhetoric did nothing to heal the racial divide. He called the sites "detrimental to all the people of Chicago" and said public housing should be built "where this kind of housing is most needed and accepted," that is, in black neighborhoods. Like Pucinski, he maintained that class, not race, was behind his objection to public housing: "Those who claim that public housing is solely an issue of race ignore the experience of communities, black and white, which have rejected public housing because of economic reasons." Continuing the metropolitan theme developed by the CHA, Daley added after his prepared remarks: "Those who occupy public housing through no fault of their own require many local governmental services and the cost of providing them should not be borne disproportionately by the taxpayers of Chicago."[25] The comment linked public housing with welfare, again pandering to anxieties of whites.

Even the CHA offered only lukewarm support for its own site list. In an accompanying press release, executive director Buck Humphrey noted that "it is premature to speculate which sites will be developed" and that "considerable time could elapse" before development begins. Pointing a finger at Austin, he said the CHA "had no choice" but to release the sites and that the CHA "still believes that public identification of these sites is unwise until suitable sites have been identified in suburban communities to put the housing program on a metropolitan-wide basis." The CHA planned to put a better face on the list's release and hired a public relations firm to develop a campaign called "The New Look in Public Housing for Families," emphasizing the scattered nature of the sites, the vernacular designs, and the preference for local residents as tenants. But Daley's press secretary, Earl Bush, seeking to distance the mayor from public housing in any form, contended that the photographs in the "New Look" brochures would make homeowners assume the new housing had already been built. The CHA would not launch its "New Look" campaign until July 1971—well after the election. Polikoff bitterly complained that the CHA had promised it would engage in a public relations program before the sites were released, and the Chicago *Daily Defender* judged that the CHA's actions were "designed to invite the kind of negative reaction the plan received in the white community."[26]

Thus, the CHA and city hall fulfilled Richard Wade's prophesy that a site list would be negatively politicized during the campaign. Republican mayoral candidate Richard Friedman rushed to tie Daley to the issue, playing both sides of the argument. First he charged Daley with secretly supporting the list: "He's fighting for time until the election is over with and if he wins then he is going to go ahead and okay those sites. . . . He didn't have the guts to tell the people in the neighborhoods targeted for the projects."[27] Then he reversed gears and accused the mayor of opposing the sites out of political strategy to play "race politics" and "go for panic" to get reelected. The latter accusation was more accurate. Daley's unequivocal objection to the sites had the effect of rallying the machine in white neighborhoods, and he easily won reelection. Yet victory came at a cost; he lost much of his support among middle-class African Americans, leaving him more dependent than ever on the city's white wards.[28] Reflecting his steady retreat on issues of race during his tenure, Daley had now exacerbated the racial divides that would lead to a decade of political turmoil after his death in 1976.

Following the 1971 election, the City Council Committee on Housing and Planning, true to form, snubbed Judge Austin's ruling and refused to approve the bulk of the CHA's proposed sites in white areas and, instead, added new sites in black areas. In place of 1,500 units in white areas, the committee proposed only 318 units in white neighborhoods and 417 in black ones. Some of the sites were penciled in less than an hour before the vote, allowing no room for public hearings. A week later, on June 12, 1971, the full city council approved an even smaller list, rammed through on Daley's orders. The council gambled that its actions would satisfy Austin and HUD, which had made the city's Model Cities funds conditional on progress "consistent with Austin's order." Council leaders maintained, incredibly, that they had not defied Austin and that they intended to come up with additional white sites later.[29]

The same day that the full city council approved the list that flouted Austin, President Nixon released a convoluted statement on housing policy that signaled to the aldermen that the Nixon administration would not interfere in Chicago's conflict. Nixon's statement coupled vague language supporting antidiscrimination goals with other statements undermining the federal government's will to enforce those goals. The Nixon administration would not impose public housing on the suburbs and would "not seek to impose economic integration upon an existing local jurisdiction." Nixon gratuitously added that federal agencies should not "dictate local land use policies." Some in Chicago interpreted the new policy as suggesting that Model Cities funds would no longer be used as leverage to enforce Austin's order. Soon after, HUD accepted the city council's charade and released the balance of $26 million in Model Cities funds.[30] With Daley reelected, Nixon on their side, and the HUD funds available, any urgency among aldermen on the public housing question evaporated. Again, as in 1950, the city council and Washington administrators had refused to back the integration agenda of Chicago liberals.

In the face of these obstacles, Polikoff turned to a new tactic, one that belatedly addressed the heart of the matter. He asked Austin to suspend provisions of the state housing law that gave the city council the power to approve or disapprove sites. The initial *Gautreaux* lawsuit did not challenge state statutes, first enacted in 1941 and strengthened in 1949, that put the CHA at the mercy of aldermen, because attacking a democratic process did not appear a promising legal strategy. But now Polikoff told the court that the state law was being used "without justification to frustrate a court-ordered remedy." Austin, irate as well at the city council's actions, agreed, and ordered the CHA to stop submitting sites to the city council. The CHA appealed Austin's order and lost, but it again sought a U.S. Supreme Court review as a delaying tactic. Not until January 1974 did the Court decline to accept the case. The city council had finally lost its power to veto CHA sites.[31]

Polikoff still defined relief for CHA tenants as removing as many of them as possible from the ghetto. With scattered-site housing in the city stalled, he turned to advocating them in the suburbs. But two U.S. Supreme Court cases blocked a court-enforced, scattered-site public housing program on a metropolitan-wide basis. The first involved school segregation in the Detroit area, where the court ruled that suburban school districts could not be forced to participate in a desegregation plan for that city. The second case involved Polikoff's own suit against HUD, which was delayed while the parallel case against the CHA moved forward. Surprisingly, Austin ruled against Polikoff and for HUD in 1971, but an appeals court reversed the decision, citing the 1965 letter by Marie McGuire on the Cermak and State site as key evidence of the government's complicity in the CHA's discrimination. HUD appealed to the Supreme Court, which in 1976 upheld the appeals court in a unanimous decision and found HUD guilty. The opinion was bittersweet for Polikoff, however. The Court affirmed its view in the Detroit case and insisted that public housing could not be forced on localities that did not want it, shutting out a metropolitan-wide remedy. The decision meant Polikoff lost what he called the "grail" of public policy: scattered-site public housing, distributed throughout city and suburb and administered by HUD experts or courts without interference from locally elected interests.[32]

*   *   *

After his victory-turned-loss at the Supreme Court, Polikoff shifted to a strategy that offered a way out of the seemingly never-ending litigation. Section 8 of the 1974 Housing Act had expanded the Section 23 demonstration into a new program that offered an array of subsidy options, including "tenant-based" subsidies to individual families to live in private housing. Section 8 certificates circumvented hostile municipal governments because local housing authorities or HUD could contract directly with landlords. Using his litigation stick, Polikoff convinced HUD in July 1976 to start a demonstration program using four hundred Section 8 certificates to move *Gautreaux* plaintiffs to the suburbs.

The "Gautreaux program" placed the first public housing tenants in white suburbs in 1976, and over the next two decades, 7,100 low-income African American families received counseling, assistance, and rent certificates to relocate out of Chicago's ghettos, a remarkable achievement given three decades of white resistance to residential integration. In 1992, Polikoff convinced HUD secretary Jack Kemp to try the idea, and Congress passed a "national demonstration" called the Moving to Opportunity program. Over four years, 1,700 randomly selected participants moved out of high poverty areas in Baltimore, Boston, Chicago, Los Angeles, and New

York. Social scientists tracked families over time and used control groups to measure outcomes. Results, on the whole, were positive, especially in areas of physical and mental health, though educational gains were disappointing, and some studies showed adolescent boys actually had higher arrest rates in their new, less impoverished neighborhoods than in the control groups. Still, Congress was not interested in social science results and instead responded to a white backlash in suburban Baltimore soon after the program was announced. Senator Barbara Mikulski (D-MD) led the effort to cap the demonstration program and limit its scope, effectively blocking any national-level expansion.[33]

While Polikoff's Gautreaux program successfully moved some public housing families out to the suburbs, the CHA's scattered-site public housing efforts, intending to integrate the city, languished. The CHA offered numerous excuses, including, most prominently, that construction costs exceeded HUD's cost limits, a throwback to 1959 constraints. While HUD was indeed tightfisted throughout the 1970s, and scattered-site projects experienced the same red tape as the traditional program, a court-ordered report in 1979 found that the CHA's effort was "disgraceful," conducted at minimal levels to avoid a contempt of court citation. Despite the CHA's behavior, the court refused Polikoff's request to appoint a receiver for the scattered-site program. Instead, Austin referred the issue to magistrate court, where the scattered-site program lay neglected for another nine years, with little progress before a receiver was belatedly appointed in 1987. Over the fifteen previous years, the CHA had completed only 900 scattered-site units, poorly constructed and unevenly distributed. The court-appointed receiver built another 1,800 between 1987 and 2000, a modest improvement. However, the CHA had so badly mismanaged what was built that many scattered-site units had to undergo major renovations after only a few years. Scattered sites, like the "traditional" program, suffered under the CHA's grave incompetence.[34]

★   ★   ★

Polikoff called his twenty-five-year legal battle with the CHA, the city of Chicago, and HUD "protracted and tortuous," nothing if not an understatement. But the effort did yield a significant victory in laying bare the city council's racist manipulation of sites and hindering further injustices. Moreover, the creative Gautreaux program achieved substantial success, at least in Chicago. Although his agenda had plenty of support among white liberals, Polikoff never received much enthusiasm from African American leaders. His solution said to many that what poor blacks needed most was to leave their neighborhoods and live in suburban white communities and send their children to mostly white schools. While several thousand low-income African Americans jumped at the chance, other public housing tenants wanted responsive maintenance, secure surroundings, and improved schools. They wanted housing freedoms but also job opportunities, neighborhood reinvestment, and equal treatment under the law. Abandoning the ghetto to become a pioneer in a mostly white suburb was an idea that emanated from white liberals, not black community activists, and it included a tinge of condescension toward community life in black neighborhoods.[35]

The CHA's response to the *Gautreaux* case is even more revealing. It chose not to lead and contested Polikoff at nearly every step throughout the 1970s. CHA boards appointed by machine mayors Daley, Bilandic, and Byrne viewed Polikoff and the court as the enemy, a narrow, shortsighted interpretation of the authority's interests. Instead of marshalling its resources to educate Chicagoans and urge public opinion in new directions, the CHA acceded to white prejudice and indeed in many ways sympathized with it. Rather than use the litigation as an opportunity to free itself from city control and join forces with reformers, the CHA dragged its feet. The defiance of Chicago leaders showed how little had changed in the city's attitudes toward residential integration in the twenty years since Elizabeth Wood fought for white sites in the early 1950s. Civil rights legislation and the fair housing movements of the 1960s made overt bigotry unfashionable, but easily decipherable varieties were pervasive in the 1970s and 1980s, thinly veiled as class arguments. Unwilling to move in the direction of social justice, the CHA floundered through the 1980s merely trying to stay afloat, its low-income housing mission in shambles.

Polikoff's legal battles stopped the CHA from repeating its ghettoization mistakes after 1969, but he made little headway in reversing them. Nor could scattered-site housing and relocation to the suburbs address the immediate suffering of CHA tenants. His solutions left open the question of what to do with disintegrating projects, many of which by the early 1980s had become, for all intents and purposes, slums themselves. The dogged pursuit of metropolitan options for CHA tenants offered minimal relief to tenants in the still viable low-rise and senior buildings enduring long wait times for repairs and deferred maintenance. Neither Polikoff nor the city ever launched a campaign to haul CHA into housing court to indict its chronic mismanagement.[36] Nor did Polikoff ask for a court-appointed receiver to run the entire CHA, a strategy used with success in Boston in the 1980s.[37] In hindsight, Polikoff might have used his legal leverage to force better management at the CHA without compromising his more ambitious dispersal strategy.

Not until 1995 would HUD finally step in and take over the authority, but by then the managerial chaos seemed nearly beyond hope. Few viable ideas emerged for turning around the enormous problems of Cabrini-Green, the Robert Taylor Homes, and other high-rise developments built in the 1940s and 1950s that made up 70 percent of the CHA's family housing. Instead, the continued descent of the CHA's largest projects in the 1980s and 1990s closed off possibilities for policymakers and left only the option of drastic measures.

The Long Road to Rebirth 10

By the early 1980s the Chicago Housing Authority, in a deep irony, had become a slumlord, with tenants at its large-scale projects enduring hostile surroundings. Inoperable elevators, erratic heat, leaky roofs, uncollected garbage, infested apartments, darkened hallways, and unrepaired playground equipment were norms, not aberrations. As a community builder, the CHA could not provide basic security, especially in its elevator buildings, leading to gang control of public spaces, routine gunfire, widespread drug dealing, debilitating addictions, and sexual violence against women. Not every project or even every building in the worst projects was chaotic, and resident-led efforts to maintain social order and enhance community had isolated successes. But in general, maintenance and security failures had reached devastating levels that affected the physical and mental health of residents. Many were trapped in worlds of addiction, violence, and hopelessness.

What to do about this situation bedeviled policymakers and public housing residents alike throughout the 1980s and early 1990s. Ideas on how to "clean up" CHA projects emerged from several directions, though exactly what this process should entail was contested. In Washington, Congress and HUD continued to treat big-city housing authorities as incompetent entities that would respond only to financial incentives. Even when headed by reformers, the CHA's bureaucracy had resisted institutional change for decades, and inertia and inefficiency prevailed. At the project level, tenants argued that problems could be addressed if they were given more control, and resident management began to be viewed as a viable alternative in the 1970s. But developing resident capacity took resources, tenant organizations were often fragile, and budget issues remained problematic. Then, in the late 1980s, the CHA moved in a new direction—really a return to its early years—and experimented with renovating existing high-rise projects as "mixed-income" housing. Despite initial success, however, few policymakers wanted to save the high-rise mistakes of the 1950s.

Underlying any proposal was the understanding that public housing faced three interrelated problems with no easy answers. The first problem was management capacity. Could the CHA reform itself into a functioning bureaucracy, or should HUD, a court-appointed receiver, or the tenants themselves take over? The second problem involved the vast extent of deferred maintenance, an issue that came to a head in the 1970s and 1980s as small repairs festered into ever-larger ones with each year of neglect. Could physical conditions be raised to reasonable standards with available resources? The third problem centered on security and developing basic levels of policing, both formal and informal. Could residents establish collective efficacy at large projects and could the police reclaim public space from gang control and the drug trade? One reform idea after another exhausted itself struggling against these problems. After a decade of promise and disappointment, the field opened during the Clinton administration to more radical ideas that, like welfare reform, ended public housing as it had been known since the New Deal.

*　*　*

Despite the fact that since 1945, the vast majority of the CHA's tenants were black, no African American had held the CHA board chairmanship after Robert Taylor's departure in 1950, and none had ever filled the executive director position. Mayor Jane Byrne had won much of the black vote in 1979 as a reformer, but three years into her tenure she replaced two black CHA commissioners with white political cronies in an effort to placate the Democratic Party machine. The move was a slap in the face to the city's black community and energized African Americans, now nearly one-third of the city's electorate. To protest the appointments, the Reverend Jesse Jackson's Operation PUSH organization orchestrated a 1982 boycott of Byrne's "ChicagoFest," a music and food festival. Congressman Harold Washington endorsed the boycott and marshaled surging African American political strength and support from reform-minded white liberals to win a tight, three-way 1983 election against Byrne and Richard M. Daley, who split most of the machine vote. Chicago had its first black mayor, but once in office, his reform agenda collided with stiff resistance from die-hard machine elements. During the "Council Wars" of the mid-1980s, white aldermen held up city appointments, asserted control over city budgets, and thwarted Mayor Washington at every turn.[1]

Still, an African American mayor now controlled appointments to the CHA board, and the possibility of real reform raised hope among residents. But Washington personally struggled with what to do with public housing. He privately admitted to his staff that he had no comprehensive solution; more pessimistically, he questioned if one even existed. "The CHA didn't have a problem," he told his press secretary Alton Miller, "they *were* the problem." Washington considered the high-rise projects "obscene . . . an abomination. They should never have been built in the first place." He despaired of finding a remedy: "Nobody can make the CHA work. . . . The only solution is just to get rid of it. What you need in the meantime is someone with Renault Robinson's skills to keep it all together."[2] Washington admired Robinson's leadership of the Afro-American Patrolmen's League, a crusade undertaken at great personal risk. Robinson initially said "no" to Washington when offered the CHA chairmanship in 1983, but he finally succumbed to the mayor's entreaties.[3]

The choice, as Washington himself later admitted, was not a good one. As a board member in the early 1980s, Robinson had castigated Swibel for his secrecy and control, but soon he, too, centralized power in the chairman's office, isolated the executive director and other board members, and then made rash decisions. Robinson correctly identified the CHA's maintenance operation as scandalously inefficient and a source of chronic frustration to tenants. But his reforms were crudely implemented and ultimately counterproductive. He abruptly canceled the wasteful elevator repair contract but did not have a replacement firm. Chaos ensued, with over 70 percent of the elevators out of service for the first three weeks of January 1984 at Cabrini-Green, Stateway Gardens, and Robert Taylor—home to 50,000 individuals. The CHA eventually hired eight separate elevator companies to handle repairs, but it still had little ability to measure their effectiveness. Robinson also fired 259 maintenance workers for "loafing" just before the winter of 1983–84; with few staff on hand, boilers worked erratically, apartments went unheated, and numerous pipes froze and burst. Meanwhile, the craftsmen sued on the grounds of wrongful termination and eventually won, forcing Robinson to reinstate them with back pay. Harold Washington viewed the whole episode as a blunder but did not demand Robinson's resignation.[4] Like Wood in 1946 and the PHA in 1957, Robinson had attempted to bring the CHA's maintenance operation under board control, but his clumsy efforts could not subdue the city's unions or improve tenant life.

Nor could Robinson bring order to the CHA's chaotic "firefighting" management style. Now in their third and fourth decade of operation, many projects desperately needed replacements of major systems with limited life spans, including roofs, windows, boilers, elevator cabs, water heaters, and incinerators. Any one of these tasks at a single project was a challenging undertaking, requiring skilled engineers and experienced project managers to oversee the work of contractors. While the CHA had federal modernization money available, it lacked the capacity to carry out the work either consistently or to HUD standards. In one embarrassing failure, it badly mismanaged a $7 million effort to secure lobbies at the Robert Taylor Homes, and HUD rescinded the funds. The episode, in the midst of Harold Washington's 1987 reelection campaign, led to Robinson's resignation. Soon after Washington's victory, the new CHA executive director, Brenda Gaines, a former aide to the mayor, discovered a colossal cash-flow problem and an "appalling lack of financial controls" that produced a $38 million hole in the CHA's budget. She begged HUD for $23 million to meet payroll and pay long-overdue bills. Again, the CHA's glaring failures of management and its inability to control its financial operations made any hope of a turnaround a distant dream.[5]

As the CHA's management woes persisted, public housing residents took matters into their own hands and created "resident management corporations" (RMCs) at several projects. The RMC idea first developed in St. Louis in the aftermath of a major rent strike in 1969. The Ford Foundation provided funds to train residents who by 1973 were given the reins for day-to-day management functions at several St. Louis projects. The foundation then partnered with HUD to sponsor a demonstration program in six cities, but a 1981 evaluation concluded that high implementation costs outweighed management gains and recommended against expanding the program. Two new studies, one in 1987 and another in 1992, reached a different conclusion: well-organized tenant groups could be effective managers, especially if they joined forces with capacity-building community organizations. In addition, RMCs outperformed the local housing authority in areas such as maintenance, security, and social service delivery, all at lower per-unit costs. Conservatives in the Reagan and Bush administrations latched on to these findings as a resident empowerment strategy that might lead to selling off public housing to its tenants, an idea already well underway in Britain under the Thatcher government. Conservative support for RMCs produced strange bedfellows, as HUD secretary Jack Kemp showered attention on the tenants, mostly African American women, fighting to take control of their projects.[6]

In Chicago, the concept took hold in the late 1980s, and by 1991, the city's projects had more RMCs than any housing authority in the country. The first RMC formed at Leclaire Courts, the low-rise, vacant land project that for years had been the jewel of the CHA. Deferred maintenance, however, had taken its toll, and older residents longed for the days when the CHA enforced rules and when managers had a say in admissions. With high-rises absorbing attention and resources, little money was available for the relatively stable low-rise projects, which rarely received modernization funds. Leclaire tenants wanted their buildings fixed, but they also demanded control over their community, especially to screen out "problem" families. Working with RMC advocates in St. Louis and Washington, Leclaire's leaders, almost all of whom were women, began a lengthy process of organizing their community, training residents, and overcoming resistance at the CHA, which doubted their competency to manage housing. "People thought we were crazy because we were black women on welfare," recalled Irene Johnson, president of the Leclaire RMC. In 1986, after three years of work and negotiation, the CHA board agreed to hand over control to Leclaire residents, and Renault Robinson presented the RMC with a symbolic, large-size check for $1 million for capital improvements "so that the tenant management staff can get off to a good, clean start." The money never materialized, however, and it represented another example of the CHA's broken promises to residents in the 1980s. Still, Leclaire became a darling of Kemp, who frequently invited Johnson to Washington and who identified the RMC leaders as "heroes."[7]

Chicago's RMCs, like those in other cities, had mixed results and were not a panacea for public housing's fundamental problems. At several projects they launched many women into empowering and entrepreneurial roles, producing remarkably tenacious leaders who fought for improvements to their communities. But management by committee proved fragile. The Leclaire RMC board suffered from internal conflicts, and while a 1993 audit found no fraud, it labeled management financial controls "ineffective" and "inefficient." Partnerships and advisors could not be sustained, and one long-time observer believed the Leclaire RMC had become "complacent." In 1995, the CHA temporarily suspended its powers and forced new elections because of personality clashes on the board.[8] Other RMCs had more success. Residents at a single building at Cabrini-Green (1230 North Burling Street) organized a corporation to tackle maintenance and security in their high-rise. The "1230 RMC" created "tenant patrols" consisting of teams of residents who walked each floor to police public space. Once rent rebates were offered to patrol members, the idea expanded across the CHA, with the 1230 RMC acting as a contractor to manage 900 patrolling residents by 1995. At Wentworth Gardens, a smaller project of 422 row houses and walk-ups, long-time tenant leaders established a viable RMC organization through persistence and partnerships. They successfully held the project together through lean years and oversaw a complete renovation in 2005–2007.[9] Had RMCs received more backing from CHA leadership and other capacity-building organizations, they might have thrived. Still, the RMC solution only underscored the failures of the CHA as a landlord. Tenants in private apartment complexes did not have to devote their lives to overseeing basic issues of management and upkeep of their buildings.

In their frustration with conditions, Mayor Washington and Renault Robinson blamed federal funding levels. They pointed out that the CHA ranked twelfth among U.S. housing authorities in per-unit operating subsidy under the performance funding system, ignoring the fact that the authority remained mired in "low-performing" status. In 1979, HUD established new measures for assessing housing authority managerial capacity, efficiency, and effectiveness. The CHA received failing grades. Along with a dozen other big-city housing authorities, it was placed on a "troubled" list, where it resided until 1997. Despite this lame performance, other subsidies continued to flow, including federal modernization grants, the "Targeted Projects" program in the Carter years, HUD's Community Development Block Grant money for the city in the 1980s, and anticrime funds in the 1990s. Further, the CHA stopped payments in lieu of taxes to the city in 1981. These streams of resources may have plugged holes in operating budgets, but they did nothing to build management capacity that might have elevated the CHA's performance funding score. Instead of reforming itself, the authority questioned the whole PFS formula. In 1989, it sent HUD a 320-page "recalculation" of its PFS, claiming that bad data, miscalculations, and "underestimation" of both project age and building height had cost it more than $70 million in operating subsidies since 1975.[10] But the CHA had long since lost credibility in Washington. Two years earlier, it had sent HUD a $1 billion request for modernization funds to address deferred maintenance and replacements at its projects, a figure revised downward to $724 million when the press found obvious double counting in the numbers, which the CHA dismissed as a "proofreading error." Even this lower figure was more than the entire federal modernization budget that year and amounted to $18,000 for each of the CHA's apartments. The effort underlined the desperation that paralyzed the CHA by the mid-1980s. "We have to reach up to touch bottom," executive director Zirl Smith told the press. With the CHA in disarray and struggling to spend its existing modernization money, HUD had no interest in entertaining "pie-in-the sky" funding requests.[11]

The Reagan administration was no friend of public housing, but it would be wrong to suggest that funding cuts at HUD were behind the woes of housing authorities across the country. The Reagan war on social welfare programs produced much rhetoric but few actual budget cuts in the areas most important to the CHA. Aggressive proposals from the Reagan HUD slashed construction of additional public housing and other subsidized housing production programs and instead favored using tenant-based, Section 8 rental assistance in the private market to assist families. But Congress and affordable housing advocates rescued funding for existing public housing—the all-important operating subsidy and modernization accounts—from the Reagan budget ax. Outlays for these two programs increased in inflation-adjusted terms on a per-unit basis between 1981 and 1989, and with two exceptions, local housing authorities received the full expected amount of performance funding subsidies between 1981 and 1992. The Reagan HUD and Congress did slice some programs in real terms, most prominently the Community Development Block Grant, which provided flexible funds to cities for community investment, and it did force tenants to pay more of their income toward rent, raising the percentage from 25 percent to 30 percent in 1982, to save annual contributions costs.[12]

Advocates at the time and scholars since have pointed to severe budget reductions as one reason for its demise. But budget cuts for public housing in the Reagan years were mostly illusionary, the result of confusion over highly complex federal budget concepts. In fact, federal outlays on low-income housing programs, including public housing, increased faster than the rate of inflation, and the number of families assisted grew faster than population growth.[13] At the CHA, budget information from the 1980s is infrequently available and difficult to compare year to year, but existing data suggest that federal operating subsidies were largely flat in real terms during the 1980s, rising only slightly from $180 per unit month in 1980 to $185 per unit month in 1990 (in 1984 dollars), even as the number of vacancies at the CHA soared. Yet available data also indicate that the CHA's total spending (from all sources) rose in real terms over the period from 1978 to 1995, more than doubling from $126 million to $267 million (1984 dollars) in that period.[14] While it is fair to say that the CHA's inefficiencies cost it precious operating subsidies and that the Reagan HUD was not forthcoming with infusions of new resources, it would be unfair to pin the CHA's fiscal problems on "budget cuts" in the 1980s.

Once again, managerial incapacity explains the CHA's fiscal crisis throughout the 1980s. An outside audit in 1987 found CHA records in disarray and its financial statements inaccurate; a HUD investigation concluded that "accepted standards of government procurement management, internal control, economy and efficiency were variously ignored, manipulated, or subordinated to other objectives in an unacceptable number of sampled transactions." A GAO report in 1989 listed the repeated findings of study after study conducted in the 1980s showing that the CHA had "no current management plan," "no current operational manual," and "no functional statements that clearly define the responsibilities of organizational units." Many of its middle managers "lack[ed] the necessary education, experience, or training to perform adequately," and those in lower positions were "unqualified."[15] The picture painted by Oscar Newman in 1982 had not changed in the Harold Washington years.

Until the CHA's administrative house was in order, substantive progress on improving conditions for tenants proved elusive. And neither Mayor Washington nor HUD was prepared to overhaul the authority. The new round of fiscal crises in 1987 presented yet another opportunity for HUD to intervene, and a federal takeover of the CHA was seriously contemplated. The mayor, however, feared the dismissal of CHA staff, the privatization of public housing, and perhaps even its demolition, given the Reagan administration's rhetoric. In negotiations throughout the summer of 1987, HUD wanted to hand over day-to-day management to a private management firm free from CHA board interference. The CHA countered with a reorganization plan that HUD rejected as "business as usual," and the federal government prepared to move forward with a takeover. The CHA's threat of a lawsuit delayed action, and, in a meeting with Vice President Bush in August 1987, the mayor pleaded for more time to implement reforms. Reagan officials backed off, fearing a protracted political and legal battle, and a watered-down memorandum of agreement was reached in September that included performing yet another comprehensive management study and adding a HUD liaison to the CHA's staff to represent federal interests. As with so many previous efforts, the memorandum of agreement was easily neglected by both parties. The new study never got off the ground, and the CHA's new managing director, Jerome van Gorkum, resigned after five months, citing differences with the board after finding further administrative incompetence.[16] Yet another opportunity for reform had passed.

But the next CHA head, African American housing developer Vincent Lane, promised a turnaround at the CHA, and for a while the city rallied to his charismatic leadership. In a deal with the new mayor, Eugene Sawyer, who had been chosen by the city council after Harold Washington's sudden death in November 1987, Lane became both executive director and chairman with a revamped board, accumulating more power than either Robinson or Swibel. "You have to start over," Lane told the press. "We want to take a totally new approach, with new board members who from day one believe in the concept." Lane's concept involved improving security, focusing on property management basics, and enlisting public housing tenants in both areas. He had successfully rehabbed and managed low-income properties in the city, and he viewed his private-sector tenants as "the same people who live in public housing. It's amazing what you can do when you get the residents involved." The strategy was hardly radical, but the back-to-basics approach made Lane—in a relative sense—appear as a savior.[17]

Yet the challenge Lane faced was enormous. The eighth executive director in seven years, he inherited an organization in utter disarray. Early in his tenure, Lane decided not to take on the CHA bureaucracy all at once. He resisted HUD's demand for extensive management review and instead tackled CHA departments one at a time, leaving much of its operations untouched. Lane also focused on repairing relations with HUD and tenants, ending the war of words that had lasted over a decade. He called the federal agency a "partner" in solving problems, and he stopped the practice of treating most tenant groups as adversaries. By 1989, the General Accounting Office gave Lane a vote of confidence, saying that his administration had improved communication, listened to tenants, and implemented a "crisis-management" approach that "shows much promise." Soon, HUD secretary Jack Kemp saluted him as well, and Lane became a national figure in public housing circles.[18]

★   ★   ★

Part of Lane's new approach involved mixed-income housing, which he envisioned as a return to public housing's early days. He had grown up across from Ida B. Wells in the 1940s and 1950s and recalled that "there were working families there as well as families on welfare. It was a mixed-income community." This idea of mixing incomes still divides advocates for the poor, many of whom continue to want scarce public housing resources dedicated to helping those most in need, especially the homeless. But social scientists in the late 1980s and 1990s were more in tune with Lane. No hard research indicated that mixing incomes would create viable neighborhoods, but theory pointed in that direction. The work of sociologists William Julius Wilson and Robert Putnam had convinced many that concentrated poverty compounded social ills. By deconcentrating poverty and by connecting welfare mothers and the jobless with working-class families, neighborhoods would create the networks and the know-how—what Putnam called "social capital"—needed to gain access to jobs, social services, and other elements of "community." Similarly, Robert Sampson's theories of collective efficacy also viewed concentrated poverty as a factor contributing to social disorder. For Lane, however, the mixed-income idea came from both nostalgia and an intuitive belief that a return to the past was the way to a better future.[19]

The first effort to re-create income mixes in public housing in Chicago—and the nation—began at the Lakefront Properties, a collection of six high-rises with views of Lake Michigan, where plans for renovation were already underway. Four of the six buildings, completed between 1962 and 1964, used the same blueprints as the indefensible, gallery-style, sixteen-story Robert Taylor Homes, while the other two were center-corridor, nineteen-story buildings with enclosed lobbies dating from the Elizabeth Wood era. Three years before Lane's arrival, Renault Robinson's staff had abruptly announced that the Lakefront's 700 families would be evacuated from the severely deteriorated, gang-ridden buildings, but future plans were left vague, with no guarantee that former tenants could return to the rehabilitated developments. Residents were outraged at the lack of consultation and, fearing a land grab by developers, organized to demand a voice in the future of their former homes. Thirty-two families in one building refused to leave until the CHA granted them a right to return. Robinson managed the public relations problem feebly, promising much but delivering little. Then community actors stepped into the void left by weak CHA leadership; black middle-class homeowners pressured the city council and CHA to tear the high-rises down. Developer Ferd Kramer, long involved in urban renewal in the city, proposed renovating two buildings as senior housing, demolishing the rest, and building low-rise, market-rate, private housing and scattered-site public housing in their place. Alexander Polikoff supported Kramer's plan, believing that high-rises for families were a bad idea and arguing that the area was undergoing economic revitalization that could support a racially integrated community.[20]

Lane entered the scene in 1988 and engineered a new plan that eventually became Lake Parc Place. He focused on the two, nineteen-story, center-corridor buildings, with their enclosed lobbies, and recommended renovating them to a standard that would be attractive to working-class renters. (The four gallery-style buildings had less defensible space and needed even more costly renovations). He suggested putting a cap on income-based rents and reserving half of the apartments for what HUD called "low-income" families, those earning between 50 percent and 80 percent of the city's median family income ($21,000 to $34,000 in Chicago in 1992). This income range mirrored the CHA's experience in the 1950s, when the income of its tenants was 60 percent of the city's median. The other half of the apartments would go to "very low-income" families, those earning between 30 and 50 percent of median family income, or "extremely low-income" tenants earning below 30 percent of median by HUD definitions, the latter category encompassing most welfare recipients. All of these income categories were already eligible for public housing, but without rent caps and amenities, the CHA knew from experience that few of the "low-income" households would apply. Lane lobbied Congress for a law authorizing waivers of rules to demonstrate the mixed-income idea, and while four cities were authorized to participate, only Chicago did so initially. In 1989, HUD funded Lane's plan with $14 million to renovate 282 units (or nearly $50,000 per apartment) in the two nineteen-story buildings. The other four gallery-style high-rises at Lakefront Properties, however, remained in limbo. After another thirteen years of delay and broken promises to tenants, they were imploded in 1998. In 2005—almost twenty years after residents had been scattered—a Ferd Kramer–style plan to rebuild with mostly market-rate and some scattered-site public housing began. A lack of consensus and funds had led to an agonizing redevelopment process that underscored the difficulties facing any turnaround of the CHA.[21]

But the two Lake Parc Place buildings were largely successful and promptly cemented Lane's reputation as a visionary. He not only mixed the incomes, he hired a private management firm and encouraged committees of residents to screen applicants, review management performance, and provide tenant patrols. A social director and an assistant facilitated programs for youths and residents, including a scouting troop, a teen council, and after-school programs. Lane told Congress that after three years the development had "zero crime, no vandalism, no graffiti. Over 20 percent of the families who started on welfare are now working-full time jobs." Planners and housing experts flocked to Lake Parc, and social scientists surveyed resident attitudes to see if the mixed-income model worked as theorized. While they found less cross-class interaction and social capital gains than expected, safety and security problems showed major improvement.[22] Lane had accomplished what his predecessors had been unable to in the previous twenty-five years: he had created physical and social order in a high-rise, public housing building.

But the income mix was likely only one factor in the establishment of order. First, redevelopment meant a dramatic deconcentration of youth, as the new tenants had far fewer children. In 1970, the two buildings had a youth-adult ratio of 1.72; after redevelopment the figure was roughly 0.4, below the city average and close to levels in sustainable urban renewal projects, such as Lake Meadows. Second, the tenant selection process "creamed" the applicant pool in an effort to create a model development. Over 40 percent of the former public housing residents had employment income when admitted, far higher than the CHA average of 9 percent. Third, defensible-space principles were incorporated in the renovation. A secured entranceway included a guard behind bulletproof glass who admitted residents via a buzzer, allowing tight control over access to the building. Fourth, resident organizations, supported by project managers, were able to create an effective community. Tenant patrols and tenant screening boards established a voice for residents, who reported feeling safe and secure. As well, some of those who returned to Lake Parc had been active members of the previous Lakefront Homes, allowing some degree of community stability, a salient variable in Sampson's model of collective efficacy. Finally, private managers received the budgetary resources needed to maintain the newly renovated property because of rents from working-class tenants, even though rents were still capped at an affordable $371 a month.[23] Lake Parc, then, brought together two decades of thinking on community formation and showed that, in themselves, highrises were not dysfunctional. With careful planning, limits on youths, selective admissions, active management, and substantial renovation funds ($50,000 per unit), center-corridor buildings could be viable. These numerous qualifications, however, made it unclear at the time if the success could be replicated. Most of the CHA's high-rise buildings were gallery style, and the Lake Parc tenant selection rules, if applied broadly, would have displaced most public housing residents.

★   ★   ★

By 1990, the crack cocaine epidemic had hit Chicago with full force. Public housing's indefensible space, vacant apartments, and ready supply of impoverished youths had made it the center of the city's drug trade. Heroin and cocaine had been prevalent in the largest projects for over two decades, but the lucrative and addictive form of crack sent profits and violence to record levels. Gang leaders used intimidation and payoffs to take control of building spaces, buying the collusion of building presidents and local advisory council members to stake out territory. With the Chicago Police ineffective, outmanned, and, at times, corrupt, gang leaders became de facto authority figures in the buildings they occupied. As Sudhir Venkatesh recounted in his ethnography of the Robert Taylor Homes, gang leaders enforced their own brand of order on tenants in an effort to maximize drug sales and, if possible, restrain turmoil that would drive away customers.[24] But the high stakes meant violence erupted frequently in deadly gang wars that terrified residents and police alike. With gangs controlling lobbies, stairwells, and other public spaces, the pressures on youths to join were intense, with devastating consequences. Assaults, convictions, rapes, maimings, and murders wrecked the lives of those directly involved and haunted the families around them. In speaking with former residents of high-rise projects, nearly every one could describe witnessing a murder or experiencing a violent death in their family.[25] Few were left unscarred. Tiffany Pinkson-Wheeler, who grew up in the Harold Ickes and Robert Taylor Homes in the 1980s, lost an uncle and two cousins to violence—one a ten-year-old hit by a stray bullet. She still goes into what she calls an "automatic defense mode," balling up her fist and putting on a fierce look, when she walks down the street and sees an unknown man—a legacy of her time at Taylor.[26]

Lane's efforts to tackle crime were controversial. His new policies included curfews and visitation rules, but the centerpiece effort involved "sweeps" to "take back the buildings" from gang control. The sweeps idea emerged out of the complaint Lane's staff received again and again from the vexed tenants and community groups at West Wide projects: "We've got to do something . . . these young men are getting killed every day." In a coordinated effort, CHA staff and police would cordon off a building's entrances and exits and then search every apartment, ostensibly as part of routine inspections, though in reality they targeted weapons, drugs, and unauthorized tenants. The aggressive nature of early sweeps quickly met resistance from some residents, who, with the help of the ACLU, took the CHA to court. A judge ruled the searches unconstitutional, and a consent decree in 1988 toned down the sweeps. The CHA was allowed to conduct apartment inspections and evict squatters, and if staff found illicit activity "in plain view," waiting police could be called in to make a "probable cause" judgment for further searching.[27]

Over time the effectiveness of the sweeps diminished; insiders tipped off gang members and avoidance strategies proliferated. In the summer of 1993, after a wave of gunfire at the Robert Taylor Homes and Stateway Gardens, Lane ratcheted up the sweeps again and had police conduct warrantless searches for weapons in twelve buildings at Robert Taylor and Stateway Gardens. The CHA's Central Advisory Council and local council members supported the effort, though not unanimously; one group sided with the ACLU, which again went to court to rein in the CHA. At the hearing, residents in favor of sweeps described how they slept on the floor and in bathtubs to avoid gunfire. The judge ruled against the CHA, eliciting an angry response from President Clinton, then engaged in a public campaign for his 1994 crime bill, but Jesse Jackson's Operation PUSH opposed the sweeps and decried the "police state" at the CHA. In defense of the sweeps, CHA board member and tenant Artensa Randolph, whose sixteen-year-old grandson was murdered in a gang conflict at Cabrini-Green, later told a congressional committee that she would "rather trade rights for life . . . a dead person has no rights, and the fact that we would willingly relinquish this constitutional right in order to restore some semblance of peace in our development is an indication of the 30 years of neglect by HUD toward the problem and the people in public housing communities." The clearly unconstitutional sweeps highlighted the desperation of residents and the CHA as they tried to wrestle control of buildings back from gangs in the midst of a drug-fueled, low-level war.[28]

The crack epidemic of the late 1980s and early 1990s devastated numerous public housing communities, and the sweeps proved costly and ineffective. Despite enormous expenditures, gains were transient. Spending on security and antidrug initiatives rocketed from $7 million in 1986 to $80 million in 1995. Lane asserted that the CHA's large high-rise projects were "more under the command of drug lords than the rule of law" and that until they were reclaimed from gangs renovating them was useless. Only a massive, continuing, and costly security and police presence could provide hope. Lane attempted such an effort and replaced the discouraged Chicago Police Department with his own force of six hundred police officers and five hundred deputized security guards to conduct sweeps, vertical patrols, and evictions. The strategy showed promise, but the demands were too great. At the Harold Ickes mid-rise buildings, researchers found that security improved significantly in 1995 when a combination of tenant patrols, CHA-trained security guards, and occasional sweeps were introduced. But, in a sad twist, the improvement led the CHA to assume progress was permanent, and the security guards were reassigned to a different project. Drug dealers returned to Ickes, violence and insecurity surging in their wake.[29]

Evaluations of the CHA's anticrime efforts were depressing. Researchers, funded by federal sources and the MacArthur Foundation in the 1990s, found that despite a "state-of-the-art community crime-prevention program," this "very expensive effort had little impact." In 1994, despite an intensive campaign against crime at the Henry Horner Homes, an astonishing 40 percent of residents in one building said that a bullet had entered their apartments in the past year. Life in Chicago's high-rises, where 70 percent of families lived, had become a "humanitarian disaster" on several levels. A decade of lawlessness and gang control had effected "overwhelming social disorganization" with few obvious solutions. "A different set of social rules applied," making it difficult for residents to either agree on a set of social norms or confront the social disorder. As the researchers phrased it, "The realities of their social world force CHA residents to focus primarily on survival, 'minding their own business,' and protecting themselves and their children from the war around them." The psychological costs of neglect, addiction, and violence took their toll. Conditions varied considerably from building to building, researchers found, but social disorder was so pervasive that extensive policing managed only a slight advance: "Gang conflicts and peace treaties have more impact on residents' quality of life than anything the police or the CHA tries to do improve conditions."[30]

* * *

All the focus on the sweeps and security meant continued neglect of physical conditions at the CHA's other crumbling, large projects, both high and low in design. Lead paint, vermin infestation, and uncovered scalding radiators threatened the health of children. Public housing had once prided itself on its improvements in public health over the slums, but even that advantage had dissolved. Much of the money for the security effort had been diverted from the CHA's modernization budget, intended to renovate existing projects. Again tenants organized to fight for their communities, and the Henry Horner Mothers Guild, with the assistance of legal aid lawyers, filed suit in 1991, accusing the CHA of intentionally not repairing and rerenting apartments as part of a plan to demolish the project. With half of the units vacant at Horner, Lane's policies amounted to "de facto demolition" since public housing law required that any unit demolished be replaced with new public housing on a "one-for-one" basis, so that the total number of public housing apartments remained unchanged. For two years the CHA and the Mothers Guild litigated and negotiated a plan to tear down the tallest buildings, renovate mid-rise projects, and build replacement housing on a one-for-one basis. The work would be accomplished in phases to minimize displacement and ensure that new housing was completed before old housing was torn down.[31]

The Horner litigation was the first to force the CHA's hand on rebuilding its projects. But as the Mothers Guild plan involved reconstruction of public housing in a black neighborhood, it was subject to the *Gautreaux* ruling and required the approval of Alexander Polikoff and the court. Polikoff, however, resisted the residents' plan to renovate their mid-rise gallery buildings and potentially reconcentrate the poorest families on the Horner site. The goal of the *Gautreaux* ruling was to break up the ghetto and build public housing in white areas, not to save the mistakes of the past. Still, by the early 1990s, Polikoff had begun to retreat from his idealistic stance of the 1970s, as it had become clear that many African Americans wanted community redevelopment not just ghetto dispersal. In 1995, the parties agreed to a phase 1 plan to rehabilitate some mid-rises and replace housing on a one-for-one basis, with half of the new units dedicated to existing "very low-income" families at Horner and the other half to "low-income," working class families per the Lake Parc model. After Congress repealed the one-for-one replacement rule in 1998, however, the ground slid out from under the residents during the planning for phase 2. With the number of replacement units now subject to negotiation, *Gau-*

treaux lawyers argued against renovating more mid-rises and for limiting new public housing to only 30 percent of all replacement units, with the remaining 70 percent sold or rented as market-rate, private housing. Any more than 30 percent, they maintained, "would jeopardize chances for integration" by scaring off potential white renters and buyers. Polikoff, in essence, envisioned moving whites into black neighborhoods as a complement to the *Gautreaux* program of moving blacks into white suburbs. Eventually a mediated settlement favored this view, and the phase 2 plan demolished the remaining mid-rises and granted only 32.5 percent of units to former Horner residents.[32]

The Horner Homes story played out again and again in the mid-1990s, with tenants and their supporters clashing with *Gautreaux* lawyers and, to a lesser extent, the CHA over the number of replacement units and the "mix" of incomes. At Lakefront, Cabrini, ABLA, and Wells, time-consuming legal action set policy. Redevelopment plans slowly moved forward on a mixed-income model that had changed significantly from Lane's vision. Instead of a split between "low-income" and "very low-income" tenants, mixes now included "market-rate" homeowners with buying power and their own definitions of social order. At the heart of these negotiations was an earnest debate among liberals over how to construct neighborhoods. Polikoff and the CHA wanted to tear down the mistakes of the past and to integrate the black poor into the rest of the city through planned gentrification. With new scattered-site public housing in white areas virtually a dead issue, blocked by white resistance and neglected by a CHA struggling with security, Polikoff was forced to confine his integration goals to existing public housing sites. For their part, residents wanted reinvestment and rebuilding of their communities to provide as much affordable housing as possible. In the end, court settlements made commitments only to existing project residents, while the gentrification message came through clearly. In an effort to create social order, policy had shifted toward a new "mix" that privileged the homebuyers, black or white, who could afford market rates.

*   *   *

By 1994, Lane had given up trying to rescue the CHA's large high-rise projects, believing there was little option but to tear most of them down, perhaps saving some using the Lake Parc model. The gallery-style high-rises could be turned around only at extraordinary cost because of their poorly engineered systems, and in any event, *Gautreaux* lawyers objected to preserving high rises on social grounds. Because salvage and rebuilding were expensive and required far more money than HUD provided in annual modernization funds, Lane creatively proposed leveraging the modernization money to accelerate his plans. If HUD could guarantee a steady stream of modernization money (roughly $150 million per year) for a lengthy period of time, then the CHA could borrow over $1 billion in capital funds, much as the federal annual contributions contract guaranteed repayment of housing bonds. But HUD modernization funding had no guarantees, and lenders wanted stronger collateral. Lane lobbied Congress and HUD for help in solving these problems, but legislation fell short of passage, leaving him demoralized and exhausted.[33]

During this time, Lane's leadership at the CHA had grown precarious. The CHA had remained on HUD's "troubled" housing authority list since its inception in 1979, and Lane had made little progress on the fundamental managerial and administrative weaknesses at the authority. Richard M. Daley was reluctant to intervene in his first few years as mayor, recognizing that he lacked the political capital in Chicago's black community to tackle the issues. But in early 1994, he sent Graham Grady, an African American lawyer and former commissioner in the zoning and building departments, to serve as executive director under Lane. Grady had extensive government experience but was shocked by the disarray at the CHA and the low level of financial discipline. No-bid contracts, pilot programs that became permanent, and exceptions to rules were the administrative norm. With CHA employees loyal to Lane, however, Grady struggled to reform the organization, and within ten months, he left, signaling to some that the CHA was at "the meltdown point." New scandals emerged, including a charge that the authority's benefits director had defrauded the employee benefits plan of $12 million, and an even more outrageous report that a twenty-nine-year-old director of risk management had lost $13 million in pension funds in a financial scam and then accepted a $4.1 million bribe from the scammers to cover up the crime.[34] The revelations and resulting headlines meant Lane's days at the CHA were numbered.

Ironically, the 1994 elections resulting in a Republican Congress created the political space for radical reform at the CHA. House Republicans threatened HUD's very existence, and Secretary Cisneros responded with a "Reinvention Blueprint" to save his agency's programs by repackaging them in the language of devolution and "housing choice." Some housing activists thought the blueprint a surrender plan, and it could not stave off the first substantial congressional cuts in public housing operating funding since the program's start. Moreover, the Republican Congress demanded a "viability test" for public housing projects with vacancies above

10 percent that compared the cost of renovation with the cost of giving residents Section 8 certificates to find housing in the private market. By 2000, every CHA family project put to the test—totaling 14,000 units—had failed and was expected to be demolished. (Another 9,500 units had already been slated for demolition or rehabilitation under litigation at the Cabrini, Horner, ABLA, and Lakefront properties). The new political climate and congressional mandates spurred HUD to take dramatic action with incompetent housing authorities.[35]

In a high-level meeting between CHA and HUD officials in early 1995, HUD laid out the continued poor performance of the authority on basic management tasks—"failing grades across the board," as Grady put it. Lane, laying bare his own frustration with the CHA, threw his large set of keys across the table at HUD assistant secretary Joseph Shuldiner, and told him the federal government could have Chicago's projects if it wanted them.[36] A few months later, the CHA board voted to accept a federal takeover, and Cisneros appointed Shuldiner the new CHA chairman. A receiver was contemplated but rejected because of the delays of moving through the court system. Instead, federal officials declared the CHA in breach of its annual contributions contract, a tool that had long been available to HUD but was rarely invoked. Cisneros approved the decision over the concerns of Shuldiner, who worried whether HUD itself had the capacity to manage the nation's third largest housing authority (behind New York City and Puerto Rico) and one of its most troubled. But Cisneros had spent a night at Robert Taylor in 1994, and the appalling conditions caused him to embrace the takeover. "Residents have suffered long enough," Cisneros told Congress.[37]

Shuldiner had extensive experience in public housing at the New York City Housing Authority and as executive director of the Los Angeles Housing Authority, but tackling the CHA was an entirely new proposition. He stepped down from his HUD post to devote his full attention to the CHA. Within two years, he had moved the authority off the "troubled" housing authority list for the first time in its history—without infusions of new funds and without the absolute powers of a court receiver. Instead, privatizations of aspects of the operations and the recruitment of experienced outsiders moved most management measures from failing to passing grades. Private firms were brought in at some projects, and the entire Section 8 operation—applications, tenant selection, inspection of apartments—was privatized. After six months, Shuldiner commented on the financial mess he had found: "Gaining control of the budget has proven to be one of our most difficult challenges to date. Establishing an accurate set of books and a credible accounting system is something we have been working on since day one." In 1997, the CHA received a "clean" audit, the first in at least ten years.[38] While the CHA was hardly "high performing," Shuldiner had managed a turnaround that had eluded the CHA for more than two decades.

But even Shuldiner knew Chicago's high-rises were in a hopeless condition and had to come down. The question was how to pay for a massive rebuilding of public housing and what form the new communities would take. Even before the Republican takeover of Congress, federal policy was moving in bolder directions. In 1992, Congress created the "Hope VI" initiative to fund major overhauls of projects, but in its early stages, the program still operated under many of the old modernization rules. Innovators in Louisville, Atlanta, and Boston worked with Clinton administration officials at HUD to maneuver Hope VI in new directions, suggesting that public-private partnerships and alternative funding sources, including the low-income housing tax credit (created in 1986), were the way to finance an entire makeover of projects.

At the same time, the New Urbanist movement among architects and planners emerged with a model for community development that was, in many ways, the antithesis of midcentury modernism. Building on the ideas of Jane Jacobs and Oscar Newman, New Urbanists promoted urban planning that embraced mixed-use communities (housing, retail, and work spaces), defensible space, and vernacular architecture. They proposed changing restrictive zoning regulations that produced low-density suburbs and instead called for regulations that emphasized sidewalks, verandas, smaller lot sizes, and densities intended to create community interaction. The idea was to foster Robert Putnam's "social capital"—neighborhoods organized to promote community life. When applied to public housing redevelopment, New Urbanism and Hope VI meant a return to the grid of nineteenth-century city streets, demonstrating a respect for the types of urban space once disdained by modernist reformers.[39] More important, Hope VI ended decades of stalemate over what to do with old projects and instead focused planners on envisioning a new future.

★   ★   ★

The federal takeover of the CHA was considered a temporary measure, and a year after the authority achieved the label "untroubled," the city regained control. In June 1998, Daley rushed in a new team with a mandate to accelerate change. Cobbling together the ideas of Vince Lane, New Urbanism, and Hope VI, the Daley appointees produced an aggressive "Plan for Transformation" that pictured the complete remaking of the CHA and its mission. The plan proposed privatizing management at all of its developments and to get the authority "out of the business of managing real estate." Instead, the CHA would serve as a "facilitator" for the renovation or remaking of its projects. The plan called for demolishing 18,500 of the CHA's existing 29,300 family apartments, while another 5,800 family units (mostly in low-rise and mid-rise projects) and all 9,500 senior apartments (mostly in high-rises) would be renovated. At the end of the ten-year plan, the CHA expected to have 24,700 public housing apartments in all (including senior units), slightly more than its number of occupied units in 1999, but far below its peak of 39,000. To pay for this $1.5 billion building program, the CHA proposed using Hope VI grants and, like Lane, leveraging a ten-year stream of federal capital grant funding (formerly the modernization program). Residents deemed "lease compliant" in current CHA developments would have a "right of return" to public housing in some form and, in the interim, would be offered Housing Choice vouchers (formerly the Section 8 certificate program) to pay rent in the private market. Residents would also be connected with city and private social agencies to receive job training, counseling, and other services as part of a "Moving to Work" initiative. The replacement projects would be built in the New Urbanist mold, with new row houses indistinguishable from the city's vernacular styles in order to attract working-class as well as "market-rate" families and to remove the stigma from public housing residency. To accomplish all this, the CHA asked for numerous waivers to federal public housing rules and regulations. In scale and scope, the plan was beyond anything being attempted in the country, but city officials proclaimed that three decades of crisis, incompetence, and insecurity had to come to an end.[40]

The CHA's transformation plan was contentious, however. It was formulated without consultation with elected tenant leaders or housing activists, and they soon made clear their view of its shortcomings. The first involved a macro-level objection to the plan's shrinking of the total public housing stock available. While the CHA claimed that 24,700 apartments by the end of the plan would be enough "to accommodate all existing leaseholders," critics complained about the loss of 14,000 apartments, and perhaps even more if the CHA did not keep its rebuilding promises. To distance itself from the loss of affordable housing, the plan shifted the onus on Washington, claiming that "there is no alternative" given the limits of federal funding.[41]

A second conflict in the plan arose over who would be allowed to return to rebuilt or renovated projects. The CHA would not promise that residents could return to their old developments and the "right of return" to some form of public housing extended only to those who were "lease compliant." While it pledged assistance to help residents comply with lease rules, critics feared many would fall short and be at risk of homelessness. As well, those obviously non–lease compliant—unknown numbers of squatters and transients who lived in vacant apartments—had no place in the plan. Another problem was maintaining contact with residents once they scattered with their Housing Choice voucher; the plan included little incentive to search for former residents and to help them to return. Finally, the CHA in 2004 imposed daunting new rules for those returning, including a thirty-hour-per-week work, school, or training requirement. It viewed its tough admission, screening, and eviction policies as central to its new mission and essential to avoiding a descent to its past.[42]

A third clash resumed the debate over definitions of "mixed income." While most parties agreed that a "mix" was desirable, the precise recipe was hotly contested, as it had been in the Horner litigation. The transformation plan set no precise formula and left the issue to be decided in consultation with local advisory councils and potential developers. Activists wanted, at a minimum, half of the units devoted to "extremely low-income" and "very low-income" categories, with the remainder given to the "low-income" category, following the Lane approach at Lake Parc Place. While most low-rise projects renovated under the plan would follow this model, redevelopment of projects where land values were higher—such as Cabrini and parts of ABLA—followed a different "mix." At these desirable locations, the plan prioritized the "market-rate" group, with roughly one-third of apartments programmed for "market-rate" families, one-third for a new "affordable" category (families earning between 80 and 120 percent of area median area income), and only one-third for the three low-income categories. At other projects, the mix was skewed even higher toward market rate in an effort to extract as much value from the land as possible in order to help pay for public housing production. At the Ida B. Wells Homes, 44 percent of new housing was for "market-rate" households, and only 30 percent for former public housing residents. To critics, this amounted to a land grab or state-sponsored gentrification, but the CHA asserted it needed to make its new communities attractive to market-rate buyers, who would, in effect, subsidize the development of affordable housing.[43]

Finally, as during the first wave of public housing in the late 1940s, the issue of relocation was a central, indeed crucial, issue in the fairness of the plan. If buildings were torn down, where would public housing residents go? Legal aid lawyers pointed to the Horner consent decree as a model that would protect existing tenants, with phased redevelopment involving construction of new units before old ones were torn down so as to avoid distant moves and to preserve public housing communities. But the CHA preferred to "voucher out" as many residents as possible in order to close its buildings, reduce expenses, accelerate redevelopment, and encourage market-rate gentrification in surrounding neighborhoods. This would increase CHA land values and allow it to extract more resources to help fund the plan. With thousands of families to move and a tight housing market in the plan's early years, relocation counselors loaded tenants into vans and drove to neighborhoods where they knew they would find a supply of landlords willing to accept the vouchers—mainly in some of Chicago's poorest neighborhoods, especially Englewood, Roseland, South Shore, and East Garfield Park. Only after the prodding of a 2003 lawsuit, settled in 2005, did the CHA modify its relocation policy and follow the guidelines of the Gautreaux program to "encourage moves to racially integrated areas of metropolitan Chicago." The settlement covered not only tenants still awaiting moves out of public housing but also those who had already taken a voucher and left—in effect, the CHA was required to aid them in a second move, ideally to better opportunities. While vouchers sometimes allowed former public housing residents to improve their physical housing conditions, they more often redistributed than deconcentrated poverty.[44]

Although the Daley transformation plan outlined broad strokes, project-level details were left to painstaking negotiations between the CHA, developers, and local advisory councils, the officially recognized representatives of public housing residents. Even before the plan, Shuldiner initiated efforts to achieving resident "buy-in" to redevelopment by awarding grants to LACs to hire professional planners to conceptualize what new communities might look like. Slowly, planners and the CHA convinced the LACs to accept demolition and rebuilding as the best option. Opposition groups formed to challenge the LACs, claiming they had been co-opted and did not represent real tenant interests. The Coalition to Protect Public Housing, formed in 1996, resisted the transformation plan from the start and tried unsuccessfully to save projects from the wrecking ball, resist income mixing, and increase the number of units for very low-income families in redevelopment plans. Despite rallies, editorials, and protests, the CPPH's voice was mostly ignored by the post-Shuldiner CHA. In 2000, private foundations ended their financial support for the CPPH's full-time staff, and the MacArthur Foundation, a giant in city philanthropy, threw its weight behind the plan, giving $17 million in grants to support it.[45] Opposition tenant groups were simply overrun, but given LAC support, the CHA could still say with some legitimacy that tenants had played an important role in the planning process and that their concerns had been heard.

★   ★   ★

It is far too early to tell whether the Plan for Transformation will be a long-term success. While most projects slated for demolition have come down—including all of the high-rises at Robert Taylor Homes, Stateway Gardens, ABLA, and Wells—rebuilding is proceeding slowly. The net effect is that most displaced residents will remain "vouchered out" for several more years. How many will ultimately return to the new mixed-income communities is an open question. The onerous rules set up by the CHA and enforced by private managers have embittered many; at one new development, public housing residents were required to take a drug test, while the "market-rate" renters were not. Meanwhile, the neighborhoods receiving the greatest influx of voucher recipients have seen rising social disorder as newcomers and transition create instability.[46] The plan has been especially burdensome on residents who had strong attachments to their projects, those who had looked out for one another and scratched out a community amid the violence. Moving to new neighborhoods has been often been a wrenching change with minimal support. Much of this distress might have been avoided had the Horner model of phased redevelopment been followed.[47]

While judgment may be premature, a tentative conclusion is that the Plan for Transformation was essential to pointing the CHA away from its past failings. In the previous four decades, the CHA drove itself into an abyss, building ill-conceived, poorly planned, and badly engineered buildings, while accepting inefficiencies that resulted in poorly maintained, ill-managed housing. By the 1980s, the CHA was running state-sponsored slums that were a mockery of social justice. Residents tried desperately to assert social order, but the shape of their environment, the policies governing it, and the managers running it made their task nearly impossible. Federal operating formulas certainly damaged its housing stock, but the CHA's incompetence was revealed time and again by investigators. Despite repeated opportunities for reform, the CHA was impervious to change. Federal officials only belatedly pulled the plug on this overwrought disaster in 1995. The Plan for Transformation recognized that the CHA could not be trusted to do its core function—manage housing. It acknowledged, at last, that the gallery-style, family high-rises were not worth saving and that the New Urbanist model offered a chance at more livable, defensible, and sustainable community. While opponents have legitimate criticisms about the handling of the relocation problem and the heavy regulations on returning residents, these caveats should not distract from the necessity and significance of starting over with an entirely new approach.

The Plan for Transformation, at heart and paradoxically, is about keeping public housing alive by making it nearly invisible. The CHA was an eyesore and embarrassment for decades, and now Daley's team wanted both to put a new face on public housing and to hide that face. In the New Urbanist model, Chicago's rebuilt developments are intended to be attractive and desirable to a range of incomes yet be physically indistinguishable from market-rate housing. In the effort to remove the welfare stigma attached to it and its former projects, the CHA now blends into neighborhoods, with its tenants living side-by-side with higher-income residents. Private developers, private managers, and "vouchered-out" residents represent a blurring of the line between the public and private market in public housing policy. Progressives in the 1930s directed state authority to step into the space where the market failed and lead the way with large-scale housing in the modernist mold. Administrators in the 1950s built these projects but isolated the public portion of the market. The Plan for Transformation ends this tension by allowing the CHA—and by corollary, its tenants—to become nearly imperceptible in the social fabric of the city.

The Unraveling of Chicago Public Housing

On August 1, 1998, HUD secretary Andrew Cuomo held a press conference on Chicago's West Side to dedicate the Chicago Housing Authority's newest project. The setting offered a stunning juxtaposition of the past and future of public housing, as two CHA projects sat on either side of Leavitt Street—one a recently completed collection of three-story townhouses, the other a group of abandoned fourteen-story high-rises, the remnants of the Henry Horner Extension project. Opened in 1961, the Horner Extension had by the 1980s descended into a living hell for its residents, as recounted in Alex Kotlowitz's *There Are No Children Here*.

The new project appeared nothing like the CHA's previous efforts. In conjunction with developers, marketers, and Horner residents, the CHA erected townhouses using New Urbanist concepts that embraced the older architec-

Figure 31. The Villages of West Haven and the Henry Horner Extension, 1998.
Courtesy of the CHA.

tural styles of the city. The new project included front stoops, small lawns, iron gates, and the incongruous name "The Villages of West Haven," a marketing tactic by the CHA and developers that revealed much about their ambitions to remake Chicago's West Side. Comparing the new and the old, Cuomo told the audience that CHA high-rise projects such as "the Robert Taylor Homes, the Cabrini-Greens, the Horner Homes are public housing developments of the past."[1] The Villages of West Haven, by contrast, represented the humbled but optimistic future of public housing, an implicit statement that the towers across the street had been a disastrous miscalculation. Forty years after the planning of Horner Extension, the CHA had completed an ironic full circle. In the 1950s, it leveled nineteenth-century brick and stone buildings considered irredeemable slums, then built high-rises that became altogether unviable, and finally tore these down in a 1990s version of "slum clearance" in order to erect a new mixed-income "village" that echoed the architectural conventions of the site's original dwellings.

The same summer that Cuomo trumpeted the CHA's New Urbanist vision for the West Side, Scott Fortino embarked on an unusual study at Cabrini-Green. The sprawling project had been neglected through the 1990s in anticipation of demolition and rebuilding like that at Horner. Fortino was a police officer with ten years on the beat at Cabrini, but he was also a graduate student in photography at the University of Illinois at Chicago, and for his master's thesis, he began photographing various doors at the project. At first he chose doors that intrigued him. Then he elected to document all forty-eight apartment doors at a single, six-story Cabrini building (see fig. 32). He presented the images to a faculty committee, whose reactions were immediate and visceral. Some committee members felt Fortino had invaded the privacy of Cabrini residents and insulted their dignity by displaying the stark, heavily worn, often damaged, and decidedly unwelcoming doors and damaged wooden screens. The images magnified public housing's cold, disheartening image and denied the humanity of its residents.

Others found the collection intriguing, with each scarred door showing a remarkably different character that betrayed its own troubled past. Fortino commented that the "doors have a psychological weight to them," and a *Chicago Tribune* reviewer added, "[The doors] are as complicated as faces; like faces, they both hide and reveal, keep in and keep out. To some, a closed door may be an unfinished sentence or a held breath. In the next moment, anything can happen." The *Tribune* review included a graphic of twelve of the doors in a play on tourist posters of colorful Irish and English doorways, offering a voyeuristic tour for readers never likely to get near public housing. When long-time Cabrini resident and activist Carol Steele heard about Fortino's work, she told the *Tribune*: "The media are always taking pictures of the outsides of the buildings. They don't go inside. People don't realize that [Cabrini residents] take care of their places too. They live just like everybody else."[2]

The diversity of Cabrini-Green's psychologically ambiguous front doors mirrors the complexity of public housing's failure. Steele understood that many apartment interiors were fastidiously neat and clean, as tenants sought internal order to counteract the external chaos and failures of the CHA. But despite Steele's defense, Cabrini's embattled doors—and the contrast between Horner Extension and the Villages at West Haven— do symbolize the difference between public housing and the surrounding community, evidence that its residents did not "live just like everybody else." For decades they resided in indefensible projects containing unprecedented densities of youth with limited police protection. They lived in poorly planned, badly maintained housing complexes stricken by random violence, erratic services, and oppressive mismanagement. They lived with extreme racial, economic, and social isolation in ways that few

Figure 32. Selections from "The Doors of Cabrini," 1998. Photographs by Scott Fortino. Reproduced by permission of the photographer.

Chicagoans could imagine, and their children were often deeply scarred by the experience. Residents understandably formed tight-knit bonds and clung to their own forms of community just to survive.

The divergent reactions of Fortino's professors to his photographs as well as the controversy over the Plan for Transformation reflect the competing narratives about how society should view public housing's residents and the program's outcomes. On one side are those who consider public housing tragic. Journalists such as Alex Kotlowitz in *There Are No Children Here* and radio producer David Isay in *Ghetto Life 101* employed the stories of children in Chicago projects to unmask the profound social injustice and deep-seated pain inflicted on the least advantaged. The children that Kotlowitz followed and that Isay recorded are heartbreakingly perceptive about the world around them, reinforcing the empathetic quality of the narratives. While less didactic than Jacob Riis's *How the Other Half Lives*, the Kotlowitz and Isay exposés challenge affluent America to confront its social failures.[3]

A new generation of scholars, however, has moved away from narratives of victimization. Reacting against general stereotypes of public housing residents in the media, sociologist Sudhir Venkatesh, historian Rhonda Williams, and planners Roberta Feldman and Susan Stall want to restore agency to public housing residents and allow them to speak for themselves. Their narrators are mostly women who carve out community, create their own survival networks, and confront the neglect of the state. Public housing residents are not passive victims and their communities are not "disorganized," Venkatesh suggests, but rather "organized according to a different set of principles" in response to structural inequalities and state oppression.[4] Instead of viewing residents as deviant, these writers argue, we should seek to understand them on their own terms and comprehend the community they have struggled to fashion. Residents should be listened to and empowered, rather than simply targeted for reforms that dismantle their neighborhoods.[5]

While these authors reveal the complex coping mechanisms of residents, their works are less useful in explaining the multiple forces that caused public housing to spiral downward. Policies developed over decades by activists, legislators, federal administrators, and local housing authorities were critical to public housing outcomes. Tenant leaders had little influence over budgets, maintenance, and security expenditures, and while they desperately tried to impose order on their environments, they were rarely given the resources to do so. Moreover, a bottom-up perspective alone does not provide an adequate picture of the sources of policy failure.

★   ★   ★

The answer to the question "What went wrong with public housing in Chicago?" cannot be boiled down to a simple statement. Numerous policies contributed to the unraveling of the CHA, ranging from ideological assumptions to specific implementation issues. First, a market-failure ideology, itself the product of progressive thinking and long-held considerations of the role of the American state, constrained public housing's boundaries. From inception, the program's viability was defined by the belief that public housing should not compete with the private market. The result was a narrowing of the target audience and an expectation that public housing should be less expensive than private housing. The reformers behind the 1937 Housing Act shaped this ideology and accepted these boundaries; most had no intention of displacing reasonable private housing. But assumptions regarding the extent, permanence, and nature of housing market failure proved wrong by the late 1950s. State restructuring of credit markets, rising real wages, and improved production methods spurred an unpredicted housing boom that reached down into the ranks of the working class. Moreover, once it became apparent that public housing could not be built for less than the private market, the Truman, Eisenhower, and Kennedy administrations demanded cost controls in order to justify and preserve the program.

Similarly, income-based rents were counterproductive over time. This policy emerged from a progressive impulse to distribute aid based on need. But it concentrated poverty with its economic incentives for the very poor to stay and for the upwardly mobile to leave. These incentives were mitigated for a while through tenant selection that prioritized higher-income applicants, but changing welfare policy, social disorder, and a host of other forces in the late 1960s pushed out the working class, dooming the projects to welfare housing status. By themselves, income-based rents merely redistributed rent burdens. But the policy also severed the link between rental income and project expenses, undermining managerial discipline and financial health. In Great Britain, poor families unable to afford fixed rents in council housing were provided an additional "housing benefit" payment by the state; by contrast, income-based rents in the U.S. left housing authority budgets vulnerable. It would be unfair, however, to say that public housing was "programmed to fail," in the words of Eugene Meehan, because of its funding mechanisms. Washington paid to construct buildings, local governments exempted taxes, and even after it became clear that these deep subsidies were not enough to absorb an increasingly impoverished clientele, additional subsidies were piled on. Tremendous sums poured into public housing in Chicago and other large cities, yet reasonable outcomes remained elusive.

Even less well understood were public housing policies that contributed to—if not created—social disorder. Again, the progressive mission to help those most in need directed well-meaning administrators to build numerous large apartments for large families. When such apartments were configured in indefensible high-rise buildings, the resulting youth densities proved catastrophic. Despite considerable efforts from tenants and administrators, establishing social order in these conditions was nearly impossible. As Jane Jacobs observed in 1961, neighborhoods work because responsible adults can police community behavior and impose social norms. But public housing's very shape created a community that was unmanageable to police, either formally or informally. More than any single factor, the combination of high youth-adult ratios and high-rise buildings doomed public housing in Chicago.

Finally, the federal-local partnership did not function well in Chicago. Federal officials, fearful of congressional reprisal, failed to support Elizabeth Wood's racial liberalism and forced high-rise construction. At the same time, Washington accepted widespread inefficiency in the CHA's maintenance operation and balked at removing unfit leadership. Federal powers were substantial; HUD controlled the purse strings and the annual contributions contract afforded oversight of operations. Yet HUD assumed that financial incentives would change the CHA's behavior. Instead, political push back from city mayors and bureaucratic inertia contributed to an anemic federal response. For their part, Chicago's mayors permitted inefficiency and incompetence, largely for political expediency.

Given the numerous policy choices that undermined Chicago's projects, the ready inclination to blame tenants for negative outcomes was shortsighted. Of course, the violent and destructive behavior of a portion of antisocial tenants was inexcusable (though it can be explained), and certainly some tenants contributed disproportionately to disruption in projects. But fundamentally, the policies, not the tenants, caused the unsustainable environments. Planners, housing authority commissioners, and federal administrators built large-scale, high-rise projects, filled them with numerous children and few adults, then struggled to manage the resulting social chaos. The tenants did not make these decisions—experts and political appointees did. Responsibility for Chicago's public housing fiasco lies with those in power who made unsound choices, failed to alter plans they knew were flawed, and then tolerated incompetence.

★   ★   ★

Just when this analysis points to an utter lack of state capacity to craft a public housing program and successfully implement it, two arguments give pause. Advocates for a continued federal presence in state-sponsored housing construction contend that the "failure" label placed on public housing is wrong. They cite a 1992 government commission that found only about 7 percent of the nation's housing stock—or 86,000 units— was "severely distressed." Senior housing, rural housing, and many small cities, they argue, are successful, undermining the monolithic idea that all public housing looks like the Robert Taylor Homes.[6] This is a reasonable point, but the "severely distressed" euphemism cannot cover up the devastating impact of such projects. In cities ranging from Washington to San Francisco, from Boston to New Orleans, from Glasgow, Scotland, to Caracas, Venezuela, large-scale housing projects by 1990 had become infamous ghettoes of economic, social, and often racial isolation. If "failure" is too general a term to describe all of public housing, to call the program a "success" lowers the bar so as to be nearly meaningless. The suffering in large-scale urban projects has been, by any measure, a social disaster.

More relevant is a second argument. The New York City Housing Authority continues to operate the largest housing authority in the country, consisting mostly of large-scale, superblock, high-rise family projects. They are fairly well maintained, fully tenanted, and—compared to housing projects in other cities—reasonably safe; few have been torn down. The NYCHA is, in a relative sense, a success story. How did New York do it?

Historian Nicholas Bloom shows how the NYCHA charted its own path with hard-nosed management policies. Mayor Fiorello La Guardia threw out the progressive slum reformers who initially ran the authority and installed a cadre of professional real estate managers who ran it "as a business." Tenants were screened; rules were enforced. The NYCHA acted less like the weak partner in the federal-local relationship and instead like an independent agency. This was possible in part because of an extensive city- and state-funded program that matched its federal program in size and that allowed it to experiment with management techniques without federal interference. When the NYCHA's postwar high-rises, many of them designed with weak defensible space, experienced social disorder because of youth vandalism in the mid-1950s, the city instituted an aggressive police strategy, including vertical patrols, in an effort to control crime. Fortunately, New York built significantly fewer bedrooms per apartment than Chicago, housing only 1.8 minors per unit versus Chicago's average of 3.1, aiding the social control effort. Competent maintenance and administrative professionalism made the NYCHA a "high-performing" housing authority under the federal performance funding system, allowing it to receive substantial operating subsidies. New York also actively resisted housing high proportions of welfare recipients. As late as 1968, only 15 percent of its tenants were reliant on AFDC, and even when pressured to accept the homeless in the early 1970s, NYCHA leaders fought back and restored tenant stability by using quotas to favor higher-income families and by raising income limits to HUD maximums. New York's welfare population peaked at 34 percent in 1973 and declined slowly thereafter. Working-class residents, plus copious subsidies, plus strong management kept New York's projects viable. Finally, New York's tight rental market throughout the period likely helped attract and keep working-class families in public housing.[7]

But New York is the exception, not the rule. As a model, the NYCHA's policies have run against the grain of those promoted by housing advocates for the poor. It continues to screen heavily and restrict admission from welfare applicants through quotas, imposing rules that put institutional interests first and tenants second. To some, this is a tradeoff: tenants want security and order, and they are willing to submit to housing authority regulations in return for well-managed housing at low rents. To others, these policies unfairly privilege one class—those with employment—over the most vulnerable. But the New York accomplishment suggests that public housing should first and foremost be a housing program, not an extension of a city's welfare agency. Further, as an exceptional case, New York's survival while other U.S. cities floundered says a great deal about the riskiness of trusting local governments and Congress—with all their political vulnerabilities—to perform adequately over the long run in the difficult business of building and maintaining rental housing for low-income families. The U.S. political state of the past half-century simply could not meet this challenge in most cities, with calamitous consequences.

★　★　★

Taking the long-view of Chicago's housing reform, an alternative path existed that might have avoided public housing's disasters. Political leaders and community groups organized in the late 1930s to seek state support for neighborhood-level rehabilitation, spot clearance, and reinvestment. But the slum clearance consensus of progressives crowded out those voices, and the CHA's 1946 study ambushed the idea of rehabilitation by hiding its cost-effectiveness over clearance. Public housers saw saving old neighborhoods as a flawed approach; they also rejected early proposals for housing vouchers, arguing that this would not supply new housing and would only inflate the profits on bad housing. Today, vouchers are the single largest component of affordable housing provision in the United States, in large part because of the failures of public housing but also because vouchers put the state in the role of redistributor of income and regulator of landlords, tasks it does far better than planning and managing large-scale projects. These alternatives, while far from perfect, suggest the possibility existed during the New Deal for a much gentler footprint of state-sponsored, neighborhood reform upon fragile urban fabrics. Renovation, housing code enforcement, selective demolition, targeted rebuilding, and voucher payments might have produced incremental gains without displacing tens of thousands of renters, homeowners, and businesses.

Not every area could be saved, of course. The Federal Street slum mostly consisted of rotting and unsanitary wood frame buildings, vacant lots, and abandoned rail yards. But numerous other portions of the city identified as "slums" by the CHA in the 1930s dodged the wrecking ball and survived as viable low-income communities, often housing new waves of immigrants. By the late 1960s, as public housing's mistakes grew apparent, the wholesale clearance of old neighborhoods largely ended. In some communities, highly localized, community-based, nonprofit builders began producing small-scale affordable housing developments with new sources of funding, including the 1986 low-income housing tax credit. By the 1980s, gentrification had become a concern, as former slums began filtering upward, driving out their working-class tenants and installing a new upper-middle class infatuated with the nineteenth-century streetscape. Whether widespread slum clearance was even necessary has now become an open historical question.

★   ★   ★

The lessons of public housing's disaster in Chicago are humbling. While undoing the mistakes of the past is a painful process, policy learning has taken place, albeit belatedly. High modernism was dispatched by the dispiriting results of public housing and urban renewal. Jane Jacobs began the critique, but the reaction extended well beyond her iconoclasm to cause an about-face on thinking about how cities evolve. Today planners must vet redevelopment through long periods of community input that, while imperfect, nonetheless give voice to local residents. Planners now seek to tread lightly on the urban landscape, not wipe it clean like those who defined blight in cancerous terms. They respect the street grid and think about human scale. Local authorities no longer pursue a heavy-handed model of government-planned and government-managed housing development. In many ways, the massive failure of large-scale public housing projects was necessary to end the lofty position of housing authorities, planners, and architects as a city's foremost experts. But residents who wanted a positive community paid a dreadful price, finding themselves surrounded by disorder in well-intentioned but misguided projects.

Today, the CHA's Plan for Transformation represents a daring experiment in social planning. Like the New Deal experiment, it could also founder on its assumptions about what makes a viable community. The new mixed-income concept assumes, in a somewhat patronizing fashion, that higher-income residents will provide the right kind of leadership and that contact with such families will lift the opportunities of the poor. It assumes that private managers can avoid the pitfalls that sunk CHA managers. Finally, the concept trusts that its mix of incomes will prove durable and that market-filtration forces can be managed to avoid economic and racial resegregation, another sustainability challenge that bedeviled the New Deal public housing program. Once again, policymakers have begun to clear the slums and build better housing for the poor. The ambitions are certainly less lofty, and one can only hope they are more successful. Whether this new vision has conquered the complex problem of housing the poor any better than the original vision of the 1930s remains to be seen.

ACKNOWLEDGMENTS

The questions at the heart of this book have long been on my mind. As a teenager from the western suburbs exploring Chicago in the mid-1980s, I stumbled upon public housing projects like Cabrini-Green and Stateway Gardens and discovered a built environment and a density of people unlike any I had seen before. A sociologist might call my experience a fleeting encounter with the "other," as I had little in common with the poor African American families living stacked on top of each other in neglected projects that were alien to anything in my world. But even in my ignorance and innocence, I recognized governmental neglect on a scale that begged explanation. "What went wrong here?" became the question.

Finding answers has taken the generosity of countless scholars, practitioners, former residents, archivists, family, and friends. In graduate school at the University of California, Berkeley, professors Richard Abrams, Robin Einhorn, and the late Nelson Polsby offered encouragement and constructive criticism as I wrestled with my evidence. Much of that data came from the Chicago Housing Authority, where former communications director Angela Ryan took a chance on a graduate student and unlocked doors. The late Pat MacArthur-Harris, manager of the CHA's record center, overcame initial suspicions to become a supporter of my work, as did Lee Chuc Gill, who unfailingly provided access to the CHA's minutes. Former executive director Joe Shuldiner, former chairperson Sharon Gist Gilliam, and staff members Lisa Schneider, Tim Veenstra, Derek Hill, and Bryan Zises deserve credit for a willingness to open the CHA to historical scrutiny.

While too numerous to list here, formal interviews with thirty-six former residents and staff and informal conversations with countless others greatly helped my understanding of the challenges they faced. I thank them for telling me their stories. Many connections with former residents came through Roosevelt University, where I have been fortunate to work with students and colleagues interested in my research and committed to issues of social justice. Jim Fuerst, a special friend and CHA staff member from 1947 to 1953, shared with me transcripts of 130 interviews, many of which we compiled into a book, *When Public Housing Was Paradise: Building Community in Chicago* (University of Illinois Press, 2005). This generosity of time and life stories has greatly added to this book.

Help also came from other educational and cultural institutions. Lyle Benedict and Ellen O'Brien of the Chicago Public Library's Municipal Reference Collection searched for obscure CHA reports, and the late Archie Motley at the Chicago Historical Society (now the Chicago History Museum) offered his bibliographic memory. Audiences at the Chicago Urban History Seminar, a National Endowment for the Humanities Summer Institute, the Temple Hoyne Buell Center at Columbia University, the Newberry Library, Northwestern University's sociology colloquium, and a University of Chicago graduate history seminar provided helpful feedback. I am grateful to Michael Ebner, Robert Bruegmann, Richard John, Juan Onesimo Sandoval, and Jim Grossman for their invitations to these forums. Financial support came from a research leave and summer grants from Roosevelt University, and Cornell University provided a grant to visit its valuable collection of planning history.

Versions of this book were read in their entirety by Daniel Headrick, Alexander von Hoffman, Scott Henderson, Joseph Biggott, Alex Polikoff, Kevin Skelly, series editor Tim Gilfoyle, and two anonymous readers. Each offered a keen eye and thoughtful criticism, and I am grateful for their comprehensive reactions to my work. Jason Scott Smith, Dominic Pacyga, David Erickson, Amanda Seligman, Nicholas Bloom, Richard Harris, Dennis McClendon, and Cassie Fennell helped me with key problems at important times. At the University of Chicago Press, Robert Devens skillfully guided me through numerous challenges, Carlisle Rex-Waller patiently copyedited the manuscript, and Emilie Sandoz held the book together at the finish.

I am blessed with an amazing family. My mother, Jane Cockerill Hunt, read every word of every iteration of this book with the eye of a former English teacher. She taught me to write as a youth and has been teaching me with loving patience ever since. My sister, Marcia Hunt, also read chapters and gave energetic pep talks. My father, Donald S. Hunt has always embraced my work and my career with enthusiasm. My wonderful wife, Page Hartzell, and our two young children, Sam and Chloe, have been exceptionally patient with a husband and father often absorbed in his own world, pondering troublesome questions about housing, planning, and social order. I cannot possibly thank them enough for all that they have given me.

A NOTE ON SOURCES

The Chicago Housing Authority granted me access to its surviving official records beginning in 1998, including statistical reports, development files, legal proceedings, photographs, and board minutes. While these sources proved invaluable, much material has been lost over various moves, floods, and managerial changes. Records before 1955 are slim, and the loss of administrative capacity at the CHA by the 1980s is readily apparent in the breakdown of filing systems.

The CHA retains all its records. This collection has not been cataloged and is not publicly available. Unless noted otherwise, the records cited are stored in a CHA warehouse. Photocopies of many of the sources cited in this book are held by the author, with the exception of the CHA's *Official Minutes*, which were not photocopied. To cite the records in this book, the following system is used:

- "CHA Development files": Subsection of files on individual developments, sorted by development number. For example, "CHA Development files, IL 2-37" refers to the files for the creation of the Robert Taylor Homes, project IL 2-37.
- "CHA Subject files": Subsection of files sorted by subject matter, sometimes with folder titles.
- "CHA Gautreaux files": Subsection of files relating to the *Gautreaux* litigation described in chapter 9.
- "CHA Public Affairs files": Subsection of files stored at the CHA's central office, including clipping files and selected published reports.
- "CHA Legal files": Subsection of files on legal cases other than *Gautreaux*.

NOTES

INTRODUCTION

1. J. S. Fuerst, *When Public Housing Was Paradise: Building Community in Chicago*, with the assistance of D. Bradford Hunt (Champaign: University of Illinois Press, 2005), 144–45.

2. Ibid., 137, 153, 175.

3. Ibid., 145, 154, 175; Addie and Claude Wyatt, former residents of Altgeld Gardens, transcript of interview by Jim Fuerst, no date, in author's possession. For more recollections of public housing as early paradise and later hell, see Susan J. Popkin et al., *The Hidden War: Crime and the Tragedy of Public Housing in Chicago* (New Brunswick: Rutgers University Press, 2000), 39–43, 85–91, and 138–42.

4. Popkin et al., *The Hidden War*; House Committee on Government Reform and Oversight, *HUD's Takeover of the Chicago Housing Authority: Hearing before the U.S. House of Representatives, Committee on Government Reform and Oversight*, 104th Congr., 1st sess., September 5, 1995, 21; U.S. Bureau of the Census, *The 100 Poorest Tracts in the United States: 1989*, Report CPH-L-188 (Washington, DC, 1989).

5. Alex Kotlowitz, *There Are No Children Here* (New York: Double-

day, 1991). For other stories of growing up in public housing, see LeAlan Jones and Lloyd Newman, *Our America: Life and Death on the South Side of Chicago*, with David Isay (New York: Scribner, 1997); Doreen Ambrose-Van Lee, *Diary of a Midwestern Getto Gurl* (Baltimore: Publish America, 2007).

6. Histories of public housing are extensive. See John Bauman, *Public Housing, Race, and Renewal: Philadelphia* (Philadelphia: Temple University Press, 1987); Arnold Hirsch, *Making the Second Ghetto: Race and Housing in Chicago, 1940–1960* (New York: Oxford University Press, 1983); Rachel Bratt, *Rebuilding a Low-Income Housing Policy* (Philadelphia: Temple Press, 1989); Eugene Meehan, *The Quality of Federal Policymaking* (Columbia: University of Missouri Press, 1979); Gail Radford, *Modern Housing for America* (Chicago: University of Chicago Press, 1996); Lawrence Vale, *From the Puritans to the Projects* (Cambridge: Harvard University Press, 2000); Devereux Bouly, *The Poorhouse: Subsidized Housing in Chicago, 1895–1976* (Carbondale: Southern Illinois University Press, 1978). Owing to superior management, New York City has avoided crisis. See Nicholas Dagen Bloom, *Public Housing That Worked: New York in the Twentieth Century* (Philadelphia: University of Pennsylvania Press, 2008).

7. Jeffrey L. Pressman and Aaron Wildavsky, *Implementation*, expanded edition (Berkeley and Los Angeles: University of California Press, 1984); Peter deLeon and Linda deLeon, "What Ever Happened to Policy Implementation? An Alternative Approach," *Journal of Public Administration Research and Theory* 12, no. 4 (2002): 467–92; Paul Sabatier, "Top-down and Bottom-up Approaches to Implementation Research: A Critical Analysis and Suggested Synthesis," *Journal of Public Policy* 6, no. 1 (1986): 21–48.

8. See Gerald D. Suttles, *Social Order of the Slum* (Chicago: University of Chicago Press, 1968); Lee Rainwater, *Behind Ghetto Walls* (Chicago: Aldine, 1970); William Moore Jr., *The Vertical Ghetto: Everyday Life in a Housing Project* (New York: Random House, 1969); Sudhir Venkatesh, *American Project: The Rise and Fall of a Modern Ghetto* (Cambridge: Harvard University Press, 2000); Sudhir Venkatesh, *Gang Leader for a Day: A Rogue Sociologist Takes to the Streets* (New York: Penguin, 2008); Roberta M. Feldman and Susan Stall, *The Dignity of Resistance: Women Residents' Activism in Chicago Public Housing* (New York: Cambridge University Press, 2004); Rhonda Y. Williams, *The Politics of Public Housing: Black Women's Struggles against Urban Inequality* (New York: Oxford University Press, 2004); Amy Howard, "'More than Shelter': Community, Identity, and Spatial Politics in San Francisco Public Housing, 1938–2000" (Ph.D. diss., College of William and Mary, 2005); Kelly A. Quinn, "Making Modern Homes: A History of Langston Terrace Dwellings, a New Deal Housing Program in Washington, D.C." (Ph.D. diss., University of Maryland, 2007).

9. CHA, *Plan for Transformation*, January 6, 2000, Harold Washington Library Center, Municipal Reference Collection, 16–17 (hereafter HWLC-MRC).

10. Edith Elmer Wood, *Recent Trends in American Housing* (New York: Macmillan, 1931); William Leuchtenberg, *Franklin D. Roosevelt and the New Deal, 1932–1940* (New York: Harper Collins, 1963); Jason Scott Smith, *Building New Deal Liberalism* (New York: Cambridge University Press, 2006); Alan Brinkley, *The End of Reform: New Deal Liberalism in Depression and War* (New York: Knopf, 1995).

11. Kent Colton, *Housing in the 21st Century* (Cambridge: Harvard University Press, 2003), 3–33.

12. James C. Scott, *Seeing Like a State: How Certain Schemes to Improve the Human Condition Have Failed* (New Haven: Yale University Press, 1998).

13. Arnold R. Hirsch, *Making the Second Ghetto: Race and Housing in Chicago, 1940–*

1960 (Cambridge: Cambridge University Press, 1983; reprint, Chicago: University of Chicago Press, 1998).

14. See a special issue devoted to the "second ghetto" school in the *Journal of Urban History* (March 2003), as well as Hirsch's preface to the 1998 edition of *Making the Second Ghetto*. Among the "second ghetto" works are the following: John F. Bauman, *Public Housing, Race, and Renewal: Urban Planning in Philadelphia, 1920–1974* (Philadelphia: Temple University Press, 1987); Robert Fairbanks, *Making Better Citizens: Housing Reform and Community Development Strategy in Cincinnati, 1890–1960* (Champaign: University of Illinois, 1988); Thomas Sugrue, *The Origins of the Urban Crisis: Race and Inequality in Postwar Detroit* (Princeton: Princeton University Press, 1996); Ronald H. Bayor, *Race and the Shaping of Twentieth-Century Atlanta* (Chapel Hill: University of North Carolina Press, 1996); Raymond Mohl, "Making the Second Ghetto in Metropolitan Miami, 1940–1960," *Journal of Urban History* 21, no. 3 (1995): 395–427.

15. Jane Jacobs, *The Death and Life of Great American Cities* (New York: Vintage Books, 1992); Oscar Newman, *Defensible Space: Crime Prevention through Urban Design* (New York: Macmillan, 1972); Robert J. Sampson and Byron W. Groves, "Community Structure and Crime: Testing Social-Disorganization Theory," *American Journal of Sociology* 94, no. 4 (1989): 774–802.

CHAPTER ONE

1. Catherine Bauer, "Now, at Last: Housing," *New Republic*, September 8, 1937, 119–21.

2. The historical literature overwhelmingly blames real estate interests and conservatives for forcing policies that led to public housing failure. I challenge this argument in detail in D. Bradford Hunt, "Was the 1937 Housing Act a Pyrrhic Victory?" *Journal of Planning History* 4, no. 3 (2005): 195–222. The critical historical works that blame real estate interests for bad public housing policy include James Patterson, *Congressional Conservatism and the New Deal: The Growth of the Conservative Coalition in Congress, 1933–1939* (Lexington: University of Kentucky Press, 1967), 153, 183; Daniel T. Rodgers, *Atlantic Crossings: Social Politics in a Progressive Age* (Cambridge: Harvard University Press, 1998), 461–79; Lawrence M. Friedman, *Government and Slum Housing: A Century of Frustration* (Chicago: Rand McNally, 1968), 104–13; Mark Gelfand, *A Nation of Cities* (New York: Oxford University Press, 1975), 62–65; Gail Radford, *Modern Housing for America* (Chicago: University of Chicago Press, 1996), 189–91; Bratt, *Rebuilding a Low-Income Housing Policy*, 56–60; and Nathaniel Keith, *The Housing Crisis since 1930* (New York: Universe, 1973), chap. 5; Alex Schwartz, *Housing Policies in the U.S.* (New York: Routledge, 2006), 105.

3. Roy Lubove, *The Progressives and the Slums: Tenement House Reform in New York City, 1890–1917* (Pittsburgh: University of Pittsburgh Press, 1962); John F. Bauman, "The Eternal War on the Slums," in *From Tenements to the Taylor Homes*, edited by John F. Bauman, Roger Biles, and Kristin M. Szylvian (University Park: Pennsylvania State University Press, 2000), 21–42; Alexander von Hoffman, "The End of the Dream: The Political Struggle of America's Public Housers," *Journal of Planning History* 4, no. 3 (2005): 222–53.

4. Thomas Philpott, *The Slum and the Ghetto* (New York: Oxford University Press, 1978); Robert Hunter, *Tenement Conditions in Chicago* (Chicago: City Homes Association, 1901).

5. Lubove, *The Progressives and the Slums*; Friedman, *Government and Slum Housing*, 59–67; Max Page, *The Creative Destruction of Manhattan* (Chicago: University of Chicago Press, 1999), 72–85; Robert M. Fogelson, *Downtown: Its Rise and Fall, 1880–1950* (New Haven: Yale University Press, 2001), chap. 7; von Hoffman, "The End of the Dream," 223–25; Peter Hall, *Cities of Tomorrow*, 3rd ed. (Oxford: Blackwell, 2002), 36–47.

6. Edith Abbott, *The Tenements of Chicago, 1908–1935* (Chicago: University of Chicago Press, 1935), 61–66, 121–25, 197–93, 232.

7. Lubove, *Progressives and the Slums*, 179–83; Edith Elmer Wood, *The Housing of the Unskilled Wage Earner* (New York: Macmillan, 1919).

8. Wood, *Recent Trends in American Housing*, 1; Friedman, *Government and Slum Housing*, 75–103.

9. For the progressive slum reformer view, see the plan released by the National Association of Housing Officials (NAHO), *A Housing Program for the United States* (Chicago, 1934), and the explanation of the 1937 Housing Act published by the United States Housing Authority (USHA), *What the Housing Act Can Do for Your City*, 1938. See also speeches by Senator Robert F. Wagner: *Congressional Record*, January 16, 1936, 475–76, April 28, 1936, 6259, and June 15, 1936, 9347.

10. Mary Simkovitch, "Housing," excerpt from her book *Here Is God's Plenty: Reflections on American Social Advance* (1949), in *The American Planner: Biographies and Recollections*, 2nd ed., edited by Donald A. Krueckeberg (New Brunswick: Center for Urban Policy Research, 1994), 106–7.

11. The divides among housing reformers have been well described by historians. See Bauman, *Public Housing, Race, and Renewal*, 3–10; Rodgers, *Atlantic Crossings*, 391–404, 474–75; von Hoffman, "The End of the Dream."

12. Catherine Bauer, "'Slum Clearance' or 'Housing,'" *Nation* 137, no. 3573 (1933): 730–31; Catherine Bauer, *Modern Housing* (Cambridge, MA: Riverside Press, 1934), 228, 247.

13. Bauer, *Modern Housing*, xv–xvii, 125–29, 242; H. Peter Oberlander and Eva Newbrun, *Houser: The Life and Work of Catherine Bauer* (Vancouver: University of British Columbia Press, 1999); Radford, *Modern Housing for America*; Hall, *Cities of Tomorrow*, 116–74.

14. Bauman, *Public Housing, Race, and Renewal*, 4–8; von Hoffman, "The End of the Dream," 223–31; Langdon W. Post, *The Challenge of Housing* (New York: Farrar and Rinehart, 1938), 223–27. See also Rogers, *Atlantic Crossings*, 461–67. John Bauman labels the two progressive camps "professionals" and "communitarians." I have chosen "progressive slum reformers" and "modern housing planners" to describe these same groups.

15. Timothy L. McDonnell, *The Wagner Housing Act: A Case Study of the Legislative Process* (Chicago: Loyola University Press, 1957), 29–30, 54–55; von Hoffman, "The End of the Dream," 229–30. During World War I, the federal government built housing for war workers but quickly sold off properties at the end of the war.

16. Harold Ickes, *The Secret Diary of Harold L. Ickes*, vol. 1 (New York: Simon and Schuster, 1953), 610; Bauer, *Modern Housing*, 255; Radford, *Modern Housing for America*, 105–6; Lyle John Woodyatt, "The Origins and Evolution of the New Deal Public Housing Program" (Ph.D. diss., Washington University, 1968), 79–80, 148–52; Post, *The Challenge of Housing*; Robert E. Wood to PWA administrator, July 23, 1936, folder H-1400, Public Works Administration Housing Division files, RG 196, National

Archives II, Suitland, Maryland (hereafter PWA Housing Division files); Charles Abrams, *The Future of Housing* (New York: 1946), 253; Michael W. Straus and Talbot Wegg, *Housing Comes of Age* (New York: Oxford University Press, 1938); NAHO, "*A Housing Program for the United States*; Metropolitan Housing Council, "Report of the Committee on Public Housing," no date [1937?], folder "Public Housing Committee, 1947," box 23, accession 74-20, Metropolitan Housing and Planning Council Papers, University of Illinois at Chicago, Special Collections (hereafter UIC Special Collections).

17. Senate Committee on Education and Labor, *Hearings on S. 4424*, 74th Congr., 2nd sess., April 20–29, 1936, 21. Some scholars view local control in public housing as driven by racial considerations, especially by southerners seeking to protect segregation. See Michael K. Brown, *Race, Money and the American Welfare State* (Ithaca, NY: Cornell University Press, 1999), 104–6.

18. *Congressional Record*, June 6, 1936, 9155–56; "Correspondence with Chicago General Advisory Board on Housing, July 23, 1936, through November 27, 1936," November 28, 1936, box 80, PWA Housing Division files; Arthur Bohnen, "Report of the Committee on Public Housing of the Metropolitan Housing Council," October 7, 1937, folder 59, Graham Aldis Papers, UIC Special Collections; Warren J. Vinton, "Contemporary Public Housing in the USA," lecture, October 26, 1938, box 1, Warren Vinton Papers, Cornell University Special Collections Library (hereafter Vinton Papers); Richard Pommer, "The Architecture of Urban Housing in the United States during the Early 1930s," *Journal of the Society of Architectural Historians* 37, no. 4. (1978): 242–43.

19. Von Hoffman, "The End of the Dream," 233; Dorothy Schaffter, *State Housing Agencies* (New York: Columbia University Press, 1942); NAHO, *State Housing Agencies: A Comparative Summary of State Enabling Laws* (Chicago, 1937).

20. Bauer's outline of the Ellenbogen bill is available at Catherine Bauer to Ernest Bohn, March 13, 1935, folder 10, box 2, Ernest Bohn Papers, Case Western Reserve University Special Collections, Cleveland (hereafter Bohn Papers). For the text of the Ellenbogen bill (HR 7399, 74th Congr., 1st sess.), see McDonnell, *The Wagner Housing Act*, 404–22.

21. McDonnell, *The Wagner Housing Act*, 92; Mary S. Cole, "Catherine Bauer and the Public Housing Movement, 1926–1937" (Ph.D. diss., George Washington University, 1975); Oberlander and Newbrun, *Houser*, 118–56; Radford, *Modern Housing for America*, 182–85; McDonnell, *The Wagner Housing Act*, 67–72, 100, 113.

22. Senate Committee on Education and Labor, *Slum and Low-Rent Public Housing: Hearings on S. 2392*, 74th Congr., 1st sess., June 4–7, 1935, 87, 94; Bauer to Robert F. Wagner, December 5, 1935, box 2, Vinton Papers.

23. McDonnell, *The Wagner Housing Act*, 111, 116–21, 433–34; Hunt, "Was the 1937 Housing Act a Pyrrhic Victory?" 201; von Hoffman, "The End of the Dream," 240–41.

24. The men in Bauer's circle deferred to her knowledge and political instincts. See Coleman Woodbury to Catherine Bauer, February 12, 1937, folder "NAHO," box 2, American Federation of Labor Papers, Wisconsin State Historical Society, Madison (hereafter AFL Papers); Bauer to Ernest Bohn, May 16, 1937, folder 11, box 2, Bohn Papers; Cole, "Catherine Bauer," 456–627; Eugenie. L. Birch, "Woman-Made America: The Case of Early Public Housing Policy," *American Institute of Planners Journal*, April 1978, 140; von Hoffman, "The End of the Dream," 236–42.

25. Catherine Bauer to Franklin Roosevelt, May 17, 1934, folder 10, box 2, Bohn Papers; Coleman Woodbury to Stacy May, September 21, 1936, box 16, Coleman Woodbury Papers, Cornell University Special Collections Library.

26. McDonnell, *The Wagner Housing Act*, 126–29.

27. Catherine Bauer to Dorothy Schoell, February 9, 1937, folder "S," box 1, AFL Papers; Bauer to J. David Stern, *Philadelphia Record*, February 22, 1936, folder "P," box 2, AFL Papers; Bauer to Bruce Bliven, June 22, 1936, folder "New Republic," box 2, AFL Papers; Bauer to Ernest Bohn, January 10, 1937, folder "Bohn," box 2, AFL Papers; Bohn to Bauer, June 4, 1937, folder "Bohn," box 1, AFL Papers; Bauer to Thomas Kennedy of Pennsylvania, June 14, 1937, folder "K," box 1, AFL Papers; Bohn to Coleman Woodbury, June 1, 1936, folder 10, box 1, Bohn Papers.

28. Vinton worked at the Resettlement Administration as a protégé of Columbia economist Rexford Tugwell in 1936. The year before Vinton had published a book critical of the New Deal from the left. See Benjamin Stolberg and Warren Jay Vinton, *The Economic Consequences of the New Deal* (New York: Harcourt Brace, 1935).

29. For an example of how the financing provisions worked, see Senate Committee on Education and Labor, *Creating a United States Housing Authority*, Senate Report 933, July 22, 1937, 12. For an international comparison of subsidies, see Bauer, *Modern Housing*, 125–28. Only Vienna's state funding in the 1920s compared to the depth of U.S. subsidies. Also, Hunt, "Was the 1937 Housing Act a Pyrrhic Victory?"

30. Meehan, *The Quality of Federal Policymaking*, 29; Friedman, *Government and Slum Housing*, 107–9.

31. Fisher, *Twenty Years of Public Housing*, 128–35.

32. The 1937 Housing Act actually contained both the annual contribution and Morgenthau's capital grant ideas, but in practice, only the former was used (McDonnell, *The Wagner Housing Act*, 274–88, 320). See also Catherine Bauer to the Right Honorable Herbert S. Morrison, June 29, 1937, folder "M," box 1, AFL Papers.

33. James Patterson suggests that Walsh was on the fringes of the "conservative" bloc in the Senate and was "sympathetic" to a conservative manifesto that argued for an end to New Deal regulation of business and for less progressive taxation. But Walsh supported Wagner's public housing bill in concept and practice, though he wanted to ensure that it served the poor who needed it most. Nearly all of the "conservatives" who form the core of Patterson's analysis opposed the Wagner housing bill altogether on purely ideological grounds. See Patterson, *Congressional Conservatism and the New Deal*, 50–51, 155, 202, 293; see also Dorothy G. Wayman, *David Walsh: Citizen Patriot* (Milwaukee: Bruce Publishing, 1952).

34. *Congressional Record*, June 16, 1936, 9558–59, and August 2, 1937, 7987; Vale, *From the Puritans to the Projects*, 177–78.

35. Robert M. Fisher, *Twenty Years of Public Housing* (New York: Harper and Brothers, 1959), 87–88; *Congressional Record*, June 19, 1936, 10212–13; McDonnell, *Wagner Housing Act*, 391.

36. Bratt, *Rebuilding A Low-Income Housing Policy*, 56; Rodgers, *Atlantic Crossings*, 478; Radford, *Modern Housing for America*, 189–90.

37. *Congressional Record*, June 16, 1936, 9553–65; Friedman, *Government and Slum Housing*, 109–10, 123; McDonnell, *Wagner Housing Act*, 323, 338, 393.

38. Hunt, "Was the 1937 U.S. Housing Act a Pyrrhic Victory?" 205–6; *Congressional Record*, August 2, 1937, 7974, 7990, 8099. In 1938, Wagner successfully sponsored legislation to add noncommercial groups including cooperative societies, limited-

dividend corporations, and "quasi-public housing agencies" to the FHA's portfolio, but the amended FHA Section 207 program never received much institutional support and produced little housing. The 1938 Housing Act is explained in the Conference Report on H.R. 8730, found in the *Congressional Record*, January 21, 1938, 923–30.

39. Catherine Bauer to Bruce Bliven, April 5, 1936, folder "New Republic," box 2, AFL Papers. Later historians have seen the loss of alternative agencies as a major missed historical opportunity, cementing a "two-tiered" housing policy in the United States, with a "top tier" of FHA-induced housing for the middle-class and a "bottom tier" of public housing for the poor. See, for example, Radford, *Modern Housing for America*, 185–95. Daniel Rodgers argues that nongovernmental housing agencies would have been far more successful than local housing authorities (*Atlantic Crossings*, 467). On alternative housing production modes during World War II, see Kristin M. Szylvian, "The Federal Housing Program during World War II," in Bauman, Biles, and Szylvian, *From Tenements to the Taylor Homes*, 120–38.

40. *Congressional Record*, August 4, 1937, 8190, 8196; McDonnell, *The Wagner Housing Act*, 330–32, 349, 353–54, 394–95; Bauer, "Now, at Last: Housing." The 1937 Housing Act actually included three clauses on construction: the modified Byrd cost limits, vague language suggested by real estate interests that prohibited "elaborate or expensive design and material," and a third clause written by Bauer that restricted public housing costs to the "average costs of similar new dwellings in a given locality, constructed with prevailing wage labor rates."

41. McDonnell, *The Wagner Housing Act*, 347–48, 353.

42. CHA, *Annual Report*, 1947, appendix, table 4.

43. National Public Housing Conference, "Conference on Federal Public Housing Legislation held at Christodora House, New York City," August 20, 1935, folder "National Public Housing Conference," box 2, AFL Papers.

44. Bauer, "Now, at Last: Housing"; Coleman Woodbury, *U.S. Housing Act of 1937, Will It Work?* NAHO Bulletin no. 119, August 24, 1937.

45. Patterson, *Congressional Conservatism and the New Deal*, 153, 183; Meehan, *The Quality of Federal Policymaking*, 12; Rodgers, *Atlantic Crossings*, 461–79. Bauer's biographers are among the few historians who see the bill as overall a victory for her. See Oberlander and Newbrun, *Houser*, 154–58. See note 2 of this chapter for the literature on the 1937 Housing Act and government's role in public housing generally.

46. For a summary of legislative history of U.S. housing policy, see House Committee on Finances, *A Chronology of Housing Legislation and Selected Executive Actions, 1892–2003*, report prepared by the Congressional Research Service, 108th Congr., 2nd sess., March 2004.

CHAPTER TWO

1. Roger Biles, "Nathan Straus and the Failure of U.S. Public Housing, 1937–1942," *Historian* 53, no. 1 (1990): 40.

2. CHA, *Official Minutes*, October 28, 1938; Roger Biles, *Big City Boss in Depression and War: Mayor Edward J. Kelly of Chicago* (DeKalb: Northern Illinois University Press, 1984), 91. The 1937 slate of CHA commissioners was Kelly's second; his first nominees in 1934 were rejected by the Illinois State Housing Board as being "not well qualified" and too political in nature. In an effort to improve his reputation among liberals, Kelly agreed to a more progressive board in 1937. See Coleman Woodbury

to Edward J. Kelly, June 20, 1934, box 78, A. R. Clas to Horatio B. Hackett, July 6, 1934, box 78, and Trevvett to chief of branch 1, "Re: The Chicago Housing Authority, a Grimm Fairy Tale," February 3, 1936, box 79, all in PWA Housing Division files.

3. *Chicago Defender,* March 2 and 4, 1957; *Chicago Tribune,* March 4, 1957; Martin Meyerson and Edward C. Banfield, *Politics, Planning, and the Public Interest: The Case of Public Housing in Chicago* (Glencoe, IL: Free Press, 1955), 42–43; Barbara Bowman (daughter of Robert R. Taylor), discussion with the author, September 10, 2004, notes in author's possession.

4. Woodbury and Crane also recommended a fourth vacant land site adjacent to Riverview Amusement Park. But the PWA held this fourth site in "reserve," explaining it would "encounter serious objections from real estate interests because of the use of vacant land." See the following documents from the PWA Housing Division files: Jacob Crane and Coleman Woodbury, "Preliminary Report on Areas for Housing Projects under the Federal Housing Corporation," IL State Housing Board Report to the PWA, December 1, 1933, folder H-1400(2), box 78; Crane and Woodbury, "Supplement to Proposed Housing Program for Chicago," March 29, 1934, box 88; George Warnecke to Harold Ickes, "Proposed Area of Operations, Chicago, IL," May 8, 1934, box 78.

5. Adolph Sabath to Franklin Roosevelt, October 1, 1934, and C. A. Inman, district manager, to Clas, October 4, 1935, "Re: Interview with Congressman Sabath," both in folder H-1400(2), box 78, PWA Housing Division files. For entreaties of private property owners, see folder H-1400(1), box 78, PWA Housing Division files; PWA, Press Release 1315, no date [April 1935?], Jane Addams Memorial Collection, UIC Special Collections; *Chicago Tribune,* April 22, 1934, and June 30, 1935; Arthur Bohnen, "Report of the Committee on Public Housing of the Metropolitan Housing Council," October 7, 1937, folder 59, Graham Aldis Papers; Friedman, *Government and Slum Housing,* 106.

6. E. B. Johnson, PWA chief of branch 1, to Clas, "Report on Mr. Carrel's Memorandum of June 25 re allocations for Chicago housing projects," July 11, 1935, and B. M. Pettit, PWA initiation branch chief, to Clas, September 25, 1935, both in box 78, PWA Housing Division files; George Warnecke to Harold Ickes, May 8, 1934; "Statement of M. D. Carrel, Associate Projects manager, Chicago General Advisory Board on Housing, Meeting of September 10, 1935," in folder 3, box 56, Edith and Grace Abbott Papers, University of Chicago.

7. H. H. Haylett to Horatio B. Hackett, May 13, 1935, box 93, PWA Housing Division files; Chicago Real Estate Board, "Accompanying Exhibits on the South Side Federal Housing Project, Chicago, IL," May 15, 1935, box 93, PWA Housing Division files; Robert C. Weaver to Clas, March 29, 1935, box 78, PWA Housing Division files; Kamenjarin Real Estate to Harold Ickes, April 12, 1935, box 93, PWA Housing Division files; *Chicago Tribune,* March 7, 1935; A. B. Gallion to Pettit, February 25, 1935, box 94, PWA Housing Division files; Ickes, *The Secret Diary of Harold L. Ickes,* 1:645, 673; Bohnen, "Report of the Committee on Public Housing"; Weaver to Nathan Straus, December 2, 1937, box 94, PWA Housing Division files.

8. *Chicago Defender,* September 17, 1938, and October 14, 1939; Coleman Woodbury, "Project Design and Development by the Chicago Housing Authority," February 19, 1940, CHA, *Official Minutes,* February 12, 1940.

9. Biles, *Big City Boss in Depression and War,* 22–26; Vera Miller, "Tax Delinquency and Housing in Chicago," report to the CHA, 1942, CHA Subject files; "Copy of Statement of Chicago Association of Commerce," November 3, 1937, folder 59,

Graham Aldis Papers; Chicago City Council, *Journal of Proceedings*, May 18, 1938, 6010. Becky Nicolaides, *My Blue Heaven* (Chicago: University of Chicago Press, 2002), describes the often intense politics of property taxes in a low-income Los Angeles suburb in the late 1920s and early 1930s.

10. See reports in the *Chicago Tribune*, November 22, 1937, December 10, 1938, August 8, and 11, 1939, and January 18, 1940. Also, Elizabeth Wood to the commissioners, September 5, 1939, in CHA, *Official Minutes*, September 12, 1939; Chicago Housing Authority, *The Chicago Housing Authority: Manager and Builder of Low-Rent Communities*, January 1, 1940, 17, 32 (hereafter cited as CHA, *Annual Report*, 1940); CHA, *Annual Report*, 1947, appendix, table 4.

11. Fisher, *Twenty Years of Public Housing*, 115.

12. Chicago City Council, *Journal of Proceedings*, December 21, 1939, 1469, and January 17, 1940, 1760; CHA, *Official Minutes*, February 12, 1940, April 8, 1940; Chicago City Council, *Journal of Proceedings*, March 8, 1940, 2152; Elizabeth Wood to the commissioners, September 5, 1939, in CHA, *Official Minutes*, September 12, 1939; *Chicago Tribune*, January 18, 1940; Chicago City Council, *Journal of Proceedings*, March 8, 1940, 2152; *Chicago Tribune*, August 11, 1939.

13. Chicago City Council, Committee on Housing, hearing, January 31, 1941, in the files of the Chicago City Clerk, City Council Division, City Hall, Chicago (hereafter Chicago City Clerk files); Chicago City Council, *Journal of Proceedings*, March 8, 1940, 2120, December 20, 1940, 3671–80, January 27, 1941, 4157, and March 5, 1941, 4402; S.B. 423, approved July 21, 1941, in *Final Legislative Synopsis and Digest of the Sixty-second General Assembly, State of Illinois* (Springfield: Secretary of State of Illinois, 1941), 180–81; *Laws of Illinois*, 1941, 824; CHA, *Annual Report*, 1940, 25.

14. Hirsch, *Making the Second Ghetto*, 223–24, suggests that 1948 was the year that aldermen first exerted control over site selection at the CHA by forcing a change in state law to require a city council ordinance to approve public housing sites. But the 1948 amendment to the Illinois Housing Authorities Act only sealed tight the 1941 amendment to state law, which had some loopholes that the CHA and the mayor had exploited in 1945 when selecting sites for the veterans' housing program. The veterans' program did not require a cooperation agreement since it was not governed by the 1937 Housing Act. On Kelly's power over the Chicago City Council, see Biles, *Big City Boss in Depression and War*, 49, 158. See also Elizabeth Wood, *The Beautiful Beginnings, the Failure to Learn: Fifty Years of Public Housing in America* (Washington, D.C.: National Center for Housing Management, 1982), 112.

15. Proposals for sites came from two aldermen, William Rowan (vacant site at 87th and Baltimore) and George Kells (Ashland and California), as well as from the Citizens' Committee on Improved Housing (site near Cabrini Homes) and the Southtown Planning Association (unknown site in Englewood). Several of these areas contained tiny enclaves of African Americans, and the sites may have been proposed on the assumption that CHA projects, operated in strict adherence to the neighborhood composition rule as at Jane Addams Homes, might prevent the enlargement of these black enclaves. See Citizens' Committee on Improved Housing, "Low Cost Housing Project for the Near North Side of Chicago," January 7, 1937, folder 59, Graham Aldis Papers; Elizabeth Wood to the commissioners, April 8, 1939, in CHA, *Official Minutes*, April 10, 1939; CHA, *Official Minutes*, June 14, 1937, and May 22, 1939; William Rowan to John Fugard, April 19, 1938, and George Kells to Elizabeth Wood, July 28, 1941, City Council folder, CHA Subject files.

16. CHA, *Official Minutes*, May 12 and June 16, 1941. As I discuss in chapter 3, the Father Dorney Homes site was eventually abandoned in 1949 because of racial opposition from Bridgeport whites at the end of the decade.

17. Bauman, *Public Housing, Race, and Renewal*, 54, 121.

18. "Report on Land Acquisition for IL 2-2," January 5, 1941, in CHA, *Official Minutes*, January 8, 1941; CHA, *Official Minutes*, January 13, 1941; *Chicago Daily News*, July 19, May 31, and August 23, 1941; Thomas Guglielmo, *White on Arrival: Italians, Race, Color, and Power in Chicago, 1890–1945* (New York: Oxford University Press, 2003), 147, 155–59.

19. "Report on Land Acquisition for IL 2-2"; CHA, *Annual Report*, 1940, 15, and 1941, 16.

20. Elizabeth Wood, "The Realities of Urban Redevelopment," *Journal of Housing*, January 1946, 12–13; CHA, *The Cost of Acquiring Chicago's Blighted Areas*, April 1948, HWLC-MRC; Hirsch, *Making the Second Ghetto*, 125–28.

21. USHA, *Equivalent Elimination of Unsafe or Insanitary Dwellings*, Bulletin no. 3, January 31, 1938 (a revision of this bulletin was issued on April 15, 1940), and USHA, *Site Selection*, Bulletin no. 18, February 1, 1939, all three in box 2, series "Bulletins on Policy and Procedure," RG 196, National Archives II, Suitland, Maryland (hereafter RG 196).

22. USHA, *Equivalent Elimination of Unsafe or Insanitary Dwellings as of June 30, 1946* Report S-133, September 13, 1946, box 132, series "Reports Containing Statistics on Public Housing Operations, 1939–1969," RG 196. Non–public housing demolition accounted for another 67,000 units eliminated.

23. Elizabeth Wood later reminisced that "equivalent elimination" did have an impact in forcing slum sites, yet I can find no evidence in Chicago, or any other city, to support her memory. See Wood, *The Beautiful Beginnings*, 11. For evidence that equivalent elimination did not influence site choices, see USHA Press Release 150, September 22, 1938; Fisher, *Twenty Years of Public Housing*, 234.

24. Illinois State Housing Board, *Report of State Housing Board Demolition Project* (1935); Metropolitan Housing Council, "Housing News," May 1938, UIC Special Collections.

25. Warren Vinton, A. C. Shire, and Catherine Bauer to Nathan Straus, December 19, 1938, and Warren Vinton to Nathan Straus, February 23, 1938, both in box 3, Vinton Papers; USHA Document 699, revised June 3, 1940, in box 3, Vinton Papers; untitled piece by Catherine Bauer in *Shelter* 3, no. 4 (November 1938).

26. USHA Press Release HA-29, February 3, 1938; USHA Press Release 261, April 14, 1939; Nathan Straus, *Seven Myths of Housing* (New York: Holt, 1944), 94–103; Radford, *Modern Housing for America*, 192; Edith Elmer Wood to Warren Vinton, August 21, 1941, box 18, Vinton Papers.

27. USHA, *Planning the Site: Design of Low-Rent Housing Projects*, Bulletin no. 11, May 1939, box 1, series "Bulletins on Policy and Procedure," RG 196; Bauer, *Modern Housing*, 112; Richard Plunz, *A History of Housing in New York City* (New York: Columbia University Press, 1990), 180–81, 235–40; Radford, *Modern Housing for America*, 192; Charles Abrams, *The Future of Housing* (New York: Harper and Brothers, 1946), 271–72; Joseph Hudnut, "The Art in Housing," *Architectural Record* 93, no. 1 (1943): 57–62; Jill Pearlman, *Inventing American Modernism: Joseph Hudnut, Walter Gropius, and the Bauhaus Legacy at Harvard* (Charlottesville: University of Virginia Press, 2007), 162–66; Richard Pommer, "The Architecture of Urban Housing in the United States

during the Early 1930s," *Journal of the Society of Architectural Historians* 37, no. 4. (1978): 242–43.

28. CHA, *Annual Report*, 1941, 17; Bauer, "'Slum Clearance' or 'Housing'"; Bauer, *Modern Housing*, 146–47, 176–87.

29. Straus, *Seven Myths of Housing*, 99–103; USHA, *Annual Report*, 1941, 35; Catherine Bauer, *A Citizens' Guide to Public Housing* (Poughkeepsie, NY: Vassar College, 1940), 41.

30. For a critique, see Pommer, "The Architecture of Urban Housing."

31. An example can best explain how income limits were set. If community surveys determined that the lowest "widely available" rent for "standard" private housing was $30 per month or $360 per year (including utilities), then the private market served families earning over $1,800 per year (assuming only one-fifth of income should be spent on rent). Straus wanted a "gap" of at least 20 percent between public housing income limits and the point of market failure. Therefore, the USHA allowed income limits up to $1,500. See Nathan Straus, "Memorandum on Rent and Tenancy Policies," September 12, 1939, box 3, Vinton Papers; see also Meehan, *The Quality of Federal Policymaking*, 24.

32. USHA, "Memorandum on Rent and Tenant Policies," September 25, 1939, and *Income Limits and Rents for USHA-Aided Projects*, Bulletin no. 24, revised, December 14, 1940, both in box 3, Vinton Papers; Leon Keyserling, Warren Vinton, and Jacob Crane to Nathan Straus, "Maximum Income Limits for Admission to Projects," March 22, 1940, and Keyserling to Straus, "Your Memorandum of March 15," March 21, 1940, both also in box 3, Vinton Papers; Straus, *The Seven Myths of Housing*, 127–143.

33. CHA, "The Procedure of Tenant Selection, CHA, January 1938 [CHA Procedure no. 1]," January 17, 1938, box 87, PWA Housing Division files; CHA, "Report on Applications, Leasing, and Occupancy," November 9, 1938, box 93, PWA Housing Division files; CHA, *Annual Report*, 1940, 23; USHA, *Initial Steps in Tenant Selection*, Bulletin no. 22, May 1, 1939, box 2, series "Bulletins on Policy and Procedure," RG 196.

34. Elizabeth Wood to alderman Earl Dickerson, October 7, 1940, City Council folder, CHA Subject files; CHA, *Official Minutes*, October 14, 1940; *Chicago Tribune*, March 9, 1940; Public Service Administration, "A Summary of Discussion at the Joint Conference of Housing and Welfare Officials, Chicago, May 11–13, 1939," Library of Congress. On the treatment of welfare families in the early years of public housing, see Vale, *From the Puritans to the Projects*, 178–83; Williams, *The Politics of Public Housing*, 38–39; Kenneth Jackson, *Crabgrass Frontier: The Suburbanization of the United States* (New York: Oxford University Press, 1985), 227; Bratt, *Rebuilding a Low-Income Housing Policy*, 57.

35. CHA, *Annual Report*, 1940, 25–29. On selecting the "submerged" middle class in other cities, see Vale, *From the Puritans to the Projects*, 178–83.

36. Fuerst, *When Public Housing Was Paradise*, 11; St. Clair Drake and Horace Cayton, *Black Metropolis: A Study of Negro Life in a Northern City*, (Chicago: University of Chicago Press, 1993), 660–61.

37. Alderman William Rowan to CHA chairman John Fugard, February 29, 1938, City Council folder, CHA Subject files; Chicago City Council, Committee on Housing, hearing, March 31, 1938, Chicago City Clerk files.

38. CHA, *Official Minutes*, May 22, 1939, and September 9 and October 14, 1940; CHA, *Annual Report*, 1940, 6, 24, and 1941, 6–8; Elizabeth Wood to Jacob Crane, "Re-

port on the Committee on Operations and Expenditures," May 15, 1939, box 79, PWA Housing Division files; *Chicago Tribune*, December 20, 1939.

39. CHA, *Official Minutes*, December 9 and April 29, 1940, October 13, 1941; CHA, *Annual Report*, 1941, 9; Metropolitan Housing Council, "Report of the Activities of the Metropolitan Housing Council for 1940," folder 21, box 2, Metropolitan Housing and Planning Council Papers, UIC.

40. May Lumsden to Richard F. Voell, December 15, 1937, box 87, PWA Housing Division files; Elizabeth Wood to Roger Kiley, January 4, 1940; CHA, *Annual Report*, 1941, 8; Wood to Jacob Crane, April 1, 1940, box 3, Vinton Papers; Elizabeth Wood to Philip Klutznick, February 7, 1945, box 1, Vinton Papers.

41. Nathan Straus, "Memorandum on Rent and Tenancy Policies," September 12, 1939, in box 3, Vinton Papers; USHA, *Establishing Rent Schedules for USHA-Aided Projects*, Bulletin no. 24, box 3, series "Bulletins on Policy and Procedure," RG 196.

42. Edith Elmer Wood to Nathan Straus, "Management Policies as to Tenant Incomes at Entrance and Later," March 11, 1940, box 3, Vinton Papers; Wood to Jacob Crane, "Statement on Rent Differentials and Amenities," March 19, 1940, box 3, Vinton Papers.

43. Warren Vinton to Nathan Straus, "Memorandum on Important Policy Questions implicit in Bulletin no. 24," May 9, 1940; USHA, *Income Limits and Rents for USHA-Aided Projects*, Bulletin no. 24, preliminary revised draft, May 16, 1940, and revised version, December 14, 1940, box 3, series "Bulletins on Policy and Procedure," box 3, RG 196; Catherine Bauer, "Housing: Paper Plans or a Workers' Movement?" in *America Can't Have Housing*, edited by Carol Aronvici (New York: Museum of Modern Art, 1934), 21; Wood, *The Beautiful Beginnings*, 19–21.

44. Fisher, *Twenty Years of Public Housing*, 160.

45. CHA, *Official Minutes*, July 14, 1941, September 14, 1942, February 17, November 19, and December 19, 1943; CHA, *Monthly Report*, February 1942, July 1942, September 1942; Elizabeth Wood to the commissioners, August 2, 1943, "An analysis of the occupancy trends in the low rent and war housing projects from January to June 1943," CHA Gautreaux files; CHA, *Annual Report*, 1943–44, 1945, and 1947, 18–19; *Chicago Tribune*, June 13, 1943.

46. Wood to the commissioners, August 2, 1943; Lawrence Bloomberg, "Mobility and Motivations: Survey of Families Moving from Low-Rent Housing," PHA report, April 1958. Interestingly, the survey did not find jealousies due to differential rent payments by neighbors. Instead, tenants were disgruntled by the bureaucratic hassles of income-based rents.

47. F. J. C. Dresser to Horatio B. Hackett, March 7, 1935, H. H. Haylett to Hackett, March 13, 1935, and Chicago Real Estate Board, "Accompanying Exhibits on the South Side Federal Housing Project," May 15, 1935, all in box 93, PWA project files, RG 196. Also, Guglielmo, *White on Arrival*, 150, especially note 13; Arnold Hirsch, "Containment on the Home Front: Race and Federal Housing Policy from the New Deal to the Cold War," *Journal of Urban History* 26, no. 2 (2000): 161, and *Making the Second Ghetto*, 14; Wendell Pritchett, *Robert Clifton Weaver and the American City* (Chicago: University of Chicago Press, 2008), 82–83.

48. Organic and unplanned integration had existed in many northern cities before the 1930s, but on a limited scale. See Spear, *Black Chicago*, 20–27; Olivier Zunz, *The Changing Face of Inequality* (Chicago: University of Chicago Press, 1982), 41–47; Homer Hoyt, *The Structure and Growth of Residential Neighborhoods in American Cities*

(Washington, DC: Federal Housing Administration, 1939), 62–71; Douglas Massey and Nancy Denton, *American Apartheid: Segregation and the Making of the Underclass* (Cambridge: Harvard University Press, 1993), 17–42. But deliberate, planned residential integration in an urban setting appears to have had no precedent before public housing. See Morton Deutsch and Mary Evans Collins, *Interracial Housing: A Psychological Evaluation of a Social Experiment* (Minneapolis: University of Minnesota Press, 1951).

49. CHA, *Official Minutes*, September 27, 1937; Elizabeth Wood to Mr. McGuire, South Deering Improvement Association, April 13, 1940, CHA Gautreaux files; Guglielmo, *White on Arrival*, 150.

50. CHA, *Official Minutes*, March 29, 1937, and January 9, 17, and 21, 1938; Elizabeth Wood to May Lumsen, May 23, 1938, CHA Gautreaux files; Guglielmo, *White on Arrival*, 149–53; Pritchett, *Robert Clifton Weaver*, 61, 81–85.

51. *Chicago Tribune*, June 28, 1939; Elizabeth Wood to Catherine Henck, Vallejo Housing Authority, September 10, 1942, CHA Gautreaux files.

52. Wood to Henck, September 10, 1942; CHA, *Official Minutes*, January 9, February 13, and March 13, 1939; Wood to Raymond Voight, Parklawn Management Office, Milwaukee, October 28, 1940, CHA Gautreaux files.

53. City Council, Committee on Housing, minutes, March 1, 1940, City Clerk files; CHA, *Official Minutes*, February 17 and August 2, 1943; Wood to Henck, September 10, 1942; Hirsch, *Making the Second Ghetto*, 45–46; Guglielmo, *White on Arrival*, 155–59.

54. Wood to Henck, September 10, 1942; Meyerson and Banfield, *Politics, Planning, and the Public Interest*, 123. Meyerson and Banfield indicate that whites left Brooks Homes "often with the encouragement of the Negro families, who felt the whites were occupying places that should rightfully be given to Negroes. Finally, despite the intention of the Authority, Brooks became entirely Negro."

55. *Chicago Defender*, August 7, 1943; on wartime housing conditions in the black belt, see Hirsch, *Making the Second Ghetto*, 16–28; Nicholas Lemann, *The Promised Land* (New York: Vintage, 1991), 61–71; Williams, *The Politics of Public Housing*, 57.

56. Timuel Black, *Bridges of Memory: Chicago's Second Generation of Black Migration* (Evanston, IL: Northwestern University Press, 2007); Richard Wright, *Twelve Million Black Voices* (New York: Thunder Mouth Press, 1988), 105–11.

57. CHA, *Annual Statistical Report*, 1948; CHA, *Official Minutes*, December 19, 1943, and February 11 and April 12, 1944. See also CHA, *Official Minutes*, August 10, 1944, and CHA, *Monthly Report*, September 1943; Robert C. Weaver, *The Negro Ghetto* (New York: Harcourt, Brace, 1948), 96–96 and 193–94.

58. CHA, *Monthly Report*, September 1943; CHA, *Official Minutes*, July 20, 1943. The CHA submitted several sites near black enclaves to federal officials, who ultimately approved the Altgeld site.

59. CHA, *Monthly Report*, September 1943. The CHA did hope to integrate Altgeld, but overwhelming demand from African Americans made this impossible. See "Development Program, IL 2-11," pt. 2, December 1950, 29–30, CHA Development files, IL 2-11.

60. CHA, *Official Minutes*, June 10, 1947; Fuerst, *When Public Housing Was Paradise*, 57–59, 76–78, 92–93, 114–15, 137–39, 152–55.

61. CHA, *Official Minutes*, February 11, 1943.

62. Arthur Lindell to Robert Taylor, January 27, 1944, in City Council folder, CHA Subject files.

63. *Chicago Tribune*, June 11, 1944, and November 16, 1945; CHA, *Official Minutes*, February 12, 1943. Of the 15,848 permits for private housing starts issued in the city of Chicago with NHA approval between January 1, 1940, and September 1, 1944, 6 percent were made available to black families. See CHA, "Application for Allotment of Funds for Post-War Low-Rent Public Housing," CHA Development files, IL 2-7.

64. CHA, *Official Minutes*, March 14, 1944; *United States Petitioner vs. Certain Parcels of Land in the City of Chicago, County of Cook, and State of Illinois, and Robinson Clay Production Company, et al.*, No. 44 C 851, District Court of USA for the Northern District of IL, Eastern Division, dated August 15, 1944, found in folder "CHA, Development Contract, IL-11208," undescribed box numbered 33001, Legal Records, Records Administration, RG 196, National Archives, Chicago Branch, Chicago; *Chicago Sun*, August 19, 1944; Devereux Bowly, *The Poorhouse: Subsidized Housing in Chicago, 1895–1976* (Carbondale: Southern Illinois University Press, 1978), 45–47; CHA, *Monthly Report*, May 1949. For a detailed look at the West Chesterfield controversy, see Preston H. Smith II, "The Quest for Racial Democracy: Black Civic Ideology and Housing Interests in Postwar Chicago," *Journal of Urban History* 26, no. 2 (2000): 131–57.

65. CHA, *Official Minutes*, September 11, 1944; People's Welfare Organization of Chicago, "History of Dearborn Homes," 1950, Chicago History Museum (hereafter CHM); Hirsch, "Containment on the Home Front," 161–62.

66. Chicago Liaison Committee (John Fugard, Elizabeth Wood, Arthur Bohnen), "A Housing Project for the South Side of Chicago," May 24, 1935, folder H-1402, box 94, PWA Housing Division files, RG 196.

67. Don R. Bonaparte to Milt Shufro, March 23, 1948, "Tenant Selection for IL 2-9," CHA Gautreaux files.

68. Dorothea Kahn, "Pioneer in Public Housing, Elizabeth Wood Blazes Way for Other Women," *Christian Science Monitor*, March 4, 1941.

69. CHA, *Annual Report*, 1940, 25, 29–30; CHA, *Monthly Report*, October 1941; Elizabeth Wood, "Ideals and Realities in Subsidized Housing since 1934," in *Housing Form and Public Policy in the United States*, edited by Richard Plunz (New York: Praeger, 1980), 64.

70. CHA, *Annual Report*, 1943–44 and 1947; Mary Bolton Wirth to Jane Addams Homes manager, "Report of Community and Tenant Relations Aide to the Manager, 1953," folder 13, box 2, Mary Bolton Wirth Papers, University of Chicago Special Collections (hereafter Mary Wirth Papers).

71. CHA, *Flowers Grow Where Slums Once Stood*, pamphlet, 1945, HWLC-MRC; Fuerst, *When Public Housing Was Paradise*, 137, 11, 25, 45, 59, 89, 115, 167, 175.

72. CHA, *Monthly Report*, March 1942 and September 1943; CHA, *Annual Report*, 1947; CHA, *Handbook for Residents of Altgeld Gardens*, 1944, HWLC-MRC. Claude and Addie Wyatt, interview; Doris Smith (former resident of Dearborn Homes), transcript of interview by Jim Fuerst (former CHA staff member), no date, in author's possession; Jim Fuerst, interview by the author, March 19, 1998, Chicago, tape in author's possession; Fuerst, *When Public Housing Was Paradise*, 75, 145, 182, 191; Kahn, "Pioneer in Public Housing." For tenants who chafed against these rules, see the *Daily Calumet* (Chicago), April 1, 1958, and the *Chicago Sun-Times*, June 20, 1958.

73. Fuerst, *When Public Housing Was Paradise*, 52.

74. Ibid., 45, 48, 114.

75. Ibid., 10–33; Emil Hirsch, former CHA public relations official, interview by

Kathleen McCourt, February 9, 1989, transcript in author's possession; Fuerst-Hunt interview.

76. CHA, *Annual Report*, 1945; Wood, "The Realities of Urban Development." See also John Dean, "The Myths of Housing Reform," *American Sociological Review* 14, no. 2 (1949): 281–88. Dean had been an early supporter of public housing but then challenged its environmental determinist assumptions.

77. Catherine Bauer to Herbert Emmerich, no date [1942?], in folder "Bauer Correspondence," box 4, Vinton Papers. For more doubts from Bauer, see Catherine Bauer Wurster to Warren Vinton, January 2, 1945, also in box 4, Vinton Papers.

78. Catherine Bauer to Fritz [Gutheim?], April 17, 1948, outgoing correspondence, box 4, Bauer Papers. See also Catherine Bauer, "Planning Is Politics," *Pencil Points* 25, no. 3 (1944): 66–70.

79. Woodyatt, "The Origins and Evolution of the New Deal Public Housing Program," 206–7; Biles, "Nathan Straus and the Failure of U.S. Public Housing," 40–41; Nathaniel Keith, *Politics and the Housing Crisis since 1930* (New York: Universe Books, 1973), 38; Kyle Longley, *Senator Albert Gore, Sr.: Tennessee Maverick* (Baton Rouge: Louisiana State University Press, 2004), 43–44.

80. Warren Vinton, handwritten note, October 30, 1941, box 1, Vinton Papers; Dorothy Gazzolo, former NAHRO official, interview by πMorton Schussheim, April 21, 1995, transcript, "Pioneers in Housing" series, Library of Congress; Philip J. Funigiello, *The Challenge to Urban Liberalism* (Knoxville: University of Tennessee Press, 1978), 105–6; Pritchett, *Robert Clifton Weaver*, 85–86. The FPHA (1942–47) and its successor agency, the PHA (1947–65), came under the control of the new Housing and Home Finance Agency (HHFA) in 1947, which was eventually reconstituted as HUD in 1965.

81. CHA, *Annual Statistical Report*, 1948.

82. See also Dean, "The Myths of Housing Reform," 281–88.

CHAPTER THREE

1. *Chicago Tribune*, December 7, 1986; CHA, *Annual Statistical Report*, 1967; Hirsch, *Making the Second Ghetto*. Amanda Seligman argues that Hirsch's conception of the second ghetto was both "temporal and spatial," and I concur. The second ghetto involved both a new set of policies in postwar Chicago and a physical location that rebuilt former ghetto neighborhoods. See Amanda Seligman, "What Is the Second Ghetto?" *Journal of Urban History* 29, no. 3 (2003): 272–80.

2. Wood, "The Realities of Urban Redevelopment"; Fogelson, *Downtown*, 349.

3. On later definitions of "blight," see Amanda Seligman, *Block by Block: Neighborhoods and Public Policy on Chicago's West Side* (Chicago: University of Chicago Press, 2005), 41, 53–54.

4. Chicago Plan Commission (CPC), *Chicago Land Use Survey*, vol. 1, *Residential Chicago* (Chicago, 1942);CPC, *Master Plan of Residential Land Use of Chicago* (Chicago, 1943), tables 17 and 81; Chicago City Council, *Journal of Proceedings*, March 18, 1943, 8420–22; CHA, "Application for Allotment of Funds for Post-War Low-Rent Public Housing," January 4, 1945, CHA Development files, IL 2-7. See also CHA, *Chicago's Housing Needs, an Interim Measurement*, July 1949, CHA, *The Kit of Tools for Slum Clearance*, 1947, and Metropolitan Housing Council, *Reclaiming Chicago's Blighted Areas*, 1946, all at HWLC-MRC.

5. On the postwar consensus on slum clearance and the drive for urban redevelopment, see Gelfand, *A Nation of Cities*; John Mollenkopf, *The Contested City* (Princeton: Princeton University Press, 1983); Jon Teaford, *The Rough Road to Renaissance: Urban Revitalization in America, 1940–1985* (Baltimore: Johns Hopkins University Press, 1990); Fogelson, *Downtown*, 319–21; Alison Isenberg, *Downtown America: A History of the Place and the People Who Made It* (Chicago: University of Chicago Press, 2004).

6. CHA, *Report to the Mayor*, January 1, 1940; CPC, *Chicago Land Use Survey*, vol. 1, table 17A.

7. See the City of Chicago tracts, sorted by "dilapidated or without private bath," in U.S. Bureau of the Census, "Census Tract Statistics: Chicago, Illinois, and Adjacent Area," chap. 10 of *1950 Population Census Report* (Washington, DC, 1952), vol. 3.

8. CHA, "Application for Allotment of Funds for Post-War Low-Rent Public Housing."

9. CHA, *Annual Report*, 1945; Richard O. Davies, *Housing Reform during the Truman Administration* (Columbia: University of Missouri Press, 1966).

10. CHA, *Official Minutes*, June 14, 1937; House Resolution 47, Illinois State Legislature, debated April 26, 1937, passed May 3, 1937; Chicago City Council, Committee on Housing, hearings, February 18, 1938, City Clerk files; Arthur Lindell, *A Proposed Housing Program for the City of Chicago*, November 1939; *Chicago Tribune*, April 20, 1938; CHA, *Official Minutes*, July 25 and November 14, 1939; Chicago City Council, *Journal of Proceedings*, December 20, 1940, 3671–80, and June 19, 1941, 4982–87.

11. CHA, *Official Minutes*, November 14, 1939; CHA, *Report to the Mayor*, August 1, 1941, 30–31.

12. CHA, *The Slum . . . Is Rehabilitation Possible?* 1946, HWLC-MRC. On Vernon Avenue, see Philpott, *The Slum and the Ghetto*, 149–51.

13. See CHA, *The Slum . . . Is Rehabilitation Possible?* 24–25.

14. In late 1953, the CHA experimented with rehabilitating a handful of buildings at its Rockwell Gardens site, but implementation languished through the decade. See CHA, *Monthly Report*, July 15, 1954, and CHA, *Official Minutes*, April 25, 1961. After 1964, the CHA began a more extensive rehabilitation program, especially to produce senior housing. See CHA, "Highlights of the Operation," March 31, 1965, CHA Public Affairs files.

15. Daniel Bluestone, "Preservation and Renewal in Post-World War II Chicago," in *Chicago Architecture: Histories, Revisions, Alternatives*, edited by Charles Waldheim and Katerina Ruedi Ray (Chicago: University of Chicago Press, 2005), 61–81. For the backlash against slum clearance, see Herbert Gans, *The Urban Villagers: Group and Class in the Life of Italian Americans*, (New York: Free Press, 1982). The city of Chicago did create a conservation program in 1953 to try to prevent older neighborhoods from reaching "slum" status, and the U.S. Housing Act of 1954 required cities to produce "workable plans" that included an effort to prevent further deterioration. In Philadelphia, postwar planners and housers focused on code enforcement, rehabilitation, and conservation. See Bauman, *Public Housing, Race, and Renewal*, 105–10.

16. *Chicago Tribune*, September 28, 1938; S.B. 264 and H.B. 759 in *Final Legislative Synopsis and Digest of the Sixty-first General Assembly, State of Illinois* (Springfield: Secretary of State of Illinois, 1939); Chicago City Council, *Journal of Proceedings*, May 3, 1939, 164, and June 14, 1939, 369–73; Chicago City Council, Committee on Housing, hearing, May 5, 1939, Chicago City Clerk files; *Chicago Tribune*, December 19, 1940. The Daley bill returned in a slightly different form two years later as the Neighbor-

hood Redevelopment Corporation Act of 1941 and passed the state legislature over the concerns of the CHA. See *Chicago Tribune*, April 9, April 16, April 30, May 28, 1941, and January 18, 1945.

17. Catherine Bauer, "Basic Principles for a Redevelopment Program," 1942, box 1, Vinton Papers; Ashley Foard and Hilbert Fefferman, "Federal Urban Renewal Legislation," in *Urban Renewal: The Record and the Controversy*, edited by James Q. Wilson (Cambridge: MIT Press, 1966), 71–125; Marc Weiss, "The Origins and Legacy of Urban Renewal," in *Urban and Regional Planning in an Age of Austerity*, edited by Pierre Clavel, John Forester, and William W. Goldsmith (New York: Pergamon, 1980), 63–65; Alexander von Hoffman, "A Study in Contradictions: The Origins and Legacy of the 1949 Housing Act" *Housing Policy Debate* 11, no. 2 (2000): 299–326.

18. *Laws of Illinois*, 1945, 940–46; Chicago City Council, *Journal of Proceedings*, October 25, 1945, 4256–59; CHA, *Report to the Mayor*, August 15, 1946.

19. CHA, *The Kit of Tools for Slum Clearance*, 1947, in HWLC-MRC; CHA, *The Tenth Year of the Chicago Housing Authority*, 1947, 28; Wood, "The Realities of Urban Redevelopment"; CHA, *Official Minutes*, May 5, 1947.

20. Chicago City Council, *Journal of Proceedings*, October 25, 1945, 4256–262, and November 8, 1945, 4401–4; CHA, *Annual Report*, 1945; CHA, *Annual Report*, 1947, 17, 27; Elizabeth Wood to George Kells, November 7, 1945, City Council folder, CHA Subject files.

21. South Side Planning Board (SSPB), *An Opportunity for Private and Public Investment in Rebuilding Chicago*," 1947, in HWLC-MRC.

22. Hirsch, *Making the Second Ghetto*, 120–34; Sarah Whiting, "Bas-Relief Urbanism: Chicago's Figured Field," in *Mies in America*, edited by Phyllis Lambert et al. (New York, Abrams, 2001), 671–73; Weaver, *The Negro Ghetto*, 339–340.

23. SSPB, *An Opportunity for Private and Public Investment*, 40; CHA, *Monthly Report*, September 1949; Wood, "Realities of Urban Development," 11.

24. See CHA, *Annual Report*, 1950, 12–13, and 1951, 42–43; CHA, *Annual Statistical Report*, 1951–57. Arnold Hirsch, citing Metropolitan Housing and Planning Council sources, writes that "between 1950 and 1954, more than half of all public housing units constructed (2,363 apartments out of 4,636) were allocated directly to families displaced" by slum clearance (Hirsch, *Making the Second Ghetto*, 124). The MHPC appears to have misinterpreted CHA data, which shows 28 percent of all CHA housing (including that already built) went to families displaced during this time period (2,845 out of 10,112 move-ins). By 1958, this figure had dropped to 7 percent. Relocation families were never a numerical burden, but CHA staff believed that they were more likely to be "problem" families.

25. CHA, "Memorandum on Relocation, Chicago Housing Authority Experience," draft, July 1, 1948, in HWLC-MRC, and final version, May 1949, in CHA Subject files; CHA, *Official Minutes*, August 11, 1952; Hirsch, *Making the Second Ghetto*, 121–24; CHA, "Relocation of Families to Private Housing: Character and Quality of Dwellings Obtained by Relocated families, 1952–1954," CHA Development files, IL 2-34; Wood, "Realities of Urban Redevelopment"; CHA, *The Kit of Tools for Slum Clearance*.

26. CHA, *Annual Report*, 1947, 20–25; CHA, *Official Minutes*, November 23 and December 4, 1945; Elizabeth Wood to aldermen Moss and Lindell, November 28, 1945, City Council folder, CHA Subject files; City Council Committee on Housing, minutes, February 8, 1946, City Clerk files; CHA, *Temporary Housing for Chicago's Veterans*, 1948, HWLC-MRC.

27. Ed Fruchtman (CHA general counsel), "Legal Aspects of Inter-Racial policy at Fernwood Project," undated memo [1946?], folder "Veterans," CHA Subject files; Meyerson and Banfield, *Politics, Planning, and the Public Interest,* 121–25.

28. Hirsch, *Making the Second Ghetto,* chap. 2; Mayor's Commission on Human Relations (CHR), "Memorandum on Airport Homes," in folder "Veterans," CHA Subject files; Chicago Council against Racial and Religious Discrimination (CCARD), "Racial Violence at Fernwood Housing Project," 1947, in folder "Veterans," CHA Subject files; Weaver, *The Negro Ghetto,* 195–96.

29. CHR, "Memorandum on Airport Homes"; Hirsch *Making the Second Ghetto,* 88–94.

30. Biles, *Big City Boss in Depression and War,* 146–47; Arnold Hirsch, "The Cook County Democratic Organization and the Dilemma of Race, 1931–1987," in *Snowbelt Cities: Metropolitan Politics in the Northeast and Midwest since World War II* (Blooming-ton: Indiana University Press, 1990), 69–71; Hirsch-McCourt interview.

31. *Chicago Tribune,* October 31, 1945, December 1, 1946, January 8, 1947, January 9, 1947, February 21, 1947; Chicago City Council, Committee on Housing, hearings, September 19, 1945, City Clerk files; CHA, *Report to the Mayor,* August 15, 1946. For various private redevelopment plans put forth in 1946, see *Chicago Tribune,* June 21, November 24, and December 29, 1946.

32. Hirsch, *Making the Second Ghetto,* xiv, 103–15, 133, 269–71. The legislative his-tory of the 1947 Blighted Areas Redevelopment Act is well spelled out by Hirsch. However, his account misses the 1945 law as context for the 1947 law. Further, Hirsch accepts the claim of its authors that the 1947 Blighted Areas Redevelopment Act was an innovative piece of legislation and a "model" for the nation. But in 1945, ten other states passed urban redevelopment laws. Further, the "write-down" of land values in the 1947 state act was not an Illinois innovation; the 1945 Wagner-Ellender-Taft bill (S. 1592) included a similar provision. See Hugh Pomeroy, "Housing Developments in 1945," *Journal of Housing,* May 1946; von Hoffman, "A Study in Contradictions."

33. CCAD, "Racial Violence at Fernwood Housing Project"; Hirsch, *Making the Second Ghetto,* 202.

34. CCARD, "Racial Violence at Fernwood"; *Chicago Daily News,* August 13, 1948. For a detailed discussion of the rioting and violence used by whites to "defend" their neighborhoods, see Hirsch, *Making the Second Ghetto,* 171–211.

35. Chicago City Council, *Journal of Proceedings,* March 15, 1948, 2040–49; Hirsch, *Making the Second Ghetto,* 223; Meyerson and Banfield, *Politics, Planning, and the Public Interest,* 136–37, 258. Hirsch, relying on Meyerson and Banfield, says that without additional state legislation in 1949, the city council "would exercise no control over this new program [the 1949 U.S. Housing Act authorizing more public housing]." This is inaccurate. As discussed in chapter 2, amendments to Illinois state law in 1941 required the CHA to reveal sites to win a cooperation agreement with the city, and the cooperation agreement remained a central requirement under 1937 Housing Act and, later, the 1949 Housing Act. However, the federal Veterans' Emergency Housing Program, authorized under different federal legislation, had not required a coopera-tion agreement, and the 1949 state law closed this loophole.

36. CHA, *Official Minutes,* June 3, 1946, June 10,1947, and September 21, 1948; Chicago City Council, *Journal of Proceedings,* October 28, 1949, 4952; *Chicago Tribune,* October 24, 1948, September 20, 1949, and April 10, 1956. The CHA eventually repaid

$1 million of the $2 million loan. See William B. Kean to Richard J. Daley, July 28, 1957, "Mayor's File," CHA Subject files.

37. John Ducey to Elizabeth Wood, "Relocation Housing Sites," March 24, 1948, and "Statement of Mr. Taylor in re: Relocation Sites," June 23, 1948, both in CHA Gautreaux files; CHA, *Official Minutes*, June 17, 1948.

38. *Chicago Daily News*, July 27, 1948; *Chicago Construction News*, June 29, 1948; CHA, *Monthly Report*, June 1948.

39. *Chicago Daily News*, July 1, 1948; *Chicago Sun-Times*, July 1, 1948; *Chicago Tribune*, July 8, 1948.

40. Meyerson and Banfield, *Politics, Planning, and the Public Interest*, 248, 262–67.

41. *Chicago Sun-Times*, August 8, 1948; *Chicago Construction News*, August 12, 1948; Ducey to Wood, March 24, 1948; Meyerson and Banfield, *Politics, Planning, and the Public Interest*, 131–36.

42. John Ducey, former CHA director of planning, interview by the author, November 17, 1998, Northridge, CA, tape in author's possession.

43. Elizabeth Wood quoted in Jim Fuerst, *Public Housing in Europe and America* (London: Croom Helm, 1974), 157–58.

44. CHA, "Application for Reservation of Urban Low-Rent Public Housing and for a Preliminary Loan," August 12, 1949, CHA Development files, IL 2-7; Meyerson and Banfield, *Politics, Planning, and the Public Interest*, 246–51.

45. The site in Bridgeport had been approved by the city council in 1941 for 108 units, but the CHA lacked funds to construct the project, named the Father Dorney Homes, during the war. In 1948, the CHA proposed the site for relocation housing, but an aide to Mayor Kennelly told Elizabeth Wood that it was "a poor project on which to fight out the race issue." The CHA again proposed the site for public housing in 1949 but dropped it in 1950, most likely because it could not win council approval owing to the overwhelming issues of race. The site was sold in 1957 to a cooperative. See CHA, *Official Minutes*, February 9, 1942; Elizabeth Wood to Orvil Olmsted, August 20, 1943; Wood to the commissioners, February 19, 1948, CHA Gautreaux files; CHA, *Official Minutes*, January 10, 1949, November 3, 1952, and May 6, 1957; *Chicago Daily News*, April 23, 1959.

46. Meyerson and Banfield, *Politics, Planning, and the Public Interest*, 138–50; *Chicago Tribune*, February 24, 1950; *Chicago Daily News*, February 23, 1950.

47. Robert Taylor to William Lancaster, March 31, 1948, Committee on Housing, City Clerk's files; *Chicago Tribune*, July 10, 1948; Meyerson and Banfield, *Politics, Planning, and the Public Interest*, 169. Between 1948 and 1954, the CHA never proposed vacant land sites on the North Side, likely because land was significantly more costly than on the South Side.

48. Meyerson and Banfield, *Politics, Planning, and the Public Interest*, 153–93; CHA, *Monthly Report*, April 1950; Chicago City Council, Committee on Housing, "Committee Pamphlet no. 17," July 26, 1950, in HWLC-MRC; Chicago City Council, *Journal of Proceedings*, August 4, 1950, 6781–95.

49. Hirsch, *Making the Second Ghetto*, 226–27; see also "The Plot to Kill Public Housing," *Ebony*, June 1950, 92; *Chicago Sun-Times*, April 27, April 30, and June 28, 1950; Minority report of aldermen Benjamin Becker and Archibald Carey, in Chicago City Council, Committee on Housing, "Committee Pamphlet no. 17," July 26, 1950, 13–15.

50. George Nesbitt to C. L. Farris, "Chicago, Illinois Field Trip, July 24–28, 1950," August 3, 1950, folder "Chicago," box 750, RG 207, National Archives II, Suitland, Maryland (hereafter RG 207); Frank Horne to Raymond Foley, "Proposed Public Housing Program in Chicago," October 16, 1950, folder "Racial Relations Service," entry 55, box 2, RG 207; Hirsch, "Containment on the Home Front," 167–68.

51. Meyerson and Banfield, *Politics, Planning, and the Public Interest*, 205–22, 242–51; Arnold Hirsch, "Searching for a 'Sound Negro Policy': A Racial Agenda for the Housing Acts of 1949 and 1954," *Housing Policy Debate* 11, no. 2 (2000): 404–10; Hirsch, *Making the Second Ghetto*, 225–27.

52. CHA, *Official Minutes*, August 8, September 13, November 16, and December 20, 1950, January 9 and 15, 1951, November 3 and December 22, 1952, March 9 and May 25, 1953; CHA, *Monthly Report*, July, August, and December 1950; *Chicago Tribune*, July 24, 1952; Meyerson and Banfield, *Politics, Planning, and the Public Interest*, 242; Chicago Plan Commission, *A Survey of Vacant Land Suitable for Residential Use*, October 1949.

53. *Chicago Sun-Times*, June 28, 1950; Meyerson and Banfield, *Politics, Planning, and the Public Interest*, 87.

54. Sugrue, *Origins of the Urban Crisis*, 72–88; Williams, *The Politics of Public Housing*, 97–99; Don Parson, *Making a Better World: Public Housing, the Red Scare, and the Direction of Modern Los Angeles* (Minneapolis: University of Minnesota Press, 2005), chap. 4.

55. CHA, *Annual Report*, 1952, 28; Chicago City Council, Committee on Housing, minutes of meeting, June 6, 1952, Chicago City Clerk files; CHA, *Official Minutes*, April 9 and 30, October 8, November 26, and December 10, 1951, and February 11, June 13, July 14, November 10, December 8 and 22, 1952; CHA, *Official Minutes*, January 8, 1953; Metropolitan Housing and Planning Council, Minutes of the Meeting of the Board of Governors, October 5, 1951, Louis Wirth Papers, University of Chicago.

56. The legal case *Gautreaux vs. the Chicago Housing Authority* would later stake a claim that CHA complicity with city council racism began in the mid-1950s, under the leadership of CHA executive director William B. Kean. But the CHA's subordination to the city council was evident by 1952. See Alexander Polikoff, *Waiting for Gautreaux* (Evanston, IL: Northwestern University Press, 2006), 56–58.

57. William Mullen, "Cabrini-Green: The Road to Hell," *Chicago Tribune Magazine*, March 31, 1985.

58. Chicago City Council, *Journal of Proceedings*, December 3, 1940, 3607; *Chicago Tribune*, January 12, 1940.

59. "Development Program, IL 2-37," June 27, 1956, CHA Development files, IL 2–37; *Chicago American*, September 18, 1957. For a negative reaction to the site, see *Chicago Defender*, December 17, 1957. For issues surrounding the highway, see *Chicago Tribune*, February 24 and March 29, 1956; *Chicago Sun-Times*, June 6, 1956. Many observers view the location of the South Expressway (renamed the Dan Ryan Expressway) as a deliberate attempt to separate public housing residents from the white neighborhoods to the west. However, the historical record provides little evidence for this. The South Expressway had been planned since the 1930s to run through the Federal Street slum. After the city council picked the area for CHA housing in the 1950s, the expressway was moved slightly to the west, on the west side of the Pennsylvania Railroad that paralleled Federal Street. The council, likely influenced by Richard J. Daley, did reroute a northern portion of the South Expressway to the east in 1947 to

avoid destruction of the north end of Bridgeport. But this was far from what became the "State Street corridor." Still, the mammoth Dan Ryan Expressway certainly formed a psychological boundary for public housing residents, even if it did not represent much of a racial one by the time it opened in 1962. See Domnic A. Pacyga, "The Busiest, the Most Dangerous, the Dan Ryan," in Jay Wolke, *Along the Divide: Photographs of the Dan Ryan Expressway* (Chicago: University of Chicago Press, 2004).

60. Mary B. Wirth, "Memorandum of Record, Interview with Robert Taylor," June 27, 1956, folder 1, box 1, Mary Wirth Papers. Taylor feared that small-scale projects would be swallowed by surrounding blight. Robert Taylor's daughters, however, believe that their father would not have been happy with the scale or size of the Robert Taylor Homes. See *Chicago Tribune*, December 3, 1986.

61. These projects include Ida B. Wells and the Wells Extension (2,300 units); Dearborn (800 units); Brooks and Abbott (2,052 units); Altgeld Gardens and Murray Extension (2,000 units); Cabrini and Cabrini Extension (2,500 units).

62. See Douglas Massey and Nancy Denton, *American Apartheid: Segregation and the Making of the Underclass* (Cambridge: Harvard University Press, 1993), 56; Masey and Shaun Kanaiaupuni, "Public Housing and the Concentration of Poverty," *Social Science Quarterly* 74, no. 1 (1993): 111; Lemann, *The Promised Land*, 73; Adam Cohen and Elizabeth Taylor, *American Pharaoh, Richard J. Daley: His Battle for Chicago and the Nation* (Boston: Little, Brown, 2000), 86.

CHAPTER FOUR

1. Robert Weaver, *The Negro Ghetto*, 318–41 and 359–69; Pritchett, *Robert Clifton Weaver*, 121–29, 143–46, 157–61, 165–67.

2. Deutsch and Collins, *Interracial Housing*; Leon Festinger and Harold Kelley, *Changing Attitudes through Social Contact: An Experimental Study of a Housing Project* (Ann Arbor: University of Michigan Press, 1951).

3. CHA, *Official Minutes*, January 6, 1950, and November 3, 1952; CHA, *Monthly Report*, December 1950; and the following documents from the Gautreaux files: "Statement of Elizabeth Wood," August 30, 1953; Paul Freedman to the commissioners, "Analysis of situation at Lathrop Homes," January 28, 1953; Wood to Wilfred Sykes, April 3, 1953; "Interview of John Yancey, October 11, 1967"; Wood to the commissioners, "Evaluation of 'Report on Certain Policies and Procedures of the CHA' by Griffenhagen & Associates, August 17, 1953," April 30, 1954. Also, Hirsch, *Making the Second Ghetto*, 230–31; Meyerson and Banfield, *Politics, Planning, and the Public Interest*, 45.

4. Arnold Hirsch, "Massive Resistance in the Urban North, 1953–1966," *Journal of American History*, September 1995, 522–50. See also CHA, *Monthly Report*, September 15 and October 15, 1953.

5. CHA, *Official Minutes*, August 24 and September 14, 1953; CHA, *Monthly Report*, October 15, 1953.

6. Hirsch, "Massive Resistance," 539; Hirsch, *Making the Second Ghetto*, 232; CHA, *Official Minutes*, January 25, 1954.

7. CHA, *Official Minutes*, April 22, 1954; Hirsch, *Making the Second Ghetto*, 236–237; Griffenhagen and Associates to John Fugard, August 18, 1954, in Griffenhagen file, CHA subject files; Hirsch-McCourt interview.

8. "Statement of Elizabeth Wood," August 30, 1954; Hirsch, *Making the Second*

Ghetto, 235; Robert Gruenberg, "Trumbull Park: Act II, Elizabeth Wood Story," *Nation*, September 18, 1954; Elizabeth Wood to Catherine Bauer Wurster, November 9, 1955, Catherine Bauer [Wurster] Papers, University of California, Berkeley (hereafter cited as Bauer Papers).

9. Elizabeth Wood to the commissioners, "The Tenant Selection Process," December 22, 1952, CHA Gautreaux files; Griffenhagen and Associates, *Report on Certain Policies and Procedures of the Chicago Housing Authority*, August 13, 1953, 12, CHA Subject files; Meyerson and Banfield, *Politics, Planning, and the Public Interest*, 134.

10. Hirsch, "Containment on the Home Front," 158–19; U.S. Housing and Home Finance Agency (HHFA), *Open Occupancy in Public Housing* (Washington, DC, 1953).

11. Hirsch, "Containment on the Home Front," 169–75; Frank Horne to Albert M. Cole, "An Approach to Racial Policy in the Housing and Home Finance Agency," August 12, 1954, and Horne to Cole, "Living Space Procedures: Equity in Public Housing," June 4, 1953, files of the HHFA, box 11, RG 207.

12. See Brian J. L. Berry, *The Open Housing Question: Race and Housing in Chicago, 1966–1976* (Cambridge: Ballinger, 1979).

13. Charles Abrams, *Forbidden Neighbors: A Study of Prejudice in Housing* (New York: Harper and Brothers, 1955), 311–13; Wendell Pritchett, "Where Shall We Live? Class and the Limitations of Fair Housing Law," *Urban Lawyer* (2003): 453–54; Scott Henderson, *Housing and the Democratic Ideal* (New York: Columbia University Press, 2000), 152. On efforts by New York City liberals to sustain integration without mentioning quotas, see Citizens' Housing and Planning Council of New York, *A Report to the New York City Housing Authority*, June 4, 1958.

14. Mayer and O'Brien, Inc., *Report and Recommendations of the Chicago Housing Authority Information Program*, July 28, 1955, 11, folder "CHA Facts—History," CHA Subject files.

15. See Jim Fuerst to Elizabeth Wood, *Quarterly Statistical Report*, for periods ending March 31, 1952, June 30, 1953, and December 31, 1953, CHA Gautreaux files; "Management Aide Minutes," April 8, 1954, CHA Gautreaux files.

16. Hirsch, *Making the Second Ghetto*, 238; Matthew B. Ridgeway, *The Korean War* (New York: Doubleday, 1967), 192. On the controversy over the Twenty-fourth Infantry Regiment's performance in Korea, see William T. Bowers, William M. Hammond, and George L. MacGarrigle, *Black Soldier, White Army: The 24th Infantry Regiment in Korea* (Washington, DC: Center for Military History, U.S. Army, 1996).

17. "Affidavit of Tamaara Tabb," December 7, 1966, CHA Gautreaux files. Also, Hirsch, *Making the Second Ghetto*, 238–39; CHA, *Annual Report*, 1955; *Journal of Housing*, June 1954, 197; CHA, *Annual Statistical Report*, 1955–66; Hirsch-McCourt interview.

18. See CHA, *Annual Statistical Report*, 1951–65; Hirsch, *Making the Second Ghetto*, 238–39; CHA, "Management Aide Minutes," April 8, 1954, CHA Gautreaux files.

19. CHA, *Annual Statistical Report*, 1954–64.

20. Seligman, *Block by Block*; Hirsch, *Making the Second Ghetto*; Harvey Molotch, *Managed Integration: The Dilemmas of Doing Good* (Berkeley and Los Angeles: University of California Press, 1972); Carole Goodwin, *The Oak Park Strategy* (Chicago: University of Chicago Press, 1979); Berry, *The Open Housing Question*; Michael T. Maly, *Beyond Segregation: Multiracial and Multiethnic Neighborhoods in the United States* (Philadelphia: Temple University Press, 2005); Ingrid Gould Ellen, *Sharing America's*

Neighborhoods: The Prospects for Stable Racial Integration (Cambridge: Harvard University Press, 2000).

21. Gerald Suttles, *The Man-Made City* (Chicago: University of Chicago Press, 1990), 158–68.

22. Griffenhagen and Associates, *Report on Certain Policies and Procedures"; Chicago Tribune*, October 9, 1955.

23. CHA, *Annual Report*, 1954 and 1956.

24. Mayer and O'Brien, *Report and Recommendations on the CHA Information Program*, 14–15, 48–49; Chicago City Council, *Journal of Proceedings*, November 4, 1954, 8386, and December 9, 1954, 8730.

25. Deposition of C. E. Humphrey, March 22, 1968, CHA Gautreaux files; Boyd L. Gillilan, former assistant to William Kean, telephone interview by the author, August 27, 1998, notes in author's possession.

26. "Minutes of the City Council Housing and Planning Committee, May 6, 1955," folder labeled "Sites rejected, 1949–1959," CHA Gautreaux files.

27. William B. Kean to the commissioners, "Selection of Sites," June 30, 1955, CHA Gautreaux files; Chicago City Council, Housing and Planning Committee, minutes, September 26, 1955, City Council files; CHA, *Official Minutes*, September 27 and November 14, 1955; *Chicago Tribune*, October 9, 1955; "Interview of John Yancey, October 11, 1967," CHA Gautreaux files; Hirsch, *Making the Second Ghetto*, 240–41; Bowly, *The Poorhouse*, 190.

28. CHA, "1956 Program—Sites approved by CHA and submitted to City Council for Approval," CHA Gautreaux files; *Chicago American*, February 20, 1956. An undated news article (almost certainly from 1956) from an unnamed newspaper, found in a CHA clipping folio in the CHA's Public Affairs files, quotes Nineteenth Ward alderman David T. McKiernan, a Republican, as claiming, "No one has cleared this site with me at any time."

29. *Southtown Economist*, March 4 and February 26, 1956; *Calumet Index*, March 7 and 12, 1956; *Chicago Tribune*, February 24, 1956. Thanks to Will Cooley for explaining Morgan Park's black enclave.

30. *Calumet Index*, March 12, 1956; *Chicago Daily News*, March 9, 1956; Chicago City Council, Committee on Housing, minutes, May 9, 1956, folder labeled "Sites rejected, 1949–1959," CHA Gautreaux files.

31. Emil Hirsh to file, May 28, 1958, CHA Gautreaux files; *Chicago Daily News*, August 9, 1962; Kale Williams to file, "Conference with Alvin Rose, February 3, 1959," CHA Gautreaux files; Hirsch, *Making the Second Ghetto*, chap. 7.

32. *Chicago Tribune*, March 10, 1956; *Southtown Economist*, March 11, 1956; *Chicago American*, February 20, 1956; *Chicago Tribune*, May 10, 1956; "Interview with John Yancey, October 11, 1967," CHA Gautreaux files; Meyerson and Banfield, *Politics, Planning, and the Public Interest*, 221.

33. On black aldermen in the 1950s, see William Grimshaw, *Bitter Fruit: Black Politics and the Chicago Machine, 1931–1991* (Chicago: University of Chicago Press, 1992), 108–12. In 1955, alderman Claude Holman disingenuously joined Hyde Park reform alderman Leon Despres in calling for an "open occupancy" ordinance to battle housing discrimination. A year later in 1956, Holman betrayed Despres by substituting a watered-down measure that proved meaningless but scored him political points in his middle-class ward. Throughout the 1960s, Daley's "silent six" aldermen said nothing

on the issue of open occupancy and housing discrimination. See Leon M. Despres, *Challenging the Daley Machine: A Chicago Alderman's Memoir* (Evanston: Northwestern University Press, 2005), 82–83.

34. See *Chicago Defender*, May 14, 1956, June 5, 1958, and March 4, 1959; *Chicago Daily News*, August 9, 1962; *Chicago Sun-Times*, September 11, 1963.

35. *Chicago American*, March 2, 1956; Hirsch, *Making the Second Ghetto*, 241.

36. Welfare Council of Metropolitan Chicago, *Report on Site Selection in Public Housing in Chicago*, December 1956, Gautreaux exhibits, CHA Gautreaux files.

37. Joseph P. Sullivan to the commissioners, January 31, 1957, CHA Gautreaux files; C. E. Humphrey deposition, March 22, 1968, CHA Gautreaux files.

38. CHA, *Official Minutes*, Resolution 62-CHA-192, December 12, 1962; CHA, *Official Minutes*, Resolution 64-CHA-63, April 22, 1964; CHA, *Official Minutes*, December 14, 1960, April 25, 1962, and August 29, 1963; Alvin Rose to William Bergeron, October 23, 1963, and Joseph Burstein to Marie McGuire, "Equal opportunity—admission to project based on residence in neighborhood," December 11, 1963, both in PHA Dispute folder, CHA Legal files; *Chicago Daily News*, July 19, 1962. See also Hirsch, *Making the Second Ghetto*, 244–45.

39. "Manager's Meeting, July 17, 1963," CHA Gautreaux files; "Statement of Edwin C. Berry, Executive Director, Chicago Urban League, before the Board of Commissioners, CHA, September 11, 1963," and the Reverend Carl A. Fuqua, "Statement of the Chicago Branch, National Association for the Advancement of Colored People before the CHA on Housing for the Elderly, September 11, 1963," both in CHA, *Official Minutes*, September 11, 1963; Burstein to McGuire, December 11, 1963, 3.

40. Kathryn Kula to Alvin Rose, "Legality of CHA's Priority Policy—Housing for the Elderly," January 20,1964, 8–10, in PHA Dispute folder, CHA Legal files (emphasis in the original); CHA, *Official Minutes*, April 22, 1964.

41. Burstein to McGuire, December 11, 1963; "Affidavit of Tamaara Tabb," December 7, 1966, CHA Gautreaux files.

42. CHA, *Annual Statistical Report*, 1969.

43. *Chicago Tribune*, December 6 and 31, 1956; *Chicago Sun-Times*, June 25, 1965; *Chicago Tribune*, January 20, 1990.

44. CHA, *Official Minutes*, May 28, June 27, October 24, and December 7, 1956; Chicago City Council, Housing and Planning Committee, minutes, December 27, 1956, and hearings, January 11, 1957, Chicago City Clerk files; Ed Marciniak, "Lots of Charges, No Facts in Housing Authority Ruckus," *Work*, January 1957; *Chicago Tribune*, November 22 and December 7 and 31, 1956; *Chicago Sun-Times*, December 13 and 31, 1956; CHA Press Release, November 21, 1956, CHA clipping folio, Public Affairs files; Gillilan-Hunt interview.

45. *Chicago Tribune*, January 28, 1957; *Chicago Daily News*, January 11, 12, and 17, 1957; *Chicago Defender*, January 26, 1957; *Chicago Daily News*, February 7, 1957; Cohen and Taylor, *American Pharaoh*, 199–201. On "plantation politics," see Roger Biles, *Richard J. Daley: Politics, Race, and the Governing of Chicago* (DeKalb: Northern Illinois Press, 1995), 93–94.

46. *Chicago Sun-Times*, July 3 and 9, 1957; CHA, *Official Minutes*, July 12, 1957. S.B. 706, introduced May 13, passed the Illinois State Senate on June 11, and was tabled by the House, June 28, 1957. H.B. 1284 was introduced May 28, passed June 19, and was stricken by the Senate, June 26, 1957. See *Final Legislative Synopsis and Digest, of the*

Seventieth General Assembly, State of Illinois (Springfield: Secretary of State of Illinois, 1957), 310, 927.

47. Transcript of Charles Swibel deposition, October 10, 1967, CHA Gautreaux files; *Chicago Sun-Times*, November 25, 1956, and *Chicago Tribune*, December 6, 1956; Gustave (Gus) Master, former CHA executive director, interview by the author, August 4, 1998, notes in author's possession; Biles, *Richard J. Daley*, 46, 61.

48. On patronage in other city agencies under Mayor Daley, see Biles, *Richard J. Daley*, 59–60, 186–88; "Patronage," in *The Encyclopedia of Chicago*, edited by James R. Grossman, Ann Durkin Keating, and Janice L. Reiff, (Chicago: University of Chicago Press, 2004), 603.

49. *Chicago Defender*, July 11, 1963; CHA, *Official Minutes*, March 14, 1968; *Chicago American*, March 24, 1969; Scott Jacobs, "Re: Chicago Housing Authority," no date, folder "Swibel," box 106, Better Government Association Papers, CHM (hereafter cited as BGA Papers); Charles McCall, former CHA comptroller (1965–86), interview by the author, August 3, 1999, Arlington Heights, IL, notes in author's possession.

50. On Swibel and Rose's relationship, see Scott Jacobs, "Interview with Humphrey, April 15," folder "CHA Contracts," box 66, BGA Papers; *Chicago Sun-Times*, August 23, 1964, and November 10, 1967. Rose was recommended for the CHA job by the Metropolitan Housing and Planning Council. See Joseph Pois to CHA, December 12, 1956, folder 277, box 23, accession 74-20, Metropolitan Housing Council papers, UIC Special Collections.

51. Howard Kurtz, "HUD-Chicago Housing Fight Brings New Faces, Same Problems," *Washington Post*, October 8, 1982; Steve Gittleson, "The Secret Battle over Charlie Swibel," *Chicago Magazine*, July 1982, 100. On accusations of patronage in general, see Mike Royko, *Boss: Richard J. Daley of Chicago* (New York: Signet, 1971), 22–23.

52. James Ralph, *Northern Protest: Martin Luther King, Jr., Chicago, and the Civil Rights Movement* (Cambridge: Harvard University Press, 1993).

53. Charles Lamb, *Housing Segregation in Suburban America since 1960* (New York: Cambridge University Press, 2005), 26–56; Massey and Denton, *American Apartheid*, 83–114.

54. Bruce Ackerman, "Integration for Subsidized Housing and the Question of Racial Occupancy Controls," *Stanford Law Review* 26, no. 2 (1974): 251–60; Ankur J. Goel, "Maintaining Integration against Minority Interests," *Urban Lawyer*, 22 (1990): 369–416; Morris Milgram, *Good Neighborhood: The Challenge of Open Housing* (New York: Norton, 1977).

CHAPTER FIVE

1. Catherine Bauer, "Comments on 'The Search for the Ideal City,'" January 9, 1954, box 4, Vinton Papers; *Chicago Defender*, December 2, 1957.

2. Newman, *Defensible Space*, 1972. On various criticisms of Corbusier and Gropius, see Charles Jencks, *The Language of Post-Modern Architecture* (New York: Rizzoli, 1977); Jane Jacobs, *Death and Life of Great American Cities*; Tom Wolfe, *From Bauhaus to Our House* (New York: Farrar, Straus, and Giroux, 1981); Pearlman, *Inventing American Modernism*; Nicholas Dagen Bloom, "Architects, Architecture, and Planning," *Journal of Planning History*, 7, no. 1 (2008), 72–79.

3. On Pruitt-Igoe, see Mary C. Comerio, "Pruitt-Igoe and Other Stories," *Journal of Architectural Education* 34, no. 1 (1981): 25–31; Roger Montgomery, "Pruitt-Igoe: Policy Failure or Societal Symptom," in *The Midwest Metropolis: Policy Problems and Prospects for Change*, edited by Barry Checkoway and Carl V. Patton (Urbana: University of Illinois Press, 1985); and Katherine G. Bristol, "The Pruitt-Igoe Myth," *Journal of Architectural Education* 44, no. 3 (1991): 163–71. All three authors make the crucial point that architecture is less important than other factors in public housing's downfall, and their work is influential to this chapter. See also Lee Rainwater, *Behind Ghetto Walls: Black Life in a Federal Slum* (Chicago: Aldine, 1970). Dell Upton, *Architecture in the United States* (New York: Oxford University Press, 1998), 239; and Sam Davis, *The Architecture of Affordable Housing* (Berkeley and Los Angeles: University of California Press, 1995), 11–13.

4. *Chicago Tribune*, April 14, 1982.

5. Elizabeth Wood to alderman George D. Kells, September 21, 1945, City Council folder, CHA Subject files; Wood to PHA administrator Orvil Olmsted, October 14, 1946, CHA Development files, IL 2-9; People's Welfare Organization of Chicago, *History of Dearborn Homes*, 1950, CHM.

6. See Elizabeth Wood to Loebl and Schlossman, February 16, 1946, and Wood to Orvil Olmsted, October 14, 1946, both in CHA Development files, IL 2-9; Robert Taylor to alderman William J. Lancaster, October 28, 1948, CHA Subject files. On St. Louis, see Alexander von Hoffman, "Why They Built Pruitt-Igoe," in *From Tenements to Taylor Homes*, edited by John F. Bauman, Roger Biles, and Kristin Szylvian (University Park: Pennsylvania State University Press, 2000), 189–91.

7. CHA, "Development Program for IL 2-9," CHA Development files.

8. Phyllis Lambert, "Mies Immersion," in Lambert et al., *Mies in America*, 356–57; Eric Mumford, "More than Mies: Architecture of Chicago Multifamily Housing, 1935–1965," in Waldheim and Ray, *Chicago Architecture*, 85.

9. Julian Whittlesley, "New Dimensions in Housing Design," *Progressive Architecture*, April 1951, 57–68.

10. "Experiment in Multi-Story Housing" and "Architects Act as Editorial Board," *Journal of Housing*, October 1951, 367–69 and 338, respectively.

11. Catherine Bauer to Nathan Straus, October 31, 1949, box 4, outgoing correspondence, Bauer Papers.

12. "Address by John Taylor Egan, Commissioner, Public Housing Administration, at the 17th Annual Conference of the National Association of Housing Officials, Detroit, Michigan, October 16–19," box 10, "Miscellaneous Records of the Liaison Division," RG 196; Housing and Home Finance Agency, *18th Annual Report, 1964* (Washington, DC: Government Printing Office, 1965), table II-35, 123–24; CHA, *Monthly Report*, February and October 1950; CHA, *Annual Statistical Report*, 1955. The construction cost figure for public housing excludes other nondwelling structures but includes dwelling equipment (refrigerators, stoves).

13. William Bergeron to Charles Slusser, October 30, 1953, "Field Office Director's Monthly Report," box 1, Correspondence of the Commissioner of Public Housing, RG 196.

14. NAHO, Local Authority Letter no. 85, July 27, 1950, "Minutes of Federal-Local Relations Committee Meeting, July 7, 1950," in box 2, "Miscellaneous Records of the Liaison Division," RG 196. The 1949 Housing Act changed construction cost limits from per-unit to per-room and raised the limits substantially.

15. NAHO, Local Authority Letter no. 88, October 9, 1950, "The Cost Situation and PHA Policies," in "Miscellaneous Records of the Liaison Division," box 2, RG 196.

16. "Address by John Taylor Egan" (emphasis in the original).

17. David M. P. Fruend, *Colored Property* (Chicago: University of Chicago Press, 2007).

18. Leonard Freedman, *Public Housing, the Politics of Poverty* (Chicago: Rand Mc-Nally, 1968), 45–53; Warren Vinton, "Places in Which the City Council Voted against Public Housing or Slum Clearance," June 13, 1950, in box 16, Vinton Papers; Roger Biles, "Public Housing and the Postwar Urban Renaissance, 1949–1973," in Bauman, Biles, and Szylvian, *From Tenements to the Taylor Homes*, 143–62.

19. Catherine Bauer, "The Dreary Deadlock of Public Housing," *Architectural Forum*, May 1957, 140–42; D. Bradford Hunt, "How Did Public Housing Survive the 1950s?" *Journal of Policy History* 17, no. 2 (2005): 193–216.

20. Catherine Bauer to Leon Keyserling, April 22, 1952, box 4, outgoing correspondence, Bauer Papers; Oberlander and Newbrun, *Houser*, 256–60; Freedman, *Public Housing, the Politics of Poverty*, 160. For a dissenting view, see Parson, *Making a Better World*.

21. Public Housing Administration (PHA), *"Low-Rent Public Housing: Planning, Design, and Construction for Economy*, December 1950.

22. CHA, *Monthly Report*, October 1950 and January 1951; CHA, *Official Minutes*, January 25, 1951; CHA, *The Livability of Low-Rent Public Housing*, 1950, HWLC-MRC; Jack Bryan to Neal Hardy, "Vinton Memo to Architectural Forum," May 31, 1950, in box 1, Vinton Papers. On changes in minimum room sizes, compare FPHA, *Minimum Physical Standards and Criteria for the Planning and Design of FPHA-Aided Urban Low-Rent Housing*, November 1945, 7, and PHA, *Low-Rent Public Housing*. See also Eric Mumford, "The Tower in the Park in America," *Planning Perspectives* 10 (1995): 17–41.

23. PHA, *Low-Rent Public Housing*, 4, 31–33.

24. Catherine Bauer to Elizabeth Wood, February 18, 1948, and Bauer to Gilbert Rodier, February 7, 1952, both in box 4, outgoing correspondence, Bauer Papers.

25. Elizabeth Wood, "The Case for the Low Apartment," *Architectural Forum*, January 1952, 102. On Wood's concerns with the livability of high-rises, see Hirsch-McCourt interview.

26. Douglas Haskell, "The Case for the High Apartment," *Architectural Forum*, January 1952, 103–6.

27. Catherine Bauer, "Clients for Housing: The Low-Income Tenant—Does He Want Supertenements?" *Progressive Architecture*, May 1952, 61–64.

28. "Address made by Minoru Yamasaki in Pittsburgh at the MARC of NAHO Conference on Friday, May 23, 1952," outgoing correspondence, box 4, Bauer Papers.

29. CHA, *Official Minutes*, April 13, 1953; CHA, "Addendum no. IV to Development Program for Project IL 2-20," CHA Development files, IL 2-20. The PHA forced similar changes in other cities, including Buffalo in 1952 and Baltimore in 1953. See Gilbert Rodier to Charles Slusser, December 18, 1953, and Rodier to John Taylor Egan, January 7, 1953, box 5, "Correspondence of the Commissioner of Public Housing," RG 196; Wood, "Ideals and Realities in Subsidized Housing since 1934," 67. Data for "Construction Cost per Room" and "Total Development Cost per Unit" from CHA, *Actual Development Cost Statement*, a report to the Public Housing Administration found in CHA Development files for individual projects.

30. Bauer had also envisioned the use of Title I funds to secure vacant land tracts for public or private housing projects. She pleaded with Warren Vinton and Nathaniel Keith to do more in this area, but the Urban Redevelopment Administration did little. See Bauer to Vinton, August 30, 1949, box 4, Vinton Papers; Bauer to Keith, September 18, 1949, box 4, outgoing correspondence, Bauer Papers.

31. From Warren Vinton, see the following: "Urban Redevelopment and Public Housing Programs Must Work Together," *American City*, December 1949, 117–18; "Summary of Legislative History in Respect to Use of Urban Redevelopment Funds to Cover Write-Downs on Cost of Slum Lands Used for Low-Rent Housing," February 28, 1950, in box 19, Vinton Papers; "The Low Rent Public Housing Program," June 5, 1956, box 1, Vinton Papers.

32. *Chicago Sun-Times*, September 4, 1957, and October 31, 1958; *Chicago Daily News*, March 8, 1958; Henry F. Lewelling, former CHA planner, telephone interview by the author, August 13, 1998, notes in author's possession.

33. Senate Committee on Banking and Currency, *President's Message Disapproving S. 57*, 86th Congr., 1st sess., July 23–31, 1959, 610; Alvin Rose to Dorothy Gazzolo, June 16, 1958, CHA Gautreaux files; CHA to Charles Slusser, February 5, 1959, folder "PHA Development Dispute," CHA Legal files; *Chicago Sun-Times*, February 1, 1958. Plans for the first iteration of the "row-on-row" design have not survived. However, a sketch of the second version appeared in the CHA's *Monthly Report*, March 1958.

34. CHA to Slusser, February 5, 1959; PHA acting regional director Hugo Schwartz to CHA, September 5, 1957, CHA Development files, IL 2-37; Lewelling-Hunt interview; Ernst Schranz, former CHA architect, telephone interview by the author, April 17, 1998, notes in author's possession.

35. Kathryn Kula to Alvin Rose, January 30, 1958, and CHA to Richard J. Daley, July 29, 1959, all in folder "PHA Development Dispute," CHA Legal files; CHA to Slusser, February 5, 1959, CHA Development files, IL 2-37.

36. CHA to Slusser, February 5, 1959.

37. Alvin Rose to William Bergeron, January 6, 1959, CHA Development files, IL 2-30; CHA to Slusser, September 5, 1959; "Development Program, IL 2-37, Revision 3," CHA Development files, IL 2-37. See also *Chicago Sun-Times*, May 14, 1959. Only 7.5 percent of families moving into CHA housing in 1958 were "priority" families displaced by public action (CHA, *Annual Statistical Report*, 1958).

38. "President's Message Disapproving S. 57," 329–36; CHA to Congressman Sidney Yates, June 23, 1959, folder "PHA Development Dispute," CHA Legal files.

39. "President's Message Disapproving S. 57," 604; "Comparison on bids received on Project IL 2-34, Chicago with Project NY 5-34, New York," June 11, 1958, folder "Chicago Development Dispute," box 5, "Historical Publications," RG 196. The comparison underestimated the difference between the projects; a construction cost index showed that high-rise buildings in New York cost 17.8 percent more in New York than in Chicago.

40. "Mayor Daley's Charges before the Sparkman Committee," internal memo, September 1, 1959, folder "Chicago Development Dispute," box 5, "Historical Publications," RG 196. The CHA later countered that the gallery concept had proved to be highly successful and no more expensive than center corridor buildings, submitting data to bolster its case. See Sumner Sollitt Company to CHA, August 28, 1959, and Sollitt to Metz and Associates, August 31, 1959, both in folder "PHA Development Dispute," CHA Legal files.

41. *Report of the Special Committee to the Commissioners of the Chicago Housing Authority on the Subject of Project Illinois 2-34*, August 3, 1959, in folder "PHA Development Dispute," CHA Legal files.

42. CHA to Slusser, September 2, 1959, in folder "PHA Development Dispute," CHA Legal files; Slusser to CHA, September 4, 1959, CHA Development files, IL 2-37. Among the "1959 projects," only the Washington Park Homes used any row houses, which were distributed in small numbers on individual parcels in the black belt.

43. "Development program for IL 2-37, Revision IV," February 1960, CHA Development files, IL 2-37; *Chicago Sun-Times*, March 24 and April 13, 1960; CHA, *Official Minutes*, March 31, 1960; "Notes of Commissioners' Meeting," in CHA, *Official Minutes*, April 4, 1960; CHA development director J. W. Hasskarl to PHA regional director William Bergeron, August 21, 1964, CHA Development files, IL 2-37.

44. Egan was quoted in Mullen, "Cabrini-Green: The Road to Hell."

CHAPTER SIX

1. Wesley Skogan, *Disorder and Decline: Crime and the Spiral of Decay in American Neighborhoods* (New York: Free Press, 1990), 2.

2. The sociological literature on social disorder has a long pedigree going back to the Chicago School of Sociology in the 1920s. Influential books include Clifford R. Shaw and Henry D. McKay, *Juvenile Delinquency and Urban Areas* (Chicago: University of Chicago Press, 1942); Gerald Suttles, *The Social Construction of Communities* (Chicago: University of Chicago Press, 1972); Ruth Kornhauser, *Social Sources of Delinquency* (Chicago: University of Chicago Press, 1978). I am most influenced in this chapter by the work of Robert Sampson and his colleagues. See especially Robert J. Sampson, Jeffrey D. Morenoff, and Thomas Gannon-Rowley, "Assessing 'Neighborhood Effects': Social Processes and New Directions for Research." *Annual Review of Sociology* 28 (2002): 443–78; Robert J. Sampson and Byron W. Groves, "Community Structure and Crime: Testing Social-Disorganization Theory," *American Journal of Sociology* 94, no. 4 (1989): 774–802; Robert J. Sampson, Jeffrey D. Morenoff, and Felton Earls, "Beyond Social Capital: Spatial Dynamics of Collective Efficacy for Children," *American Sociological Review* 64, no. 5 (1999): 633–60; Robert J. Sampson and Stephen W. Raudenbush, "Systematic Social Observation of Public Spaces: A New Look at Disorder in Urban Neighborhoods," *American Journal of Sociology* 105, no. 3 (1999): 603–51.

3. The direct connection between youth density and public housing's demise is nearly absent from the literature on planning or public housing. The earliest mention can be found in Anthony F. C. Wallace, *Housing and Social Structure: A Preliminary Survey*, (Philadelphia: Philadelphia Housing Association, 1952), 89. Wallace noted the managerial problems faced in the high-rise Jacob Riis houses with their "very high proportion of small children." But no serious comparative work on youth densities or its effect on public housing management has been completed. One study of "problem families" in Boston makes a hesitant link between child density and negative "project reputation," finding Boston's managers connected high concentrations of children with "problem areas" in their projects. See Richard S. Scobie, *Problem Tenants in Public Housing: Who, Where, and Why Are They?* (New York: Praeger Publishers, 1975), 63. A planning treatise from 1986 encourages housing developers to be careful

about youth densities: "Ratios of adults to children of less than 3 to 1 [i.e. youth density greater than 0.30] and densities of more than 30 children to the acre are 'warning devices.' They signal the need for careful planning, special provision for child recreation, and more-than-adequate maintenance." See Clare Cooper Marcus and Wendy Sarkissian, Housing As If People Mattered (Berkeley and Los Angeles: University of California, 1986), 280–81. Marcus and Sarkissian cite a handful of British reports from the late 1970s. Extensive research in the late 1960s and 1970s asked how children adapted to high-rise buildings and public project grounds, especially in Great Britain and Canada. See also Clare Cooper Marcus and Robin C. Moore, "Children and Their Environments: A Review of Research" Journal of Architectural Education (April 1976), 22–25; E. W. Cooney, "High Flats in Local Authority Housing in England and Wales since 1945," in Multi-Storey Living, the British Working Class Experience, edited by Anthony Sutcliffe (London: Croom Helm, 1974), 161; Vancouver City Planning Department, Housing Families at High Densities, 1978, 11, 17, 26; Joan Maizel, Two to Five in High Flats: An Enquiry into Play Provision for Children Aged Two to Five Years Living in High Flats (London: Housing Centre Trust, 1961); Pearl Jephcott, Homes in High Flats (Edinburgh: Oliver and Boyd, 1971), 65–67. Mark Baldassare, in Residential Crowding in Urban America (Berkeley and Los Angeles: University of California Press, 1979), an important work on residential densities, only examines "persons per residential acre" but never addresses youth-adult ratios.

4. Youth-adult ratios are defined as the number of people under age twenty-one divided by the number of people age twenty-one and over. Demographers often use percentage of minors to describe age composition, and this is a valid measure, but using youth-adult ratios highlights the relative numbers of each more clearly. Like a student-teacher ratio for measuring classroom conditions, the youth-adult ratio is one measure of the capacity of adults to manage the youths in their environment.

5. Sources for table 1: U.S. Bureau of the Census, U.S. Census of Population: 1970, vol. 1 (Washington, DC, 1973), pt. 1, sec. 1, table 52, 1–269, also pt. 15, Illinois—sec. 1, table 24, 111–13, and table 28, 15–183; Sixteenth Census of the United States: 1940, vol. 2, Population (Washington, 1943), pt. 1, table 7, 22, and pt. 2, Florida-Iowa, table A-35, 639; Report on Population of the United States at the Tenth Census (Washington, 1883), table 20, 548; Report on Population of the United States at the Eleventh Census: 1890 (Washington, 1897), pt. 2, table 8, 117; Robert Hunter, Tenement Conditions in Chicago (Chicago: City Homes Association, 1901), 195–96; Census of Population: 1960, vol. 1 (Washington, 1963), pt. 34, New York, table 20; U.S. Census of Population and Housing: 1960 (Washington, 1962), Census Tracts, Final Report PHC(1)-104, pt. 1, table P-2, 371, and Final Report PHC(1)-26, table P-1, 58; Chicago Housing Authority, Annual Statistical Report, 1951, 1960, 1965, 1970, and 1975.

6. The standard deviation calculation uses youth-adult ratios for census tracts in the city of Chicago for 1960 and a definition of youth as eighteen or under, because of limitations in census data at the tract level. Twelve census tracts that year consisted of 90 percent or more public housing. See U.S. Census of Population and Housing: 1960, Final Report PHC(1)-26, Census Tracts for Chicago, IL, Standard Metropolitan Statistical Area, table P-1.

7. U.S. Bureau of the Census, Census of Population: 1970, vol. 1, Characteristics of the Population (Washington, DC, 1973), pt. 1, Illinois, table 155.

8. CHA, What Is a Low Income Family? November 1947, 17; CHA, Annual Report, 1945; CHA, Facts about Public Housing in Chicago, June 1947, 28; CHA, Annual Statisti-

cal Report, 1952, chart 7; CHA, *Children's Cities*, pamphlet, 1945, HWLC-MRC; CHA operating manual, 1940, HWLC-MRC.

9. "Meeting for discussion of desirable legislation," July 13 and 14, 1944, box 1, Vinton Papers; CHA, *Facts about Public Housing in Chicago*, 10; CHA, *Monthly Report*, November 1948; John Taylor Egan, "Supplemental Statement on Costs of Public Housing and Appropriate Cost Limits," testimony before the Senate Committee on Banking and Commerce, February 7, 1949, and "Address by John T. Egan, NAHO Conference, October 16–19, 1950," both in box 10, "Miscellaneous Records of the Liaison Division," RG 196; Abrams, *The Future of Housing*, 272.

10. Major federal planning documents include: USHA, *Planning the Site: Design of Low-Rent Housing Projects*, Bulletin no. 11, May 1939; FPHA, *Minimum Physical Standards and Criteria for Planning and Design of FPHA-Aided Public Housing Projects*, 1945; FPHA, *The Livability Problems of 1,000 Families*, 1945; PHA, *Low-Rent Public Housing*. Only one document makes brief mention of the problems of youth, quoting without explanation an unnamed housing official from Ohio: "Multi-story buildings containing dwelling units housing a number of children are, we find, extremely unsatisfactory." See FPHA, *Public Housing Design: A Review of Experience in Low-Rent Housing*, 1946, 88.

11. CHA, *Annual Statistical Report*, 1951–60.

12. Theodore A. Veenstra to Stanley W. Hahn, June 23, 1954, CHA Development files, IL 2-22.

13. CHA, *Annual Statistical Report*, 1951–67; CHA, *Monthly Report*, April 1955; CHA to Richard J. Daley, July 19, 1957, in "Mayor's file," CHA Subject files; CHA, *Official Minutes*, December 6, 1957, CHA files; *Chicago Tribune*, November 28, 1957, January 10 and 14, 1958.

14. Elizabeth Wood to the commissioners, "The Tenant Selection Process," December 22, 1952, CHA Gautreaux files; *Chicago Tribune*, January 14, 1958. Pruitt-Igoe also had difficulty renting smaller apartments. See Rainwater, *Behind Ghetto Walls*, 13.

15. William Moore, *The Vertical Ghetto*, xv; Frank de Leeuw, *Operating Costs in Public Housing: A Financial Crisis* (Washington: Urban Institute, 1968), 24.

16. Jane Jacobs, *The Death and Life of Great American Cities* (New York: Vintage Books, 1992), 35, 50, 82 (emphasis in the original).

17. Fuerst, *When Public Housing Was Paradise*, 48, 79, 114, 127, 131, 174.

18. Elizabeth Wood, *Housing Design: A Social Theory* (New York: Citizens' Housing and Planning Council, 1961).

19. See Newman, *Defensible Space*, 234–37, especially tables A-6 and A-7.

20. Criminologists have attributed some of the drop in overall crime in the 1990s to the decline in the youth population following the baby-boom "echo." See Robert Agnew, "An Integrated Theory of the Adolescent Peak in Offending," *Youth and Society* 34, no. 3 (March 2003): 263–300; Alfred Blumstein and Joel Wallman, *The Crime Drop in America* (New York: Cambridge University Press, 2000); Sampson and Rauderbusch, "Systematic Social Observation of Public Spaces."

21. Alvin Rose to William Bergeron, January 6, 1959, CHA Development files, IL 2-30; CHA, *Official Minutes*, January 25, 1961; *Chicago Sun-Times*, April 5, 1959; *Chicago Daily News*, March 8, 1958; Robert H. Murphy, "City within a City: Robert R. Taylor Homes," *FREE: A Roosevelt University Magazine* 2, no. 1 (spring 1963): 6–13, CHM; Wolf Von Eckardt, "The Black Neck in the White Noose," *New Republic*, October 19, 1963, 14–18; Robert H. Murphy to Harry J. Schneider, "Taylor (37): Comments on

Magazine Article," October 28, 1963, manager's folder, Robert Taylor Homes, CHA Subject files. For descriptions of youth-inspired social disorder in other cities, see Rainwater, *Behind Ghetto Walls*, 66.

22. See reports in the *Chicago Daily News*, April 25, 1959; *Chicago Sun-Times*, September 4, 1957, March 12, 1956, February 4, 1959, and August 25, 1967; and *Chicago Tribune*, June 27, 1980. Also the CHA records: Robert Murphy, internal memo, September 16, 1963, manager's folder, Robert Taylor Homes, CHA Subject files; Jack Doppelt to file, "Interviews with Virgil Cross, CHA Chief of Central Maintenance," July 31, 1980, box 134, BGA Papers.

23. *Chicago American*, April 5, 1958; *Chicago Sun-Times*, September 4, 1957; *Chicago Defender*, September 2, 1960; *Chicago Daily News*, April 12–17, 1965; see also *Chicago Daily Defender*, editorial, October 19, 1966. For earlier examples of similar concerns with the large number of youths, see *Chicago Sun-Times*, September 4, 1957, May 7, 1958, and April 4, 1959.

24. Sociologists studying gang behavior have explained that the term "gang" covers a wide range of organization and activity. Some of the city's more violent and organized gangs did stake out turf at projects soon after they were opened. On the first identification of the Vice Lords and Cobras in public housing, see CHA, *Official Minutes*, February 28, 1962. For the complex identities of gang members within a community, see Mary Pattillo-McCoy, *Picket Fences: Privilege and Peril among the Black Middle Class* (Chicago: University of Chicago Press, 1999). On gangs in the 1990s in public housing, see the work of Sudhir Venkatesh, including *American Project* (Cambridge: Harvard University Press, 2000).

25. James Baldwin, *The Price of the Ticket: Collected Nonfiction, 1948–1985* (New York: Macmillan, 1985), 209–10.

26. Murphy to Schneider, "Taylor (37): Comments on Magazine Article."

27. Rainwater, *Behind Ghetto Walls*, 4, 66.

28. USHA, *Community Activities in Public Housing*, May 1941; CHA, *Annual Report*, 1945.

29. PHA, Chicago Regional Office, *Management Review, Chicago Housing Authority*, January 1958, HWLC-MRC, 31–32.

30. Mary Bolton Wirth studied with Edith Abbott at the University of Chicago in the 1920s and then supervised WPA social workers during the 1930s. After the death of her husband, she went to work for the CHA in 1952 as a community and tenant relations aide at the Jane Addams Homes. Her papers, housed at the University of Chicago, are a rich source on public housing management in the city.

31. Mary Bolton Wirth, "Reminiscences of My Assignment As an 'Aide'— 1953–1954," "Report on Activities at the Jane Addams Homes," and Wirth to Albert Rosenberg, May 15, 1953, all in folder 1, box 1, Mary Wirth Papers. See also "Mary Bolton Wirth," in *Women Making Chicago*, edited by Rima Schultz (Bloomington: Indiana University Press, 1995), 998–91.

32. Mary Bolton Wirth, "Meeting with Recreation Agencies of Near West Side" April 23, 1953; Mary Bolton Wirth to Albert Rosenberg, May 15, 1953; Wirth, "Memorandum of Record," August 17, 1954, folder 1, box 1, Mary Wirth Papers. Also, Albert Rosenberg, "The Community and Tenant Relations Program of the Chicago Housing Authority," May 25, 1953; Wirth, "Memorandum of Record: Re: Meeting on March 19, 1957 with the Chicago Park District," March 27, 1957, folder 2, box 1; Mary Bolton Wirth, "Recreation and Group Work at CHA Projects," June 28, 1958.

33. CHA Press Release, February 10, 1959, CHA clipping folio, CHA Public Affairs files; *Chicago Sun-Times*, June 1, 1958; *Chicago Daily News*, October 16, 1958; CHA, *Official Minutes*, June 8, 1960, and March 25, 1965; Chicago Metropolitan Welfare Council, *Proposed Co-operative Survey and Planning Project on Social Welfare and Health Services in Public Housing*, appendix, March 1967, folder "Management—General," CHA Legal files. On Rose, see Edward Banfield, *Political Influence: A New Theory of Urban Politics* (New York: Free Press, 1961), 65–66.

34. Alvin Rose, "A Public Houser Speaks," *Public Welfare*, 20, no. 2 (1962): 91–92, 137; CHA Press Release, February 10, 1959, CHA clipping folio, CHA Public Affairs files; *Chicago Daily News*, October 16, 1958; *Chicago Sun-Times*, June 14, 1960, and August 10, 1961; CHA, *Official Minutes*, June 8, 1960.

35. CHA, *Official Minutes*, May 25 (Kay Kula to Theophilus Mann, May 23) and June 13, 1962; March 9, 1967; March 28, 1968. Also Better Government Association, "Memo to Hoge, re: CHA," no date [1975?], folder "background," box 66, BGA Papers.

36. CHA, *Official Minutes*, July 22, 1965. On Rose and the National Scouts, see CHA, *Official Minutes*, August 12, 1965.

37. Chicago *Sun-Times*, November 10, 1967.

38. Undated, unnotated clip from unknown newspaper, folder "Authorities—Miscellaneous," CHA Subject files, likely from late 1964.

39. CHA director of development J. W. Hasskarl to William Bergeron, February 15, 1962, CHA Development files, IL 2-37.

40. Harry J. Schneider to Bergeron, August 25, 1964, CHA Development files, IL 2-37.

41. Gus Master to Bergeron, July 29, 1969, and Alvin Rose to Bergeron, November 4, 1964, CHA Development files, IL 2-37. In 1962, the CHA estimated that 6,700 Taylor residents would be prekindergarten age (Rose to Bergeron, February 8, 1962, CHA Development files, IL 2-37).

42. Claude P. Miller, chief of community and tenant relations, to Harry J. Schneider, January 21, 1966, folder "Management—General," CHA Legal files.

43. *Chicago Tribune*, October 24, 1968; Master to Bergeron, July 29, 1969, CHA Development files, IL 2-37.

44. In 1944, the all-black Altgeld Gardens project opened on the far South Side without sufficient school space, and the CHA had little choice but to offer thirty-six apartments to the school board for use as classrooms. A new school finally opened in 1947, but only after federal officials intervened by threatening to block renewal of the temporary solution. See CHA, *Official Minutes*, June 10, 1947.

45. Noel Naisbitt, telephone interview by the author, March 28, 2000, notes in author's possession; Noel Naisbitt to William Bergeron, January 21, 1962, CHA Development files, IL 2-37; CHA, *Official Minutes*, January 24, 1962.

46. CHA, *Official Minutes*, April 11, 1962, May 11, 1967, June 8, 1972; *Chicago Defender*, October 21 and 22 and November 10, 1964. For more on the challenge by African Americans to the school board's leadership, see Arvarh E. Strickland, *A History of the Chicago Urban League*, (Champaign: University of Illinois Press, 1966), 235–41; Christopher Reed, *The Chicago NAACP and the Rise of Black Professional Leadership, 1910–1966* (Bloomington: Indiana University Press, 1997), 168.

47. Murphy, "City within a City"; CHA, "Managers' Meeting, September 19, 1962," CHA Subject files.

48. CHA director of management Harry J. Schneider to Thomas A. Williams, 4352 S. State St., no. 1003, September 21, 1966, manager's folder, Robert Taylor Homes, CHA Subject files; CHA, "Response to the *Daily News*," April 26, 1965, HWLC-MRC.

49. CHA director of management Gus Master to Carolyn Lennear, 4410 S. State Street, no. 903, August 30, 1968, manager's folder, Robert Taylor Homes, CHA Subject files.

50. *Chicago Daily News*, April 25, 1959; Mary Bolton Wirth, "Interview—Mr. Joe Ford, Supervisor, Robert Taylor Park, Chicago Park District," February 18, 1965, in Mary Wirth Papers; Alvin Rose to C. L. Farris, December 9, 1960, folder "Authorities—Miscellaneous," CHA Subject files; *Chicago Defender*, May 14 and December 14, 1963, January 6, 1964, and March 13, 1965; *Chicago Tribune*, September 9, 1963, and September 9, 1965; Master to Bergeron, June 8, 1967, CHA Development files, IL 2-37. See also Mullen, "Cabrini-Green: The Road to Hell."

51. Dorothea Washington, former Dearborn Homes resident and CHA administrator, interview by the author, October 29, 2007, Chicago, digital recording in the author's possession. Similar sentiments were expressed in several interviews. See also Travis Yarborough, Cynthia Yarborough, Douglas Austin, KathyAnn Kendall, all former residents of ABLA, joint interview by the author, November 13, 2004, Hazel Crest, IL, notes in the author's possession; Annie Smith Stubenfield, former resident of Ida B. Wells and Darrow Homes, interview by the author, October 5, 2007, Chicago, digital recording in the author's possession; Raymond E. Gunn, former resident of Cabrini-Green, interview by the author, October 2, 2007, Chicago, digital recording in the author's possession; Doreen Ambrose-Van Lee, former resident of Cabrini-Green, interview by the author, May 9, 2008, Chicago, digital recording in the author's possession. See also Venkatesh, *American Project*, 36, 73.

52. Venkatesh, *American Project*, 77–83.

53. Mary Bolton Wirth, notes, no date, no title, likely 1965, folder 2, box 11, Mary Wirth Papers.

54. *Chicago Defender*, December 14, 1963.

55. *Chicago Defender*, November 30 and December 14, 1963; January 15, 22, and 28, February 4 and 25, March 9 and 31, May 2 and 30, 1964; Harry J. Schneider to William Bergeron, June 23, 1964, CHA Development files, IL 2-37; *Chicago Tribune*, February 27, 1964. For more on the efforts of Taylor residents to exert collective efficacy in the 1970s, see Venkatesh, *American Projects*, 77–83.

56. *Chicago Defender*, February 24 and 29, 1964; Gus Master to Bergeron, May 27, 1964, CHA Development files, IL 2-27; Schneider to Bergeron, November 15, 1966, CHA Development files, IL 2-22; CHA, "Annual Report on Operations, Year Ended December 31, 1970," CHA Subject files; William Lebsock to John Waner, April 19, 1972, CHA Development files, IL 2-37; Schneider to Rose Cunningham, building president, 5326 S. State, April 20, 1972, CHA Development files, IL 2-37.

57. Wood, "The Realities of Urban Redevelopment" and *Public Housing and Mrs. McGee* (New York: Citizens' Housing and Planning Council, 1957). On early mentions of "problem" families, see *Journal of Housing*, August 1951, 283.

58. Wood, *Public Housing and Mrs. McGee*; see also by Wood, *The Small Hard Core: The Housing of Problem Families in New York City, a Study and Recommendations* (New York: Citizens' Housing and Planning Council, 1957).

59. On the Wells Extension, see "Minutes of Meeting, Advisory Committee to

the CHA, Welfare Council of Metropolitan Chicago," April 11, 1956, CHA Gautreaux files. On problem families and evictions, see also L. G. McDougal to Elizabeth Wood, May 22, 1952, Subject: "Undesirable Families," folder 13, box 1, Mary Wirth Papers; also Mary Bolton Wirth, "Those Ivory Notices," no date, likely 1956, and Mary Bolton Wirth, memo, July 9, 1956, both in folder 1, box 1, Mary Wirth Papers. See also Richard Scobie, *Problem Families in Public Housing* (New York: Praeger, 1975), 63.

60. "Minutes of Meeting, Advisory Committee to the CHA, Welfare Council of Metropolitan Chicago," April 11, 1956, folder "Elson," box 1, Business People for the Public Interest Papers, CHM.

61. Cook County Department of Public Aid, Public Assistance Division, *The Rockwell Gardens Project (A Progress Report)*, December 1, 1960, folder "Cook County Departments," CHA Subject files.

62. Charles Swibel to the *Chicago Daily News*, April 26, 1965, folder "Charles Swibel," CHA Subject file.

63. Mary Bolton Wirth, "Standards of Social Eligibility," March 1, 1957, Mary Wirth Papers; Roberta Coffee, former CHA staff member, telephone interview by the author, September 9, 1998, notes in author's possession. See also *Chicago Daily News*, March 9, 1968.

64. Master-Hunt interview.

65. CHA, *Monthly Report*, June 1950; Mary Bolton Wirth, typed notes, July 9, 1956, folder 1, box 1, Mary Wirth Papers; Lemann, *The Promised Land*, 233; *Chicago Defender*, August 6 and October 19, 1966; *Chicago Sun-Times*, March 14, 1968.

66. Jim Fuerst and Roy Petty, "Public Housing in the Courts, Pyrrhic Victories for the Poor," *Urban Lawyer*, summer 1977. The court cases include *Thorpe v. Housing Authority of Durham*, 386 U.S. 670, January 13, 1969; *Neddo v. Housing Authority of Milwaukee*, 335 F. Supp. 1397 (E.D. Wis 1971); *Thomas v. Housing Authority of Little Rock*, 282 F. Supp. 575 (E.D. Arkansas, 1967).

67. Muriel Chadwick, former CHA project manager and senior administrator, interview by Jim Fuerst, no date, transcript in author's possession.

68. Daisy Brumfield, former CHA project manager, interview by Jim Fuerst, no date, transcript in author's possession.

69. See Thomas Grippando, Arthur Scheller, and Victoria Haas, eds., *John Marshall Law Manual for Community Developers and Social Workers*, 6th ed., 1980, in box 134, BGA files, CHM.

70. Mary Bolton Wirth, "The CHA dilemma," no date [1957?], folder 1, box 1, Mary Wirth Papers. For a dissenting view that argues the problem family was an exaggerated problem, see Scobie, *Problem Tenants in Public Housing*.

71. *Chicago Defender*, April 28, 1960, and January 6, 1964; *New Crusader*, September 19, 1959, CHA clipping folio, CHA Public Affairs files; Venkatesh, *American Project*, 68–76.

72. CHA, *Comprehensive Security Program for the Cabrini-Green Homes*, April 12, 1972, HWLC-MRC; CHA, *Official Minutes*, February 26, 1970; Doug Longhini to file, "Crime in Cabrini-Green," May 28, 1975, box 66, BGA files; *Chicago Sun-Times*, November 8, 1974, and January 29, 1978; *Chicago Defender*, November 11, 1974; *Chicago Tribune*, December 3, 1986; Tiffany Pinkston-Wheeler, former resident of Ickes and Taylor, telephone interview by the author, August 6, 2007, notes in author's possession.

73. See David J. Garrow, editor, *Chicago 1966: Open Housing Marches, Summit Negotiations, and Operation Breadbasket* (New York: Carlson Publishing, 1989), 70–79.

74. CHA, *Official Minutes*, August 11, 1966, July 9 and August 28, 1970; Alvin Rose to William Bergeron, December 23, 1966, CHA Development files, IL 2-37; news clipping, Tom Littlewood, "U.S. Blocks Financing Plan for CHA Project Guards," January 26, 1967, in CHA clipping files, HWLC-MRC.

75. CHA, *Official Minutes*, March 23, 1971; House Committee on Banking, Finance, and Urban Affairs (hereafter House Banking Committee), *Safety and Security in Public Housing: Field Hearing before the Subcommittee on Housing and Community Development, Chicago, Illinois*, 103rd Congr., 2nd sess., April 22, 1994, 65–66.

76. CHA, *Official Minutes*, August 27, 1970; CHA, *Comprehensive Security Program for the Cabrini-Green Homes; Chicago Defender*, August 11, 1973; Chicago City Department of Planning, *Cabrini-Green: A Model Project for Public Housing Security, A Final Report*, 1980, HWLC-MRC. See also W. Victor Rouse and Herb Rubenstein, *Crime in Public Housing: A Review of Major Issues and Selected Crime Reduction Strategies*, Report for the Department of Housing and Urban Development, December 1978.

77. *Chicago Defender*, November 29, 1973; Charles Swibel to Lawrence B. Simons, August 22, 1979, CHA Development files, IL 2-37. For an extended discussion on the lack of policing, see Venkatesh, *American Project*, 68–77.

78. Harry J. Schneider to H. R. Crawford, June 17, 1974, CHA Development files, IL 2-22. On the complicated relationships between residents and criminals and drug dealers in public housing, see Popkin et al, *The Hidden War*, and Pattillo-McCoy, *Picket Fences*. For public housing residents' perceptions of police, see transcripts of interviews of eleven residents of Stateway Gardens in 1989 and 1990 by Tracye Matthews, archived at the CHM.

79. *Chicago Sun-Times*, March 11 and September 13, 1981, and March 28, 1982; Jane Byrne, *My Chicago* (New York: Norton, 1992), 313–23; Suttles, *Man-Made City*, 63–65.

80. Lack of data makes a regression analysis of the CHA's social disorder difficult to generate. Finding a proxy for the dependent variable of "social disorder" proved impossible. The CHA did record repair costs due to vandalism, but data is largely unavailable, and its reliability in the 1970s would be difficult to ascertain. Crime data, as used by Newman in *Defensible Space*, is also not available on a project basis in Chicago, and crime data is itself problematic. However, a Rand Institute study of New York City Housing Authority projects found that "average unit size" was the most important variable affecting maintenance cost. Large units, of course, likely had more children. See C. Peter Rydell, *Factors Affecting Maintenance and Operating Costs in Federal Public Housing Projects*, Report R-634-NYC (New York: Rand Institute, 1970).

81. CHA, *Official Minutes*, August 11, 1966. The five projects targeted for extra security were ABLA, Stateway Gardens, Cabrini-Green, Henry Horner Homes, and Robert Taylor. For turnover rates, see CHA, *Annual Statistical Report*, 1948–84.

82. CHA, *Tenant Assignment Plan Report*, 1970–76, CHA Gautreaux files; Barbara M. Knox, "Title VI Compliance Review Fact Sheet," July 3, 1975, folder "Elderly," box 66, BGA Papers. On vacancies, see CHA, *Annual Statistical Report*. Wait list data from before 1970 does not survive at the project level.

83. See CHA, *Annual Statistical Report*, 1959–84.

84. *Chicago Defender*, July 10, 1978.

85. Williams, *The Politics of Public Housing*; Feldman and Stall, *The Dignity of Resistance*; Venkatesh, *American Project*; Venkatesh, *Gang Leader for a Day*.

86. Some will undoubtedly disagree that projects were doomed from the start.

See especially Venkatesh, *American Project*; also Feldman and Stall, *The Dignity of Resistance*.

87. As discussed above, measures of relative numbers of youth are almost entirely absent from models of social disorder, and when they are included, even though social scientists find a strong link, it remains undeveloped. Youth densities are taken for granted, not explored as a social construction. The research of Jeanne Brooks-Gunn and her colleagues, for example, notes that "[t]he presence of more single-parent families [in poor neighborhoods] reduces the supply of adults for monitoring and socializing children and adolescents, which in turn probably increases peer influences [on youth behavior]." See Jeanne Brooks-Gunn, Greg J. Duncan, Pamela Kato, and Naomi Sealand, "Do Neighborhoods Influence Child and Adolescent Behavior?" *American Journal of Sociology* 99, no. 2 (1999): 360.

88. For a critique of ghetto sociology, see Loïc Wacquant, "Three Pernicious Premises in the Study of the American Ghetto," *International Journal of Urban and Regional Research* 21, no. 2 (1997): 341–53.

CHAPTER SEVEN

1. CHA, *Annual Statistical Report*, 1948, CHA Public Affairs files. Black tenants had median incomes equal to 92 percent of whites in 1948. Figures do not include temporary veterans' projects.

2. CHA, *Annual Statistical Report*, 1984–85; U.S. Bureau of the Census, *The 100 Poorest Tracts in the United States: 1989*, Report CPH-L-188 (Washington, DC, 1989). On the "underclass," see Michael B. Katz, ed., *The Underclass Debate: Views from History* (Princeton: Princeton University Press, 1992). On concentrated poverty, see William Julius Wilson, *The Truly Disadvantaged: The Inner City, the Underclass, and Public Policy* (Chicago: University of Chicago Press, 1987).

3. See Kathryn Edin and Laura Lein, *Making Ends Meet: How Single Mothers Survive Welfare and Low-Wage Work* (New York: Russell Sage, 1997); Christopher Jencks, *Rethinking Social Policy* (Cambridge: Harvard University Press, 1992), chap. 6; and Venkatesh, *American Project*, 67–68.

4. CHA, *Official Minutes*, December 28, 1945, July 7, 1947, and January 8, 1948; CHA, *Monthly Report*, January 1948, June 1948, and December 1949; *Amendments to the U.S. Housing Act of 1937*, Public Law 301, 80th Congr., 1st sess., July 31, 1947; CHA, *Annual Report*, 1948, 13–14.

5. Robert Taylor to alderman William J. Lancaster, October 28, 1948, City Council folder, CHA Subject files; Chicago City Council, Committee on Housing, minutes, January 16, 1950, Chicago City Clerk files; CHA, *Annual Statistical Report*, 1953.

6. CHA, *Annual Report* for 1945, August 1946; CHA, *Monthly Report*, April 1948 and September 1949.

7. CHA, *Official Minutes*, January 6, 1950; CHA, *Monthly Report*, February 1948, April 1948, July and December 1950; CHA, *Annual Report*, 1948, 14; *Chicago Sun-Times*, November 28, 1957; *Chicago Daily News*, November 29, 1957; CHA Press Release, June 13, 1956, CHA clipping folio, CHA Public Affairs files.

8. CHA, *Official Minutes*, May 10, 1948; *Chicago Daily News*, October 13, 1948. See also Morton Bodfish's testimony before the McCarthy Housing Committee hearings: Joint Committee on Housing, *Study and Investigation of Housing*, pt. 1, 80th Congr., 1st

sess., November 6, 1947, 2090–94. For evidence that federal officials such as Warren Vinton shared a desire to remove excess-income families, see "Summary of Commissioner's Staff Meeting," November 26, 1948, box 3, folder "Staff Meetings," Vinton Papers.

9. On the origins of the 20 percent "gap" provision, see above, chap. 2, n. 31. See also U.S. Senate, *Special Senate Committee on Post-War Economic Policy and Planning*, pt. 15, 79th Congr., 1st sess., February 7, 1945, 1567–69; Edward Weinfield to President Truman, December 15, 1948, folder "NPHC releases," box 2, Vinton Papers; Warren Vinton, "The Low-Rent Public Housing Program," June 5, 1956, box 1, folder "Important memos," Vinton Papers; "Notes on Meeting of Postwar Committee," November 25, 1943, box 16, Vinton Papers; "Meeting for discussion of desirable legislation," July 13 and 14, 1944, box 1, Vinton Papers; Nathan Straus, "Memorandum on Rent and Tenancy Policies," September 12, 1939, box 3, Vinton Papers. The gap policy was ended in the 1974 Housing Act.

10. CHA, *Official Minutes*, June 17, 1948; C. E. Humphrey to Charles Swibel, June 4, 1969, CHA Subject files, folder "Swibel correspondence"; CHA, *Determination of Lowest Private Rents for the City of Chicago*, February 1963, HWLC-MRC. The gaps described by the CHA were exaggerated, however, as housing authorities used unrepresentative data, including rental listings in newspapers, to judge market pricing. A larger gap suited their purposes, demonstrating private market failure and the need for public housing. See also Daniel R. Mandelker, *Housing Subsidies in the United States and England* (Indianapolis: Bobbs-Merrill, 1973), 51.

11. Wood, "Ideals and Realities in Subsidized Housing since 1934," 65; CHA, *Official Minutes*, January 10, 1949; Wood, *The Beautiful Beginnings*, 22–23, 28–29.

12. Wood, *Public Housing and Mrs. McGee*, 13 (emphasis in the original).

13. Bloom, *Public Housing That Worked*, 209–212.

14. U.S. Bureau of the Census, *Census of Population: 1960*, vol. 1, *Characteristics of the Population* (Washington, 1963), pt. 15, Illinois, tables 76 and 78. The median family income of whites in Chicago is not recorded in the census, but it is estimated using figures in tables 76 and 78.

15. CHA, *Annual Statistical Report*, 1958.

16. Fisher, *Twenty Years of Public Housing*, 158–71.

17. Data on CHA wages found in the folder "Housing Assistance Administration Correspondence" folder, CHA Subject files. See also Meehan, *The Quality of Federal Policymaking*, 61.

18. Title to the PWA projects was not transferred from the federal government to the CHA until 1956; under the terms of the transfer, housing authorities received additional construction funds to perform upgrades. See CHA, *Official Minutes*, July 11, 1956; *Chicago Tribune*, July 12 and September 10, 1956; William Kean to James Downs, July 18, 1956, folder "Chicago Housing and Redevelopment Coordinator," CHA Subject files.

19. *Chicago Tribune*, January 10, 1956; William Kean to Raymond Hilliard, February 6, 1957, in folder "Cook County Departments," CHA Subject files; *Chicago Daily News*, June 26, 1958; *Chicago Sun-Times*, March 29, 1968; CHA, *Modernization Program, 1968*, April 11, 1968, CHA Subject files.

20. CHA, *Official Minutes*, memorandum of record, "Commissioners Meeting, November 27, 1957," December 6, 1957; *Chicago Tribune*, editorial, May 29, 1956; CHA, *Monthly Report*, March 1958; CHA, *Official Minutes*, November 14, 1962.

21. *Chicago Tribune*, editorial, May 29, 1956; PHA, *Management Review of the Chicago Housing Authority*, January 1958, HWLC-MRC; CHA, *Annual Statistical Report*, 1957.

22. George B. O'Malley to Bruce Savage, "Legislative Proposals," December 22, 1960, in box 18, "Correspondence of the Commissioner of Public Housing, 1952–1967," RG 196.

23. See CHA, *Annual Statistical Report*, 1957–63.

24. PHA, *Management Review of the Chicago Housing Authority*, 4.

25. CHA, operating budget for 1963, *Official Minutes*, April 1962.

26. CHA, *Official Minutes*, September 13, 1961, and March 11, 1964.

27. CHA, "Highlights of the Operation for 1964," March 31, 1965, CHA Public Affairs files.

28. CHA, *Official Minutes*, October 8, 1964.

29. CHA, *Official Minutes*, May 12 and December 8, 1966; CHA, *Annual Statistical Report*, 1960–70; CHA, operating budgets, 1966–67, published in the *Official Minutes* for those years.

30. CHA, *Official Minutes*, January 18, 1946; FPHA, *Report on the Operations of the Chicago Housing Authority*, June 1946, Library of the Department of Housing and Urban Development, Washington, DC. This library has since been dismantled, and the location of the report is unknown. A copy is in the possession of the author. This report was labeled "Confidential," and its contents did not make their way into the press.

31. On the close connection between the city's unions and Mayor Daley, see Biles, *Richard J. Daley*, 53, 215; Cohen and Taylor, *American Pharaoh*, 170–71, 200; William L. Goetz to Mr. Luke Coleman, June 3, 1976, box 223, "Patronage—Goetz, William, 1976," BGA files. On labor support for public housing, see McDonnell, *The Wagner Housing Act*, 116–23.

32. CHA, *Official Minutes*, August 27, 1946, June 10 and November 10, 1947, and January 8, 1948; Hirsch-McCourt interview.

33. J. S. Fuerst, *How Many Employees Are Required for Efficient Local Authority Operation?* NAHO Publication no. N253, March 1948, in the private files of Jim Fuerst; CHA, *Monthly Report*, March 1948; J. S. Fuerst, "Housing Management Costs Compared for 16 Public and Private Projects," *American City*, May 1950.

34. *Southtown Economist* (Chicago), June 9, 1948; CHA, *Official Minutes*, June 17, 1948; *Chicago Tribune*, September 2, 1948.

35. PHA, *Management Review of the Chicago Housing Authority*.

36. *Chicago Tribune*, March 27, 28, and 29, April 14 and 29, and July 15, 1958; *Chicago Sun-Times*, March 27, 1958; *Chicago American*, March 27, 1958. PHA, *Management Review of the Chicago Housing Authority*.

37. Brice Martin to Casey Ireland, May 29, 1958, folder "Chicago," box 5, "Records of the Special Assistant to the Commissioner for Liaison, 1930–1960," RG 196; *Chicago Tribune*, March 27, 1958; CHA, *Official Minutes*, March 26, 1958.

38. CHA, *Official Minutes*, April 9 and 23, June 11, and July 9, 1958; *Chicago Sun-Times*, April 24 and May 7, 1958; *Chicago Tribune*, April 24, May 15 and 21, and July 10, 1958; *Chicago Daily News*, July 9, 1958.

39. CHA, *Official Minutes*, July 9, 1958; *Journal of Housing*, September 1959, 285–88.

40. William Bergeron to Alvin Rose, August 7, 1958, in "Clipping books relating to the Chicago Housing Authority, volume 1," CHM; CHA Press Release, November 12, 1958, CHA clipping folio, CHA Public Affairs files; *Chicago Daily News*, August 4 and 5 and November 12, 1958.

41. CHA, *Annual Statistical Report*, 1970.

42. See the CHA's operating budgets for 1960–68, published in the *Official Minutes*.

43. *Chicago Daily News*, March 28, 1968; CHA, *Annual Statistical Report*, 1967–69.

44. *Chicago Daily News*, March 28, 1968; Frank de Leeuw, *Operating Costs in Public Housing: A Financial Crisis* (New York: Urban Institute, 1970), 20–21; Meehan, *The Quality of Federal Policymaking*, 61–70; CHA, Memorandum of Record, in *Official Minutes*, July 23, 1970.

45. De Leeuw, *Operating Costs in Public Housing*, 15–16, 40–42. See Senate Committee on Banking and Currency, *Housing and Urban Development Legislation of 1969: Hearings before the Subcommittee on Housing and Urban Affairs on S. 2620*, 91st Congr., 1st sess., July 15–25, 1969; Meehan, *The Quality of Federal Policymaking*, 61.

46. *Chicago Daily News*, February 24, 1972; *Chicago Today*, February 24, 1972.

47. See James T. Patterson, *America's Struggle against Poverty*, (Cambridge: Harvard University Press, 1994), 171–84; Michael B. Katz, *In the Shadow of the Poorhouse: A Social History of Welfare in America* (New York: Basic Books, 1996), 275–76; Frances Fox Piven and Richard Cloward, *Regulating the Poor: The Functions of Public Welfare* (New York: Pantheon, 1971), 181–96, 296–312, and 337–38; Premillia Nadesen, *Welfare Warriors: The Welfare Rights Movement in the United States* (New York: Routledge, 2005).

48. Official unemployment rates for the Chicago Metropolitan Statistical Area reached a 1960s low of 2.3 percent in 1969. While African Americans had higher rates, in 1972, the first year data are available by race, unemployment among African American males age twenty and over was officially 8.1 percent for Chicago. See State of Illinois, Department of Labor, *Labor Market Trends, 1950–64*, and *Trends in Employment and Unemployment, 1965–73*. For other research that points to the 1970s and 1980s as the key decades for job loss, see Joel Rast, *Remaking Chicago: The Political Origins of Urban Industrial Change* (DeKalb: Northern Illinois University Press, 1999), 88–90; William Julius Wilson, *When Work Disappears* (New York: Knopf, 1996), 12–17 and 249–51; Gregory Squires, Larry Bennett, Kathleen McCourt, and Philip Nyden, *Chicago: Race, Class and the Response to Urban Decline* (Philadelphia: Temple University Press, 1987), 25–41. In Detroit, Thomas Sugrue found an exodus of industrial employment from that city to the suburbs beginning in the 1950s (Sugrue, *Origins of the Urban Crisis*). Yet Chicago appears to have had a different trajectory, with crisis coming in the 1970s and after.

49. Alvin Rose to William Bergeron, August 9, 1967, CHA Gautreaux files. This letter refers at length to a HUD circular of July 10, 1967, entitled *Revised Requirements for Administration of Low-Rent Housing under Title VI of the Civil Rights Act of 1964*. See also Paul Messenger, "Public Housing Perversity: A View from the Trenches," *Public Interest* 108 (summer 1992): 133.

50. Why HUD agreed to the court-approved plan with quotas is unclear. The court case, *Gautreaux v. Chicago Housing Authority*, is more famous for its site-selection proscriptions. But the case also hinged on discriminatory tenant selection at the four all-white projects. For the new tenant selection policy, see CHA, *Official Minutes*, November 13, 1969.

51. CHA, *Annual Statistical Report*, 1978–79.

52. Three Brooke amendments were passed in 1969, 1970, and 1972. The first capped rents at 25 percent of income, the second refined the operating subsidy program, and the third required that welfare agencies not decrease benefits in response to the lowering of rents by the first Brooke amendment.

53. Many point to the first Brooke amendment and its change in rental policy as a pivotal moment in public housing policy. But at the CHA, the policy had little effect, other than to decrease revenues. For an explanation of how the Brooke Amendments were implemented in Chicago, see CHA, *Annual Statistical Report*, 1972, 1. See also, *Chicago Sun-Times*, March 28, 1982, and Hayes, *The Federal Government and Urban Housing*, 130–32. For more on the Brooke Amendments, see Roger Starr, "Which of the Poor Shall Live in Public Housing?" *Public Interest* 23 (spring 1971): 116–24; U.S. General Accounting Office (GAO), *Local Housing Authorities Can Improve their Operations and Reduce Dependence on Operating Subsidies*, Report B-118718, February 11, 1975; Meehan, *The Quality of Federal Policymaking*, 102–3; Roberto G. Quercia and George C. Galster, "The Challenges Facing Public Housing Authorities in a Brave New World," *Housing Policy Debate* 8, no. 3 (1997): 538.

54. GAO, *Serving a Broader Economic Range of Families in Public Housing Could Reduce Operating Subsidies*, Report CED-80-2, November 7, 1979; Raymond J. Struyk, *A New System for Public Housing: Salvaging a National Resource* (Washington, DC: Urban Institute, 1980), 100–9; *Chicago Daily News*, November 16, 1967.

55. Vale, *From the Puritans to the Projects*, 362; Public Law 96-153, *Housing and Community Development Amendments of 1979*, 96th Congr., 2nd sess., December 21, 1979; Public Law 101-625, *Cranston-Gonzalez National Affordable Housing Act*, 101st Cong., 2nd sess., November 28, 1990.

56. See U.S. census reports for Chicago for the years 1950, 1960, 1970. Also, compare maps for 1950 and 1960 in Arnold Hirsch, *Making the Second Ghetto*, 7–8, with the map for 1980 in Squires et al., *Chicago*, 95. The maps show a massive dispersion between 1960 and 1980 in the areas where African Americans live. While true integration remained rare, African Americans by 1980 had "transitioned" into wide areas of the city with the conspicuous exception of the North and Northwest Side.

57. Brian J. L. Berry, "Ghetto Expansion and Single-Family Housing Prices, Chicago, 1968–1972," *Journal of Urban Economics* 3 (1976): 417. See also George Sternlieb and James Hughes, *America's Housing: Prospects and Problems* (New Brunswick, NJ: Center For Urban Policy Research, 1980), 546–50.

58. Richard P. Taub, D. Garth Taylor, and Jan D. Dunham, *Paths of Neighborhood Change* (Chicago: University of Chicago Press, 1984), 7–9; Community Fact Book Consortium, *Local Community Fact Book, Chicago Metropolitan Area, 1990* (Chicago, 1995). Abandonment has complex causes; see George Sternlieb and Robert W. Burchell, *Residential Abandonment: The Tenement Landlord Revisited* (New Brunswick, NJ: Rutgers University Press, 1973).

59. *Chicago Defender*, June 22, 1971; CHA, *Tenant Assignment Plan Report*, 1970–76; CHA, *Official Minutes*, October 27, 1966, and November 13, 1969; *Chicago Tribune*, October 26, 1971; *Chicago Sun-Times*, October 26, 1971; *Chicago Daily News*, February 24, 1972, and December 29, 1975.

60. *Chicago Tribune*, June 7, 1972; *Chicago Sun-Times*, July 27, 1972; *Chicago Daily News*, December 29, 1975.

61. Senate Committee on Banking and Urban Affairs, *Housing and Urban Development Legislation of 1969*, 211.

62. R. Allen Hays, *The Federal Government and Urban Housing*, 2nd ed. (Albany: State University of New York, 1995) 101–8.

63. CHA, *Modernization Program, 1968*, April 11, 1968; HUD circular, *Program for*

Upgrading Low-Rent Housing Projects, November 14, 1967, both in folder "Modernization," CHA Subject files; *Chicago Tribune*, December 5, 1986.

64. Senate Committee on Banking and Currency, *Housing and Urban Development Legislation of 1970*, 91st Congr., 2nd. sess., July 13–23, 1970, 936; Meehan, *The Quality of Federal Policymaking*, 101–106; Hayes, *The Federal Government and Urban Housing*, 130–132.

65. Senate Committee on Banking and Currency, *Housing and Urban Development Legislation of 1970*, 13.

66. Senate Banking, Housing, and Urban Affairs Committee, *Financial Condition of Local Housing Authorities*,, 94th Congr., 1st sess., March 11, 1975; Robert Schafer, *Operating Subsidies for Public Housing: A Critical Appraisal of the Formula Approach* (Boston: Citizens Housing and Planning Association of Metropolitan Boston, 1975); Vince Lane to Gertrude Jordan, June 30, 1989, folder "Reports," CHA Subject files.

67. See HUD, *Budget of the U.S. Government*, (Washington, DC, 1970–84). On CHA operating subsidy, see CHA, "Statement of Operating Receipts and Expenditures," in CHA, *Official Minutes*, 1969–83.

68. CHA, "Budget and Income statements," 1973–74, CHA Subject files. Historically, tenants had not been charged for heat or electricity, under the argument that these were essential items of housing cost and could be purchased more cheaply in bulk by the CHA. The 1937 Housing Act, however, made no mention of utility costs, and local housing authorities were free to adopt various policies. The CHA elected to pay all tenant utility costs in the 1930s, though it did assess an "excess utility" charge if specific levels of consumption were exceeded.

69. CHA, "Statement of Operating Receipts and Expenditures," in CHA, *Official Minutes*, 1970–80.

70. *Chicago Sun-Times*, February 16, 1975; Gus Master to the residents of the Robert Taylor Homes, January 16 and July 19, 1980, CHA manager's files, Robert Taylor Homes; Judy Stevens to file, "Re: Current Cost-cutting measures being undertaken by CHA," March 2, 1982, box 135, BGA Papers; GAO to Harold Washington, "Examinations of Allegations Concerning the CHA," GAO-RCED 83–144, April 28, 1983, box 135, BGA Papers.

71. Steven Gittleson, "The Secret Battle over Charles Swibel," *Chicago Magazine*, July 1982, 100.

72. Institute for Community Design Analysis, *Review and Analysis of the CHA and Implementation of Recommended Changes: Final Report of Phase 1, Recommended Changes and Resulting Savings*, March 31, 1982, 104, in HWLC-MRC (hereafter cited as the Newman Report, 1982).

73. Catherine Bauer to Fritz Gutheim, April 17, 1948, outgoing correspondence, box 4, Catherine Bauer Papers; CHA, *Official Minutes*, May 12, 1952; Wood, *Public Housing and Mrs. McGee* and *The Small Hard Core*.

74. Elizabeth Wood to Norman Mason, in *Views on Public Housing: Symposium of Letters* (Washington, DC: Housing and Home Finance Agency, 1960), 116–21.

75. On the debate over who should live in public housing, see Al Hirschen and Vivian Brown, "Too Poor for Public Housing: Roger Starr's Poverty Preferences," *Social Policy* 3, no. 1 (1972): 28–32; Kathryn P. Nelson and Jill Khadduri, "To Whom Should Limited Housing Resources Be Directed?" *Housing Policy Debate* 3, no. 1 (1992): 1–55.

CHAPTER EIGHT

1. PHA, *Management Review of the CHA*; CHA, *Modernization Program, 1968*, 21.
2. CHA, "Managers Meeting, April 19, 1967," CHA Subject files.
3. Meehan, *The Quality of Federal Policymaking*, 88–101; Williams, *The Politics of Public Housing*; Julia Rabig, "The Fixers: Devolution, Development, and Civil Society in Newark, NJ, 1960–1990" (Ph.D. diss., University of Pennsylvania, 2007), chap. 4.
4. CHA, *Modernization Program, 1968*, 36.
5. *Chicago Defender*, August 3, 8, and 25, 1970.
6. CHA, *Official Minutes*, August 27, 1970; *Chicago Tribune*, August 28 and September 10, 1970; *Chicago Defender*, July 25 and September 8, 1970; *Chicago Sun-Times*, September 11, 1970.
7. CHA, *Official Minutes*, July 23, 1970.
8. CHA, *Official Minutes*, July 9 and August 27, 1970.
9. *Chicago Tribune*, September 25 and November 26, 1970; *Chicago Defender*, August 17, 1970; CHA, *Official Minutes*, September 24, 1970.
10. *Chicago Sun-Times*, November 7, 1970; *Chicago Tribune*, November 12 and 26, 1970; *Chicago Today*, November 14, 1970.
11. "Memorandum of Accord," CHA, *Official Minutes*, April 8, 1971; *Chicago Sun-Times*, April 15, 1971.
12. "Memorandum of Accord," April 8, 1971.
13. *Chicago Tribune*, November 11, 1970; *Chicago Daily News*, April 8, 1971.
14. *Chicago Defender*, May 26 and June 29, 1971; *Chicago Tribune*, July 4 and 11, 1971; *Chicago Sun-Times*, July 4, 1971; *Chicago Lerner Booster*, July 18, 1971.
15. Venkatesh, *American Project*, 57–62; *Chicago Tribune*, July 13, 15, and 21 and August 1, 1971; *Chicago Daily News*, July 20, 1971; CHA, *Official Minutes*, November 11, 1972. In 1971, the American Arbitration Association, an independent group, oversaw the special election in CHA projects.
16. Transcript of hearing on November 16, 1970, in case *Eddie Shepard, et al. v. CHA*, 70-CV-2685, Northern District Court of Illinois, Federal Records Center, Chicago. See also *Chicago Tribune*, November 22, 1970. The favorable ruling in the Shepard case did not mean the end of litigation; the CHTO returned to court in 1973 to again sue CHA for its implementation of grievance procedures. See *CHTO v. CHA*, 73-C-1419, Northern District Court of Illinois. In a separate case, *Dorinda Mays, et al. v. CHA*, 71-CV-21, CHTO successfully sued the CHA to drop a late-fee charge for welfare recipients. On continued tenant protests in the 1970s, see *Chicago Tribune*, March 10, 1972, and *Chicago Daily Defender*, October 11, 1972, and September 17, 1974.
17. "Reply Memorandum in Support of Plaintiff's Motion for Summary Judgment, February 19, 1976," *CHTO vs. CHA*, 75-C-501, Northern District Court of Illinois, Federal Records Center.
18. *Chicago Tribune*, July 25 and August 22, 1991, March 2, 1992, February 5, June 8, and June 12, 1994; *Chicago Sun-Times*, March 7, 1981, and March 28, 1982; Vale, *From the Puritans to the Projects*, 344.
19. *Chicago Defender*, July 21, 1979.
20. *Chicago Sun Times*, March 5, 1980; *Chicago Tribune*, March 5, 1980.
21. Sudhir Venkatesh, "American Project: An Historical-Ethnography of Chicago's Robert Taylor Homes" (Ph.D. diss., University of Chicago, June 1997), 76–131.

22. Venkatesh, *American Project*, 52–55, 72–78.

23. Jacobs, "Re: Chicago Housing Authority."

24. *Chicago Sun-Times*, June 25 and July 7, 1965.

25. *Chicago Sun-Times*, June 16, 1967, and August 10, 1975; *Chicago Daily News*, June 16, 1967; Scott Jacobs, "Notes from interview with Lou and Myra Mervis, May 19, 1975," folder "CHA—Miscellaneous," box 67, BGA Papers.

26. *Chicago Daily News*, August 7, 1969, and November 3, 1972; *Chicago Sun-Times*, March 10, 1972 . See also, Christopher Chandler, "*Sun-Times* Kills Exposé of Swibel Renewal Deal," *Chicago Journalism Review* 2, no. 11 (November 1969): 3–5. The Madison-Canal site would later be developed as the controversial Presidential Towers project.

27. *Chicago Sun-Times*, April 6, 1975, and August 27, 1976; Chicago *Tribune*, July 20, 1975.

28. See *Chicago Sun-Times*, July 24 and 28 and September 10, 1975, January 9, 1977; also the following documents from the BGA Papers: Bert Rice to Peter Manikas, "Re: the criminal law and Charles Swibel," July 24, 1975, folder "CHA, Charles Swibel, Financial Dealings," box 66; Scott Jacobs, "Interview with Humphrey, April 15," folder "CHA, Contracts," box 66; Barbara Knox, "Title VI Compliance Review Fact sheet," July 3, 1975, folder "CHA, Elderly," box 66; and Edward Pound, "Memo re: Wells Fargo burglar alarm system / Swibel home," May 27, 1975, folder "CHA—Wells Fargo," box 67.

29. *Chicago Sun-Times*, September 12, 1975; Cohen and Taylor, *American Pharaoh*, 532–39. Swibel's lengthy defense of his practices, sent to Mayor Daley, is found in the "Mayor's File," 1975, CHA Subject files.

30. Elizabeth C. Warren, *The Legacy of Judicial Policy-Making: Gautreaux v. Chicago Housing Authority* (Lanham, MD: University Press of America, 1988), 9; Howard Kurtz, "HUD-Chicago Housing Fight Brings New faces, Same Problems," *Washington Post*, October 8, 1982; Steve Gittleson, "The Secret Battle over Charlie Swibel," *Chicago Magazine*, July 1982, 100. On accusations of patronage in general, see Royko, *Boss*, 22–23; CHA, *Official Minutes*, November 13, 1963.

31. Master-Hunt interview; McCall-Hunt interview; Eric Ellison, former deputy comptroller, interview by the author, September 17, 1999, Mt. Prospect, IL, notes in author's possession; Tom Costello to Oscar Newman, December 11, 1981, box 268, BGA Papers.

32. CHA, "Payroll List, December 31, 1955," folder "Chicago," box 15, Records of the Intergroup Branch, RG 207; CHA, *Annual Statistical Report*, 1975; CHA, "Administrative Staff as of March 31, 1980," CHA Subject files.

33. *Chicago Sun-Times*, September 11, 1975, and July 16, 1979; *Chicago Defender*, December 18, 1978.

34. *Chicago Sun-Times*, September 13 and December 17, 1981.

35. AIC Security president Dennis E. Burke to Virgil Cross, "Re: Confidential Investigation," December 15, 1978; Al Lanier to file, "Re: Status of Things as of July 8, 1980," July 8, 1980; Jack Doppelt to file, "Interviews with Virgil Cross, CHA Chief of Central Maintenance," July 31, 1980; CHA, "Administrative Staff as of March 31, 1980"; Jack Doppelt to *Chicago Magazine* and CHA file, "CHA Elevator Fact Sheet," August 29, 1980, all in box 134, "CHA Interviews and Statements," BGA Papers.

36. *Chicago Sun-Times*, August 27, 1976; CHA, *Official Minutes*, October 27, 1966; Doppelt, "Interview with Virgil Cross."

37. Paul McGrath, "Shafted: Housing Project Elevators Are Deathtraps," *Chicago Magazine*, October 1980, 23–26; Doppelt, "CHA Elevator Fact Sheet."

38. William Miller to CHA, February 3, 1976, CHA Development files, IL 2-37. For an important analysis of heat in public housing and its social implications, see Cassie Fennell, "Project Heat: Warmth and Entitlement in Redeveloping Chicago Public Housing," paper presented at the American Anthropological Association, November 2006.

39. Harry J. Schneider to HUD regional director John Waner, February 14, 1974; Schneider to William Bergeron, October 8, 1965; CHA general counsel Kathryn Kula to PHA official Albert F. Muench, November 3, 1965; C. E. Humphrey to Bergeron, September 17, 1963, all in CHA Development files, IL 2-37; *Chicago Tribune*, March 13. 1962. The only previous heating system of Taylor's size had been built at the Air Force Academy in Colorado.

40. *Chicago American*, April 5, 1958; CHA, *Official Minutes*, August 9, 1961; Wisconsin Chemical and Testing Company, "Air Pollution Studies at the Robert Taylor Homes Project of the CHA," September 12, 1962, CHA Contract files, IL 2-37; Illinois Pollution Control Board, "Opinion and Order of the Board, EPA, vs. CHA," September 19, 1974, box 66, BGA Papers; *Chicago Daily News*, January 26, 1974; Jacobs to Hoge, "re: CHA," no date [1975], in folder "Background," box 66, BGA Papers; CHA to Elmer Binford, December 30, 1981, box 134, BGA Papers.

41. *Chicago Tribune*, December 5, 1986, April 20, 1987, and June 20, 1995.

42. *Chicago Tribune*, June 20, 1981. The nine studies are the Costello management review of 1978, the Ernst and Whinney IPA audit of 1979, the Albert Ramond maintenance improvement program of 1979, the GAO purchasing and procurement audit of 1980, the Ernst and Whinney management study of June 1981, the HUD wage rate study of August 1981, the HUD management reviews of August 1980 and August 1981, and the Institute for Community Design analysis study in 1982. For a summary, see Institute for Community Design Analysis, *Review and Analysis of the CHA: Report on Task 1, Assessment of the Findings and Recommendations of the Previous Studies*, November 26, 1981, available in box 268, BGA Papers. The last (a preliminary study for the final Newman Report) gives a brief summary of the other eight.

43. Newman Report, 1982, 104.

44. Ibid., 94–102.

45. Institute for Community Design Analysis, *Review and Analysis of the CHA: Report on Task 1*; Newman Report, 1982, 4–18; Judy Stevens to John Laing, February 18, 1982, box 268, BGA Papers; Oscar Newman to Samuel R. Pierce, "Re: CHA Study," March 30, 1982, box 135, BGA Papers; Lynne Borrell, interview by the author, April 22, 2008, notes in author's possession.

46. HUD Chicago Regional Office official Ron Gatton to HUD assistant secretary for housing Philip D. Winn, "Draft Chicago Housing Authority Task Force Report, April 30, 1981, box 265, BGA Papers; *Chicago Sun-Times*, March 28, 1982; Vale, *From the Puritans to the Projects*, 344–53.

47. HUD regional director Donald Hovde to Chicago mayor Jane Byrne, January 22, 1982, folder "CHA: HUD Financial Review," box 135, BGA Papers. Also Steve Gittleson, "The Secret Battle over Charlie Swibel," *Chicago Magazine*, July 1982, 100.

48. Gittleson, "The Secret Battle over Charlie Swibel."

49. *Chicago Sun-Times*, March 21, 24, and 28, 1982. The full-page ads defending the

CHA appeared in the *Chicago Tribune, Chicago Sun-Times,* and the *Chicago Defender* on April 12, 1982.

50. *Chicago Tribune,* March 20, 1982; *Chicago Sun-Times,* Mach 24, 1982; Andrew Mooney to Samuel Pierce, March 12, 1982, box 135, BGA Papers; House Banking Committee, *Housing and Urban-Rural Recovery Act of 1982, Part 2,* 97th Cong., 2nd sess., March 18, 1982, 1265–71.

51. Gittleson, "The Secret Battle over Charlie Swibel"; *Chicago Sun-Times,* April 10, 1982; WGN Editorial, March 24 and April 7, 1982; WLS-TV, March 15, 1982; WBBM, March 19, 1982; Walter Jacobsen, WBBM, April 5 and April 9, 1982; WMAQ-TV, March 22 and April 7, 1982, all in box 268, BGA Papers; see also, *Chicago Sun-Times,* March 19 and April 15, 1982; *Chicago Tribune,* March 20 and April 14, 1982.

52. *Chicago Sun-Times,* September 13, 1981.

53. Byrne, *My Chicago,* 1992, 313–23; Gittleson, "The Secret Battle over Charles Swibel"; Oscar Newman to UPI managing editor Ron Cohen, February 13, 1983, box 135, BGA Papers; Newman to David Hovde, September 8, 1982, box 135, BGA Papers; *Chicago Tribune,* November 20, 1982.

54. WMAQ editorial, April 7, 1982, in folder "Swibel," box 268, BGA Papers; Mike Royko, "Byrne's Bad Boys," *Chicago Sun-Times,* December 17, 1981; WBBM, "Walter Jacobsen Perspective," April 9, 1982, in folder "Swibel," box 268, BGA Papers.

CHAPTER NINE

1. CHA, *Official Minutes,* April 24 and July 24, and December 10, 1964; *Chicago Daily News,* May 28, 1962, June 28, July 24, and October 23, 1963; Chicago City Council, *Journal of Proceedings,* May 8, 1963; CHA, *Official Minutes,* October 23, 1963.

2. "Statement of Thomas L. Nicholson to the Chicago Housing Authority," in CHA, *Official Minutes,* February 1, 1965; CHA, *Official Minutes,* February 11, 1965; Carl Gardner and Associates, *Land Use Analysis, CHA tract, Cermak and State,* January 5, 1965, HWLC-MRC.

3. See the following documents from the CHA Gautreaux files: Deposition of C. E. Humphrey, March 22, 1968; CHA, "1965 Program for Family Housing (As Proposed by CHA to Department of City Planning)," Exhibit E; CHA, "1966 Program for Family Housing (As Proposed by CHA to Department of Development and Planning)," Exhibit F,; deposition of Charles Swibel, October 10, 1967. See also Hirsch, *Making the Second Ghetto,* 241–43.

4. West Side Federation chairman, the Reverend S. Jerome Hall, to HHFA administrator Robert Weaver, August 26, 1965, CHA Gautreaux files; Alexander Polikoff, *Housing the Poor: The Case for Heroism* (Cambridge, MA: Ballinger, 1978), 147.

5. See *Chicago Sun-Times,* September 14, 1965; Keith, *Politics and the Housing Crisis,* 166–67. Pritchett, *Robert Clifton Weaver,* 262–78. Weaver was finally appointed the first HUD secretary in early January 1966.

6. PHA commissioner Marie C. McGuire to West Side Federation chairman Jerome Hall, October 14, 1965, CHA Legal files, folder "PHA Disputes—West Side Federation" folder; Keith, *Politics and the Housing Crisis,* 183–85.

7. There are at least four excellent sources for understanding the Gautreaux case: Polikoff's *Waiting for Gautreaux* and *Housing the Poor;* Frederick A. Lazin's "Public Housing in Chicago, 1963–1971—*Gautreaux vs. Chicago Housing Authority:* A Case

Study of the Co-optation of a Federal Agency by Its Local Constituency" (Ph.D. diss., University of Chicago, March 1973); and Elizabeth Warren's *The Legacy of Judicial Policy-Making.*

8. Polikoff, *Housing the Poor,* 149.

9. Cohen and Taylor, *American Pharaoh,* 195–96, 487; Len O'Connor, *Clout: Mayor Daley and His City* (New York: Avalon, 1975), 147; Polikoff, *Housing the Poor,* 149–50; Lazin, "Public Housing in Chicago," 158–60, 178.

10. Lazin, "Public Housing in Chicago," 163; Polikoff, *Waiting for Gautreaux.* Lazin cites a memo from CHA chief counsel Kathryn Kula to executive director C. E. Humphrey, dated December 18, 1967.

11. Lazin, "Public Housing in Chicago," 162–72.

12. Ibid., 172–73; CHA, *Annual Statistical Report,* 1967; "Deposition of Harry J. Schneider, June 11, 1968," CHA Gautreaux files. Most landlords in the Section 23 program approached the CHA, rather than the other way around. Schneider estimated that "85 percent of landlords [in the Section 23 program] select or refer the tenant [to the CHA]—they find the poor tenants and bring them in."

13. Charles Swibel to Alexander Polikoff, January 5, 1968, quoted in Lazin, "Public Housing in Chicago," 170.

14. Polikoff's desire for affirmative integration was shared by the mid-1960s by the National Committee against Housing Discrimination (NCAHD). See NCAHD, *How the Federal Government Builds Ghettos,* February 1967; Polikoff, *Waiting for Gautreaux.*

15. Lazin, "Public Housing in Chicago," 178–83.

16. *Gautreaux v. Chicago Housing Authority,* 296 F. Supp. 907 (N.D. Ill., 1969).

17. Ronald J. Gilson, "Public Housing and Urban Policy: *Gautreaux v. Chicago Housing Authority," Yale Law Review* 79, no. 4 (March 1970): 712.

18. Lazin, "Public Housing in Chicago," 199–206; Polikoff, *Housing the Poor,* 153; Polikoff, *Waiting for Gautreaux.*

19. Judgment Order, *Gautreaux v. Chicago Housing Authority,* 304 F. Supp. 736 (N.D. Ill., 1969); Lazin, "Public Housing in Chicago," 194–99; Polikoff, *Housing the Poor,* 154; Polikoff, *Waiting for Gautreaux.*

20. Kathryn Kula to Charles Swibel, June 7, 1969, quoted in Lazin, "Public Housing in Chicago," 221–25.

21. Lazin, "Public Housing in Chicago," 236–39, Polikoff, *Waiting for Gautreaux,* 94–95; C. E. Humphrey to Lewis Hill, December 1, 1969; Humphrey to Edward F. Arnolds, December 29, 1969; Francis Fisher to Humphrey, March 3, 1970; Fisher to Humphrey, March 13, 1970, all in CHA Gautreaux files; CHA, *Official Minutes,* August 14, 1970; *Chicago Sun-Times,* August 10, 1970.

22. Lazin, "Public Housing in Chicago," 239; *Chicago Tribune,* March 25, 1971. The letter from Wade to Austin is dated July 19, 1970.

23. Lazin, "Public Housing in Chicago," 245–47; *Chicago Sun-Times,* March 6, 1971; *Chicago Tribune,* March 6, 7, and 8, 1971; *Chicago Daily News,* March 6, 1971. For interviews with white Chicagoans, see *Economist Newspapers,* March 10, 1971; for interviews with black Chicagoans, see *Chicago Daily News,* March 12, 1971.

24. *Daily Calumet,* March 10, 1971; *Chicago Daily News,* March 10, 1971; David M. P. Freund, *Colored Property: State Policy and White Racial Politics in Suburban America* (Chicago: University of Chicago Press, 2007).

25. *Chicago Tribune,* March 7, 1971; *Chicago Daily News,* March 8, 1971.

26. *Chicago Tribune,* March 6 and July 11, 1971; *Chicago Sun-Times,* March 8 and 9,

1971; *Chicago Daily Defender*, March 9, 1971; Lazin, "Public Housing in Chicago," 245–47; see CHA, *Annual Report*, 1971, for "New Look" material.

27. *Chicago Tribune*, March 9, 1971; Lazin, "Public Housing in Chicago," 239.

28. Cohen and Taylor, *American Pharaoh*, 507–13; Biles, *Richard J. Daley*, 182–85; Hirsch, "The Cook County Democratic Organization and the Dilemma of Race," 85.

29. *Lerner Booster Newspapers*, week of June 9, 1971, CHA Gautreaux clipping files; *Chicago Tribune*, June 4, 1971; *Chicago Daily News*, June 13, 1971; *Daily Calumet*, June 15, 1971; *Chicago Sun-Times*, June 16, 1971; Polikoff, *Housing the Poor*, 155–156.

30. *Chicago Tribune*, June 12, 1971; *Chicago Sun-Times*, June 11, 1971; Polikoff, *Housing the Poor*, 156; Polikoff, *Waiting for Gautreaux*, 90–91.

31. Polikoff, *Housing the Poor*, 157–58; Polikoff, *Waiting for Gautreaux*, 107–8.

32. Polikoff, *Waiting for Gautreaux*, 149–51.

33. Leonard S. Rubinowitz and James E. Rosenbaum, *Crossing the Class and Color Lines: From Public Housing to White Suburbia* (Chicago: University of Chicago Press, 2000); Polikoff, *Waiting for Gautreaux*; Susan Clampet-Lundquist, Kathryn Edin, Jeffrey R. Kling, and Greg J. Duncan, "Moving At-Risk Teenagers Out of High-Risk Neighborhoods: Why Girls Fare Better Than Boys" (Working Paper no. 509, Industrial Relations Section, Princeton University, March 2006).

34. Polikoff, *Housing the Poor*, 159; Rubinowitz and Rosenbaum, *Crossing the Class and Color Lines*, 27–35; CHA, *Residential Statistical Summary, Year End 1997*, HWLC-MRC; Polikoff, *Waiting for Gautreaux*, 177–212.

35. Polikoff, *Housing the Poor*, 159. On resistance to Polikoff from the black community, see the report prepared for the House Committee on Government Operations, *The Gautreaux Decision and Its Effect on Subsidized Housing*, 95th Congr., 2nd. sess., September 22, 1978. See also, Polikoff, *Waiting for Gautreaux*, 215–16, 241–42.

36. Robert Slayton advocated this strategy in June 1988 in a report he prepared for the Chicago Urban League. See Slayton, *Chicago's Public Housing Crisis: Causes and Solutions* (Chicago: Chicago Urban League, 1988).

37. Vale, *From the Puritans to the Projects*, 344–65.

CHAPTER TEN

1. Paul Kleppner, *The Making of a Black Mayor* (DeKalb: Northern Illinois University Press, 1985); Gary Rivlin, *Fire on the Prairie* (New York: Henry Holt, 1992).

2. Alton Miller, *Harold Washington: The Mayor, the Man* (Chicago: Bonus Books, 1989), 308–9.

3. Kleppner, *The Making of a Black Mayor*, 142–43; Gary Rivlin, *Fire on the Prairie*, 76–77, 384–92.

4. *Chicago Tribune*, January 4 and 27, 1984; Miller, *Harold Washington*, 308–9.

5. Polikoff, *Waiting for Gautreaux*, 189–93; *Chicago Tribune*, December 5, 1986, January 18 and April 20, 1987; Brenda Gaines, *Preliminary Report on the Authority's Financial Position, April 1987*, HWLC-MRC; GAO, *CHA Addressing Long-Standing Problems*, Report GAO/RCED-89-100, June 1989, 24.

6. William Peterman, *Neighborhood Planning and Community-Based Development* (Thousand Oaks, CA: Sage, 2000), 111–28; see also the report prepared for the U.S. Department of Housing and Urban Development, *Evaluation of Resident Management in Public Housing*, December 1992.

7. *Chicago Tribune*, May 10, 1989; Peterman, *Neighborhood Planning*, 126–28.

8. Peterman, *Neighborhood Planning*, 126; Feldman and Stall, *The Dignity of Resistance*; *Chicago Tribune*, June 11, 1995, and July 17, 1996.

9. *Chicago Sun-Times*, July 30, 1975; *Chicago Tribune*, November 14, 1991; statement by Ms. Cora Moore, in *HUD's Takeover of the Chicago Housing Authority*, 87–89; Maryann Mason, "Mixed Income Public Housing: Outcomes for Tenants and Their Community, A Case Study of the Lake Parc Place Development in Chicago,"(Ph.D. diss., Loyola University, 1989), 107–10; Feldman and Stall, *The Dignity of Resistance*.

10. Vince Lane to Gertrude Jordan, June 30, 1989, folder "Reports," CHA Subject files; Mayor Jane Byrne to HUD secretary Samuel R. Pierce Jr., June 15, 1981, folder "CHA correspondence," box 133, BGA files; CHA, *1986 Budget Reduction Program*, July 25, 1986, and CHA, *Long-Term Plan, 1996-2000*, February 15, 1996, both in HWLC-MRC; *Chicago Tribune*, August 2, 1998.

11. *Chicago Tribune*, December 5, 1986; Miller, *Harold Washington*, 308–9; Rivlin, *Fire on the Prairie*, 394.

12. Abt Associates, "Revised Methods of Providing Federal Funds for Public Housing Agencies, Final Report, H-5889," April 23, 1993, Exhibit 1-5; Irving Welfeld, *HUD Scandals: Howling Headlines and Silent Fiascoes* (New Brunswick, NJ: Transaction, 1992). For criticism of how the Reagan HUD handled operating subsidies, see House Banking Committee, *Public Housing Operating Subsidies*, 97th Congr., 1st sess., October 29, 1981; and "Prepared Statement of John A. McCauley, Baltimore Department of Housing and Community Development," in House Banking Committee, *Housing and Urban-Rural Recovery Act of 1982, Part 2*, 1239–62.

13. The idea of "Reagan budget cuts" at HUD in the 1980s is so widespread that it reaches the level of an urban myth. For examples, see Charles H. Moore and Patricia A. Hoban-Moore, "Some Lessons from Reagan's HUD: Housing Policy and Public Service," *Political Science and Society* 23, no. 1 (1990): 14; Venkatesh, *American Project*, 112, 116, 148, 274; Gregory D. Squires, *Capital and Communities in Black and White* (Albany: SUNY Press, 1994), 46; Peter Drier and John Atlas, "U.S. Housing Policy at the Crossroads," *Journal of Urban Affairs* 18, no. 4 (1996): 344; James D. Wright, Beth A. Rubin, and Joel A. Divine, *Beside the Golden Door: Policy, Politics, and the Homeless* (New York: Aldine de Gruyter, 1998), 79. While HUD's Budget Authority was substantially cut, this did not affect outlays in the 1980s. Outlays are the actual funds dispensed from the Treasury to real organizations like the CHA. It should be noted that HUD outlays did decline in the mid-1990s. For a brief discussion of the myth and the confusion over HUD's federal budget, see D. Bradford Hunt, "Rethinking the Retrenchment Narrative in U.S. Housing Policy History," *Journal of Urban History* 32, no. 6 (2006): 943–45.

14. CHA, operating budgets, 1979–84, published in the *Official Minutes* for those years; CHA, *Annual Report*, 1980, 1983–84; Gaines, "Preliminary Report on the Authority's Financial Position"; CHA, *Progress Report, 1995-1998* (1998), HWLC-MRC.

15. GAO, *Chicago Housing Authority Taking Steps to Address Long-Standing Problems*, 33.

16. Ibid.; Miller, *Harold Washington*, 309.

17. *Chicago Tribune*, May 15, 1988.

18. GAO, *CHA Taking Steps to Address Long-Standing Problems*.

19. Lewis H. Spence, "Rethinking the Social Role of Public Housing," *Housing Policy Debate* 4, no. 3 (1993): 355–68; Yan Zhang and Gretchen Weismann, "Public Housing's Cinderella: Policy Dynamics of HOPE VI in the Mid-1990s," in *Where Are Poor People to Live? Transforming Public Housing Communities*, edited by Larry Bennett,

Janet L. Smith, and Patricia A. Wright (Armonk, NY: M. E. Sharpe, 2006), 46–47; Wilson, *The Truly Disadvantaged*; Robert Putnam, *Bowling Alone: The Collapse and Revival of American Community* (New York: Simon and Schuster, 2000).

20. House Banking Committee, *Safety and Security in Public Housing*, 37. For an in-depth account of the saga of the Lakefront Properties, see Mary Pattillo, *Black on the Block: The Politics of Race and Class in the City* (Chicago: University of Chicago Press, 2007), 181–257.

21. Mason, "Mixed Income Public Housing," 83–113; Pattillo, *Black on the Block*.

22. House Banking Committee, *Safety and Security in Public Housing*, 38; Mason, "Mixed Income Public Housing," 83–113; James E. Rosenbaum, Linda K. Stroh, and Cathy A. Flynn, "Lake Parc Place: A Study of Mixed-Income Housing," and Philip Nyden, "Comment," *Housing Policy Debate* 9, no. 4 (1998): 703–40 and 741–48, respectively.

23. Mason, "Mixed Income Public Housing," 83–113. Mason says that 38 percent of residents were under eighteen in 1995. See also Lawrence Vale, "Comment," *Housing Policy Debate* 9, no. 4 (1998): 749–55.

24. Venkatesh, *Gang Leader for a Day*.

25. Darryl MacArthur, interview by the author, March 25, 1998, notes in author's possession; Stubenfield-Hunt interview; Gunn-Hunt interview; Ambrose-Van Lee–Hunt interview; Eddie L. Easley, interview by Tracye Matthews, May 5, 1998, CHM; Barbara Moore, interview by Tracye Matthews, December 10, 1998, CHM.

26. Tiffany Pinkston-Wheeler, interview by the author, August 6, 2007, notes in author's possession.

27. Washington-Hunt interview; House Banking Committee, *Safety and Security in Public Housing*, 112–75.

28. Popkin et al., *The Hidden War*, 16–18, 100; *Chicago Tribune*, April 12, 1994; House Banking Committee, *Safety and Security in Public Housing*, 53–54.

29. Popkin et al., *The Hidden War*, 17, 32, 138–73.

30. Ibid., 2–5.

31. William P. Wilen and Wendy L. Stasell, "Gautreaux and Chicago's Public Housing Crisis: The Conflict between Achieving Integration and Providing Decent Housing for Very Low-Income African Americans," *Clearinghouse Review* 34, nos. 3–4 (2000): 117–45.

32. Wilen and Stasell, "Gautreaux and Chicago's Public Housing Crisis"; Alexander Polikoff, "Comment," *Clearinghouse Review* 34, nos. 3–4 (2000): 146.

33. House Banking Committee, *Safety and Security in Public Housing*, 36; *Chicago Tribune*, June 16 and October 5, 1994.

34. Graham Grady, former CHA chief operating officer, interview by the author, August 29, 2007, Chicago, notes in author's possession; *Chicago Tribune*, April 29 and May 28, 1995, and July 27, 1996.

35. Zhang and Weismann, "Public Housing's Cinderella," 41–67; CHA, *Plan for Transformation*, January 6, 2000, HWLC-MRC.

36. Grady-Hunt interview.

37. House Committee on Government Reform and Oversight, *HUD's Takeover of the Chicago Housing Authority*, 22; Joseph Shuldiner, former CHA executive director, interview by the author, February 21, 2007, notes in author's possession; Janet Smith, "The Chicago Housing Authority's Plan for Transformation," in Bennett, Smith, and Wright, *Where Are Poor People to Live?* 93–124; *Chicago Tribune*, April 24, 1994.

38. CHA, *1996 Budget Statement*, January 12, 1996, HWLC-MRC; Shuldiner-Hunt interview; Smith, "The CHA's Plan for Transformation," 100.

39. Zhang and Weismann, "Public Housing's Cinderella"; Lawrence Vale, *Reclaiming Public Housing* (Cambridge, MA: Harvard University Press, 2002).

40. CHA, *Plan for Transformation*; Smith, "The CHA's Plan for Transformation."

41. Smith, "The CHA's Plan for Transformation"; CHA, *Plan for Transformation*, 2.

42. Brian J. Rogal, "Uncertain Prospects," *Chicago Reporter*, March 2005; Angela Caputo, "Forgotten People," *Chicago Reporter*, March 2004; William P. Wilen and Rajesh D. Nayak, "Relocated Public Housing Residents Have Little Hope of Returning," in Bennett, Smith, and Wright, *Where Are Poor People to Live?* 216–36.

43. For the mix at various developments, see CHA, *FY 2008 Moving to Work Annual Plan*, November 7, 2007, HWLC-MRC.

44. Paul Fisher, "Where Are the Public Housing Families Going? An Update," January 21, 2003, paper available on the Web site of the Sargent Shriver National Center on Poverty Law, http://www.povertylaw.org/; Bennett, Smith, and Wright, epilogue to *Where Are Poor People to Live?* 306–7.

45. Patricia A. Wright, "Community Resistance to CHA Transformation," in Bennett, Smith, and Wright, *Where Are Poor People to Live?* 125–67; *Chicago Sun-Times*, June 20, 2001; Shuldiner-Hunt interview.

46. Journalists and social scientists have recently debated the effects of public housing deconcentration on crime rates. See Hanna Rosin, "American Murder," *Atlantic Monthly* 301, no. 6 (July/August 2008): 40–54, and response from critics: Xavier de Souza Briggs and Peter Drier, "Memphis Murder Mystery? No, Just Mistaken Identity," *Shelterforce* (Journal of the National Housing Institute), July 22, 2008, http://www.shelterforce.org/article/special/1043/.

47. Stubenfield-Hunt interview; Wilen and Nayak, "Relocated Public Housing Residents"; Wilen and Stassel, "Gautreaux and Chicago's Public Housing Crisis." On the pain experienced by residents leaving public housing, see the film *DisLocation* (2005) by Sudhir Venkatesh.

CONCLUSION

1. *Chicago Tribune*, August 2, 1998; Henry Horner residents sued the CHA to gain leverage over the redevelopment process. The "Horner Consent Decree" of 1995 governed the rebuilding with relatively generous terms to former Horner residents. See *Chicago Tribune*, March 31, 1998; CHA, Office of Public Affairs, "Community Developments," fall 1998.

2. Julia Keller, "Threshold: A quality of light opens the door to seeing beauty in an unlikely place," *Chicago Tribune*, January 7, 1999. See also Scott Fortino, *Institutional: Photographs of Jails, Schools, and Other Chicago Buildings* (Chicago: Center for American Places, 2005).

3. Kotlowitz, *There Are No Children Here*; Jones and Newman, *Our America: Life and Death on the South Side of Chicago* (New York: Scribner, 1997).

4. Venkatesh, *American Project*, 234–35. Quote from Loic Wacquant, "Three Pernicious Premises in the Study of the American Ghetto," *International Journal of Urban and Regional Research* 21, no. 2 (1997): 341–53.

5. Venkatesh, *American Project*; Feldman and Stall, *The Dignity of Resistance*; Williams, *The Politics of Public Housing*.

6. For works challenging the word "failure," see James G. Stockard Jr., "Public Housing—the Next Sixty Years?" in *New Directions in Urban Public Housing*, edited by David P. Varady, Wolfgang F. E. Preiser, and Francis P. Russell (New Brunswick, NJ: Center for Urban Policy Research, 1998), 237–64; Bratt, *Rebuilding a Low-Income Housing Policy*, 66.

7. Bloom, *Public Housing That Worked*, 39. Bloom, however, discounts New York's tight housing market as a factor in New York's success.